# Business Essentials

# Business Essentials

By

David Vance

**Cambridge
Scholars**
Publishing

Business Essentials

By David Vance

This book first published 2018

Cambridge Scholars Publishing

Lady Stephenson Library, Newcastle upon Tyne, NE6 2PA, UK

British Library Cataloguing in Publication Data
A catalogue record for this book is available from the British Library

ISBN (10): 1-5275-1311-4
ISBN (13): 978-1-5275-1311-2

Dedicated to Roberta Ann Vance,
my wife and my inspiration.

# TABLE OF CONTENTS

# PREFACE

This book is for the next generation of leaders in business, industry, and society. As such, it is important for them to understand where wealth and jobs come from, how the government generates tax revenue and the principles which help society function best.

This book assumes no prior business knowledge. It starts with first principles and plunges into some of the most important issues in business. What is the nature of leadership? How can it be developed? What is the importance of self-reliance? Chapter One explores these topics and provides readers with a leadership development strategy.

Entrepreneurs create most of the new jobs in the economy and introduce most of the new goods and services, so the second chapter is devoted to entrepreneurship.

Business operates in the context of the society at large, so chapters three and four explore capitalism and tax policy. Business also operates within the context of the law. Chapter Twelve introduces the reader to legal analysis and contract law.

Soft skills are highly valued, so Chapter Five discusses ethics, manners and civility. Critical thinking should be brought to bear on every aspect of business and society. Elements of critical thinking are analyzed in Chapter Seven. This chapter also discusses specialized applications of critical thinking such as negotiation strategy, and challenging statistics.

Chapter Six explains how to read and analyze financial statements. Chapter Thirteen provides a set of tools for projecting the payoff of investments. It also discusses how to compute loan payments. Such analyses provide a basis for developing and testing strategy.

Chapters Eight, Nine and Ten discuss important marketing issues, starting with the economics of supply and demand, and proceeding through insights on consumer behavior and how to close a sale.

Business is awash in data. Chapter Eleven discusses how to use analytics to convert raw data into actionable intelligence.

Chapter Fourteen explores business valuation, a topic rarely covered in either undergraduate or MBA programs. Company valuation shows how all the other threads of business practice come together to create wealth for the entrepreneur and shareholder.

The insights in this book have been developed over a thirty-year business career, and the material in this book has been field tested on more than a thousand students. Many of the insights in this text have been triggered by questions from undergraduate and MBA students, and fellow professionals. I give them the credit. The faults are my own.

David E. Vance, MBA, JD

# Chapter One

# Leadership, Character, Self-Reliance and Execution

---

After completing this chapter, you should be able to:

1.1 Understand the nature and importance of leadership.

1.2 Understand how self-awareness and attitude affect performance, and identify characteristics that lead to success.

1.3 Discuss the importance of character, and how good character can be developed.

1.4 Explain self-reliance and its importance in success.

1.5 Explain the principles of effective execution, which is how to get things done.

---

## Introduction

What separates life's winners and losers? Are winners born, or can winning life strategies be learned? These questions have been asked since the days of the ancient Greeks, and perhaps before.

To a considerable extent, we can create our own selves. We can learn through study and experience what works and what doesn't. We can also build on the experience of the hundred-plus generations since the Greeks. History and literature provide clear signals as to why some people succeed and others fail.

The foundation of success is to know who you want to become. Few of us are born with all the knowledge, insight, and discipline needed to succeed. But through study, we can learn what we need to know, and we can develop habits of character, self-reliance and discipline that will help us succeed.

In this chapter, we explore the nature of leadership, the importance of character, the nature of self-reliance and how to get things done. We begin with that most elusive quality, leadership.

# Leadership

For a dozen years two large retailers dominated the consumer electronics, computer and music business, Circuit City and Best Buys. Their stores were the same size and they sold the same mix of merchandise in the same markets. Sometimes their stores were within walking distance of one another. In 2006, Circuit City had sales of $12.4 billion and 46,000 employees; Best Buys had sales of $35.9 billion and 140,000 employees.[1] The race was on. But in 2008, Circuit filed for Chapter 7 bankruptcy and went out of business.[2] By 2008, Best Buys increased sales to $45.0 billion. It had 155,000 employees and profits of $1.0 billion a year. What happened?

The answer is leadership. **When a business or organization fails, it is always the leader's fault.** That may sound harsh, but one element of leadership is taking responsibility for what happens. Leadership means anticipating bad circumstances and navigating around them. Leadership also means knowing where to take an organization, getting people to follow your lead, and getting the job done.

Circuit City failed for several reasons. One was poor customer service.[3] It violated **the first rule of leadership,** which **is take care of your people.** Philip J. Schoonover, Chief Executive Officer (CEO) of Circuit City laid off 3,400 of his most experienced sales people because, he said, their wages were too high. The company replaced these experienced salespeople with inexperienced salespeople at a much lower wage.[4] **When a company takes care of its people, its people take care**

---

[1] Standard & Poor's Compustat Services. 2012. Data Guide. Englewood.

[2] Rosenbloom, Stephanie 2008. "Circuit City Seeks Bankruptcy Protection", *New York Times*. Nov. 11. NYTimes.com.
www.nyutimes.com/2008/11/11/technology/11circuit.html

[3] Arnst, Cathy. 2009. "Memo to CEOs: Experience IS Worth the Money", *Businessweek*. Jan.19.
http://www.businessweek.com/careers/workingparents/blog/archives/2009/01/mem o_to_ceos_experience_is_worth_the_money.html

[4] Carr, David. 2007. "The Media Equation; Thousands Are Laid Off. What's New?" *New York Times*. April 2.

**of its customers and customers make a company profitable.** When a company fails to take care of its people, they don't take care of customers, and the company fails.

---

**First Rule of Leadership**

The first rule of leadership is to **take care of your people**.

This doesn't mean throwing money at them or coddling them. It means treating them fairly, with respect, and understanding their goals.

Everything flows from the bond created by taking care of your people.

---

Corporations put a high premium on leadership. Jack Welsh, former CEO of General Electric, was widely considered to be one of the most effective leaders of the twentieth, or twenty-first century. He believed development of a broad and deep leadership team would help the company succeed, in any market and under any economic conditions. GE has a 53-acre campus at Crotonville, New York, dedicated to leadership development. General Electric spends a billion dollars a year on employee training, much of that on leadership development. The GE program combines classroom study with rotating assignments, exposure to top innovators and close mentoring.[5]

Since its founding in 1968, Intel has been a pioneer in semi-conductor manufacturing and it invented the microprocessor chip. Intel also places a high value on leadership and leadership development. Several authors have attributed Intel's success to superior leadership.

In Peter Drucker's book, *The Practice of Management*, he says that the CEO's job is too varied to be performed by a single individual. Rather, a company needs a 'thought man'. The job of the 'thought man' is to see the big picture. Companies need a 'man of action', to get things done, and a 'front man', someone who can provide an attractive and engaging face for the company.[6] Intel has been able to develop leaders who can assume each of these roles over their careers.

---

http://www.nytimes.com/2007/04/02/business/media/02carr.html
[5] ___ 2012. "Leadership and Learning", General Electric. Fairfield, CT. http://www.ge.com/company/culture/leadership_learning.html
[6] Drucker, Peter. 1954. The Practice of Management. HarperBusiness. Reprinted 2006.

Gordon Moore, a former Intel CEO, was initially the 'thought man'. He was the originator of Moore's law, which says the number of transistors on a chip doubles every two years. It was his job to see the big picture, determine where the company had to go, and how to get there. Andrew Grove was the 'man of action', who implemented Moore's vision, and Robert Noyce was the public face of the company. When Grove replaced Moore as the CEO, he took over the duties of the 'thought man', and the 'man of action' job was transferred to Craig Barrett.

Andrew Grove's management principles were: (i) be honest and tell the truth. Never shade the truth for fear of offending someone; (ii) be a fast learner and know when the rules of the game have been changed; (iii) hire people with the right kind of ambition, the ambition that provides a person with the internal motivation to push, push, push, but don't hire people with the kind of ambition that will cause them to elbow others out of the way; (vi) mitigate risk when pushing the edge of the performance envelope by over-preparation; study, prepare, check everything, then check it again; and (v) once one decides a particular employee isn't working out, terminate them right away, don't wait.[7]

Intel moves about 300 people a year from management to leadership positions. Intel has created a set of 'Management and Leadership Expectations', and supports leadership development with self-study courses and face-to-face sessions with established leaders. This is designed to show how managers aspiring to become leaders must change to be effective.[8]

The conclusions to be drawn from both General Electric and Intel are: (i) leadership is one of the most critical elements of success for any enterprise; (ii) leadership is something that can be learned, enhanced and refined; and (iii) companies are willing to pay to get, and develop, good leaders.

Clearly leadership is bigger than a few good or bad decisions. So, what is it exactly? Socrates summed up the importance of leadership by saying that, "A group of donkeys led by a lion can defeat a group of lions led by a donkey."

---

[7] Mukul, Pandya, Jeffrey Brown, Sandeep Junnarkar, Robbie Shell and Susan Warner. 2004. "Best of the Best: Inside Andy Grove's Leadership at Intel" *Financial Times Press*. Pearson Publishing. Dec. 10. http://www.ftpress.com/ articles/article.aspx?p=345010. With excerpts from *Nightly Business Report Presents Lasting Leadership: What You Can Learn from the Top 25 Business People of our Times*, by Mukul, Pandya, Jeffrey Brown, Sandeep Junnarkar, Robbie Shell and Susan Warner. Pearson Prentice Hall. 2006.

[8] Grove, Andy. 1995, High Output Management. Vintage. 2nd edition, NY. NY.

> **Leadership**
> Leadership is getting people to *want* to do what needs to be done.

## Nature of Leadership

Few people achieve greatness alone. Most must work with others. Getting other people to channel their effort toward common goals requires leadership.

There are two separate and distinct components to leadership. One element is knowing where to take a company. Some call this strategic vision. The other component of leadership is getting people to follow. In some cultures, people are coerced into doing what needs to be done through fear of punishment. But in a capitalist democracy, coercion is not an option. People will only do what they want to do. Even among people who work for a good firm, there is a broad range of contributions. There are those who just do the minimum to keep their jobs; and there are those who are committed to the company and its objectives. This second group of people feel like they are part of something big and wonderful. They feel like they can contribute, and those contributions will be recognized. These people produce many times the value of the worker who just wants to keep his or her job. Good leadership makes people want to contribute. Bad leadership makes people want to do the minimum to get by.

Many people have written about leadership. Kirkpatrick and Loche argued that leaders differ from followers in six important traits: (i) **drive,** which includes motivation, ambition, energy, tenacity and initiative; (ii) the **desire to lead;** (iii) **honesty and integrity;** (iv) **self-confidence;** (v) **cognitive ability;** and (vi) **knowledge** of the business. They also argue that leaders can be born with these traits, or they can learn them.[9]

Gergen argued that one should look for three traits in a leader: character, vision, and political capacity. Political capacity is skill in dealing with people.[10] Clowney emphasized the traits of a leader ought to include sincerity, honesty and humbleness.[11] Josephson held that character is the foundation of leadership, and a leader's ability to get results is more closely related to his or her, habits and attitudes than to education and

---

[9] Kirkpatrick, S.A. and Loche, E.A. 1991. "Leadership: Do Traits Matter?" *The Executive*. 5 pp48-60.
[10] Gergen, D. 2001. "Character of Leadership", *Executive Excellence*. 18, pp.5-7.
[11] Clowney, K. 2001. "New Definition of Leadership", *Executive Excellence*. 18. Pp8-10.

technical skills. General Omar Bradley said a leader must have lofty ideals and stand by them. A leader must be trusted absolutely. His or her character must be ingrained, an internal part of his or her make-up, not a role worn like a suit of clothes. In-grained ideas must include honesty, loyalty, courage, self-confidence, humility and self-sacrifice.[12]

Jack Welsh said leaders must have fault tolerance. If a person does their best and still falls short of goals, a leader should support that person. However, fault tolerance should not extend to people who can't, won't or don't do their jobs. Fault tolerance should not be extended to people who always have an excuse as to why they couldn't achieve goals.

In short, a leader must have the skills and knowledge to form and execute a successful strategic vision, and a leader must have those character traits that cause people to want to make an extra effort. That extra effort often makes the difference between success or failure in business or in any organization. Now let's consider leadership from the point of view of followers.

## What do Followers Need?

One of the hardest, yet most useful things to do, is to look at a situation from someone else's point of view. What do followers want in a leader? What do they need? If a leader provides followers with what they want and need, they will gladly work, contribute and produce, and do it at levels far above expectations. But, if a leader fails to provide what people want or need, their efforts will be minimal and stinting, lackluster and not innovative. People may contribute their time and bodies, but not their heart, mind or creative energy.

Followers need confidence in their leaders. They need to know their leaders have a vision as to what needs to be done, and that they know how to do it. They need to know the leader's goals in some way fulfill their own goals. This is called **goal congruence**. Goal congruence is important because leadership is not a one-way street. It is a mutual exchange between leaders and followers. It can't just be about what the leader wants. If it is, the leader-follower relationship will break down and followers will become mere employees doing the minimum to keep their jobs. This gives rise to **the first rule of leadership,** which is **take care of your people**. Everything else flows from the bond created by this rule. Taking care of

---

[12] Barlow, Cassie B. Mark Jordan, William Hendrix. 2003. "Character Assessment: An Examination of Leadership Levels", *Journal of Business and Psychology*. Vol. 17, No. 4 Summer.

people doesn't mean coddling them or throwing money at them. It means treating them fairly and with respect, and it means understanding their goals.

---

**Leaders**

A leader should have the **vision** to know what to do and the **competence** to know how to do it.

A leader should be interested in his or her people as **individuals**, have their best interests at heart, consistent with the goals of the organization, and help them achieve their **goals**.

A leader must have the **character** to be truthful, honest, and follow through on promises. A leader must have **integrity**; that is, his or her actions must match his or her words.

A leader must have **compassion**. This is often expressed as **fault tolerance**. When a person tries his or her best, but fails, a compassionate leader gives them a hand up, rather than punishment for failure.

---

Followers need to know they are accepted and respected, by both the leader and others in the organization. Finally, followers need to know the leader is compassionate. Cole believed every leader must possess five 'soft' skills.

First, the leader must be sensitive to follower expectations. **Followers expect competence**. This is accomplished through study, attention to detail, and surrounding oneself with competent people. When leaders demonstrate competence, followers will follow. But followers are constantly evaluating their leaders, and if leaders appear incompetent, or if they appear to lack confidence, or if they are indecisive, followers will stop following. In the Navy, cool, unemotional, competence, coupled with decisive and disciplined action, is called **command presence**. Officers are encouraged to work on, and practice, command presence.

Second, followers want a leader that inspires them to **work toward a 'higher' cause**. That could range from introducing a revolutionary product, to reviving a failing company, to making the best bricks in the world. This higher cause gives people self-satisfaction about their work, generates group acceptance, and provides a kind of status.

Third, **followers want clarity and clear standards** against which they can be judged. Clarity is often missing in business communications. Followers need the leader to clarify the murky and simplify the complex. Leaders need to see the world through the eyes of their followers and explain goals, objectives, means and methods in their followers' terms.

Fourth, **followers need a leader who actively listens to what they are saying**. Often people on the factory floor, in the field doing repairs, or in sales, identify problems and opportunities long before they show up in financial records or customer service reports. Leaders need to listen to their followers and carefully consider their input. If leaders don't listen, a company is likely to make the same mistakes, and miss the same opportunities, again and again. Listening also gives followers a sense of self-esteem and a feeling that they are part of the enterprise and not just a replaceable part.

Fifth, **followers want leaders who are introspective and self-critical**. Not self-critical to the point of indecision or inaction, but self-critical in the sense they are humble enough to admit mistakes, and self-critical enough that they are not complacent. Followers want leaders who work to become better leaders. Followers want leaders who can acknowledge their weaknesses and take steps to eliminate them. Humility and self-deprecating humor go a long way in this regard.[13]

---

**Followers want a leader who:**

is competent, disciplined and decisive;

can motivate them to work toward a 'higher' cause;

can clearly articulate goals, means and methods, and the basis for measuring performance;

will actively listen to what they are saying; and

is introspective, self-critical, willing to admit mistakes, and is continually trying to improve themselves.

---

[13] Cole, Michael. 1999. "Become the Leader Followers Want to Follow", *Supervision*. Dec. pp.9-11.

# Character

Character is the sum of how a person thinks and acts. It is something internal and cannot be put on or taken off like a suit of clothes. In a very real sense, character is who we are. When people speak of character they mean good character.

Character is the foundation of leadership. In fact, character is the foundation of any successful career, profession, job, or calling. Good character is important because people want to know who they can rely upon, and who they can't. Many people have tried to articulate the principles of good character. Table 1.1 summarizes Benjamin Franklin's Thirteen Moral Virtues and Two Questions.[14]

---

[14] Franklin, Benjamin. 1791. "Memoires De La Vie Privee", was published in Paris in March of 1791. The first English translation, "The Private Life of the Late Benjamin Franklin, LL.D."

## Table 1.1 Benjamin Franklin's Thirteen Moral Virtues

---

**Temperance** – Do not eat or drink to excess.

**Silence** – Only speak when it helps yourself or others. Avoid trifling conversation.

**Order** – Let everything have its place and every part of business have its time.

**Resolution** – Resolve to perform what you ought. Perform without fail what you resolve.

**Frugality** – Make no expense unless it benefits yourself or others. Waste nothing.

**Industry** – Lose no time. Always be employed doing something useful. Cut off all unnecessary actions.

**Sincerity** – Use no hurtful deceit. Think innocently and justly, and if you speak, speak accordingly.

**Justice** – Wrong no one by doing injuries or by omitting the benefits that are your duty.

**Moderation** – Avoid extremes. Do not resent injuries as much as they deserve.

**Cleanliness** – Tolerate no uncleanness in body, clothes or home.

**Tranquility** – Do not be bothered by the little things or common unavoidable accidents.

**Chastity** – Manage your sexual appetites so you don't injure your reputation or that of others.

**Humility** – Imitate Jesus and Socrates.

The Morning Question: What good shall I do this day?

The Evening Question: What good have I done this day?

---

A more contemporary analysis of character is Likona's Model, which has three primary components: (i) Moral Knowing; (ii) Moral Feeling; and (iii) Moral Action. Moral knowing is understanding that there are moral consequences to every interaction with other people. Moral feeling is based on internal sign-posts as to what is right or wrong. Those internal sign posts are developed through thought, study and analysis. Moral Action involves competence, will and habit. Competence is necessary to turn moral feeling into action. Will has been defined as the mobilization of the necessary physical and mental energy to act. People act morally when they have practiced acting morally. Habits of character can be developed and should be practiced.[15]

Aristotle believed that "by doing... acts with other men we become just or unjust... and by doing acts in the presence of danger, being habituated to feel fear or confidence, we become brave or cowardly... Some men become temperate and good-tempered, others self-indulgent and irascible, by behaving in one way or another." **The basic thrust of his argument is that virtue, like the arts, is acquired through practice and corresponding actions.**[16]

---

**Good character**, like any art, is developed through **study** and **practice**.

---

Table 1.2 Air Force Character Attributes provides a good model for evaluating one's character, and the character of co-workers, employees and potential business partners.[17]

---

[15] Likona, T. 1991. Educating for Character. New York. Bantam Books.
[16] Annas, Julia. 1999. "Aristotle on Virtue and Happiness", *Aristotle's Ethics*. Edited by Nancy Sherman. New York. Rowman and Littlefield.
[17] Katz, D. and Kahn, R. 1976. *Leadership*. New York. John Wiley & Sons. Pp.525-576.

**Table 1.2 Air Force Character Attributes**

---

**Integrity** – Consistently choosing to do the 'right' thing.

**Honesty** – Consistently being truthful with others.

**Loyalty** – Being committed to one's organization, coworkers and subordinates.

**Selflessness** – Genuine concern for the welfare of others and putting that welfare ahead of one's own.

**Compassion** – Concern for the suffering of others, providing aid, and showing mercy.

**Competency** – Capable of excelling at all tasks assigned; efficiency and effectiveness.

**Respectfulness** – Shows esteem for, and consideration of others.

**Fairness** – Treats people in an equitable, impartial, and just manner.

**Responsibility and Self-Discipline** – Can be depended upon to make rational decisions and to perform tasks assigned without supervision.

**Decisiveness** – Capable of making logical and effective decisions in a timely manner. Does not shoot from the hip, but makes decisions promptly after considering appropriate information.

**Spiritual Appreciation** – Values spiritual diversity among individuals.

**Cooperativeness** – Willingness to work or act together with others in accomplishing a common purpose.

---

# Self-Reliance

Self-reliance is a belief one can do things, by oneself, without help or guidance from others. The self-reliant person relies on his or her own resources. He or she takes charge of any task or job presented to her or him and completes it in an efficient, effective and timely manner.

Self-reliance requires self-confidence. Anyone who lacks self-confidence will subordinate his or her judgment to the opinions of others and when those opinions conflict, as they often do, they will procrastinate and be indecisive.

The self-reliant person never drifts along. He or she sets and completes goals; not because someone tells them to, but because they have an inner voice, an inner drive that propels them forward. The self-reliant person takes responsibility for completing any assigned task or job. The self-reliant person never makes excuses or lays blame when things don't work out.

Once you strap-on the mindset that the responsibility for something is yours and yours alone, you can focus on how to get the job done. The resulting concentrated effort usually leads to success.

Think of a successful person as the sum of thousands of small successes that lead to a successful life. Small successes beget larger ones and so forth, until people look at a person and judge them successful. Self-reliance leads to a peaceful and satisfying life.

Contrast this with the person who is not self-reliant. They either wait for others to do things for them, or they wait for others to help them, or they wait for instructions. In many of life's most critical situations such help will never come. Waiting and procrastination lead to failure. And as failures accumulate, the sum of a person's life looks more and more dismal. Some might reject self-reliance because they think they are too poor, or too weak, or too uneducated, or too old. Such rejection leads to a life without achievement and without dignity. The more you do for people, the less self-reliant and the more dependent they become. Dependent people are not happy people.

People aren't born self-reliant; they learn it, study it, practice it, and after a while, it becomes second nature. Take a challenge, a task, a job and decide you are going to figure out how to do it yourself. Determine you will succeed and you will succeed. Never let up. Never give in. During the Battle of Britain, two years after World War II began in Europe, while London was being bombed, an exhausted Winston Churchill gave a speech that put steel in the backbone of every man and woman in England. The nine key words in that speech were, "Never give in. Never give in. Never, never, never."[18]

In the movie "To Have and To Have Not", Humphrey Bogart plays Captain Morgan. A frightened French patriot says: "I wish I could borrow

---

[18] Churchill, Winston. 1941. Speech given to the Harrow School October 29, a time when Europe had been at war for two years. The Unrelenting Struggle. London: Cassell and Boston: Little Brown 1942, pp. 274-76 English edition.

your nature for a while Captain Morgan. You never consider the possibility of defeat; only how to achieve your goals." Captain Morgan was a man who practiced self-reliance every day.

Elbert Hubbard wrote one of the greatest essays ever on the importance of self-reliance. It was published in 1899. It is called "A Message to Garcia." An abridged version is reproduced in Table 1.3. It should be read often.

**Table 1.3 A Message to Garcia** by Elbert Hubbard

---

In all this Cuban business one man stands out on the horizon of my memory like Mars at perihelion. When war broke out between Spain and the United States (in 1899), it was necessary to communicate quickly with the leader of the insurgents, General Garcia. He was somewhere in the mountain vastness of Cuba; no one knew where. No mail nor telegraph message could reach him. President McKinley had to secure his cooperation, and quickly.

What to do?

Someone said to the President, "There's a fellow by the name of Rowan who will find Garcia for you, if anybody can."

Rowan was given a letter to be delivered to Garcia. Rowan took the letter, sealed it in an oil-skin pouch and strapped it over his heart. In four days he landed by night off the coast of Cuba from an open boat, disappeared into the jungle, and in three weeks came out on the other side of the island, having traversed a hostile country on foot, and delivered his letter to Garcia. I have no special desire to tell how he did it in detail.

The point I wish to make is this: McKinley gave Rowan a letter to be delivered to Garcia; Rowan took the letter and did not ask, "Where is he?" By the Eternal! There is a man whose form should be cast in deathless bronze and the statue placed in every college of the land. It is not book-learning young men need, nor instruction about this and that, but a stiffening of the vertebrae which will cause them to be loyal to a trust, to act promptly, concentrate their energies: do the thing- "Carry a message to Garcia!"

General Garcia is dead now, but there are other Garcias.

Every man or woman, who has endeavored to carry out an enterprise where many hands were needed, has probably been appalled at times by the imbecility of the average man; by their inability or unwillingness to concentrate on a thing and do it. Slip-shod assistance, foolish inattention, dowdy indifference, and half-hearted work seem the rule; and no man succeeds, unless by hook or crook, or threat, he forces or bribes other men to assist him; or perhaps, God in His goodness performs a miracle, and sends him an Angel of Light for an assistant. You, reader, put this matter to a test: You are sitting now in your office, six clerks are within call. Summon any one and make this request: "Please look in the encyclopedia and make a brief memorandum for me concerning the life of Correggio."

Will the clerk quietly say, "Yes, sir", and go do the task?

On your life, he will not. He will look at you out of a fishy eye and ask one or more of the following questions:

Who was he? Which encyclopedia? Where is the encyclopedia? Was I hired for that? Don't you mean Bismarck? What's the matter with Charlie doing it? Is he dead? Is there any hurry? Shan't I bring you the book and let you look it up yourself? What do you want to know for?

And I will lay you ten-to-one, that after you have answered the questions, and explained how to find the information, and why you want it, the clerk will go off and get one of the other clerks to help him try to find Correggio, and then come back and tell you there is no such man. Of course, I may lose my bet, but according to the Law of Averages, I will not.

Now if you are wise, you will not bother to explain to your 'assistant' that Correggio is indexed under the C's, not in the K's, but you will smile sweetly and say, "Never mind", and go look it up yourself.

And this incapacity for independent action, this moral stupidity, this infirmity of the will, this unwillingness to cheerfully catch hold and lift, are the things that put pure Socialism so far into the future. If men will not act for themselves, what will they do when the benefit of their effort is for all? A first-mate with knotted club seems necessary; and the dread of getting 'the bounce' Saturday night, holds many a worker to his place.

Advertise for a stenographer, and nine out of ten who apply can neither spell nor punctuate, and do not think it necessary to.

Can such a one write a letter to Garcia?

We have recently been hearing much maudlin sympathy expressed for the 'downtrodden denizen of the sweat-shop' and the 'homeless wanderer searching for honest employment', and with it all, often go many hard words for the men in power.

Nothing is said about the employer who grows old before his time in a vain attempt to get frowsy ne'er-do-wells to do intelligent work, and his long, patient, striving with 'help' that does nothing but loaf when his back is turned. In every store and factory there is a constant weeding-out process going on. The employer is constantly sending away 'help' that have shown their incapacity to further the interests of the business, and others are being taken on. No matter how good times are, this sorting continues; only if times are hard and work is scarce, the sorting is done finer, but out and forever out, the incompetent and unworthy go.

It is the survival of the fittest. Self-interest prompts every employer to keep the best, those who can carry a message to Garcia.

I know one man of brilliant parts who has not the ability to manage a business of his own, and yet who is worthless to anyone else, because he carries with him constantly the insane suspicion that his employer is oppressing, or intending to oppress, him. He cannot give orders, and he will not receive them. Should a message be given him to take to Garcia, his answer would probably be, "Take it yourself."

Tonight, this man walks the streets looking for work, the wind whistling through his threadbare coat. No one who knows him dare employ him, for he is a regular fire-brand of discontent. He is impervious to reason, and the only thing that can impress him is the toe of a thick-soled No. 9 boot.

Of course, I know that one so morally deformed is no less to be pitied than a physical cripple; but in our pitying, let us drop a tear, too, for the men who are striving to carry on a great enterprise, whose working hours are not limited by the whistle, and whose hair is fast turning white through the struggle to hold in line employees with dowdy indifference, slip-shod imbecility, and the heartless ingratitude, which, but for their enterprise, would be both hungry and homeless.

Have I put the matter too strongly? Possibly I have, but when all the world has gone a-slumming I wish to speak a word of sympathy for the man who succeeds, the man who, against great odds, has directed the efforts of others, and having succeeded, finds there's nothing in it; nothing but bare board and clothes.

I have carried a dinner pail and worked for day's wages, and I have also been an employer of labor, and I know there is something to be said on both sides. There is no excellence, per se, in poverty; rags are no recommendation; and all employers are not rapacious and high-handed, any more than all poor men are virtuous.

My heart goes out to the man who does his work when the boss is away, as well as when he is at home. And the man who, when given a letter for Garcia, quietly takes it, without asking any idiotic questions, and with no lurking intention of throwing it into the nearest sewer, or of doing anything but deliver it; that man or woman never gets laid off, nor has to go on a strike for higher wages.

Civilization is one long anxious search for just such individuals. Anything such a man or woman asks shall be granted; their kind is so rare that no employer can afford to let them go. They are wanted in every city, town and village; in every office, shop, store and factory. The world cries out for such; they are needed and needed badly; the people who can carry a message to Garcia.          ~ Elbert Hubbard

---

**Self-reliant** people can be thrown into any situation. They **take the initiative** and the **responsibility;** they have the **drive** to **get things done.** They **never complain.** They only ask themselves, "How can I overcome obstacles?" These are the inventors and entrepreneurs, the people who push civilization (and companies) forward. They are the most valuable people on earth. **This is the attitude we should all strive for.**

On the other hand, few people are self-reliant. Most need to be poked, prodded, cajoled, coaxed, persuaded, wheedled, enticed, sweet-talked, inveigled, charmed and flattered into doing what they should do, and then the result is often a half-hearted attempt to get a job done.

Self-reliance is an indispensable attribute for success. **Self-reliance is a habit of thought and action that can be developed. The self-reliant person improvises, adapts and overcomes.**

---

**Attitude is Everything**

Whether you think you can… or you think you can't, you're right.

Positive mental attitude is a force multiplier.

The **attitude** you bring to work, school and life is a **bigger determinant of success than IQ**, parents' income or almost any other factor.

Your attitude is something you choose every day. **Choose wisely.**

---

## Execution

Execution is the art and science of getting things done. A Harvard study found that on average, large companies only achieve about 63% of their goals and a third of companies achieve less than half their goals.[19]

---

[19] Mankins, Michael C. and Richard Steele. 2005. "Turning Great Strategy Into Great Performance", Harvard Business Review. Jul.-Aug. pp.65-72.

Another study found that 60% of planned productivity gains were lost because of failure to execute.[20] The American Management Association's survey of Chief Executive Officers (CEOs) found that only 3% of companies were successful at implementing strategy, and 62% said their ability to execute strategy was moderate or worse.[21]

Overall, this shows the gap between ideas and achievement, between plans and completion, are enormous. The question is why? Why don't organizations achieve their goals? Why don't individuals achieve their goals?

## Organizational Achievement

**Plans should be simple, concrete and measurable**. Organizations fail to implement plans because they don't: (i) prioritize; (ii) adequately communicate goals; (iii) hold people accountable; or (iv) they have the wrong people.

### *Prioritize*

A common problem is that companies fail to prioritize goals. When a company tries to do everything, management time and attention is so diffused that nothing gets done. Jack Welsh was one of the most successful CEO's of the twentieth century. In his eighteen years as CEO of General Electric he launched only five major initiatives.[22]

### *Communicate Goals*

Followers need leaders who clearly communicate goals and what is expected of them. A major problem with many business plans is that they are vague and un-executable. Suppose the business plan says, "Our goal is to be the premier supplier of popcorn to movie theatres." What exactly does that mean? Without clarification, managers and workers are left to guess what it means, or to wait for clarification that may never come.

---

[20] Neiman, Robert A. and Harvey Thomson. 2004. "Execution Plain and Simple", *Canadian Manager*. Fall. pp17-19, 17.

[21] AMA. 2007. "The Keys to Strategy Execution." AMA/HRI Survey. March 19. https://www.amanet.org/training/articles/printversion/the-keys-to-strategy-execution-06.aspx.

[22] Charan, Ram and Geoffrey Colvin. 1999. "Why CEOs Fail", *Fortune*. Vol. 139, Iss. 12. June 21. Cvr.

Suppose on the other hand, management says the company's goal is to out-perform other popcorn on taste tests 90% of the time. This is a clear goal. Research and development can test a variety of popcorns and find out what people like best. Maybe the type of corn makes a difference; maybe the amount of salt needs to be adjusted; maybe the type and amount of butter could be changed; maybe the way popcorn is cooked, stored or served, impacts performance on flavor tests. The point is that an executable plan is specific enough to provide a basis for action. It is concrete.

### Hold People Accountable

If a person is assigned a goal and they know they won't be held accountable for that goal, other priorities will take the place of the company's goal. Those other priorities might be increasing a person or department's prestige, angling for a bigger bonus, or other things that don't advance the company's agenda. On the other hand, when people know they will be held accountable for specific goals, they focus their time and energy on those goals.

### Wrong People

The leader's first job is to make sure people understand the goal. Second, the leader must make sure people have the knowledge and training to reach the goal. Third, leaders must make sure that people have the time and resources to reach the goal. One way to help assure these three things is to ask people whether they understand the goal, know how to reach it, and have adequate time and resources. After the leader has made sure that he or she has done their duty, then failure to execute falls on those assigned a task.

In every organization, there **are people who can't, won't or don't meet goals.** They may not have the drive or energy to meet goals, or they might not have the character needed to work with others. Or they may simply be malcontents. Whatever the reason is, these people must be eliminated for the good of the organization.

How does eliminating non-performers square with the first rule of leadership which is to take care of your people? When one person on a team or in an organization fails to do his or her duty, the burden shifts to his or her co-workers. Such burden shifting is fundamentally unfair to others and the organization is probably better off without the underperforming person. Taking care of your people includes terminating employees who don't do their share of the work.

## Execution Cycle

Table 1.4 Execution: Planning to Measurement summarizes the link between planning, measurement and execution. One of the most important elements of successful execution is ongoing progress monitoring. If a company waits until year-end to determine whether goals were met, it will be too late to take corrective action.

All plans should be monitored at least monthly, but weekly is better for most companies. Some things, like sales, cash, and shipments should be monitored daily. When monthly, weekly or daily results veer in an unexpected direction, enhanced monitoring and corrective action should begin immediately.

**Table 1.4 Execution: Planning to Measurement**

| **PLAN** Develop a specific, executable plan and assign people responsible for results | **MONITOR** Monitor progress monthly, weekly or daily | **MEASURE** Measure achievement of plan goals. Hold those responsible accountable. |
|---|---|---|

**CORRECTIVE ACTION** Take corrective action needed to achieve goals including retraining and personnel changes

## Personal Achievement

Why do some people achieve much, and others go through the motions, but never seem to get things done? In large measure, those who succeed, those who achieve, those who get things done, are those who develop good habits. Not just any good habits, but specific habits.

**Time management is one of the most important keys to success**. It is an old, but true saying that, "He who wastes time, wastes life." That's not to say one must work twenty-four hours a day, seven days a week. It means time should be budgeted for work, study and play. Two important-time management tools are the Weekly Planner and the Plan of the Day.

### Plan of the Day

A Plan of the Day is a way of pushing your agenda forward every day. Winston Churchill was famous for getting things done. He demanded "Action this Day", when something needed to be done. Likewise, "Carpe diem", seize the day, was Julius Caesar's advice to his men.

A Plan of the Day is simply a list of things to be accomplished this day. Recall Ben Franklin's morning question, "What good should I do this day?" In effect, he was thinking about his plan of the day. A plan of the day need not be fancy; a simple, hand-written list is usually sufficient to keep one focused. As tasks get completed, check them off. As new tasks come up, add them to the list. As time runs out, re-prioritize the list.

### Weekly, Monthly and Annual Planner

One of the reasons **people** fail to achieve their goals is they **don't space work out over the time available**. As tasks come up, they should be posted in a weekly, monthly or annual planner. Tasks should also be subdivided. For example, assigned projects might be subdivided into the research, design, prototyping, production planning, equipment acquisition, installation and test runs.

Few substantive projects can be completed in a few hours, or even a few days. So, the important thing when faced with any project is to begin early and chip away at it day after day. By starting projects as soon as assigned, and spacing work over time, there is less stress and a better chance of completing the project efficiently and on time.

## Expectations Management

Many people get frustrated and fail to achieve all they can because of unrealistic expectations. Once a person understands that the world was not created for their convenience, they will be in a better position to deal with the world as it is, full of imperfections, and yes unfairness. People that accept the world as it is, and expect nothing from it, can perform brilliantly because they will have been freed from unrealistic expectations. Table 1.5, Life Lessons, presents a couple of steps on the road to taking on the world as it is, rather than how we hope it will be.

**Table 1.5 Life Lessons**

---

1.  **If you want something, you must ask for it.** You cannot expect people to read your mind. You cannot expect others to know what you need. If you want something you have to ask for it.

2.  **Asking and getting are two different things.** Just because you ask for something doesn't mean you will get it. Most people must balance competing interests. If someone doesn't grant you what you want, when you want it, don't take that as an insult. Take it as a challenge to work harder.

3.  **Everything in life is a negotiation.** If you want something from someone, you must be willing to give something in return. If you can't get exactly what you want, try asking for something less that moves you in the right direction. Everything in life is a negotiation.

4.  **Nothing in life is free.** When someone offers something for free, step back and ask what the other party will get out of it. Often things that are 'free' end up costing more than things that are paid for.

5.  **Networking smooths negotiation.** Make it your business to get to know people in a lot of diverse groups. Knowing someone before negotiation builds trust.

6.  Successful negotiation means **finding what the other person wants** and giving it to him or her, if possible. Negotiation is only partly about what you want.

---

# Conclusion

Leadership makes the difference between organizations that succeed and those that fail. A leader must understand what must be done, how to do it, anticipate problems, and to solve them. A leader must also get people to want to do what needs to be done.

To get followers to follow, leaders need to set clear objectives, demonstrate competence, show followers how their personal goals can be achieved by doing what the leader asks, and followers need to know the leader has compassion. The first rule of leadership is to take care of your people.

Good character is essential for anyone who aspires to leadership and it is important, so that co-workers, employees, customers, suppliers and investors know they can trust you to do what is right. Ben Franklin defined good character in terms of thirteen virtues: (i) temperance, (ii) silence, (iii) order, (iv) resolution, (v) frugality, (vi) industry, (vii) sincerity, (viii) justice, (ix) moderation, (x) cleanliness, (xi) tranquility, (xii) chastity, and (xiii) humility. The Air Force has identified a dozen character traits that are important to leadership. These are: (i) integrity, (ii) honesty, (iii) loyalty, (iv) selflessness, (v) compassion, (vi) competency, (vii) respectfulness, (viii) fairness, (ix) responsibility, (x) self-discipline, (xi) decisiveness, and (xii) cooperativeness.

Self-reliance is an indispensable character trait. People who are self-reliant have the self-confidence to rely on their own judgment, and the drive to figure out what must be done; how to do it; and get it done. Self-reliant people don't wait for others to tell them what to do or how to do it. Self-reliance is a habit that can be developed through practice.

People who are self-reliant have the satisfaction of knowing they can control their lives. Those who are not self-reliant, who do not have confidence in their own opinions, who wait for others to tell them what to do, will forever be dependent on others. Dependence does not breed happiness.

Execution is the art and science of getting things done. Few companies and few individuals reach the goals they set for themselves. Execution requires plans that are simple, concrete and measurable. People also need to know they will be held accountable for assigned work. Organizations need the right people to succeed. In most organizations, there are people who can't, won't, or don't, follow through and meet goals. They must be eliminated.

Some people achieve much while others in similar circumstances achieve little. One of the keys to achievement is time management. Industry is one of Ben Franklin's Thirteen Virtues, and it means one should always be doing something to improve one's skills and value. He or she who wastes time, wastes life.

Two devices that help people improve productivity are a 'Plan of the Day', and a 'Weekly, Monthly or Annual Planner.' The plan of the day is a list of tasks to be accomplished that day. It can be as simple as a slip of paper, but it is a useful device to keep one focused on priorities.

The Weekly, Monthly, or Annual planner helps spread work over the time allotted to do it. Few substantial tasks can be accomplished in a matter of hours or even days, so it is important to start tasks as soon as they are assigned, and chip away at them every day until complete.

Many people approach life with unreasonable expectations, get frustrated, and give up when the universe doesn't behave to their liking. People need to realize the world does not exist for their convenience. Life isn't always fair. Successful people don't let unfairness derail them from achieving their goals. They must work with the world as it is, with all its imperfections.

Success in business, or in life, does not occur through random chance. There are well defined strategies for achieving success. Developing leadership skills, building character, learning self-reliance and learning to execute assigned tasks all contribute to success. Each of them can be learned. All of them must be practiced.

## Appendix 1a: Networking

What is networking and why is it important? There is an old adage, "It's not what you know, it's who you know." It's still true. Networking is building connections with people. Connections are important because this is a complicated world, and people with connections are in a better position to navigate the world than people who lack connections.

There are several reasons for the power of connections. First, people are more likely to talk to you if they know you; if they feel comfortable with you; if they feel that you are not going to be judgmental; if they feel safe dealing with you; and if they feel they can trust you. Second, each of us has a limited amount of knowledge. Yes, the internet and social media spread knowledge a little wider, but not all relevant information is on the web, or is easily identified, or appropriately filtered to eliminate misinformation. A network of friends and acquaintances can facilitate access to relevant knowledge. Third, a network of relationships can lead to new relationships. People are more likely to accept and trust you if you are introduced by a mutual acquaintance. Fourth, most people gain a sense of pleasure and well-being when they are around others who share mutual experiences and have common bonds.

As a practical matter, a network of contacts can help a person get a job, or a better job. Not all jobs are advertised or posted on the web or social media. Networking can help a person break through the clutter. Suppose a company posts a job opening on the internet, and five hundred people apply. What are the odds your resume will get a fair hearing? On the other hand, if someone who works for a company hand-delivers your résumé to the hiring manager, the odds of a fair hearing improve dramatically.

Networking can help a company make sales by identifying those who might be in the market for a good or service and when they will be ready to buy. Purchasers want to feel confident they have made the right decision, and personal referrals reduce the risk of buyer's remorse. Networking can also help a person find investors for his or her company. Finally, networking is a way to meet new people, experience new things, and make new friends.

Networking is a life skill, not a task to be performed and set aside. Networking is about making connections, but such connections must be a two-way street. It can't just be about finding the next job, next sale or next investor. A good networker must take a genuine interest in the people he or she meets. Often, you will discover a job that isn't right for you or someone is looking to invest at a time when you don't need money, or a customer might need goods or a service you can't provide. Consider whether someone else in your network could use that opportunity. Networking is not a zero-sum game. The more referrals you give, the more you get. Some say such referrals are returned tenfold.

Networking skills can be developed, and, like any skill, must be practiced. Make it your business to attend conferences, meetings, charity functions, and professional associations where people get together and have an opportunity to talk. Make it a goal to introduce yourself to three to five new people at each event. Avoid the comfortable temptation to talk only to the people you know. Get out of your comfort zone. Wear a name tag to help people remember you and carry a fresh supply of business cards. Ask for other people's business cards.

When introducing yourself, smile, give people a firm hand-shake and look them in the eye. Make sure to pronounce your name slowly and distinctly. Your self-confidence will put others at ease. Ask them their name. Repeat their name to make sure you are pronouncing it correctly. Introduce the person you are speaking to, to anyone else who joins the conversation as a way of practicing their name and signaling their importance. Think about something interesting to say before you go to a networking event. For example, if someone asks what you do, you might say, "I bring order out of chaos", if that is your specialty. Or, you might say, "I shape young minds", if you are a teacher.

Get the other person to talk about themselves and listen intently. People's attention spans are short. Few people are skilled listeners. When someone is speaking to you, give them one hundred percent of your attention. Nothing is ruder than looking around the room or playing with your phone when someone is talking to you.

Sometimes the best thing you can do for a person is to listen to them. One way to get people to talk is to ask open ended questions, like, "What's the most exciting thing you've ever done?" Or, "What plans do you have for the coming year?" Try to establish some common ground, a common interest, something that connects you. Alternatively, you can state a problem and ask for their advice. For example, "I'm putting together a course on Private Equity. How would you do it?" If you let people talk, they will think you are a brilliant conversationalist.

Adding a new contact to your network is a game of first impressions. So, dress and groom yourself neatly; dress one level better than those around you; and of course, your clothes should be clean and wrinkle-free. After a networking event, take a few minutes to write down the names of the people you met, or make notes on their business card about their job and interests. It is good practice to follow up with a note or email, to remind people who you are and cement your impression in their mind. For example, "I enjoyed meeting you the other day at the Quarterly Business Outlook. At that time, you mentioned you were interested in art. I noticed the Barnes is having an exhibit on Friday that you might be interested in." After your name, you might add a postscript line, "In case you forgot, I was the tall guy from Rutgers."

Some people are shy about making new contacts. Rest assured, the more you network, the less shy you will be, so the cure for shyness is to get in the game as often as possible. One way to do that is to volunteer to work the reception desk at professional events. This will give you a chance to greet people, "Hello. Welcome to Expo 3000. Let me help you find your name tag." People might assume you are one of the hosts of the event and that will make subsequent conversation easier.

Finally, a good networker makes a point of developing contacts with a wide variety of groups. Again, this pushes people out of their comfort zone, but by being a connector between groups one gains influence. Make it a point to network with people who are younger and older, who work in other professions as well as your own. Make it a point to network with people who travel in different social circles than your own. Networks are a way of exchanging problems, challenges and ideas. Often, one group confronts a problem that seems insuperable, but other groups facing similar problems have already found a solution. Being a connector and sharing information among groups will profoundly increase your influence. Maybe networking isn't everything, but it goes a long way toward everything.

## Appendix 1b: Literature of Character

Literature has much to say about good character. The forces that shape human nature have not changed much over the last twenty-five centuries, so to understand how people think and act today, we should examine how they thought and acted in the past. Three classic discussions of character are Polonius' advice to his son Laertes before he leaves for University in Paris; Rudyard Kipling's poem "If"; and William Ernest Henley's poem "Invictus."

### A Father's Advice

William Shakespeare (1564–1616) provided many models of human behavior. One of the best is in "Hamlet." In Act I, Scene iii, Polonius, an adviser to the king, gives his son Laertes advice before he goes to University in Paris. This is thought to be among the best advice any father has given in literature, and it still applies today.[23]

**Polonius**

"These few precepts in your memory inscribe.
Don't say everything that's on your mind, and don't act unless you've thought things over carefully.
Be friendly to everyone, but not overly personal.
Those friends you have that are tried and true, grapple them to your soul with hoops of steel;
Don't waste your time or money entertaining every new acquaintance.
Avoid quarrels, but once pulled into one, conduct yourself so that those opposed will be wary of you in the future.
Listen to everyone, but say little.
Take each man's opinion, but hold your own.
Buy the best clothes you can afford, not flashy, but of good quality, not extreme or outrageous, for clothes oft make the man (or the woman), and those (in France and elsewhere) of the best rank and station dress well.
Neither a borrower nor a lender be; for loan oft loses both itself and friend, and borrowing dulls the edge of thrift.

---

[23] Shakespeare, William. (1564–1616) "Hamlet." In Act I, Scene iii.

This above all, to thine own self be true, and it must follow, as the night the day; you cannot then be false to any man.

This advice is full of nuance and to get the most out of it, you must read it, think about it, put it aside and then read it again.

**Being a Man**

What does it mean to be a man? Is it about one's gender or is it about being a stand-up person? Rudyard Kipling's poem "If" is about character, and applies equally to men and women.[24]

---

[24] Kipling, Rudyard. 1895. "If" Complete Verses. New York: Anchor Books, 1989.

-------------------                **If**                ---------------------

If you can keep your head when
all about you
Are losing theirs and blaming it
on you;
If you can trust yourself when
all men doubt you,
But make allowance for their
doubting too;
If you can wait and not be tired
by waiting,
Or, being lied about, don't deal
in lies,
Or, being hated, don't give way
to hating,
And yet don't look too good, nor
talk too wise;
If you can dream - and not make
dreams your master;
If you can think - and not make
thoughts your aim;
If you can meet with triumph
and disaster
And treat those two imposters
just the same;
If you can bear to hear the truth
you've spoken
Twisted by knaves to make a
trap for fools,
Or watch the things you gave
your life to broken,
And stoop and build 'em up with
worn out tools;

If you can make one heap of all
your winnings
And risk it on one turn of pitch-
and-toss,
And lose, and start again at your
beginnings
And never breathe a word about
your loss;
If you can force your heart and
nerve and sinew
To serve your turn long after
they are gone,
And so hold on when there is
nothing in you
Except the Will which says to
them: "Hold on";
If you can talk with crowds and
keep your virtue,
Or walk with kings - nor lose the
common touch;
If neither foes nor loving friends
can hurt you;
If all men count with you, but
none too much;
If you can fill the unforgiving
minute
With sixty seconds' worth of
distance run -
Yours is the Earth and
everything that's in it,
And - which is more - you'll be a
Man my son!

## Knowing and Being Confident in Oneself

Self-reliance is closely related to the idea of self; the idea that a person
is responsible for shaping his or her own future. One of the best essays on

the idea that a person is responsible for shaping his or her own future is the
William Ernest Henley poem "Invictus."[1]

--------------            **Invictus**            ----------------

Out of the night that covers me,
Black as the pit from pole to pole,
I thank whatever gods may be,
For my unconquerable soul.
In the fall clutch of circumstances,
I have not winced nor cried aloud,
Under the bludgeoning of chance,
My head is bloody, but unbowed.
Beyond this place of wrath and tears,
Looms but the horror of the shade,
And yet the menace of the years,
Finds, and shall find me unafraid.
It matters not how straight the gate,
How charged with punishment the scroll,
I am the master of my fate,
I am the captain of my soul.

---

[1] Henley, William Ernest. 1875. "Invictus." Leopold Classic Library (April 30, 2016).

# Terms and Concepts

**Accountability** – Unless specific people are responsible for specific tasks, are measured on achievement of those tasks, and rewarded or punished based on objective performance, there is no accountability.

**Attitude** - The attitude you bring to work, school and life is a bigger determinant of success than IQ, parents' income or almost any other factor. Your attitude is something you choose every day.

**Character** - Character is the sum total of how a person thinks and acts. It is something internal and cannot be put on or taken off like a suit of clothes. In a very real sense, character is who we are.

**Character, Attributes of, Air Force** – The Air Force looks for the following character attributes: integrity, honesty, loyalty, selflessness, compassion, competency, respectfulness, fairness, responsibility and self-discipline, decisiveness, spiritual appreciation, and cooperativeness.

**Character, Ben Franklin defined as** – Ben Franklin's Thirteen Moral Virtues include temperance, silence, order, resolution, frugality, industry, sincerity, justice, moderation, cleanliness, tranquility, chastity, and humility.

**Character, Development of** – Good character, like any art, is developed through practice.

**Character, Likona's Model** - (i) Moral Knowing, (ii) Moral Feeling, and (iii) Moral Action.

**Chastity** – Manage your sexual appetites so you don't injure your reputation or that of others.

**Cleanliness** – Tolerate no uncleanness in body, clothes or home.

**Command Presence** - In the Navy, cool, unemotional, competence, coupled with decisive and disciplined action, is called command presence.

**Communications** – Failure to communicate goals and responsibilities clearly and concisely is a major contributor to plan failure.

**Compassion** – Concern for the suffering of others, provides aid and shows mercy.

**Competency** – Capable of excelling at all tasks assigned; effective and efficient.

**Cooperativeness** – Willingness to work or act together with others in accomplishing a task toward some common purpose.

**Decisiveness** – Capable of making logical and effective decisions in a timely manner. Does not shoot from the hip, but makes decisions promptly, after considering appropriate information.

**Execution** - Execution is the art and science of getting things done.

**Execution Cycle** – Plan, monitor, measure and take corrective action.

**Executable Plan** – See Plan, Executable.

**Fairness** – Treat people in an equitable, impartial and just manner.

**Followers, Needs of** – Followers need a leader who is competent, disciplined and decisive; who can motivate them to work toward a higher goal; who can clearly articulate goals, means and methods, and the basis for measuring performance; who can show how the organization's goals align with their own; who will actively listen to what they are saying; and who are introspective, self-critical, willing to admit mistakes, and are continually trying to improve themselves.

**Frugality** – Make no expense unless it benefits yourself or others. Waste nothing.

**Honesty** – Consistently being truthful with others.

**Humility** – Ability to be self-critical and listen to others.

**Industry** – Lose no time. Always be employed doing something useful. Cut off all unnecessary actions.

**Initiative** – An internal drive or motivation to get things done without being told to do them.

**Integrity** – Consistently choosing to do the 'right' thing.

**Justice** – Wrong no one by doing injuries or by omitting the benefits that are your duty.

**Leadership** – Leadership is knowing what to do and getting people to want to do what needs to be done.

**Leader, Characteristics of** – vision, competence, interest in his or her people, understanding of his or her people's needs and goals, character, integrity, compassion and fault tolerance.

**Leadership, First Rule of** – Take care of your people.

**Loyalty** – Being committed to one's organization, coworkers and subordinates.

**Moderation** – Avoid extremes. Do not resent injuries as much as they deserve.

**Moral Action** – Moral action requires: (i) knowing what must be done; (ii) the determination to make things happen; and (iii) habit, which is the practiced expression of moral action.

**Moral Feeling** – These are internal sign-posts as to what is right or wrong.

**Moral Knowing** – This is understanding that there are moral consequences to every human interaction.

**Order** – Let everything have its place, and every part of business have its time.

**People** – Few individuals can achieve much without other people. However, in every organization there are people who can't, won't or don't, do what is necessary to meet goals. These people should be eliminated.

**Plan, Executable** – A plan is executable when it lays out specific goals, allocates responsibility, and has a clear means of measuring progress or completion. Plans should be simple, concrete and measurable.

**Planner** – Weekly, Monthly and Annual Planners are calendars that record significant deadlines, milestones and events. Planners are a way to help manage time efficiently and spread work out over the time available.

**Plans, Failure to Meet** - Organizations generally fail to meet plans because they fail to: (i) prioritize, (ii) adequately communicate goals, (iii) hold people accountable, and (iv) have the wrong people.

**Plan of the Day** – This is a list of tasks to be performed today. It is a way of focusing attention on things that are important.

**Priority** – Companies often fail to meet plans when they fail to prioritize. Trying to do everything often results in doing nothing.

**Resolution** – Resolve to perform what you ought. Perform without fail what you resolve.

**Respectfulness** – Shows esteem for, and consideration of, others.

**Responsibility and Self-Discipline** – Can be depended upon to make rational decisions and to perform tasks assigned without supervision.

**Self-reliance** – The belief you can do things by yourself; rely on your own resources; take charge of any task or job presented and complete it in an efficient and effective manner, without the advice or guidance of others. Self-reliance is a habit of thought and action that can be developed. The self-reliant person improvises, adapts and overcomes.

**Self-reliance, Developing** - People aren't born with self-reliance; they learn it; study it; practice it; and after a while it becomes second nature.

**Selflessness** – Genuine concern for the welfare of others and putting that welfare ahead of one's own.

**Silence** – Only speak when it helps yourself or others. Avoid trifling conversation.

**Sincerity** – Use no hurtful deceit. Think innocently and justly, and if you speak, speak accordingly.

**Spiritual Appreciation** – Values spiritual diversity among individuals.

**Strategic Vision** – Knowing where an organization needs to go and how to get there.

**Temperance** – Do not eat or drink to excess.

**Time Management** –is one of the most important keys to success. He or she who wastes time, wastes life.

**Tranquility** – Do not be bothered by the trivial things or common unavoidable accidents.

**Virtue** – Aristotle said that virtue, like the arts, is acquired through practice and corresponding actions.

# References

AMA. 2007. "The Keys to Strategy Execution." AMA/HRI Survey. March 19. https://www.amanet.org/training/articles/printversion/the-keys-to-strategy-execution-06.aspx.

Annas, Julia. 1999. "Aristotle on Virtue and Happiness", Aristotle's Ethics. Edited by Nancy Sherman. New York. Rowman and Littlefield.

Arnst, Cathy. 2009. "Memo to CEOs: Experience IS Worth the Money", Businessweek. Jan.19. http://www.businessweek.com/careers/workingparents/blog/archives/2009/01/memo_to_ceos_experience_is_worth_the_money.html

Barlow, Cassie B. Mark Jordan, William Hendrix. 2003. "Character Assessment: An Examination of Leadership Levels", Journal of Business and Psychology. Vol. 17, No. 4 Summer.

Carr, David. 2007. "The Media Equation; Thousands Are Laid Off. What's New?" New York Times. April 2. http://www.nytimes.com/2007/04/02/business/media/02carr.html

Charan, Ram and Geoffrey Colvin. 1999. "Why CEOs Fail", Fortune. Vol. 139, Iss. 12. June 21.

Churchill, Winston. 1941. Speech given to the Harrow School October 29, a time when Europe had been at war for two years. *The Unrelenting Struggle*. London: Cassell and Boston: Little Brown 1942, pp. 274-76 English edition.

Clowney, K. 2001. "New Definition of Leadership", *Executive Excellence*. 18. Pp8-10.

Cole, Michael. 1999. "Become the Leader Followers Want to Follow", *Supervision*. Dec. pp.9-11.

Drucker, Peter. 1954. The Practice of Management. HarperBusiness. Reprinted 2006.

Franklin, Benjamin. 1791. "Memoires De La Vie Privee", was published in Paris in March of 1791. The first English translation, "The Private Life of the Late Benjamin Franklin, LL.D."

General Electric. 2012. "Leadership and Learning", General Electric. Fairfield, CT.
http://www.ge.com/company/culture/leadership_learning.html

Gergen, D. 2001. "Character of Leadership", *Executive Excellence*. 18, pp.5-7.

Grove, Andy. 1995, High Output Management. Vintage. 2nd edition, NY. NY.

Henley, William Ernest. 1875. "Invictus." Leopold Classic Library (April 30, 2016).

Hubbard, Elbert. 1917. "A Message to Garcia: Being a Preachment," The Roycrofters. East Aurora, N.Y.

Katz, D. and Kahn, R. 1976. *Leadership*. New York. John Wiley & Sons. Pp.525-576.

Kipling, Rudyard. 1895. "If" Complete Verses. New York: Anchor Books, 1989.

Kirkpatrick, S.A. and Loche, E.A. 1991. "Leadership: Do Traits Matter?" *The Executive*. 5 pp48-60.

Likona, T. 1991. Educating for Character. New York. Bantam Books.

Mankins, Michael C. and Richard Steele. 2005. "Turning Great Strategy Into Great Performance", Harvard Business Review. Jul.-Aug. pp.65-72.

Mukul, Pandya, Jeffrey Brown, Sandeep Junnarkar, Robbie Shell and Susan Warner. "Nightly Business Report Presents Lasting Leadership: What You Can Learn from the Top 25 Business People of our Times," Pearson Prentice Hall. 2006.

—. 2004. "Best of the Best: Inside Andy Grove's Leadership at Intel" Financial Times Press. Pearson Publishing. Dec. 10.
http://www.ftpress.com/ articles/article.aspx?p=345010.

Neiman, Robert A. and Harvey Thomson. 2004. "Execution Plain and Simple", *Canadian Manager*. Fall. pp17-19, 17.

Rosenbloom, Stephanie. 2008. "Circuit City Seeks Bankruptcy Protection", New York Times. Nov. 11. NYTimes.com.
www.nyutimes.com/2008/11/11/technology/11circuit.html

Shakespeare, William. (1564–1616) "Hamlet." In Act I, Scene iii.

Standard & Poor's Compustat Services. 2012. Data Guide. Englewood.

# CHAPTER TWO

# ENTREPRENEURSHIP AND RAISING CAPITAL

After completing this chapter, you should be able to:

2.1 Define entrepreneurship and explain the importance of entrepreneurs to the economy.

2.2 Discuss the foundations of a successful business.

2.3 Identify the most important personal factors that lead to entrepreneurial success.

2.4 Explain the relationship between entrepreneurship and raising capital.

2.5 Understand what it takes to pitch a business to investors and close a deal.

## Introduction

In the mid-1970s, only businesses and a few wealthy individuals owned computers. In 1975, IBM introduced its low-cost personal computer, the IBM 5100, priced at $10,975 including software.[1] That same year, a new Ford Mustang cost $3,529, or about a third as much as a personal computer.[2] Steve Wozniak, co-founder of Apple Computer thought everyone should have a computer, so he and Steve Jobs started a company in a garage and raised $1,300 by selling Job's Volkswagen van

---

[1] Blinkenlights. 2007. "Pop Quiz: What was the first personal computer?" Blinkenlights Archeological Institute. www.blinkenlights.com/pc.shtml
[2] VerticalScope Inc. 2011. "1975 Mustang II"
http://muscularmustangs.com/database/1975.php

and Wozniak's programmable calculator. A few weeks later, Steve Jobs made the company's first sale, 50 Apple I computers priced at $666 each. Six years later, the company was listed in the Fortune 500.[3]

In 1994, Jeff Bezos, founder and CEO of Amazon read a report projecting the annual growth of the web would be 2,300 percent per year. He saw it as a retailing opportunity. Web sales have a huge advantage over store sales because the cost of renting multiple stores and stocking them with inventory can be avoided. Web sales have an advantage over traditional mail order catalogs, because the cost of printing and mailing catalogs can be avoided, and websites can be quickly updated as consumer tastes change. Bezos drew up a list of things that could be sold on the web and decided to start with books, because there were a million titles in print and he could provide them at low cost. Amazon is now one of the most successful retailers on the planet.[4]

Berry Gordy, founder of Motown Records didn't set out to be a record producer. He just liked to write music. Because producers of the day didn't treat him fairly, he decided to take-charge of his destiny by starting his own record label, using $800 borrowed from his family. Motown, his second record label, went on to become a staple of American music.[5]

Many of the people who start businesses, don't set out to build a business. They set out to fill a need. Dineh Mohajer, a pre-med student with a passion for fashion was wearing pale blue sandals one day and couldn't find a nail polish to match. Her solution? She created her own nail polish color in her bathroom. Others liked her colors and wanted them. To supply the demand, she started a company called Hard Candy, which has over three dozen employees churning out five dozen colors. Many of her colors have provocative names, like Trailer Trash (metallic silver) and Sushi (aqua). According to some reports, these colors are popular with Hollywood stars.[6]

Sometimes, necessity is the mother of invention or at least the inspiration for a business. When Jasmine Lawrence was 11 she got a bad

---

[3] __. 2011. "The Little Entrepreneur", The Business-Adventure Series. Harper-Arrington Publishing. http://www.thelittlee.com/html/famous_entrepreneurs.html

[4] Funding Universe. 2004. "Amazon.com, Inc." Funding Universe. *International Directory of Company Histories*, Vol. 56. St. James Press. http://www.fundinguniverse.com/company-histories/Amazoncom-Inc-Company-History.html.

[5] __. 2011. "The Little Entrepreneur", The Business-Adventure Series. Harper-Arrington Publishing. http://www.thelittlee.com/html/famous_entrepreneurs.html.

[6] __. 2011. "The Little Entrepreneur", The Business-Adventure Series. Harper-Arrington Publishing. http://www.thelittlee.com/html/famous_entrepreneurs.html

relaxing perm. The harsh chemicals caused her hair to fall out. This led her to search for a hair relaxer that didn't use harsh chemicals. After a year of experimentation, she discovered an all-natural product that gave the results she wanted. After attending an entrepreneurship camp, she decided to start her own company, and at age 15, she founded Eden Body Works.[7]

Entrepreneurs are all around us, inventing new products and services, making our lives better, and getting rich in the process. This chapter discusses: what it takes to be a successful entrepreneur; the importance of capital to a start-up company; the best places for an entrepreneur to find capital; the cost; and how to persuade an investor to invest in a company.

## Entrepreneurs and the Economy

What is an entrepreneur? An economist might define an entrepreneur as someone who combines land, labor and capital to create a new enterprise. But a more down-to-earth definition of an entrepreneur is someone who can **make something out of nothing**. Or, stated differently, build a business from the ground up.

Entrepreneurs are the engine of the economy. Studies have shown that entrepreneurs create more jobs than firms led by non-entrepreneurs. People working for entrepreneurial firms also have higher job satisfaction than people working for non-entrepreneurial firms, even though their pay, on average, is lower. Entrepreneurs also commercialize, that is, convert to marketable goods and services, innovations at a higher rate than non-entrepreneurial firms. Entrepreneurial activity has a positive impact on hiring by non-entrepreneurial firms, as they try to catch up with breakthroughs and innovations created by entrepreneurs. [8]

New businesses account for about 70% of job creation. While it's true that many new businesses fail in the first five years, job destruction from such failure is far outweighed by job creation.

Entrepreneurs do more than generate employment. They also bring innovative goods and services to the market, and that improves productivity and the quality of people's lives. A nation which encourages entrepreneurship will prosper. A nation which over-regulates and over taxes entrepreneurship will fail.

---

[7] NFM Staff. 2008. "40 Under 40: Jasmine Lawrence", *Natural Foods Merchandiser*. Jul. 23.
http://newhope360.com/personal-care/40-under-40-jasmine-lawrence.
[8] Praag, C. Mirjam van and Peter H. Vershoot. 2007. "What is the value of entrepreneurship? A view of recent research." Small Business Economics. 29:351-382.

---
**Entrepreneurs**

Create new businesses to **fill a need** or **solve a problem**.

Can be **inspired** by an intense interest in a product or service, or a desire to fill a personal need.

Drive most of the net **increase** in **jobs** in the economy.

Bring innovative goods and services to market; **improve productivity** and improve the **quality of people's lives.**

---

## Personal Factors

The payoffs for a successful entrepreneur can be wealth, independence, and the ability to be one's own boss. Entrepreneurs usually have higher job satisfaction than employees. On the other hand, 30% of new businesses fail in the first two years, and only half of new firms survive five years or more.[9] So, what separates winners and losers?

### Energy and Determination

Entrepreneurs need a lot of energy and determination. Most people can sustain enthusiasm for short periods of time. Entrepreneurs must sustain it over prolonged periods, even when things aren't working out. There is no certainty when starting a business. There are likely to be roadblocks, failures and partial successes. Most people give up after a certain number of tries. Those who persist in the face of adversity almost always succeed. Whether you think you can, or you can't, you are probably right. Many businesses fail because the entrepreneur has lost his or her enthusiasm and drive to succeed. Success means trying a lot of different things.[10]

---

[9] __. 2011. "What is the survival rate for new firms?" Small Business Administration Office of Advocacy Research and Statistics. www.sba.gov/advocacy/7495/8430.

[10] Spolsky, Joel. 2009. "Start-up Static", Inc. March. Pp.33-34.

## Experience

Experience is a factor in separating those who succeed from those who fail. A person who is not an engineer, who has never worked for an aircraft manufacturer, and who has never flown a plane, probably isn't the right person to start an aircraft company. On the other hand, a person who has put solar panels on her house, on her brother's house and has electrified the local summer camp with solar panels is probably a good person to start a solar installation business.

In every business, in every profession, there are a thousand details one needs to know, a thousand trap doors one needs to avoid, and a few 'secret handshakes', call them trade secrets, that one needs to know. The best way to learn about these details, trap doors and secrets is to work in the field you want to start your business in.

Sometimes, one can get experience through intense study and experimentation. Jeff Bezos, Dineh Mohajer, and Jasmine Lawrence fit into the study and experimentation model. Steve Jobs and Steve Wozniak gained experience working for computer gaming companies. Berry Gordy learned the music business by writing songs and working in the music industry before he launched his first record label.

The point is that learning and experience are essential for entrepreneurial success. If you can find work in the industry you want to start your business in, that's a way to get experience and get paid for it. If you can't get a job in the field you want to go into, make that field your hobby; talk to others in the field; join clubs of people with similar interest; experiment. But get experience and all the knowledge you can before you launch your business.

## Character

Good character is an essential for entrepreneurial success. Customers, suppliers, employees and investors all need to know you can be trusted; that you will be fair and honest; that you are reliable; and that you will follow through.

People will judge you by your track record. If you have a record of setting and completing goals, of getting the job done with no excuses, they will trust you. On the other hand, if they perceive you as slapdash, committed one day and not the next, inconsistent, or if you make excuses, they won't trust you.

Trust is important for a start-up because it is often the only currency it has. Start-ups don't have much of a track record and usually have little collateral.

What investors are investing in is not a 'gee-whiz' technology, or a clever business plan. Investors invest in people; therefore, the entrepreneur's character is critical to raising capital and getting people to do business with a new company.

---

**Characteristics of Successful Entrepreneurs**

Successful entrepreneurs have the following characteristics:

**Energy and determination**

**Knowledge and experience**

**Good character**

---

## Foundations of Business Success

Dig down in every successful business and you will find it is built on a couple of key principles. They provide something that people want, that people are willing to pay for, and that can be provided at a profit.

### What People Want

People purchase goods and services for two basic reasons: (i) to solve a problem, or (ii), to feel good about themselves. Steve Wozniak, co-founder of Apple Computer solved the problem of high-cost computers. Jeff Bezos, founder of Amazon lowered the cost of books, made more book titles available, and improved convenience through at-home shopping.

Some people solve problems and make people feel good about themselves at the same time. Dineh Mohajer, founder of Hard Candy, built on her passion for fashion by creating nail polish colors that weren't available anywhere else. Jasmine Lawrence, founder of Eden Body Works, solved the problem of harsh chemical hair relaxers by going 'all natural'.

It is often said, "Do what you love to do, and you'll never work a day in your life." But doing what you want doesn't necessarily translate into what others want. A good entrepreneur must see things from the perspective of others.

How does an entrepreneur find out what people want? It turns out the signs are all around us. The potential entrepreneur must become sensitive to those signs.

One way to think of a hospital is as a billing machine. The typical hospital bill is pages and pages of itemized services that add up to thousands, or tens of thousands, of dollars. It also turns out that hospital bills are full of errors. Insurance companies don't like to pay medical bills, but they are obligated to pay unless they find an error. A handful of people figured out that insurance companies wanted to find billing errors to reduce their costs. These people set up medical bill audit companies which look for duplicate billing, inappropriate treatment, for example, charges for leg braces when a person was hospitalized for ulcers, and so forth. Medical bill auditors usually charge a percentage of the errors found. For example, a hospital might bill $36,000; the audit service might find that $5,000 was billed in error; and might charge an insurance company $1,000 for the audit. The result? The insurer saves $4,000.

What might an entrepreneurial student do with such an example? How about starting a service that audits tuition bills? Between the cost of tuition, fees, credits, discounts and so forth, there is substantial room for error in tuition bills. The author used to audit his undergraduate tuition bills and often found errors. An entrepreneur might audit student bills in exchange for a fee equal to a percentage of errors found.

In addition to money, people want to save time. Homemade soup gave way to condensed soup. Condensed soup gave way to ready-to-heat soup, and that has given way to soup in microwavable bowls. Time and convenience are closely linked. People often buy frozen vegetables in preference to fresh vegetables and microwave-in-bag vegetables in preference to conventional frozen vegetables, to save time and effort.

However, sensitivity to customer needs can be a trap. Henry Ford said, "If I listened to my customers, I would have built a faster horse." Steve Jobs wanted to provide people with totally new products, rather than simply making improvements to existing products. The result was the iPhone, the iPad, and a dozen other innovative products.[11]

People rarely buy products or services in isolation. They are usually trying to solve a problem. Identify a problem, and then think about a new, more effective, more convenient, or less costly way of solving it.

People want to feel good about themselves, and some are willing to pay handsomely for it. If all people wanted, was to get from point A to

---

[11] Rees, Matthew 2014. "The Real Market Makers: Knowledge and Power", Wall Street Journal. March 18 A13.

point B, no-one would pay $120,000 for a Maserati. They pay because they want to feel good about themselves. That's also why people pay $1,000 an ounce for Caron's Poivre perfume;[12] shop at Nordstroms; and have Facebook pages. If you can find something that makes people feel good about themselves, you might have an idea for a successful business.

## Profitable Products and Services

Goods and services must be profitable. One way to measure profitability is Gross Margin, which is the percentage of every dollar of sales left over after the product is made or service is provided. Gross margin for a product can be estimated using equation Eq.2.1.

$$\text{Gross Margin} = (\text{Price} - \text{Cost})/\text{Price} \qquad \text{Eq.2.1}$$

When a company's gross margin on goods or services is too small, it is likely to fail. Target gross margins vary by industry, but for most companies, gross margins under 20% mean trouble. A gross margin around 50% is much better, and gross margins over 60% are not unheard of.

## Avoid the Ordinary

A common mistake 'would be' entrepreneurs make is to offer 'me too' products or services. They want to start restaurants, retail stores, T-shirt companies, lawn care services, or other similar businesses. There are two problems with 'me too' companies. First, they are a commodity and second, there is limited potential for growth.

Commodities are goods and services offered by many companies with few things to distinguish one company's offerings from another company's. There is no reason a customer should choose to do business with a new company if they are satisfied with their old one. Because commodities are interchangeable, it is also difficult to raise price. If two companies are offering essentially the same product, and one raises its price, customers will simply buy from the other company. When a company loses control over price, it becomes difficult to generate the superior profits that investors want.

---

[12] Rich, Richie. 2011. "The 8 Most Expensive Perfumes in the World", Luxury Lists. http://luxatic.com/the-8-most-expensive-perfumes-in-the-world/

When offering commodity goods and services, there is limited opportunity for growth because there is so much competition. Real growth comes from break-out products and services.

There is a great divide between entrepreneurs with 'me too' products and services, and those with break-out products and services. Entrepreneurs with 'me too' products may have the satisfaction of working for themselves, and may make a decent living. However, these entrepreneurs probably make less than they would as large company employees. On the other hand, entrepreneurs with break-out products and services can make significantly more in their own companies than if they worked for others, and they get the satisfaction of working for themselves.

What differentiates a company with 'me too' products from a company with break-out products and services? 'Me too' products are merely copies of what others have done. Break-out products and services create value for customers in new and unexpected ways.

## Scalability

One of the differences between successful and marginal companies is scalability. Scalability refers to whether a business can replicate its success on a larger and larger scale.

A person can make T-shirts in his or her basement or garage and sell them at a profit. But can this be scaled up ten times? A hundred times? Companies that are scalable are much more likely to be successful than companies that cannot be scaled up.

### Franchises

'Hamburger joints' are a dime a dozen. Anyone can start a small restaurant to make hamburgers. It's a 'me too' product and a 'me too' service. But what if the menu were pared down to a handful of items that could be prepared in advance, so people could walk in, buy their meal and leave in a matter of minutes. People could get food, fast. But is it scalable? Yes, of course it is. Build small, standardized restaurants, with limited menus and pre-prepared food. Standardize preparation to eliminate the need for experienced short-order cooks. But, how can anyone manage large numbers of small restaurants? They might sell franchises.

A franchise is the right to use the trade mark and trade name of another company, to use its methods, formulae and procedures in a limited geographic area. A franchisor develops a concept for something, a restaurant, store, lawn care service, something, and tests it to make sure it is successful. The testing process often means building a small chain of restaurants, or stores and experimenting with different formats and combinations of products or services. When the franchisor has a proven template for a successful business, the franchisor sells the right to use that template in a limited geographic area.

Typically, the franchisor gets an initial franchise fee, which can range from tens of thousands of dollars to a million dollars, plus some percentage of the franchisee's gross sales. Ongoing fees typically range from about 4% to 10% of sales. Franchisees are also required to pay 4% to 10% of sales toward brand advertising.[13] Obviously, the 'hamburger joint' discussed above is McDonalds, one of the most successful franchises ever. Their business model is highly scalable.

### Retail Distribution

Another way to achieve scalability is to produce a product that retailers want to sell. Successful retailers consider their shelf space valuable real estate. They are not about to put just anyone's products on their shelves. But if a company can demonstrate that the public likes, even demands, its products, and the retailer can make a superior profit from the company's products, the retailer might take a chance on a new company. If a company's manufacturing is scalable, and it can get many retailers to sell its products, it can be highly successful.

### Direct Sales

If a company needs to rent or build stores to sell its products, the cost of real estate becomes a limiting factor in how rapidly it can expand. An alternative might be direct sales. Catalog sales have been around for at least a hundred and fifty years, and can still be successful, though catalog selling is expensive. Catalog sales are scalable because products are generally stored and shipped from a single point, and commercially available mailing lists provide large numbers of individuals that catalogs may be mailed to. So, catalog sales are highly scalable. The challenges are finding products people want to buy, offering them at prices people can afford, and sending catalogs only to those most likely to buy.

There are other forms of direct marketing in addition to catalog sales. For example, there is telemarketing, where people are called at home and

---

[13] World Franchising. 2011. World Franchising Network. www.worldfranchising.com/,

offered goods and services. There are television programs that offer products, backed up by phone banks of order takers. There are programs like Amway and Avon, wherein individuals are recruited to sell products door-to-door, or through their own personal networks. However, one of the most dynamic means of direct selling is through the internet.

Jeff Bezos was among the first to realize the power of the internet as a means of selling goods. The cost and difficulty of setting up a website is very low compared to setting up a bricks and mortar store. The difficulty with the internet is driving people to one's website because there are so many websites competing for attention.

## Customers

One of the mistakes start-up businesses make is to assume their product or service is so insanely-great that people will come running, with cash in hand. A successful entrepreneur will spend a lot of time thinking about potential customers.

An entrepreneur should ask him or herself: (i) who is the ideal customer? (ii) how many of these customers are there? (iii) where are they located? (iv) how can they be found and contacted? (v) how will they find out about the company? and (vi) can they afford to pay? If the entrepreneur says everyone is an ideal customer, they aren't thinking, and are doomed to fail.

Start with an even simpler question. Who will be the company's first customer? The first customer should be the one who values the company's product or service most. Be specific. If the first customer won't buy, that means other customers are unlikely to buy. Friends and family don't qualify as the first customer, because they might buy out of sympathy or support.

## Start Small

Companies that risk everything on one toss of the dice are very likely to fail. But when a company starts small, it can afford to make mistakes, regroup, and try again. Starting small might mean launching a business out of a garage, bedroom or basement, with limited invested capital.

Few people get their business model right on the first try. Most entrepreneurs try something, learn from it, change their approach, and try again. Every attempt at developing a product or making a sale, even if unsuccessful, can be a learning experience that increases the probability of success on the next try.

Starting small doesn't mean staying small. Starting small is simply a risk management strategy. Many successful entrepreneurs start their businesses while employed by other people. That gives them some income while experimenting to find the right business model.

---

**Characteristics of Successful Start-up Companies**

Goods and services **people want or need.**

Substantial **gross margins**

Goods and services that are unique, **not 'me too' products or services.**

**Scalability** is the ability to replicate success on a larger and larger scale.

**Understand customers at a deep level.**

**Start small** to prove concepts and to learn the business.

---

## Testing Business Ideas: The Investor Test

Entrepreneur enthusiasm is necessary, but it is not sufficient to gauge whether a company is likely to succeed. Friends and family are not a reliable gauge because they may just be supportive, or they may not be equipped to fully grasp the idea or the challenges of converting an idea into a business. It would be great if there were some external measure an entrepreneur could use to test the merit of his or her idea. And fortunately, there is.

If an investor is willing to put money into a company, that is good evidence that an idea, plan, or business has merit. Investors only get their money back, plus some return, if a business succeeds. Investors are sophisticated about why companies succeed or fail. Many investors have an informal template they use to decide which businesses are likely to succeed and which are likely to fail. Companies that match that template are much more likely to survive and thrive than businesses that try to make-it-up as they go along.

One of the hardest, yet most useful things a person can do is to look at the world from someone else's point of view. If an entrepreneur can look at the world the way an investor does, and understand what investors are looking for, they have a much greater chance of getting investors to write checks.

# Capital

## Why is Capital Needed?

What is capital and why is it important? Businesses large and small need capital because of timing differences. When goods are manufactured, a company must pay for raw materials and labor, both cash outflows, before it can sell goods, and generate cash inflow. Manufacturing takes time, so a company may need capital for some prolonged period. A computer consulting company may need to pay its workers while a project is being completed for a client. Clients often pay on completion and then may not pay for 30 or more days after invoicing. Capital is needed to finance payroll while waiting for clients to pay.

Retailers, wholesalers, manufacturers and service organizations all need real estate or equipment, to one extent or another. Sometimes this real estate and equipment can be rented or leased, but some of it must be purchased. Suppose a company purchases computers, desks, and filing cabinets that will help generate cash over the next four or five years. The company is making the purchase now, a cash outflow, but the cash inflows these items will help generate will come in over an extended period of time. Capital is needed to fund those cash outflows. Capital is also needed as a company expands, and needs to fund additional inventory, equipment and facilities ahead of increased sales.

## Types of Capital

There are two basic types of capital, debt and equity. Debt is money borrowed from others. Equity is what the owner of a company has invested in the company.

Suppose an entrepreneur starts a company using $1,000 of her own money. That is equity. If a company makes a profit of $5,000 and the entrepreneur pays herself a dividend of $3,000; the $2,000 of profit left in the company is called retained earnings. This is another type of equity.

If the entrepreneur forms a corporation, small slices of ownership in that company are called shares. An entrepreneur might form a company with 10,000 shares. She might give herself 5,000 shares in exchange for her initial investment of $1,000 and issue 1,000 shares to someone else for $5,000. At this point the company will have 10,000 shares authorized and 6,000 shares outstanding; 5,000 belonging to the entrepreneur and 1,000 belonging to the investor. The money the investor paid to the company in exchange for shares is also equity. Based on this example, the company would have equity of $8,000 ($1,000 entrepreneur's initial investment, $2,000 retained earnings, and $5,000 of investor's capital).

Debt is money borrowed from others. There are many forms of debt. If company borrows money from a bank, that is debt. Money borrowed from friends and family is debt. A mortgage, usually money borrowed to buy real estate, is also debt.

Sometimes, companies issue promissory notes. These are unconditional promises to pay a certain amount of money at a certain time. For example, to meet payroll, a company may issue, that means sell, a note promising to pay $10,000 in thirty days. Why would anyone want to buy such a promise? Usually promissory notes are sold at a discount, which means they are sold for less than their payoff value. An investor might be willing to pay $9,800 today for the promise of $10,000 in thirty days. That would represent about 24.5% interest if the old note were paid off, and a new note issued every month (($200 interest/$9,800) x 12 months per year).

When a company buys supplies on credit, the supplier is lending the company the value of the supplies. For example, a garden center company may order $6,000 worth of fertilizer. That is the same as the supplier lending the company $6,000. This type of credit is called accounts payable.

Assets are all the things a company has. Examples of assets include buildings, equipment, inventory, and cash in banks. Every dollar of assets must be financed by either debt or equity. Stated differently, capital is how a company finances its assets. There are many forms of debt and equity capital, and more are being invented every day. The point is, that all assets must be financed somehow. Convincing investors or creditors that a company is on the right track is the key to getting the needed capital.

## Characteristics of Capital

If an entrepreneur wants an investor to invest, or a creditor to lend, she or he must put themselves in the point of view of the investor or creditor. To simplify the discussion, let us call all suppliers of capital, whether debt or equity, investors.

Four characteristics can help identify which investors are likely to invest: (i) risk, (ii) reward, (iii), transaction size, and (iv) time to exit. Entrepreneurs, as well as established companies, must match the investor's criteria on these four characteristics or no funds will flow. Fortunately, most investors fall into well-defined categories and the risk, reward, transaction size and time to exit of each category is well known.

## Transaction Size

Some transactions are too big for some investors and too small for others. Angel investors are wealthy private individuals who invest in small companies. Typically, they invest from $25,000 to $250,000. If a company needs $10 million, the transaction size is too large for an angel investor or even a dozen angel investors. On the other hand, $10 million is too small for a company to issue corporate bonds. Corporate bonds are promises to pay a certain amount at maturity and to pay interest twice per year. Corporate bonds are commonly used when companies want to raise hundreds of millions or even billions of dollars.

## Time to Exit

No investor wants to put his or her money into a business and leave it there forever. Different types of investors have different expectations as to when they get their money back. Banks usually want loans repaid in three years, sometimes one year, depending on the type of loan. Suppliers want to be paid in 30 days or less. Bondholders invest for the long term, so ten or twenty-year bonds are not uncommon. Angel investors usually want to get their investment back in five years. Before talking to an investor, it is important to understand their time-to-exit expectations.

## Reward

Different classes of investors have different reward expectations. Angel investors usually invest in small start-up companies with a lot of risk. In return for the risk, they expect high returns. Typically, an angel investor wants from 30% to 38% per year. The exact amount depends on the bargaining power of the parties and the riskiness of the company.

Banks, on the other hand, only demand a few percentage points above the prime rate. The prime rate is the rate that money center banks lend to their best customers.

An entrepreneur needs to know the return expectations of an investor before meeting with them. If the entrepreneur offers the investor too little, the investor will walk away. If the entrepreneur offers the investor too much, he or she will be wasting money.

## Risk

Risk is the hardest variable to estimate. Generally, start-up companies are much riskier than established companies. Companies that haven't sold any products are riskier than companies that have sales of $1,000,000. Companies with losses are riskier than companies that have been profitable. Companies with only a handful of customers are riskier than companies with lots of customers. Entrepreneurs who have no experience in a particular field of business are riskier than entrepreneurs who have lots of experience in that field.

---

### Characteristics of Capital Investments

Entrepreneurs must match the characteristics of what they **need and can offer** to what investors **need and** are willing to **tolerate**. They must match on four criteria:

**Risk** – the odds the investor will get promised returns.

**Reward** – what is the investor's return on investment.

**Transaction size** – some transactions are too big or too small for certain investors.

**Time to exit** – this is how long before the investor gets his or her money back.

---

## Sources of Capital

Banks are not your friend if you are trying to start a company. They are not in the business of taking a chance on a new business. Banks are highly regulated, which means they must justify everything they do to the Federal Deposit Insurance Corporation (FDIC), and others. Banks only want to lend to companies that are tried and true; businesses that made money last year, that will make money this year, and which are likely to make money next year. Banks require substantial collateral for loans.

Start-up companies rarely meet this profile. For one thing, they may not have a last year. Banks want to know that a company has enough cash flow to pay principal and interest several times over. This gives them a cushion in case something goes wrong. Start-ups may not have sufficient cash flow.

Banks want collateral; property they can seize if a company can't repay its loan. Banks call this a secondary source of payment. Start-up companies rarely have enough collateral for a loan.

Banks also want personal guarantees. A personal guarantee is a guarantee that if the company fails, the entrepreneur will personally repay the bank. Personal guarantees involve things like giving the bank the right to seize personal assets such as cars, bank accounts, stocks and the entrepreneur's house.

Entrepreneurs have several alternatives to traditional bank loans. The art form is to figure out which combination of alternatives is the best fit for a start-up.

## Entrepreneur's Own Sources

Entrepreneurs should look to their own resources first. High on the list of capital sources should be savings. Anyone who wants to be an entrepreneur should save systematically, setting aside a certain amount each week, each pay, or each month.

Having one's own money invested in a company is important, because the first question an investor is likely to ask is, "How much of your own is invested in the company?" If the entrepreneur doesn't have enough faith in the business to invest his or her own money, why should an investor invest?

Credit cards can be a useful source of capital for a start-up. But credit cards can be dangerous if not used properly. Use some credit cards only for business and some only for personal expenses. Pay off balances completely each month. Watch for rate jumps. Pay timely so there are no late fees. Search for cards with no annual fee and no fee to transfer the balance to another card, should rates jump.

Customers can be a source of capital. Builders often ask for a third of the contract price in advance, one third halfway through the project, and one third on completion. The one third at the beginning of the contract provides capital for the builder to purchase supplies and meet initial payroll. Sometimes a software company, or a company building a custom product, can get an advance on the value of the contract.

Suppliers can be another source of capital. Think about what happens when a company buys something on credit. The supplier is lending the company money, as surely as if they handed it a check.

For those who have been working a while, and own their own home, a home equity loan can be a significant source of capital. Of course, if the entrepreneur is married, the entrepreneur will have to get the consent of his or her spouse to take out a home equity loan.

## Friends and Family

For many entrepreneurs, friends and family are one of the first sources of capital. If the people who know you best aren't willing to invest in your company, why should a stranger invest?

Friends and family may invest in the form of loans or purchase of stock. Loans require the repayment of principal and interest on a pre-set schedule. On the other hand, if friends and family purchase stock in the company, there is no requirement to pay dividends, and a stock investment is permanent, in the sense that there is no requirement to buy back the stock. Interest paid on loans is tax deductible. Dividends, if paid, are not tax deductible.

It's important to be clear as to the character of investments made by friends and family. Suppose someone hands you a $10,000 check, is that a loan or a stock purchase? Suppose your company becomes the next Google or Facebook. In that case, the investor will claim they bought stock in the company, stock which might be worth a hundred times what they invested.

If the company fails, they might claim the money was a loan. You should also be clear as to whether you are personally borrowing money, or a corporation is borrowing money. If you incorporate, and the company borrows the money, you have no legal obligation to repay the loan if the company fails. But, if you borrow the money personally, and the company fails, you are still obligated to repay the loan.

There is one final consideration when dealing with friends and family. Consider what will happen to your relationships if the company fails. Will you lose their friendship? Will family members be estranged? In the words of William Shakespeare, *"Neither a borrower, nor a lender be, for loan oft loses both self and friend." – Hamlet, Act I, Scene 3.*

## Small Business Administration (SBA) Loans

The Small Business Administration (SBA) does not make loans. The Small Business Administration guarantees up to 85% of loans under $150,000 or 75% of loans up to $5,000,000. An SBA loan is a bank loan with an SBA guarantee. The SBA guarantee may shift the bank's risk/reward calculation in favor of granting a loan. The bank can collect interest on the entire loan balance, while only risking a small fraction of the loan balance. The SBA charges a fee for such a guarantee and banks usually pass these costs onto the borrower.[14]

The Small Business Administration **always requires a personal guarantee**. If the company fails, the entrepreneur must personally repay the loan. That means the entrepreneur risks losing his or her home, savings and other assets. More details on the SBA loan guarantee program are available at www.sba.gov.

## Angel Investors

Angel investors are wealthy individuals who invest their own money. Often, they are retired executives or people who have owned their own business. Angels typically invest from $25,000 to $250,000. At a minimum, they want 30% per year return on their money, and often want five times their investment back in five years. That works out to 38% per year. Angel investors want to get in on the ground floor of the next Google or Facebook.

Since angel investors are investing their own money, they can take a chance on something new and different, whereas banks can only lend to businesses that are tried and true. Angels usually invest in businesses within a one hour's drive of their home so they can keep an eye on what they regard as 'their money.'

Most Angel Investors are very sophisticated. They screen investments very carefully before they write a check. If a company meets an Angel Investor's criteria, it is much more likely to succeed than a company untested by such scrutiny.

## Small Business Investment Companies (SBIC)

Small Business Investment Companies (SBIC) are private companies with access to low cost government funds. SBICs are chartered by the Small Business Administration specifically to support small businesses.

An SBIC can be formed by investors with a minimum of ten million dollars. Typically, the partners in an SBIC raise one or two million dollars from their own resources, then raise another twenty or thirty million of private capital from pension plans, trust funds or insurance companies. They can then borrow up to three times this private capital in the form of low cost funds raised through sale of government bonds.

---

[14] SBA 2014. "General Business Loans: 7(a)" Small Business Administration. http://www.sba.gov/content/7a-loan-amounts-fees-interest-rates downloaded 6/13/2014

SBICs invest this capital in businesses defined as 'small' by the SBA. Most investments are in the form of equity, but sometimes, an SBIC will make a loan to a small business. The term over which they want to recoup their investment varies, but five years is not unusual. Because SBICs have access to relatively inexpensive government money, they don't need as high a return as Angel Investors, however, they will need a return dramatically higher than that on SBA loans.

The investment criteria for an SBIC is tougher than for Angel Investors, but much less stringent than banks. Angel investors typically invest $25,000 to $250,000. SBICs typically invest $250,000 to $3,000,000. So, SBICs can provide money when a company outgrows Angel Investors. A list of SBICs is available at www.sba.gov.

## Venture Capital

Venture capitalists (VCs) invest money from insurance companies and pension plans. Venture capitalists demand returns of 40% a year, or more. That means a company must grow faster than 40% per year or the VCs won't invest.

Venture capitalists typically invest in high-tech or bio-medical companies with potential sales of at least a billion dollars. VCs intensely monitor the companies they invest in, demand seats on the board of directors, and typically negotiate for some form of control over a company. For example, if promised milestones aren't met, VCs reserve the right to get additional seats on the board of directors, or even fire the original entrepreneurs. Because of this intense monitoring, it is unlikely a VC would be interested in investing less than $10 million.

VCs rarely invest in start-up companies, preferring to let others take the risk of betting on early stage companies. They provide money only after a company has proven itself. Venture capitalists are very sophisticated and screen investments very carefully. Less than 1% of companies qualify for venture capital. VC funds have a limited life, often ten years. That means their time to exit is likely to be shorter than ten years, often much shorter.

## Other Sources of Capital

There are many sources of capital other than banks. Unfortunately, start-up companies rarely have the size to access this capital. A few examples include: (i) corporate bonds, (ii) public securities market, (iii) commercial paper, and (iv) asset securitization. A more complete list of sources can be found in the author's book *Raising Capital*.

Table 2.1 Analysis of Funding Sources, lists some of the more common ways that companies raise capital, and how those sources relate to risk, reward, time to exit and transaction size.[15]

## Table 2.2 Analysis of Funding Sources

In Transaction Size, k stands for thousands, M millions and B billions. In the reward column, the term 'Prime' means the prime rate of interest. That is the rate banks charge their best customers.

| Capital Source | Risk | Reward | Transaction Size | Time to Exit |
|---|---|---|---|---|
| **Entrepreneur's Own Sources** – Savings, home loans, credit cards | Very risk tolerant | Prime to 24% | $10 - $100k | 3- 4 years. |
| **Friends and Family** – Stock or loans | Very risk tolerant | 10% to 15% | $5 - $25k | 3-4 years |
| **Angel Investors** – wealthy individuals. | Risk tolerant | 30% - 38% per year | $25 to $250k | 5 years. |
| **Small Business Investment Company** – (SBICs) invest in small businesses | Moderate risk, a few start-ups | 15% - 20% per year | $250k to $3.0M | 4 to 6 years. |
| **Bank Loans** – collateral and personal guarantees. | Very, risk averse | Prime + 2% to +6% | $50k to $500M | 1 to 3 years |
| **Bank – Small Business Administration (SBA)** Partial loan guarantee. | Very risk averse | Prime +2.25% to +2.75% | $25k to $5M | 1 to 7 years |
| **Venture Capitalist** – invest insurance and pension money. | Very selective | 40% - 60% per year | $10M to $500M | 3 to 7 years. |
| **Initial Public Offering** – public stock sale. | Fairly risk tolerant | Significant potential | $30M to $3B | Never repaid |
| **Corporate Bonds** – Pay at maturity plus interest twice per year. | Moderate to low risk | Less than prime rate | $100M to $5B | 5 to 20 years |
| **Commercial Paper** – Short term promissory notes. | Extremely risk averse | 50% to 70% of Prime | $1B to $10B | 1 day to 9 months |

[15] Vance, David. 2005. Raising Capital. Springer Science + Business Media. New York.

# Pitching and Closing the Deal

Pitching is asking for money. If an entrepreneur wants someone to invest, the entrepreneur must view the world through the eyes of the investor. Is the investor primarily interested in feature number twelve on a piece of software, or how shiny the packaging is, or how insanely great the company concept is? No. The investor is interested in what is in it for him or her. Which of the following pitches is an investor most likely to respond to?

A. "This cell phone is waterproof to three atmospheres."

B. "This is an opportunity to get in on the ground floor of a $2 billion company."

A pitch should focus on what the investor is interested in, not what the entrepreneur is interested in. A pitch should briefly cover reward, transaction size, time to exit, and things that indicate the risk will be minimal, like the entrepreneur's experience. There are other things a pitch should contain as well.

## Types of Pitch

Different pitches are used in different circumstances. Each of these pitches should be concise and focused.

The 'elevator pitch', is an impromptu pitch, which provides only investment highlights, and typically lasts for less than two minutes. The objective is to test whether the investor is interested in the deal. If he or she is interested, an oral presentation can be scheduled.

The oral presentation is usually a pre-planned stand-up speech, often with PowerPoint slides, and a one-page handout. It is usually limited to ten to fifteen minutes. If investors are intrigued by the pitch, they may ask follow-up questions.

The written pitch is usually only distributed after investors have expressed interest at the oral presentation. Entrepreneurs should be wary of handing out information on their business for two reasons. First, if the idea is good, there is no point in inviting others to use it. Second, raising capital is a process which may take from three to eighteen months. As the entrepreneur learns from experience what works and what doesn't, he or she is likely to re-write their pitch. There is no benefit to having old, outdated, written pitches in circulation. Many investors use inconsistencies between old and new pitch handouts to decide against an investment. The written pitch should be limited to about ten pages and should contain forecast sales and profits through to the time of exit.

## Pitch Content

All pitches should contain the investor's potential return, the total amount the entrepreneur is trying to raise, and the time to exit. In the context of pitching, investor return and investor reward mean the same thing. Several other elements should be included in the pitch.

### *Value Proposition*

**Companies profit by creating value for customers**. Investors want to know how the company's goods and services will create value for customers. They want to know whether the value proposition gives a customer a **compelling** reason to select the entrepreneur's product or service. Angel investors **don't want** to invest in a **'me too'** product or service. 'Me too' businesses can't grow fast enough to achieve the returns investors want.

One kind of value proposition is an invention that does something no other product can. Microsoft's Windows graphical user interface provided a compelling value proposition for computer users, because prior to Window's point-and-click technology, users had to know technical commands, each of which had to be precisely input, in exactly the right order. Prior to Windows, personal computers were very difficult to use. After Windows, they were much easier to use. Reducing the difficulty of use was a compelling value proposition. Microsoft Windows and its progeny went on to dominate the market for computer operating systems.

Another kind of value proposition is a 'killer app', a concept so insanely great that it puts most competitors out of business. Home Depot & Lowes have put most local hardware stores and lumber yards out of business. In one location they provide lumber, shingles, cinder blocks, cement, plumbing, heating and ventilation supplies, nails, screws, carpet, cabinets, electrical supplies and fixtures, garden tools, fertilizer and plants. The essence of this killer app is to provide everything the do-it-yourself home improvement enthusiast might need in one location. Staples & Office Depot have had similar success by providing everything one might need for the office, or home office, including pens, paper, pencils, printers, computers, desks and chairs.

## Competitors

An investor will want to know about the company's competition. Every product, even the most revolutionary, has competition. Edison's light bulb, for example, competed against candles and kerosene lamps.

An investor might want to know who the company's top twenty competitors are. Competitor growth provides information on how fast the market is growing. Investors will want to know how a company's products, services and market position stack up to the competition. They will also want to know what will prevent competitors from simply copying the company's product or service. *Patents? Trade Secrets?*

A patent is a government grant that gives an inventor the exclusive right to use, manufacture, and sell, his or her invention for a limited period, usually 20 years. An invention, method, process or formula can also be protected by trade secret. Trade secrets arise when a company does everything it can to keep a process or method a secret. The most famous trade secret is the formula for Coca Cola.

## Customers

Investors will want to know who a company's customers will be, how many potential customers there are, and how much they are likely to purchase. Investors will also want to know how the company will get customers to try its products.

## Profitability

The entrepreneur should have summary data on the profitability of serving its customers. For example, one might have a target price in mind for a product and an estimate of the cost of that product. If a product or service doesn't have a high enough gross margin, the investor will reject the proposition out of hand. But if a product or service can be delivered inexpensively and sold at a substantial price, an investor will be more interested.

## Contours of the Deal

An investor will want to know something about the deal. First, they will want to know how much the entrepreneur has invested. If the entrepreneur doesn't have enough faith to invest, why should the investor risk his or her capital? If an investor is purchasing stock, he or she will want to know how much of the company they are purchasing. Does an investment of $25,000 buy 1% of a company, or 25%? The investor might also want to know who else has invested. No one wants to be the first one in the pool.

What is the investor's return likely to be? This is often tied to a company's exit strategy. Is the exit strategy to grow the company to a certain size and sell to a larger company? Is the exit strategy to take the company public?

### *Cash Flow*

Most start-ups use cash faster than they can generate it. The burn rate is the monthly rate of cash expenditures, less the cash generated from sales. An investor will want to know when a company will reach cash flow breakeven. Cash flow breakeven occurs when a company is generating enough cash to sustain itself.

## Building Confidence

A large part of convincing an investor to invest involves building confidence. It may take up to eighteen months to build an investor's confidence, to the point where he or she is willing to invest.

Angel investors like personal referrals. They like to know who they are dealing with. Investors don't want an entrepreneur to learn how to run a business using their money. To guard against this, they carefully examine an entrepreneur's background and experience.

One way an entrepreneur can build confidence is to make and execute plans on schedule. For example, the plan could call for: (i) getting a patent, (ii) completing a prototype, (iii) raising the first $1,000,000, or (iv) reaching the first $1,000,000 of sales.

Many of the entrepreneurs who invent wonderful gadgets are terrible at selling them. **Nothing builds confidence like real customers willing to pay real money for a company's goods and services.**

Sales to **flagship customers** builds confidence. Flagship customers are large, well-known companies with their own good reputation. The theory is that if well-known companies buy a company's products or services, those goods or services must be of superior quality.

Pre-production consulting or experience selling related products helps build confidence that the entrepreneur can do what he or she says they can do. Where a company has minimal sales or no sales, an entrepreneur should have a Sales Opportunity Schedule which: (i) lists potential customers, (ii) shows dates of sales calls, contacts, customer intentions, and (iii) shows dates, amounts and probability of expected sales.

## Conclusion

Entrepreneurs are the heroes of the economy, because new businesses tend to create more jobs than established businesses, and entrepreneurs bring new goods and services to the market.

Entrepreneurs, and those who work for entrepreneurial companies, generally have greater job satisfaction than those who work for established companies. Entrepreneurs with break-out products and services can make far more than they could working for large established companies. However, entrepreneurs with companies that sell commodity products and services generally make less than they would working for large corporations. Companies that sell commodities lose control over price, because customers can easily switch to goods or services sold by other companies.

Successful entrepreneurs have energy and determination, experience in the field in which they start companies, and good character. Good character is essential, so that customers, suppliers, employees and investors can rely on the integrity of the entrepreneur.

Successful businesses provide goods and services that people want, are profitable, are not commodities, and are scalable. Scalability means the company can replicate its success on a larger and larger scale.

Successful businesses understand their customers at a deep level. They know what the ideal customer looks like, how many there are, where they are located, and how to find them. Successful entrepreneurs often start small, to test and refine their products, services and marketing strategy without committing all their capital.

Capital is required because of timing differences. Companies need capital because expenditures for facilities, materials and labor are usually made long before customers pay. Capital can be provided through both debt and equity.

To raise capital, the needs of a company and the preferences of an investor must match on four criteria: (i) risk, (ii) reward, (iii) transaction size and (iv) time to exit. Otherwise, funds will not flow.

Banks are reluctant to lend money to start-up companies because they have limited track records, and few assets that can be used as collateral. Fortunately, there are many sources of capital other than banks. Entrepreneurs' early sources of capital include their own savings, credit cards, home equity loans, customers and suppliers, friends and family, angel investors, and SBICs. As companies grow, it may be able to get financing from venture capitalists, bonds, or selling stock to the public.

The act of asking for money is called a pitch. An elevator pitch is usually two minutes or less. It is designed to test whether there is any interest on the part of the investor. Scheduled oral pitches are usually ten to fifteen minutes, sometimes use PowerPoint slides, and are often accompanied by a one-page handout. A written pitch is generally ten pages or fewer, may contain cash flow projections through the time of exit, and is usually only provided after investors have expressed an interest in making an investment.

Pitches should lead with how the investor can profit from the deal, followed by how the company will create value for customers, profit projections, the entrepreneur's experience, competitors and how the company will differentiate itself in the marketplace.

The entrepreneur must gain the investor's confidence, or no funds will flow. Building confidence takes time, usually from three to eighteen months. An investor will want to know how much of the entrepreneur's money has been invested in the business. If the entrepreneur does not have confidence in the company, why should the investor? Investor confidence is increased if other investors have invested. Confidence can be built on personal referrals and a track record of successfully setting and completing milestones. However, nothing builds confidence like sales to real customers willing to pay real money for the company's products. Another way to build confidence is to make sales to flagship customers, customers with their own good reputation.

# Terms and Concepts

**Angel Investors** - Angel investors are wealthy private individuals who invest in small companies. Typically, they invest from $25,000 to $250,000 and want returns of 30% to 38% per year. They usually invest within a one-hour drive of their home to oversee their investment.

**Bonds** – Corporations frequently issue bonds to raise capital. A bond pays its face value at maturity, usually five to thirty years after issue, and bonds pay interest twice per year.

**Break-out products** – These are products and services which can be differentiated in the marketplace from commodities. There are few close substitutes for break-out products and services, enabling them to command higher prices and generate greater profits.

**Capital** – Capital is needed to finance assets. Both liabilities, that is, debt and equity, that is, an owner's interest in a company, are capital. Capital is needed because there are timing differences between the time a company purchases facilities, materials and labor, and when a company gets paid for completing and selling its goods or services.

**Capital, Characteristics of** – Capital can be characterized as debt or equity. Capital can also be characterized by: (i) risk, (ii) reward, (iii) transaction size, and (iv), time to exit.

**Capital, Sources of** – Banks are one of many sources of capital. Others include the entrepreneur's savings, credit cards, home equity loans, customers and suppliers, friends and family, angel investors, Small Business Investment Corporations (SBIC), venture capital, bonds, public stock offerings, and commercial paper. There are many other sources.

**Character** – Good character is important so that customers, suppliers, employees, lenders and investors can count on the entrepreneur to do the right thing.

**Confidence** –Things that build investor confidence include: personal referrals, setting and achieving milestones, investments by others, real sales to real customers, and sales to flagship customers.

**Commercial Paper** – Commercial paper are loan notes that mature in less than nine months, and don't pay a stated rate of interest, but are sold at a discount from face value. Only the best companies can issue commercial paper.

**Commodities** – A commodity is a product or service offered by many companies. Companies which sell commodities are unable to raise price because if they do, customers can purchase virtually identical goods and services from competitors.

**Competitors** – Investors want to know about a company's competitors so they can evaluate competing products and services and gauge the size and growth rate of the market.

**Determination** – see Energy and Determination.

**Direct Sales** – In direct sales, the producer sells more directly to the customer, avoiding wholesale and retail distributors. Examples include telemarketing, catalog sales, direct mail and internet-based sales.

**Energy and Determination** – The entrepreneur's energy and determination are crucial for success. Giving up on a company is one of the primary reasons start-up companies fail.

**Entrepreneur** – Someone who combines land, labor and capital to start an enterprise. Stated differently, an entrepreneur is someone who can build a company from the ground up.

**Experience** – Experience is important for entrepreneurial success. Investors don't want entrepreneurs to learn with their money.

**Failure** –Reasons start-up companies fail are, that entrepreneurs get discouraged and give up, they lack experience, or they fail to understand their customers.

**Flagship Customers** – These are customers with their own good reputation. If a flagship customer is willing to purchase a company's goods or services, that is seen by investors as an endorsement of quality.

**Franchise** – A franchise is a form of business organization in which the franchisor develops a business model, products and services, trade mark, and sells the rights to use these business elements to an independent business person. The advantage for the franchisee is that they get a proven business model and an established brand. The franchisor gets an initial fee, plus a percentage of the franchisee's gross income, plus a percentage of the franchisee's gross sales for advertising.

**Franchisee** – One who purchases a franchise. See Franchise.

**Franchisor** – One who establishes and sells franchise rights.

**Gross Margin** – Gross margin at the product or service level can be computed as (Price – Cost)/Price. Investors want to see a substantial gross margin.

**Initial Public Offering (IPO)** – An Initial Public Offering (IPO) is the first instance in which a company sells stock to the public. Only registered shares may be sold.

**Job Generation** – Small firms generate more net new jobs than large firms. Large firms are defined as those with more than 500 employees.

**'Me Too' Goods and Services** – These are goods and services which are commodities. Examples of 'me too' products include T-shirts and pizzas.

**Needs and Wants** – One of the most important steps in starting a new business is to find out what people need and want.

**Patent** - A patent is a government grant that gives an inventor the exclusive right to use, manufacture, and sell, his or her invention for a limited period, usually 20 years.

**Pitch** – A pitch is asking for money. An elevator pitch is one that is two minutes or less. Scheduled oral pitches are usually ten to fifteen minutes; sometimes use PowerPoint slides; and are often accompanied by a one-page handout. A written pitch should be ten or fewer pages, and is usually only provided after the investor has expressed interest in making an investment.

**Profitability** – Products and services must be profitable. The profitability of products and services may be gauged using gross margin.

**Securities and Exchange Commission (SEC)** – The SEC is the government agency that oversees the sale of securities to the public. Stocks, bonds, and other evidence of fractional ownership can also be classified as securities.

**SBIC** – See Small Business Investment Company.

**Scalability** – This refers to a business's ability to replicate success on a larger and larger scale.

**Small Business Investment Company** (SBIC) – These are companies which raise capital from institutional investors and low-cost government bonds, and invest that money in small businesses.

**Stock Offerings** – Companies can sell stock to raise capital. Stock can only be sold to the public, and listed on a stock exchange, if it is registered with the Securities and Exchange Commission (SEC).

**Trade Secret** - An invention, method, process or formula can be protected by trade secret. When a company takes precautions to keep a process or formula secret, it can be protected by trade secret law.

**Value Proposition** – The value proposition is the compelling reason why a customer would buy from a company. It may solve a problem, or enhance the customer's self-esteem.

**Venture Capital** – Only invest in high growth companies and aggressively manage their investment. Only about one percent of companies qualify for venture capital.

**Wants** – see Needs and Wants.

# References

Blinkenlights. 2007. "Pop Quiz: What was the first personal computer?" Blinkenlights Archeological Institute. www.blinkenlights.com/pc.shtml

Funding Universe. 2004. "Amazon.com, Inc." Funding Universe. *International Directory of Company Histories*, Vol. 56. St. James Press.

http://www.fundinguniverse.com/company-histories/Amazoncom-Inc-Company-History.html.

The Little Entrepreneur. 2011. The Business-Adventure Series. Harper-Arrington Publishing.
http://www.thelittlee.com/html/famous_entrepreneurs.html

NFM Staff. 2008. "40 Under 40: Jasmine Lawrence", *Natural Foods Merchandiser*. Jul. 23. http://www.newhope.com/news-amp-analysis/40-under-40-jasmine-lawrence

Praag, C. Mirjam van and Peter H. Vershoot. 2007. "What is the value of entrepreneurship? A view of recent research." Small Business Economics. 29:351-382.

Rees, Matthew 2014. "The Real Market Makers: Knowledge and Power", Wall Street Journal. March 18 A13.

Rich, Richie. 2011. "The 8 Most Expensive Perfumes in the World", Luxury Lists. http://luxatic.com/the-8-most-expensive-perfumes-in-the-world/

SBA. 2014. "General Business Loans: 7(a)" Small Business Administration. http://www.sba.gov/content/7a-loan-amounts-fees-interest-rates downloaded 6/13/2014

—. 2011. "What is the survival rate for new firms?" Small Business Administration Office of Advocacy Research and Statistics. www.sba.gov/advocacy/7495/8430.

Spolsky, Joel. 2009. "Start-up Static", Inc. March. Pp.33-34.

Vance, David. 2005. Raising Capital. Springer Science + Business Media. New York.

VerticalScope Inc. 2011. "1975 Mustang II"
http://muscularmustangs.com/database/1975.php

World Franchising Network. 2011. "World Franchising"
www.worldfranchising.com/,

# CHAPTER THREE

# CAPITALISM

After completing this chapter, you should be able to:

3.1 Discuss the economic systems used to organize a society and discuss the pros and cons of each.

3.2 Critically evaluate capitalism and other systems for organizing an economy.

3.3 Know the characteristics of capitalism.

3.4 Discuss the primary criticisms of capitalism, including the unequal distribution of income.

## Introduction

There are many ways to organize society. Capitalism is just one. This chapter considers several ways to organize society, and how people fare under each. The characteristics of capitalism will be examined, as well as criticisms of capitalism such as the unequal distribution of income.

## Organization of Society

Every society must have some method for determining what is produced and how production will be distributed. Do people produce willingly or are they coerced into producing? If they are coerced, what is the form of coercion? Can people avoid being coerced, and if so, at what cost? Is there any way for people to opt out of a system, or are they captives of the system?

Society must also decide how production will be distributed. Who gets the benefit of production and how much do they get? What do they have to give up to acquire some production, or to protect the production they have?

A final question about the organization of society is, how does it adapt to change? How are new products and methods introduced and old ones eliminated. Consumer demands and technology are always changing. A successful economic system must be able to adapt quickly.

## Despotism

Despotism is system in which the strong take what they want from the weak. This is the prevailing economic system in many third world countries. In a despotic society, there is no law to protect property. Hence, there is no reason to work, plan for, or invest in the future, because any gains are likely to be confiscated. Economic choice is limited to those things one can defend through force.

## Communism

Communism is a system in which the state owns all assets for the 'benefit' of the people. In its purest form, communists believe "From each according to his or her ability, and to each according to his or her needs."[1] Since reward is based on need, rather than talent or work, there is no incentive to produce more than necessary. Production is limited to goods and services those in power think will benefit the state.

Communism is a command economy in which central planners tell everyone where to work, what to do, and what to make. There is no room for individual initiative. Central planners are not good at anticipating the needs of individuals.

## Totalitarian Systems

In a totalitarian system, individuals may own property and businesses, but such ownership is honored only if those owning property are favored by those in power. When a property or business owner falls out of favor

---

[1] If pure communism were instituted, and people were required to produce according to their abilities, college professors with PhDs would be taxed on the income of an investment banker, on the theory that anyone with the intellectual ability of a PhD, could make an investment banker's income if they chose to. Pure communism leaves little no room for career choice.

with the regime, property is often confiscated through extra-judicial means; that is, by force.

Under totalitarian regimes, there are few legal protections and public statements about perceived unfairness are likely to be met with imprisonment, or worse. In a totalitarian system, there is a high degree of risk as to whether one will be able to retain what one has worked for. Some rely on their political connections and produce anyway. Some see production above subsistence levels as pointless. Some migrate to countries with greater legal protections.

## Socialism

Socialism is a system in which individuals may own property and run businesses. However, an underlying theme in socialism is equality of outcome. If one works hard, and produces too much, or has a business that is too successful, the benefits of that work are taxed away or regulated out of existence, in the name of making society's producers and non-producers more alike. In a socialist system, there is little reason to risk capital, time and energy on new inventions and new businesses, because one way or another, the benefits of that effort will be confiscated under the color of law.

Highly productive people who find themselves in a socialist country tend to migrate to a more capitalist country where they can keep the rewards of their efforts.

## Capitalism

Capitalism is a system where people are free to work, invest, produce and start businesses. In a capitalist system, the rewards of production go to those who add value by creating businesses, inventing and selling products, services and their labor in the market place.

Goods and services are distributed to those who are willing and able to pay for them. The choice of where to work, what to do, and what to purchase is left to the individual. Production is guided by what people are willing and able to pay for. When people are no longer willing to purchase an item, manufacturers stop making it. Examples of items that are no longer manufactured because most people stopped purchasing them include typewriters, telegraph equipment, and whale oil lamps.

# Equality

Equality of opportunity is a principle of capitalism. What does equality of opportunity mean? It means government should not dictate people's professions, aspirations, or limit how far they can go, if they are ambitious and hardworking enough.

Equality of outcome is a principle of communism and socialism. The only way to achieve equality of outcome is to limit the aspirations of people who want to excel. Proponents of equal outcome argue for high taxes on the rich. But, as Abraham Lincoln said, "Making the rich poor will never make the poor rich."

If we were to enforce equality of outcome in the classroom, we would add everyone's grades together and divide by the number of students. Slackers wouldn't study or do their homework, assuming the work of others would pull them up. The best students probably wouldn't invest time and energy studying, because no matter how hard they worked, they wouldn't be able to significantly change their grade. The result would be minimal or no effort by most students. Under a regime of equality of outcome, everyone would receive a D or F.

---

### Democracy versus Socialism

"Democracy extends the sphere of individual freedom, while socialism restricts it.

Democracy attaches all possible value to each man; socialism makes each man a mere agent, a mere number.

Democracy and socialism have nothing in common but one word: equality. But notice the difference.

While democracy seeks equality in liberty, socialism seeks equality in restraint and servitude."

~ F. A. Hayak

---

Consider what F. A. Hayak had to say about democracy, socialism and equality in the emphasis box above.[2] Those who want equality of outcome, economically hobble the motivated and hard-working, so the whiners, those who always have an excuse, and slackers, don't get too far behind. Equality of outcome is anti-capitalist.

**Capitalism encourages people to be all that they can be. Capitalism is a philosophy of personal achievement.**

## Benefits of Capitalism

One way to gauge the benefits of capitalism is to compare the per capita incomes of countries, with and without capitalism. Table 3.1 Analysis of Per Capita Gross Domestic Product, provides a relative measure of people's well-being in various countries. Gross Domestic Product (GDP) is the total value of goods and services produced by a country.[3] Per Capita GDP is the average produced per person. Broadly speaking, per capita GDP is the amount available to be consumed by the average person.

---

[2] F. A. Hayak, The Road to Serfdom, University of Chicago Press, Definitive Edition, p77. Here, Hayak is quoting Alexis de Tocqueville, Democracy in America 1835-1840.

[3] ___ 2011. "World Factbook", CIA. www.cia.gov/library/publications/the-world-factbook/index.html

**Table 3.1 Analysis of Per Capita Gross Domestic Product**

| Country | GDP in Billions of Dollars | Population in Millions | Per Capita GDP in Dollars |
|---|---|---|---|
| Angola | 114.1 | 13.3 | 8,553.9 |
| China | 9,872.0 | 1,336.7 | 7,385.4 |
| Columbia | 431.9 | 44.7 | 9,662.2 |
| Congo | 23.6 | 71.7 | 328.9 |
| Cuba | 114.1 | 11.1 | 10,297.8 |
| Egypt | 500.9 | 82.1 | 6,102.6 |
| France | 2,160.0 | 65.3 | 33,078.1 |
| Germany | 2,960.0 | 81.5 | 36,319.0 |
| Japan | 4,338.0 | 128.5 | 33,758.8 |
| India | 4,046.0 | 1,189.0 | 3,402.9 |
| North Korea | 40.0 | 24.5 | 1,636.0 |
| Russia | 2,229.0 | 138.7 | 16,070.7 |
| South Africa | 527.5 | 49.0 | 10,765.3 |
| South Korea | 1,467.0 | 48.8 | 30,092.3 |
| United Kingdom | 2,189.0 | 62.7 | 34,912.3 |
| **United States** | **14,720.0** | **313.2** | **46,998.7** |
| Zambia | 20.0 | 13.9 | 1,443.1 |
| Zimbabwe | 4.3 | 12.1 | 353.6 |

As can be seen from this table, capitalist countries like the United States, Japan, United Kingdom, France, Germany and South Korea have relatively high per capita GDP. North Korea and Cuba embrace communism and have much lower per capita GDP. Countries in which despotism dominates, the Democratic Republic of the Congo, Zambia and Zimbabwe, have very low per capita GDP.

No country, not even the United States, fully embraces capitalism. But countries which have embraced capitalism more fully have higher per capita GDP than countries which have embraced other economic systems.

## Characteristics of Capitalism

Capitalism is a system in which individuals work for their own benefit. Anything they produce they can keep. Those who want more, can work harder and produce more. Those who need less can work less. **Capitalism is based on maximum personal freedom and minimum government interference** in the economy, and in people's lives.

Aspects of capitalism such as investment, personal initiative and reaping the rewards of work, have been around for three millennia. However, Adam Smith, in his landmark book, *The Wealth of Nations*, published in 1776, articulated capitalism as a coherent economic system.

Prior to Adam Smith, it was widely believed that people worked and produced for God, King and country. All that was very noble, but data suggest people work, trade and invest for their own benefit and that of their loved ones. This principle is called **rational self-interest**.

## Voluntarism and Mutual Benefit

In capitalism, people only exchange goods and services (labor) for mutual benefit. No one is coerced into trading with, or working for, another. Both parties must benefit, or no exchange takes place. This is in sharp contrast to despotism, communism, totalitarianism or socialism, where people are forced to exchange goods or services (labor) with others on terms out of their control. Those who advocate other economic systems ignore their coercive nature.

In a capitalist system, if one doesn't like what an employer is willing to pay, that person is free to start their own business and compete against their former employer. This freedom to compete provides a self-correcting mechanism in capitalism. Suppose the only bakery in town charges $10 per loaf of bread. One can start their own bakery or simply sell bread out of their kitchen, at a lower price. Eventually, the original bakery would have to lower its price or face losing its customers.

Under systems of communism or socialism, people aren't free to start businesses, especially if they are competing against a state-owned business. If the government owned the bakery charging $10 per loaf of bread, they probably wouldn't let individuals compete against them and undercut price.

Capitalism, as practiced in the United States, is not pure capitalism. The government has passed many laws, rules and regulations that limit competition. In part, these rules are instituted because of lobbying. For example, accountants don't want more competition, so they constantly seek to raise the effort it takes to become a Certified Public Accountant. Lawyers and barbers do the same thing. They lobby for rules that limit access to their profession. For everyone **to benefit from capitalism** everyone must **be on guard against limits to competition**.

## Right to Own and Benefit from Property

The right to own and benefit from property is a key requirement for capitalism. There are several reasons for this. Building a business requires the accumulation of capital for plant, property and equipment, inventory, research and development and other investments. Accumulated property can serve as collateral for bank loans. Finally, property rights are necessary to preserve and protect the interests of those who invest in companies.

The right to own property means that people can keep the benefits of their work. Because they can keep the benefits of their work, they invest capital and plan for the future. Investing in the future is pointless under despotism or communism, and risky under socialism or totalitarianism.

## Price as a Means of Controlling Production

When society identifies a product or service it is willing to pay for, and the price people are willing to pay is high enough, entrepreneurs will step forward and make that product or provide that service. No government edict, command, or order is necessary to direct production in capitalism. As we have seen, if those providing a good or service are charging too much, entrepreneurs will start their own businesses and compete against the high-priced producer. Such competition inevitably drives price lower.

How much is too much in terms of price? Philosophically, a person should be able to charge whatever the market will bear. Suppose, for example, oil companies priced gasoline at $200 per gallon. That is their prerogative under capitalism. But we, as consumers, have the right to refuse to buy gasoline at that price. At $200 per gallon we might chose substitutes like alcohol or natural gas.

Suppose an oil company decided to charge $10 per gallon. If it made superior profits at that price, those profits would incentivize others to produce gasoline. To get market share, new oil companies would price their product lower than $10 per gallon. Competition would inevitably drive price down to a level at which no others are incentivized to enter the market.

Not all companies are equally efficient. Once prices have been driven down to some minimum, inefficient companies will no longer be profitable, and they will close, or convert their business to produce some new product. Sometimes companies close because the demand for their product has fallen. As more and more people began using personal computers to write, the demand for typewriters dropped dramatically. The price typewriter manufacturers could charge also dropped. Most companies left the typewriter business long ago. No government rule, edict or order told them to stop making typewriters. Market forces signaled that it was time to try something new.

## Price as a Rationing Mechanism

In capitalism, the distribution of goods and services is controlled by people's ability and willingness to pay. People always want more than their means allow, so they must make budget decisions. If I really wanted a Maserati and was willing to live in a tiny apartment so I could afford it, I would be allowed to do so under capitalism. On the other hand, I might want to live in a luxury high rise and not have a car at all. I would be allowed to do so under capitalism. Under socialism, I might have to settle for an average car and an average apartment. My options would be limited because socialism and communism seek equality of outcome.

When price is used as a means of allocating resources, everyone gets to pick exactly the right mix of goods and services that best suits their needs. No government rule or edict is needed to tell people what to buy.

## The Invisible Hand

One of Adam Smith's most remarkable insights was that when everyone pursues his or her own self-interest, society benefits more than if the government dictated their actions. This self-organizing, self-optimizing principal is called '**the invisible hand**.' While this principle sounds counter-intuitive, it has proven itself time and again.

### *John D. Rockefeller Saves the Whales*

At one time, whale oil was burned for lighting. In 1846 there were 735 ships in the US whaling fleet. This was having a devastating effect on the whale population.

In 1849, Abraham Gesner, a Canadian physician, devised a method to distill kerosene from petroleum. Kerosene is a direct replacement for whale oil. But, Mr. Gesner couldn't produce enough kerosene to make a dent in the whale oil trade.

The man most responsible for the commercial success of kerosene was John D. Rockefeller. Prior to Rockefeller, the oil industry was splintered and inefficient. Rockefeller set up an efficient network of kerosene distilleries which later developed into Standard Oil.

As kerosene became generally available, the demand for whale oil dropped. The 735-ship fleet of 1846 shrunk to 39 ships by 1876. The price of whale oil reached its high of $1.77 per gallon in 1856, but by 1896 it sold for 40 cents per gallon. Yet it could not keep pace with the price of kerosene, which dropped from 59 cents per gallon in 1865 to a fraction over seven cents per gallon in 1895.[4]

By offering an economical substitute for whale oil, Rockefeller saved the whales. He didn't set out to save the whales, he set out to make an enormous amount of money. But the by-product of his effort was to collapse the American whaling industry.

**Capitalists, acting in their own self-interest have saved more whales than Greenpeace. The whales were saved, not by government or do-gooders, but by an entrepreneur pursuing profit in the oil business.**

### Henry Ford Fights Pollution

Cars are very clean now, but there was a time in the recent past when people complained about auto pollution. But even when cars were at their dirtiest, they were much, much cleaner than the alternative. Henry Ford and his inexpensive autos dramatically reduced pollution and made cities livable.

In the eighteenth, ninetieth and early twentieth century, horses were the most common method of transportation. Every horse left fifteen to thirty-five pounds of manure a day in the streets. The manure was everywhere, ground up by the traffic, blown about by the wind, and tracked into people's homes. Manure produced vast numbers of flies that spread diseases such as typhoid fever. In 1908, 20,000 New Yorkers died from diseases related to horse manure.

And what happened when a horse died in the street? Horses were left where they dropped. In 1880, New York City removed 15,000 dead horses from its streets, and late as 1916 Chicago carted away 9,202 dead horses, weighing an average of 1,300 pounds.

The automobile dealt a severe blow to the use of the horse. Henry Ford's 1913 assembly line cut production costs, and Ford passed some of that saving onto the public. As auto prices dropped, the public embraced

---

[4] Robbins, James S. 1992. "Abraham Gesner...saved more whales than Greenpeace ever will,", *The Freeman,* August. published by the Foundation for Economic Education (FEE).

them as means of transportation.[5] When horses became more expensive than cars, people stopped using horses, the manure stopped piling up, and dead horses were no longer a feature of city life.

**Ford didn't set out to clean up the cities. He set out to make a lot of money building cars. The by-product was dramatically cleaner cities.**

### *Wal-Mart Helps the Poor*

Sam Walton, founder of Wal-Mart created a global retailing empire. His policy was to have everyday low prices, rather than attract customers from time to time with discounts. Wal-Mart's model is based on efficient distribution and tough bargaining with suppliers on price in exchange for large quantity orders. Wal-Mart's low prices have affected the prices that other retailers can charge, and as a result, overall retail prices declined about 3.1% over the period 1985 to 2006. In 2006, this translated into a savings of about $957 per person, or $2,500 per household. Since people with lower incomes shop disproportionately at stores like Wal-Mart, as compared to Neiman Marcus or Nordstrom, the individual savings for lower income people is probably higher than this average. [6]

**Sam Walton founder of Wal-Mart didn't set out to help the poor. He set out to build a profitable business. He discovered that everyday low prices and better productivity was the key to those profits. The result was that the poor, and everyone else, now face lower retail prices than they would otherwise.**

### *Wal-Mart Cuts Medicare Costs*

Wal-Mart used its market power to offer a 90-day supply of 357 different prescription drugs for just $10. Target followed suit with its own discount prescription drug program. The full price at Wal-Mart for drugs is less than the co-pay under many drug insurance plans. This saves money for those with no drug insurance. It also saves money for those with drug insurance who want to avoid high co-pays.

---

[5] Mohl, Raymond, Ed. 1997. *The Making of Urban America.* "The Centrality of the Horse to the Nineteenth-Century American City", by Clay McShane. NY: SR Publishers, pp. 105-130.

[6] ___. 2007. "The Price Impact of Wal-Mart: An Update Through 2006", Business Planning Solutions Global Insight Advisory Services Division. http://walmartstores.com/media/resources/128340111054643750.pdf

In addition to saving individuals money, Wal-Mart's drug pricing policy reduces Medicare costs. The American Medical Association *Archives of Internal Medicine* estimated that if half of the individuals on Medicare took advantage of Wal-Mart's program, they would save about $3 billion, and Medicare would save $0.9 billion in 2007 dollars. [7]

**Wal-Mart didn't set out to provide drug insurance to people. It set out to make money. The result was lower drug costs for everyone.**

### *Pollution and Energy Independence*

George P. Mitchell, a Texas entrepreneur is credited with perfecting fracking as a technique for retrieving the oil and natural gas locked in shale. Fracking is responsible for dramatically increasing oil and gas production. The increase in production has reduced gasoline prices and made natural gas so cheap it is replacing coal in electricity generation. Natural gas burns far cleaner than coal, and thus reduces air pollution. Lower natural gas prices have also encouraged expansion of the domestic chemical companies that use natural gas as feed stock. Such expansion creates jobs. The US is producing so much oil from fracking, it started exporting oil in 2016.[8] That means the $400 billion a year Americans used to spend buying foreign oil can be invested in the domestic economy.[9]

**Did George Mitchell set out to reduce air pollution, create jobs or make America energy independent? No. He set out to make a lot of money. But in pursuit of profits he has done more for energy independence than fifty years of government programs.**

### *Other Examples of the Invisible Hand*

These are five examples of individuals working for their own self-interest. They did more for society than if the government directed their actions. But are these the only examples? No. The list is endless.

---

[7] ___. 2008. "Wal-Mart $4 Prescription Program", June 5. http://i.walmart.com/i/if/hmp/fusion/genericdruglist.pdf

[8] Kumar, Devika Krishna and Marianna Parraga. 2017. "Why record U.S. oil exports are poised for even more growth", Reuters Business News. July 27. https://www.reuters.com/article/us-usa-oil-exports-idUSKBN1AC0ER downloaded 2017-07-30

[9] Kurtzman, Joel. 2013. "How Adam Smith Revived America's Oil Patch", *Wall Street Journal*. June 20. A19.

Microsoft Windows made computers usable to a wide range of non-technical people and thereby helped increase the nation's productivity. Bill Gates developed and marketed Windows for profit. Steve Wozniak and Steve Jobs designed and sold low-cost personal computers. They didn't do it because some government agency told them to, they did it to make money. The result was a range of new products and services for consumers, thousands of new jobs and personal wealth. Other examples of the 'invisible hand' would fill volumes.

---

### Characteristics of Capitalism

**Rational self-interest** - People work for their own self-interest, not for the good of society.

**Voluntary Action** - People exchange goods and labor voluntarily. In capitalism, no one is forced to work for, or trade with, another.

**Property Rights** - Capitalism cannot exist without the right to own and benefit from property.

**Price Controls Production and Distribution** - Price determines what is produced and how production is distributed.

**Invisible Hand** - People acting in their own self-interest do more good for society than if government directed their efforts.

---

## Criticisms of Capitalism

Even though capitalism has many fine qualities, no system is perfect. It has been criticized because of the unequal distribution of income, because the rich get richer and the poor get poorer, loss of jobs through layoffs and business closures, and because of conspicuous consumption.

### Income Distribution

One criticism of capitalism is the unequal distribution of income. The argument is that if capitalism were a 'fair' system, income would be distributed more equally across all people. Of course, the people who make such criticisms rarely consider income distribution under alternative systems, which is often highly unequal.

Should the educational system be likewise criticized for unequal grade distribution? Or unequal educational attainment? Or, should we look deeper? Several factors lead to the unequal income distribution, many of which are within the control of individuals.

***Education***

Education is among the greatest determinants of who will be poor and who will be well off. Among those who did not complete high school, about 14.2% live in poverty, among those with a high school diploma, only about 3.8% live in poverty, and among those with some college, only 1.2% live in poverty.[10] That is compelling evidence that personal behavior, and personal choice, in pursuing education or not pursuing education, is highly correlated with poverty. Table 3.2 Analysis of Income by Education summarizes the impact of education on income.[11]

**Table 3.2 Analysis of Income by Education**

This table is an analysis of median income by educational level. The median means that half of people in the education group have incomes higher than the reported figure and half the people in the education group have incomes that are lower than the reported income.

| Educational Level | Men | Women | Average |
|---|---|---|---|
| Less than 9$^{th}$ grade | 17,043 | 10,625 | 13,834 |
| 9$^{th}$ to 12$^{th}$ grade | 20,845 | 11,904 | 16,375 |
| High School graduate | 30,879 | 18,293 | 24,586 |
| Some college, No degree | 37,297 | 23,252 | 30,275 |
| Associate degree | 42,608 | 27,715 | 35,162 |
| Bachelor's degree | 57,278 | 36,294 | 46,786 |
| Master's degree | 70,973 | 48,000 | 59,487 |
| Professional degree | 100,000 | 58,364 | 79,182 |

[10] Bailey, Blake. 2003. "How Not to be Poor", National Center for Policy Analysis, Dallas, Texas, January 15; citing "Poverty Dynamics in Four OECD Countries", 2000. Organization for Economic Cooperation and Development.
[11] Table 701. Money Income of People – Selected Characteristics by Income Level; U.S. Census Bureau, ***Statistical Abstract of the United States: 2011***, Income, Expenditures, Poverty and Wealth.

The disparity between men and women's salaries is an artifact of the last generation. But, things are changing among jobs that require higher education. Women tend to have more self-discipline, attend more classes, do more homework, devote more time to study, and persist in the face of frustration and setbacks. This contributes to higher grades and the increased likelihood of selection for knowledge industry jobs. It also contributes to job success. It would not be surprising if the income disparity between men and women reversed in the next ten or twenty years. Men will have work harder to keep up.[12]

### Family Choices

Family choices are another factor that leads towards, or away from, poverty. As a rule, married couples are much less likely to live in poverty than single adults with dependent children. Table 3.3 Poverty by Family Type[13] is an analysis of who is in poverty, based on their family decisions.

**Table 3.3 Poverty by Family Type**

Personal choices such as whether to marry, to stay married, to have children within a marriage, or to have children outside of marriage, has an impact on the likelihood of long-term poverty.

| Family Type | Percent in Poverty |
|---|---|
| Unmarried households with 2 or more children | 51.6% |
| Married couples with 2 or more children | 7.9% |
| Single adults without children | 7.9% |
| Married couples without children | 1.2% |

The decision as to whether to marry or to have children is a personal one and should not be dictated by the government. However, these

---

[12] Gnaulati, Enrico. 2014. "Why Girls Tend to Get Better Grades Than Boys Do", The Atlantic. Sept.18.
https://www.theatlantic.com/education/archive/2014/09/why-girls-get-better-grades-than-boys-do/380318/ downloaded 11/25/2017
[13] Bailey, Blake. 2003. "How Not to be Poor", National Center for Policy Analysis, Dallas, Texas, January 15; citing "Poverty Dynamics in Four OECD Countries", 2000. Organization for Economic Cooperation and Development.

decisions have consequences that affect the likelihood that someone will live in poverty.[14]

The response of many politicians, community leaders and others, is to say that such statistics blame the victim. Such people deny that personal choice has much to do with whether a person is poor or not. Rather, they blame society for poverty. This absolves people from the consequences of their actions. And, it makes it easy for the next generation of young people to ignore the factors that are going to push them toward poverty.

Suppose you saw children playing in a field that you knew contained hidden sink-holes they could fall into. Would you let them play in the field unaware of the danger? Or would you have a moral and ethical duty to warn them?

Poverty is not just a tragedy for poor people. Poverty places a tax on those who make good decisions. The tax is levied for social services, child support, Medicaid and other goods that society provides to people who have made bad choices.

### *Special Talent*

Personal effort is probably the most important factor in the distribution of wealth. One of the things that creates unequal income distribution, is that some people have special talent that others are willing to pay for. For example, in 2008, Tiger Woods, a golfer, earned $110 million. Michael Jordan and Kobe Bryant, two remarkable basketball players, each made $45 million in a single year.[15] Athletes aren't the only ones who have a special talent people are willing to pay for.

Some entertainers command extraordinary incomes. Oprah Winfrey made $290 million from her television show, magazine, and production company in 2011.[16] She is both an entertainer and entrepreneur. While

---

[14] Bailey, Blake. 2003. "How Not to be Poor", National Center for Policy Analysis, Dallas, Texas, January 15; citing "Poverty Dynamics in Four OECD Countries", 2000. Organization for Economic Cooperation and Development.

[15] Badenhausen, Kurt. 2009. "The World's Highest Paid Athletes", Forbes Sports Valuations. 6/17.
http://www.forbes.com/2009/06/17/top-earning-athletes-business-sports-top-earning-athletes.html

[16] Staff. 2012. "Oprah Winfrey's Annual Earnings Drop by $125 Million, Says Forbes", The Hollywood Reporter. Aug.27.
https://www.hollywoodreporter.com/news/oprah-winfrey-michael-bay-highest-paid-celebrities-forbes-365703

incomes for athletes and entertainers are exceptional, other factors contribute to the unequal distribution of income.

### Small Businesses

As of 2011, there were some 437,400 businesses in the United States with 50 to 500 employees.[17] Many of these were sole proprietorships in which the owner is also the founder. Small businesses account for over half of private sector jobs, and about 64% of new jobs created over the last 15 years.[18]

Starting a business is a tough, thankless job at the beginning. Working ten to twelve hours per day six or seven days a week, is not uncommon. But for those who stick to it, and are successful, the rewards are good. A Wall Street Journal survey found that the average income of business owners or CEOs of companies with under 500 employees was about $233,600.[19]

Running a small business is risky. There are no guarantees. Those who do the thankless job of running a small business are rewarded well, and that contributes to the unequal distribution of income. But without the prospect of rewards, few if any people would create the small businesses that are the jobs engine of the economy.

The tax code also contributes to the perception of unequal distribution of income. Many businesses are set up as corporations. This separates business income from the income of a business's owners. But many small businesses are taxed as sole proprietorships, partnerships, or S-corporations. For those businesses, income is attributed to their owners and taxed as personal income. Attributing business income to individuals makes those individuals look like they have very high incomes when, in fact, much of that income is tied up in the business and cannot be used for personal expenses.

### Entrepreneurship

Entrepreneurs find a way to add value. They invent things, provide a service, or create a product that people need and want. Bill Gates, founder

---

[17] "ReferenceUSA," Infogroup Reference Division. ifoUSA Library Division, P.O. Box 27347, Omaha, NE 68127 downloaded May 10, 2011.

[18] New Jobs. 2011. U.S. Small Business Administration. www.sba.gov/advocacy/7495/8420 downloaded 5/10/2011.

[19] Spors, Kelly. 2006. "Small Business Owners, Executives Earn Less", Running A Business Column. *The Wall Street Journal.* October 19

of Microsoft, has made $84 billion in his lifetime. He has also donated $30 billion to charity. Michael Dell, founder of Dell Computer, made $1.1 billion in 2011 from stock appreciation alone.[20] Both Bill Gates and Michael Dell have done far more than simply make themselves rich. They have created jobs for tens of thousands of people. Their innovations have made it possible for others to start their own companies.

Entrepreneurship can lead to great wealth. So, what would those who criticize the unequal distribution of wealth do? Forbid invention? Forbid innovation? Or do they think people will create economic engines like Microsoft or Dell without the prospect of great wealth? Adam Smith rightly concluded that people work for their own self-interest, and by working for their own self-interest, they do more good for society than if the government directed their efforts.

### Age

While age is not a matter of personal choice, it is a factor in income inequality. On average, younger people make less than people during their peak earning years of 35 to 64. Table 3.4 Analysis of Income by Age shows that on average, men make four times more during their peak earning years than they do when they are 15 to 24. Women, during their peak earning years make three times as much as they do when they are 15 to 24.[21] This is beginning to change as women take the lead in knowledge-based work.

---

[20] Staff. 2010. "The Forbes 400: The Richest People in America", Sept. 16. http://www.forbes.com/wealth/forbes-400#p_1_s_arank_-1_
[21] Table 701. Money Income of People – Selected Characteristics by Income Level; U.S. Census Bureau, *Statistical Abstract of the United States: 2011*, Income, Expenditures, Poverty and Wealth.

## Table 3.4 Analysis of Income by Age

This table is an analysis of the median annual income by age. The median means that half of people in the age group have incomes higher than the reported figure and half the people in the age group have incomes that are lower than the reported income.

| Age | Male | Female | Average |
|-----|------|--------|---------|
| 15 to 24 years old | 10,778 | 8,901 | 9,840 |
| 25 to 34 years old | 33,415 | 25,553 | 29,484 |
| 35 to 44 years old | 44,189 | 27,371 | 35,780 |
| 45 to 54 years old | 45,540 | 28,236 | 36,888 |
| 55 to 64 years old | 41,757 | 25,515 | 33,636 |
| 65 years and older | 25,503 | 14,589 | 20,046 |

Given data on education, family type, special talent, entrepreneurship, personal effort and age, the question must be asked: "Is income inequality driven by some dark force within capitalism? Or is it the result of personal choices and age?"

## The Rich Get Richer and the Poor Get Poorer

Another criticism of capitalism is that the rich get richer and the poor get poorer. This criticism is heard all the time on radio and television, in newspapers, on the web, in blogs and in social media. But is it true?

### *Income Growth or Decline*

Table 3.5 Analysis of Income by Quintile over Time, shows that while the rich got richer, the poor got richer too.[22] A quintile is the average income of one fifth of the population. In 2009 the lowest fifth of the United States' population had an average income of $11,552 per year, as compared to $9,820 in 1970. The poor, defined as those in the lowest earnings quintile, improved their income by 17.6% over thirty years. So, in a capitalist society it looks like everyone gets richer.

---

[22] ____ 2010. "Table H-3 Mean Household Income Received by Each Fifth and Top 5Percent, All Races: 1967 to 2009." U.S. Census Department. www.census.gov/hhes/www/income/data/historical/inequality/index.html

**Table 3.5 Analysis of Income by Quintile over Time**

---

**The data in this table are inflation adjusted, so that 1970 incomes have been stated in 2009 dollars.**

|                      | 2009    | 1970    | Growth |
|----------------------|---------|---------|--------|
| Lowest Quintile      | 11,552  | 9,820   | 17.6%  |
| 2nd Lowest Quintile  | 29,257  | 26,600  | 10.0%  |
| Middle Quintile      | 49,534  | 42,833  | 15.6%  |
| 2nd Highest Quintile | 78,694  | 60,377  | 30.3%  |
| Highest Quintile     | 170,844 | 106,888 | 59.8%  |

*Income Mobility*

Another criticism of capitalism is that there is some wealthy elite that controls the economy and gets the benefits of production. There was a time in many countries when, if your father was a blacksmith, you would be a blacksmith. If your father was a peasant farmer, you would be a peasant farmer. If your father was royalty, you would be royalty.

Capitalism is dynamic. It is no respecter of persons. It only respects a person's ability to work and add value. Capitalism allows the personal freedom to reinvent oneself, and to rise as far as one's talent and effort will take one. The opposite is true as well. A person born into wealth will not necessarily keep it. If he or she doesn't work, doesn't add value, and simply tries to live off the productive efforts of their parents and grandparents, they will be downwardly mobile.

Capitalism is a meritocracy. The best are allowed and encouraged to rise to the top, and those who can't, don't, or won't work and add value, drift to the bottom. Table 3.6 is an Analysis of Income Mobility.[23] It shows the percentage of people who have moved from one income quintile to another.

---

[23]     2007. "Income Mobility in the U.S. from 1996 to 2005", Department of the Treasury, Nov. 12. Pg.7.
www.treasury.gov/resource-center/tax-policy/Documents/incomemobilitystudy03-08revise.pdf

**Table 3.6 Analysis of Income Mobility**

| 1996 Quintile | Lowest | -----------2005-----------<br>Second Lowest | Middle | Second Highest | Highest |
|---|---|---|---|---|---|
| Lowest | **42.2%** | 28.5% | 13.9% | 9.9% | 5.3% |
| Second Lowest | 17.0% | **33.3%** | 26.7% | 15.1% | 7.9% |
| Middle | 7.1% | 17.5% | **33.3%** | 29.6% | 12.5% |
| Second Highest | 4.1% | 7.3% | 18.3% | **40.2%** | 30.2% |
| Highest | 2.5% | 3.2% | 7.1% | 17.8% | **69.4%** |

What happened to the people who were in the lowest income quintile in 1996? About 42.2% of them were still there in 2005. But, 28.5% moved to the second lowest income quintile, 13.9% moved to the middle-income quintile and 5.3% made it to the highest income quintile. At the same time 2.5% of those with the highest quintile income in 1996 fell to the bottom quintile, and 3.2% fell to the second lowest income quintile. The bold diagonal percentages are those people who neither rose nor fell in terms of their income quintile.

From this table, we can see more than half of those in the lowest income quintile improved upon their circumstances. When people say the poor get poorer, one fact they overlook is that 'the poor' are not a fixed group of people. The poor includes young people, students, those just starting out, and those who are temporarily out of work. In a capitalist society, everyone can improve their circumstances if they make good decisions and work hard.

## Layoffs and Plant Closings

One of the major criticisms of capitalism is that private businesses periodically lay off large numbers of people and close plants and offices. Such actions create turmoil in people's lives through no fault of their own. Carl Marks derided capitalism as a turbulent system of production and exchange, gripped by competition and endless self-transformation. He said every firm faces the stark choice of either upgrading processes and production methods or going out of business.[24] Joseph Schumpeter called this process **creative destruction**.[25]

Marx was right. Companies must constantly reinvent themselves or they will go out of business. This raises two questions: (i) are there any benefits to such turmoil? And (ii), what are the costs of stopping the turmoil?

Customers seek value. If they have been buying a product from company A, and you produce a better product, one that does more, is easier to use, or costs less, customers will leave company A and purchase your product. Your reward for this innovation is superior sales and profits. If company A wants to survive, it must increase its value proposition. If it does, it has a chance of winning back its customers. If it doesn't, it may lose so many customers that sales will decline, and profits will become losses. Companies that fail to innovate go out of business, which results in layoffs and plant closings.

Who, if anyone, benefits from such turmoil? The short answer is practically everybody. New goods, services, and technology lowers cost, and improves the standard of living across society. Table 3.7 Examples of Creative Destruction lists a few of the new goods, services and technologies that have replaced old ones.

Progress means new products replace old ones, but it also means the businesses wedded to old technologies vanish. Jobs tied to old technologies vanish as well.

What would be the cost of stopping this turmoil? If you could stop progress as a way of preserving old industry jobs, where would you place the cut-off? After telephones, but before cell phones? After trains but before airplanes?

A politician might say, we should forbid companies from laying off people. That is the thinking in many European countries. How do companies react? If they can't lay off people when they are no longer needed, they will be extremely reluctant to hire people in the first place. Unemployment in most of Europe is consistently higher than in the United States.

---

[24] Scott, Allen J. 2006. "Entrepreneurship, Innovation and Industrial Development: Geography and the Creative Field Revisited", Small Business Economics. Vol.26 pp.1-24.
[25] Shumpeter, Joseph A. 1942. Capitalism, Socialism and Democracy. (New York: Harper, 1975) originally published in 1942. Pp.82-85

**Table 3.7 Examples of Creative Destruction**

| New Product or Service | Old Product or Service | Benefits |
| --- | --- | --- |
| Steam engines for factories | Water wheels for factories | Companies could locate anywhere |
| Electric motors | Steam engines for factories | More energy efficient, easier to use, cleaner |
| Kerosene for lighting | Whale oil for lighting | Less expensive and saved whales |
| Electric lights | Kerosene for lighting | Cleaner, less expensive, reduced fire hazard |
| Telegraph | Mail | Reduced cross country communication to minutes. |
| Telephone | Telegraph | Instant communication with no special skills |
| Cell phone | Telephone | Communication no longer tied to physical location |
| Smart Phone | Cell Phone | Touch screen and artificial intelligence |
| Train | Stage Coach | Speed increased from about three miles per hour to fifty. |
| Plane | Train | Speed increased from about fifty miles an hour to four hundred miles an hour. |

A politician might say we should subsidize industries that have fallen on tough times. Again, the question arises as to where the line for subsidies should be drawn. Should steam engine companies be subsidized because electric motors have replaced them? And of course, this raises the question of who should pay? Should taxpayers be burdened keeping alive old, obsolete, and underperforming companies? Or should the people and resources in those companies be released into the market place to find a more efficient use?

It's true that capitalism drives layoffs through creative destruction. But capitalism also creates newer, higher value jobs, in new industries.

## Conspicuous Consumption

Another criticism of capitalism is conspicuous consumption. Conspicuous consumption is spending extraordinary amounts on food, clothes, cars and houses. Conspicuous consumption is meant to show other people how much one has.

Some years ago, Vernon Hill, the founder of Commerce Bank, was criticized for conspicuous consumption when he built a $1.85 million 45,854 square foot mansion, on 44 acres in Moorestown, New Jersey. [26]

Was Vernon Hill's conspicuous consumption good or bad? To answer that question, we must think about where the money went. Suppose 40% went for building materials, 40% went for craftsmen and other laborers, 10% went to the architect, and 10% went to the prime contractor for profit and to hire supervisors.

One way to think of those expenditures is to say the $740,000 spent on building material provided employment for unskilled and semi-skilled factory labor. The $740,000 spent on craftsmen represents wages for carpenters, plumbers, sheetrock mechanics and others. The $185,000 spent on the architect, and the $185,000 spent on the prime contractor, represent wages for professionals, managers and some profit for the contractor. So, what some see as conspicuous consumption, others see as job creation.

## Navigating Capitalism

Is there a secret formula for getting ahead in a capitalist democracy known to only a select few? No, the formula is available to anyone who chooses to use it. **Benjamin Franklin said the universal principles of success were: (i) industry, (ii) thrift and (iii) prudence.**[27] The formula still works today.

Industry means one should always be working to improve one's business, craft, products or skills. Industrious people are driven by an internal desire to be all they can be. They do not drift through life. Yes, industry means working when others might be at a ball game or watching television or playing computer games. The opposite of industry is wasting

---

[26] Forder, Kenny. 2011. Villa Collina: The Largest Home In New Jersey (45,854 Sq Ft)
Apr 16. http://housing-today.com/news/villa-collina-the-largest-home-in-new-jersey-45854-sq-ft/
[27] Skousen, Mark. 2012. "Ben Franklin's Golden Rules", from *The Completed Autobiography of Benjamin Franklin*, Mark Skousen Ed. (Regnery, 2006) http://www.3rdstone.ws/Ben%20Franklin.htm. downloaded Dec. 24.

time and energy. Take two people, one who constantly improves their value through study and practice, and one who does little to improve themselves. Who will get hired? Who will get promoted? Who will be prepared to recognize and seize opportunity when it comes?

Thrift means wasting nothing, consuming only what you need, not spending lavishly, not wanting to have every gadget or possession others have. For some people, self-esteem is based on the kind and number of toys they have. For them, there will never be enough money in the world to fulfill their wants, and they will be forever broke. But successful people base their self-esteem on what they have accomplished, not the things they have.

Prudence is carefulness. Prudence means avoiding excesses. Excess eating, drinking and risk-taking can lead to disaster. Prudence also extends to those you associate with. If one associates with successful, hard-working people, one is likely to benefit from their example, advice, guidance, contacts and friendship. If one associates with people who are lazy, lack ambition, who believe in cutting corners and skirting the law, they are likely to end up in a tough situation.

The difference between success and failure, or success and lack of success, is largely one of personal choice in a capitalist democracy. One can be industrious, thrifty, and prudent if one decides to be. But no one is forced to succeed. Success is the result of good decisions and internal motivation.

## Conclusion

There are many ways to organize society. In despotism, the strong take from the weak, so there is no incentive to work or invest. In communism, the state owns all resources, and distributes output based on need, not an individual's productivity, so there is little incentive to work or invest under communism either. Totalitarian governments allow individuals to work, save, and invest in a business as long as those individuals curry favor with the government. But once an individual falls out of favor with a totalitarian government, the government will use extra judicial means to confiscate their productive output. Socialist governments permit individuals to save, invest, and build businesses, but if one becomes too successful, the benefits of success are taxed or regulated away in the name of equality and social justice. So, there is little incentive to work, save, invest, and build a substantial business under socialism.

Capitalism is a system of maximum personal freedom and minimum government interference. Individuals are free to produce as much, or as little, as they like, based on their effort, talent and needs. Capitalism is the only system free of coercion. People work, invest, buy, and sell their goods and labor on a voluntary basis. No-one is forced to work for another or sell their goods to another. Since people are free to keep the rewards of their effort, there is incentive to work hard, save and invest.

One of the most significant criticisms of capitalism is the unequal distribution of income. This criticism overlooks several factors. First, under capitalism, even the poor get richer in real dollars as the economy expands, and better and cheaper goods and services are brought to market. Second, capitalism provides income mobility. The poor can become rich, or at least improve their lot in life, and the rich can become poor if they are lazy or foolish. Third, much of income inequality can be traced to personal choices. The decision to get an education, to have children out of wedlock or not, to work 40 or 50 hours a week, or not at all, and one's attitude toward work, all contribute to whether someone is richer or poorer. In addition, people tend to accumulate wealth over their lifetime, so there is a natural disparity between the wealth of the young and old.

Capitalism has been criticized because companies lay off workers and go out of business. Companies that develop new products and methods, or invest in new machinery, thrive. Whereas those that do not adapt, lose sales and eventually go out of business. This phenomenon is known as creative destruction. But new and better goods and services, and less costly goods and services, benefit society. People released back into the economy through layoffs and plant closings, who upgrade their skills, often get better jobs.

Another criticism of capitalism is conspicuous consumption. Why should some live in million-dollar mansions when others are homeless? Why should some have yachts when others don't have cars? The answer is that when 'the rich', however that is defined, spend money for houses, yachts, cars, and shoes with complicated buckles, they make work for sales people, craft people, and factory workers. In addition, the rich invest in new businesses, directly and indirectly, which creates even more jobs.

# Terms and Concepts

**Capitalism** – A system of maximum personal freedom and minimum government interference. It is a system in which people work for their own benefit and not for the benefit of the state.

**Capitalism, Criticisms of** – Capitalism has been criticized for a) unequal income distribution, b) the rich getting richer while the poor get poorer, c) layoffs and the resulting unemployment, and d) conspicuous consumption. An analysis of these criticisms finds they lack substantial merit.

**Communism** – This is a system in which the state owns all the resources, dictates what will be produced, and how. Production is distributed based on need not effort, so incentives to work, save, and invest, are limited.

**Conspicuous Consumption** – This is expenditure of enormous sums on houses, cars, and other goods to show how wealthy one is. Such expenditures provide jobs for those who build and sell houses, cars, and other goods.

**Despotism** – This is a system where the strong take from the weak. Under despotism there is little incentive to work, save, or invest, beyond what one can defend by force.

**Equality** – In a capitalist system, equality means people are free to compete, produce, and advance themselves as far as their energy and talent will take them. In a Socialist or Communist system, equality means equality of outcome. The income of the most productive people will be redistributed to the less productive, through taxes and regulation.

**Gross Domestic Product** (GDP) – This is the total value of all the goods and services produced in a country in one year.

**Income Distribution** – Much of the difference between the highest and lowest income may be attributed to a) education, b) family choices, c) personal effort, d) entrepreneurship and e) age.

**Invisible Hand** – Individuals acting in their own self-interest will do more good for society than if the government directed everyone's actions. Though counter-intuitive, this principle has been demonstrated many, many times.

**Mutual Benefit** – See Voluntarism and Mutual Benefit.

**Per Capita GDP** – This is the gross domestic product of a country divided by the number of people in a country. It is a measure of a country's relative wealth. Capitalist countries tend to have higher per capita GDP than countries with socialist, communist, or despotic governments.

**Price** – Price controls what is produced. When the price of a good raises, entrepreneurs will provide more of it. Price serves as a rationing mechanism. Those willing and able to pay for a good or service will get it.

**Property** – The right to own and benefit from property is a requirement of capitalism. Wealth accumulation is necessary to form and invest in businesses. The right to benefit from property provides the incentive for hard work and innovation.

**Rational Self-Interest** – People work, trade, and invest, for their own benefit and that of their loved ones.

**Rich Get Richer and Poor Get Poorer** – This is a criticism of capitalism. The data show that in a capitalist system even the poor get richer over time, and there is significant income mobility. Those who start in the lowest income quintile can move up, and most do.

**Socialism** – Socialism is a system wherein a person can own property or a business, but the benefits of ownership and production are confiscated through regulations or taxes to achieve equality of outcome.

**Totalitarian Systems** – In totalitarian systems, individuals can own businesses in name, but ownership is only honored if those owning property are favored by those in power. This puts the benefits of work, savings and investment at risk, based on the favor of those in power.

**Voluntarism and Mutual Benefit** – In capitalism, people exchange goods, services and labor voluntarily. No one is forced into a transaction. Unless both parties mutually benefit from a transaction, it will not take place.

# References

Bailey, Blake. 2003. "How Not to be Poor", National Center for Policy Analysis, Dallas, Texas, January 15; citing "Poverty Dynamics in Four OECD Countries", 2000. Organization for Economic Cooperation and Development.

Badenhausen, Kurt. 2009. "The World's Highest Paid Athletes", Forbes Sports Valuations. 6/17. http://www.forbes.com/2009/06/17/top-earning-athletes-business-sports-top-earning-athletes.html

CIA. 2011. "World Factbook", Central Intelligence Agency. www.cia.gov/library/publications/the-world-factbook/index.html

de Tocqueville, Alexis. 1835-1840. Democracy in America. Reprint Bantam Classics. New York. 2000.

Forbes 400. 2010. "The Forbes 400: The Richest People in America", Sept. 16. http://www.forbes.com/wealth/forbes-400#p_1_s_arank_-1_

Forder, Kenny. 2011. "Villa Collina: The Largest Home In New Jersey" Apr 16. http://housing-today.com/news/villa-collina-the-largest-home-in-new-jersey-45854-sq-ft/

Gnaulati, Enrico. 2014. "Why Girls Tend to Get Better Grades Than Boys Do", The Atlantic. Sept.18. https://www.theatlantic.com/education/archive/2014/09/why-girls-get-better-grades-than-boys-do/380318/ downloaded 11/25/2017

Hayak, F. A. 1944. The Road to Serfdom, University of Chicago Press, Definitive Edition, p77.

Income Mobility. 2007. "Income Mobility in the U.S. from 1996 to 2005", Department of the Treasury, Nov. 12. Pg.7. www.treasury.gov/resource-center/tax-policy/Documents/incomemobilitystudy03-08revise.pdf

Kumar, Devika Krishna and Marianna Parraga. 2017. "Why record U.S. oil exports are poised for even more growth", Reuters Business News. July 27. https://www.reuters.com/article/us-usa-oil-exports-idUSKBN1AC0ER downloaded 2017-07-30

Kurtzman, Joel. 2013. "How Adam Smith Revived America's Oil Patch", Wall Street Journal. June 20. A19.

Mohl, Raymond, Ed. 1997. The Making of Urban America. "The Centrality of the Horse to the Nineteenth-Century American City", by Clay McShane. NY: SR Publishers, pp. 105-130.

Money Income of People. 2011. Money Income of People – Selected Characteristics by Income Level; Table 701. U.S. Census Bureau, Statistical Abstract of the United States: 2011, Income, Expenditures, Poverty and Wealth.

Mean Household Income. 2010. "Table H-3 Mean Household Income Received by Each Fifth and Top 5Percent, All Races: 1967 to 2009." U.S. Census Department. www.census.gov/hhes/www/income/data/historical/inequality/index.html

New Jobs. 2011. U.S. Small Business Administration. www.sba.gov/advocacy/7495/8420 downloaded 5/10/2011.

Oprah Winfrey's Annual Earnings. Staff. 2012. "Oprah Winfrey's Annual Earnings Drop by $125 Million, Says Forbes", The Hollywood Reporter. Aug.27. https://www.hollywoodreporter.com/news/oprah-winfrey-michael-bay-highest-paid-celebrities-forbes-365703

Price Impact of Walmart. 2007. "The Price Impact of Wal-Mart: An Update Through 2006", Business Planning Solutions Global Insight Advisory Services Division. http://walmartstores.com/media/resources/128340111054643750.pdf

ReferenceUSA. 2011. Infogroup Reference Division. ifoUSA Library Division, P.O. Box 27347, Omaha, NE 68127 downloaded May 10, 2011.

Robbins, James S. 1992. "Abraham Gesner...saved more whales than Greenpeace ever will,", The Freeman, August. published by the Foundation for Economic Education (FEE).

Scott, Allen J. 2006. "Entrepreneurship, Innovation and Industrial Development: Geography and the Creative Field Revisited", Small Business Economics. Vol.26 pp.1-24.

Shumpeter, Joseph A. 1942. Capitalism, Socialism and Democracy. (New York: Harper, 1975) originally published in 1942. Pp.82-85

Skousen, Mark. 2012. "Ben Franklin's Golden Rules", from *The Completed Autobiography of Benjamin Franklin*, Mark Skousen Ed. (Regnery, 2006) http://www.3rdstone.ws/Ben%20Franklin.htm. downloaded Dec. 24.

Spors, Kelly. 2006. "Small Business Owners, Executives Earn Less", Running A Business Column. *The Wall Street Journal*. October 19

Walmart $4 Prescription. 2008. "Wal-Mart $4 Prescription Program", June 5. http://i.walmart.com/i/if/hmp/fusion/genericdruglist.pdf

# CHAPTER FOUR

# TAX POLICY

---

After completing this chapter, you should be able to:

4.1   Understand the connection between taxes and capitalism.

4.2   Discuss various tax theories.

4.3   Discuss who should pay taxes and how much.

4.4   Critically evaluate tax policy issues.

4.5   Analyze the impact of tax policy on government revenue.

4.6.  Discuss what happens when people think they are being overtaxed.

---

## Introduction

Taxes are part of the price of living in a civilized society. Taxes provide funds for services that would be difficult or impossible for private citizens to acquire on their own. For example, no private citizen could provide for the national defense, police, or courts. These are public goods that benefit society at large.

Public health is another example of a service funded by taxes. Public health includes things like clean water, sewers and sanitary trash disposal. In some cases, these functions are outsourced to the private sector under government supervision.

Taxes pay for public education. No country can prosper unless its citizens are educated. Taxes for infrastructure such as roads and bridges facilitate commerce and industry and bring communities together. Few people would argue about paying taxes for such services.

Capitalism works best when people have the maximum incentives to work, save, and invest. While taxes are necessary, they reduce incentives. Balancing the need for taxes with incentives is at the heart of tax policy. A somewhat different view is the balance between personal liberty and taxation. It takes time to earn income. When income is taxed, the government is taking away time.

Other tax policy issues revolve around: (i) the overall level of taxation, (ii) what should be taxed, (iii) who should be taxed, and (iv) the economic consequences of taxation. There are no simple answers to these issues. Trade-offs must be balanced. But one thing is certain, some taxes are necessary to bind society together.

## Tax Terms

There is a certain vocabulary politicians and economists use when discussing taxes. Sometimes terms clarify issues.  Sometimes terms obscure the issues.

## Progressive v. Regressive Taxes

Taxes are said to be progressive if individuals with higher incomes pay a greater proportion of their income in taxes. Taxes are said to be regressive if people with higher incomes pay a lower effective tax rate. The terms progressive and regressive refer to tax rates, not the total taxes paid. A tax can be regressive yet those with higher incomes can pay many times the amount of a person with a lower income.

So, is a tax policy good or bad because someone gives it a name? Is progressive good because it sounds like the word progress? Is regressive bad because it sounds like the word regress which means to turn back? A better approach is to analyze the effect of tax policies on incentives to work, save, and invest, and to analyze their impact on government revenue rather than focusing on emotionally loaded terms.

A drawback to a highly progressive tax system is that government relies on a small number of individuals for a disproportionate share of revenue. For example, in California, the top 0.5% of tax filers, those making $500,000 or more per year, paid 32% of all income taxes in 2009. From 2007 to 2009 the number of people in the over $500,000 tax bracket fell from 146,221 to 98,610. In 2007, the top 1% of Californians paid $25.7 billion in taxes, but by 2009, tax collections from the top 1% fell to

$12.3 billion.[1] Using emotionally loaded words like progressive and regressive or claiming the top 1% does not pay their fair share and implementing highly a progressive tax structure might make government's tax revenue unpredictable, and therefore unreliable.

## Incidence of Tax v. Burden of Tax

The incidence of tax falls on the person who must remit a tax to the government. The burden of tax falls on the person who bears the economic cost. Most states have sales tax. Businesses are required to remit sales tax to states, so the incidence of sales tax falls on businesses. But, the economic burden of sales taxes falls principally on consumers.

The incidence of tax and the burden of tax are not obvious for Social Security and Medicare. Employees pay Social Security and Medicare taxes directly to the government, via payroll deductions. Employers pay an equal amount of Social Security and Medicare tax on employee earnings. The incidence of the employer's share of taxes falls on businesses. But who bears the economic burden of the employer's share of taxes? An employer will only hire a person if that person creates more value than they cost. The cost of an employee includes the employee's salary, benefits, and the employer's share of Social Security and Medicare taxes. So, while the incidence of the employer's share of these taxes fall on the employer, the burden of employer taxes falls on employees, because such taxes reduce the amount an employer can pay out of the value an employee creates.

# Expenditures

A discussion of tax policy must start with the level of expenditures. As more is spent, either tax revenue must rise, or deficits will rise. The European experiment in Greece, Spain, and Italy, has shown that there are limits to government deficits.

Disputes over taxes arise when government spends for purposes which go beyond national security, public safety, public health, public education, and infrastructure. When politicians fund pet projects, tax productive people to subsidize unproductive people, fund unproductive enterprises rather than letting the market decide how to allocate capital, provide government employees with lifestyles, salaries and benefits far better than

---

[1] ___. 2012. "Facebook to the Non-Rescue", Wall Street Journal. March 8. A16.

those of the governed, or use taxes as a means of controlling people's behavior, citizens object.

Often the government spends money on programs to help people using questionable and uncertain means, with questionable and uncertain results. The American Recovery and Reinvestment Act of 2009 spent $642.1 billion and created or funded the continued existence of 571,383 jobs, according to the government's website.[2] This means each job created or funded through the government cost about $1,123,765. Does this seem like a wise and thrifty use of taxpayer dollars?

Usually, individuals who lose jobs get up to 26 weeks of unemployment benefits. Extending unemployment benefits during tough economic times seems like the humane thing to do, but is it? Studies have shown that whether unemployment is high or low, a third of the unemployed get jobs immediately after their unemployment benefits run out. Expenditures for unemployment mean the unemployed don't have to make tough choices about moving or switching industries to get a job. Studies have also shown that each 13-week benefit extension increases the time a person is unemployed by two weeks. Delaying re-entry into the workforce helps neither the economy nor the unemployed individual and delay increases the tax burden.[3]

In 2013, North Carolina cut unemployment benefits from 26 weeks to 20 weeks and cut the maximum benefit from $535 a week to $350 a week. As a result, tens of thousands left the unemployment rolls and sought work. By 2015, unemployment dropped from 7.9% to 5.5%. North Carolina also cut the maximum income tax rate to 5.75% from 7.75% and cut the corporate rate from 6.9% to 5%. From 2013 to 2015, 200,000 jobs were added to the state's economy.[4]

Many well-meaning government programs have no effect or an effect that is the opposite of the one intended. Such programs increase the tax burden on productive citizens. There are also programs passed purely to get votes. For example, bills for public works that aren't needed. The General Accounting Office has documented many government programs that contain waste, or that duplicate other programs.[5]

---

[2] __ 2011. "Tracking the Money," RECOVERY.GOV. Oct. 1
www.recovery.gov/pages/default.aspx
[3] Sherk, James. 2010. "Extended Unemployment Insurance Benefits: The Heritage Foundation 2010 Labor Boot Camp", the Heritage Foundation. No. 2759. Jan.14.
[4] Moore, Stephanie. 2015. "The Tax-Cut payoff in Carolina." Wall Street Journal. June 4. A15.
[5] See "Reports and Testimony," U.S. Government Accountability Office
www.gao.gov

# Taxes and Capitalism

What is the connection between taxes and capitalism? Capitalism is voluntary. Capitalism only works when people have incentives to work, save and invest. Taxes reduce the payoff for work, investment and production. Some politicians think that people will work and produce no matter what the tax burden. Ask yourself whether that is true in your own life. Do you respond to incentives and recoil from penalties? If you do, then others probably will as well.

Consider this thought experiment. Suppose a company five minutes from your house offered you a job paying $50,000, and a company one hour away offered you a job paying $100,000. Would you take the job closer or further away? Most people would take the job further away to get the $100,000 salary.

Now let's introduce taxes into the thought experiment. Suppose the income tax on $50,000 is 10%, but the tax on $100,000 is 50%. Your after-tax income from the closer job would be $45,000 while the after-tax income from commuting an hour to work and an hour home every day would be $50,000. Still want to exert the extra effort to take the job further away?

This experiment illustrates the fact that taxes affect the amount of effort people are willing to put forth. Taxes also affect the risks people are willing to take, and the amount they are willing to invest. Capitalism works best, and society prospers most, when everyone is working full out. When people hold back, everyone's standard of living declines.

---

**GAIN**

Transistors can be found in computers, cars, phones, televisions and practically everything that uses electricity. Transistors are composed of three layers of semi-conductors. The middle layer is called a gate. By varying the gate current a little, the output current through the transistor can be changed dramatically. This is how a whisper of sound becomes rock-concert loud. The amount of amplification is called gain, which is the output current divided by the gate current.

Taxes work the same way. Small changes in tax rates dramatically affect how hard people are willing to work, and the willingness to work affects how robust the economy is. Politicians think small increases in taxes don't matter, but because tax increases and decreases affect incentives, the gain or drain on the economy is dramatic.

---

President John F. Kennedy recognized the need to balance taxes with incentives to work, save, and invest. An abridged version of his speech to the Economics Club of New York is reproduced in Appendix 4A.

## Federal Taxation

The federal government imposes taxes in five principal areas: (i) corporate income tax, (ii) individual income taxes and income taxes on trusts and estates, (iii) employment taxes, which includes Social Security taxes, Medicare taxes, and unemployment taxes, (iv) inheritance and gift taxes, and (v) excise taxes which are taxes on specific goods like gasoline and diesel fuel. Table 4.1 Federal Tax Revenue is an analysis of federal taxes for 2013 and 2012.[6]

**Table 4.1 Federal Tax Revenue**

| Source of Tax (dollars in billions) | 2013 | % | 2012 | % |
|---|---|---|---|---|
| Corporate Income Tax | $273.5 | 9.9% | $242.3 | 9.9% |
| Individual Income, Estate & Trust Taxes | $1,316.4 | 47.4% | $1,132.2 | 46.2% |
| Social Security, Medicare, & Unemployment | $947.8 | 34.2% | $845.3 | 34.5% |
| Excise Taxes | $84.0 | 3.0% | $79.1 | 3.2% |
| Inheritance and Gift Taxes | $153.4 | 5.5% | $151.3 | 6.2% |
| *Totals* | *$2,775.1* | *100.0%* | *$2,450.2* | *100.0%* |

In addition to federal taxes, businesses and individuals face state taxes. Many states have corporate income taxes, personal income taxes, sales taxes and some have personal property taxes. A personal property tax is a tax on assets. Some states levy a personal property tax on a company's inventory. Some states levy a personal property tax on its citizens' cars.

---

[6] ___ 2014. "Table 2.1 - Receipts by Source 1934-2019," Office of Management and Budget. www.whitehouse.gov/omb/budget/Historicals April 15. downloaded 2014-06-23

# Theories of Taxation

## Who Should Pay Taxes and How Much?

The French Minister of Finance under King Louis XIV, Jean Baptiste Colbert (1619-1683), said: "The art of taxation consists in so plucking the goose as to obtain the largest amount of feathers with the smallest amount of hissing." Unfortunately, maximizing tax revenue while minimizing the hissing, does not always equate with fairness.

### Apportionment

In a perfectly fair system, taxes might be apportioned based on usage. For example, does everyone require the same national defense or the same amount of police protection? If so, everyone should share equally in the cost. The same might be said for the cost of courts, jails, roads, bridges and public education.

If fair means paying for the proportion of services used, then the fair share would be the national budget of $3,456 billion divided by the population of the United States, which is about 308.7 million. That would mean a tax bill of about $11,195 for every man, woman, and child. If the cost of government were just spread over those filing tax returns instead of the entire population, each taxpayer's annual bill would be about $31,276. Unfortunately, taxes are not that systematic or orderly.[7, 8]

## Consumption Tax

A consumption tax has been proposed as an alternative to the income tax and other government taxes like social security. The virtues of a consumption tax are that: (i) it would be simple for the government to administer; (ii) individuals would not have to file income tax returns, and businesses would not have to withhold and report income and social security taxes; (iii) those who spend more would be taxed more; and (iv) a consumption tax would also tax the 'underground economy', those who pay no tax because their income is unreported, or is from illegal activities.

---

[7] __. 2011. "Table S-1 Budget Totals," Summary Tables, Budget of the United States of America.
http://www.whitehouse.gov/sites/default/files/omb/budget/fy2012/assets/tables.pdf
[8] www.census.gov

According to the Census Department, national personal expenditures for 2010 were about \$9,314 billion,[9] and the national budget was \$3,456 billion for the same year. A national consumption tax of 37.1% would pay for the national government. To put this into perspective, a \$4.00 hamburger would cost \$5.48 and a \$25,000 car would cost \$34,275. But there would be no income tax withholding, no tax returns to file, no social security, Medicare or other taxes.

That may sound like a pretty high tax rate but consider this. A single person making \$49,500 and taking a standard deduction contributes about \$10,583.50 to the federal government in taxes.[10] A consumption tax is only paid when something is purchased. A person's tax bill could be reduced by saving or investing some income. Suppose a person spent 60% of his or her income on items covered under a consumption tax, they would pay about \$11,018.70, and would not have to file tax returns.

A problem with a consumption tax is that people are already discussing how it can be modified to avoid application to food, medicine and industries with good lobbies. That means the tax on the remaining goods and services would have to be even higher.

## Corporate Tax

Maybe businesses should bear the burden of taxes. In 2011, publicly traded companies had US pre-tax income of \$666.1 billion on sales of \$27,045.5 billion. Assume there is another 25% of sales and pre-tax income in privately held companies. That raises total pre-tax income to about \$832.6 billion on sales of \$33,806.9 billion.

Taxing only corporations to cover federal government expenditures of \$3,600 billion would require a tax rate of 432.4%. At a rate of 432.4%, all businesses would close.[11]

---

[9] ___ 2012. "Table 667. Gross Domestic Product in Current and Chained Dollars," *2012 Statistical Abstract,* U.S. Census Bureau. Downloaded 03/04/2012. www.census.gov/compendia/statab/cats/income_expenditures_poverty_wealth/gro ss_domestic_product_gdp. html

[10] A single person making \$49,500 contributes about \$10,583.50 computed as follows: Gross wages of \$49,500 less standard deduction of \$5,800 less personal exemption of \$3,700 is a taxable income of \$40,000. Income in this bracket is taxed at 10% giving an income tax of \$4,000. Employee's Social Security is 4.2% this year and Medicare is 1.45% for a total of \$2,796.75. Employers pay 6.2% Social Security and 1.45% Medicare or \$3,786.75.

[11] CBO. 2011. "The US Federal Budget: Infographic" Congressional Budget Office. December 12. www.cbo.gov/publication/42636. Downloaded 2017-12-28

The federal corporate tax rate has just been reduced to 21.0% which will make the US more competitive internationally. However, state corporate income taxes must be considered in addition to federal taxes.

Texas minimizes the burden of business taxes to encourage growth. Broadly speaking, Texas levies a 1% franchise tax on the difference between revenue and the cost of goods sold. Over the period 2002 to 2011 Texas's compound annual GDP growth rate was 5.27% which was far greater than the 3.88% average for other states and the District of Columbia. Only four states had a higher growth rate than Texas (North Dakota, Wyoming, Louisiana and Alaska), and one of them, (Wyoming) had no corporate income tax.[12, 13] If an alternative to the current corporate income tax is needed, perhaps one should consider a Texas-style tax on the difference between revenue and cost of goods sold.

## Personal Income Tax

The tax that raises the most revenue, and is therefore the most problematic, is the personal income tax. The tax policy of many politicians boils down to two slogans: (i) tax the rich, and (ii) the rich should pay their fair share.

This raises two important questions. Who are the rich, and what is their fair share? These questions have led to endless arguments. But consider this, when the income tax was passed in 1913, it only applied to the rich. That is, it only applied to individuals making $3,000 per year or couples making $4,000 per year. Does $3,000 or $4,000 sound rich to you? The definition of rich often turns on how much one makes. Please tax the rich, but don't tax me.

## Who Bears the Burden of Income Taxes?

Do the rich pay their fair share? One way to think about fair share would be to say that a person who makes twice as much as another should pay twice as much in taxes. If a person who makes $25,000 pays $3,000 in taxes, a person who makes $50,000 should pay $6,000 and a person who makes $100,000 should pay $12,000. So even though the person making $100,000 uses the same amount of national defense, courts, police and so

---

[12] ___. 2012. "Regional Economic Activity Accounts," US Department of Commerce - Bureau of Economic Analysis
http://www.bea.gov/regional/downloadzip.cfm
[13] ___. 2013. "State Corporate Income Tax Rates, 2000-2013," Tax Foundation.
http://taxfoundation.org/article/state-corporate-income-tax-rates-2000-2013

forth as the person who makes $25,000 they pay four times as much. Is that their fair share? Or are they contributing more than their fair share? Table 4.2 Income Taxes analyzes personal income tax. Panel A: Analysis of Income shows the distribution of income by bracket. Panel B: Analysis of Tax Burden shows the tax paid, and effective tax rate by income bracket.[14]

**Table 4.2 Income Taxes**

---

**Adjusted Gross Income and Tax are in billions.**

**Panel A: Analysis of Income**

| Tax Bracket | Number of Returns | Percent Returns | Adjusted Gross Income |
|---|---|---|---|
| Under $25,000 | 58,096,150 | 40.7% | $293.9 |
| $25,000 - $50,000 | 34,491,665 | 24.1% | $921.0 |
| $50,000 - $75,000 | 18,949,278 | 13.3% | $1,090.6 |
| $75,000 - $100,000 | 11,926,401 | 8.3% | $1,011.0 |
| $100,000 - $200,000 | 14,755,766 | 10.3% | $1,963.0 |
| $200,000 - $500,000 | 3,801,641 | 2.7% | $1,076.6 |
| $500,000 - $1,000,000 | 597,525 | 0.4% | $401.6 |
| $1,000,000 - $2,000,000 | 134,907 | 0.1% | $162.2 |
| $2,000,000 - $5,000,000 | 79,363 | 0.1% | $234.8 |
| Over $5,000,000 | 30,634 | 0.0% | $450.1 |
| *Totals* | *142,863,330* | | *$7,605.0* |

---

[14] ___ 2011. "Table 1.1 All Returns: Selected Income and Tax Items by Size and Accumulated Size of Adjusted Gross Income, Tax Year 2011" Treasury Department.
http://www.irs.gov/uac/SOI-Tax-Stats---Individual-Statistical-Tables-by-Size-of-Adjusted-Gross-Income downloaded 2014-06-24

## Panel B: Analysis of Tax Burden

| Tax Bracket | Percent Income | Tax | Percent Tax | Effective Rate |
|---|---|---|---|---|
| Under $25,000 | 3.9% | $12.4 | 1.2% | 4.2% |
| $25,000 - $50,000 | 12.1% | $64.2 | 6.3% | 7.0% |
| $50,000 - $75,000 | 14.3% | $93.3 | 9.1% | 8.6% |
| $75,000 - $100,000 | 13.3% | $96.0 | 9.4% | 9.5% |
| $100,000 - $200,000 | 25.8% | $249.0 | 24.4% | 12.7% |
| $200,000 - $500,000 | 14.2% | $212.4 | 20.8% | 19.7% |
| $500,000 - $1,000,000 | 5.3% | $97.6 | 9.6% | 24.3% |
| $1,000,000-$2,000,000 | 2.1% | $40.5 | 4.0% | 24.9% |
| $2,000,000-$5,000,000 | 3.1% | $58.8 | 5.8% | 25.0% |
| Over $5,000,000 | 5.9% | $97.1 | 9.5% | 21.6% |
| **Totals** | | **$1,021.3** | | |

The bottom 64.8% of taxpayers, those with incomes under $50,000, have 16% of the income and pay 7.5% of total taxes. The top 13.6% of taxpayers, those with incomes over $100,000, have 56.4% of the income and pay 74.0% of the tax. The top 3.3% of taxpayers pay 49.7% of the tax. Suppose the rich are defined as those making $500,000 or more. They comprise the top 0.6% of tax payers, yet they pay 28.8% of income taxes.

Consider the effective tax rate paid by each group of taxpayers. For those making under $25,000, the effective tax rate is 4.2%. This rate rises steadily as income rises to a peak of 25.0% for taxpayers earning $2,000,000 to $5,000,000, and then drops somewhat after that.

One way to think about the tax burden is to look at the share of taxes paid divided by the share of income. For the bottom 64.8% of the population, those making under $50,000, the tax burden would be .469 (7.5% of taxes/16.0% of income). For those making over $100,000 the tax burden would be 1.312 (74.0% of taxes/56.4% of income) which is almost 2.8 times higher than for those with incomes under $50,000. The tax burden for those with incomes over $500,000 is about 1.756 (28.8% of taxes/16.4% of income) which is 3.7 times higher than for the low 64.8% of taxpayers. So, the question remains, who is paying their fair share, and who isn't?

Progressive tax rates and a 'soak the rich' political mentality is pushing the country towards two economic classes. One that works, produces and pays taxes, and one that pays little or no taxes, but enjoys the benefits of taxes: defense, roads, public safety and transfer payments.

## Taxes and Consumer Behavior

Maybe the best strategy is to tax luxury goods that only the rich buy, so politicians can say they are going to 'stick it to the rich' without affecting anyone else. Maybe a tax on yachts would be a good place to start. Most people don't need or want a yacht, so a tax on yachts would only affect the rich. Right?

In 1991, Congress imposed a 10% tax on yachts over $100,000. What was the result? Howard McMichael of McMichael Yacht Brokers sold 30 yachts priced over $100,000 in 1989 and by the middle of 1991, he had sold only 2 yachts. Viking Boat Works in New Gretna, New Jersey was building the number one sport fishing yacht in the United States, and in 1989 it employed 1,400 people. When the luxury yacht tax was passed, sales crashed. Viking's workforce dropped to just 68 people. Nationwide, the yacht tax put 100 boat builders out of business, costing the boat building industry 25,000 direct jobs and 75,000 support jobs. Prior to the tax, the United States was a major exporter of luxury boats. Even though the tax was repealed in 1993, the industry never recovered.[15, 16] As Supreme Court Justice John Marshall said, "The power to tax is the power to destroy."[17]

When politicians try to stick it to the rich, they end up sticking it to average working people. The more the rich spend on planes, cars, yachts, mansions, and fancy shoes, the more employment they provide to ordinary people. While some people want to make the rich poor through higher taxes, they forget that jobs created by the rich contribute to the fabric of society.

A person who really wanted to contribute to society should become rich, so that he or she could provide meaningful employment to others, either by creating jobs as an entrepreneur or by spending money which also creates jobs.

## Comparison of Tax Strategies

It is up to Congress to decide the level of spending, who is taxed, what is taxed, and how much they are taxed. In theory, Congress reflects the

---

[15] Singer, Penny. 1991. "New Luxury Tax Trimming Boat Sales," New York Times Archives. July 21. http://www.nytimes.com/1991/07/21/nyregion/new-luxury-tax-trimming-boat-sales.html?pagewanted=print&src=pm
[16] ___ 2009. "The Rising Tide," DVD. SLU Productions, LLC. P.O. Box 64, Caldwell, NJ 07006 www.therisingtide.info
[17] Marshall, John. 1819. McCulloch v. Maryland 17 U.S. 327.

will of the people, so it is up to citizens to provide input and guidance to Congress. Table 4.3 Comparison of Tax Strategies is an analysis of the level of taxes using various strategies. It assumes all current expenditures are paid for, which means there is no increase in the national debt.

Perhaps, rather than imposing all of the tax burden on any sector of the economy, every sector should contribute something.

**Table 4.3 Comparison of Tax Strategies**

**This analysis considers alternative tax strategies based on 2011 federal government expenditures for typical taxpayers in each category.**

| Tax Strategy | Personal Income $50,000 | Personal Income $250,000 | Small Business | Large Business |
|---|---|---|---|---|
| Apportionment by individual | $11,195 | $11,195 | $0 | $0 |
| Apportionment by taxpayer | $31,276 | $31,276 | $0 | $0 |
| Corporate income tax | $0 | $0 | 443.4% rate, no businesses. | 432.4% rate, no businesses. |
| Flat tax on all income | $11,550 | $57,750 | $0 | $0 |
| Consumption tax | $11,130 (60% of income consumed) | $55,650 (60% of income consumed) | $0 | $0 |
| Texas style corporate tax of 10% plus flat tax | $7,850 | $39,250 | $33,000 on revenue of $1M | $3,300,000 on revenue of $100M |

# Do Higher Tax Rates Generate More Tax Revenue?

Do higher tax rates generate more government revenue or just 'punish' the rich for being successful? Politicians usually say higher taxes generate more revenue for the government. Economists say, if you want to discourage something, tax it. For example, the tax on cigarettes is very high and getting higher to discourage smoking. Do high taxes on success encourage risk taking and entrepreneurship, or do they discourage it?

The Laffer Curve[18] says that when tax rates are zero or 100%, government revenue is zero. At a 100% tax rate, there is no point in working. Generally, reducing tax rates encourages work and risk-taking, which results in higher government revenue, because the tax base increases. High taxes discourage work and investment.

Since about 1950, no matter what the maximum personal tax rate was, the federal government got about 17% of GDP in taxes. Table 4.4 Tax Revenue and Marginal Tax Rates, 1950–2016 illustrates this principle. This relationship was first noticed by Kurt Hauser, a San Francisco investment banker, and is known as Hauser's law.[19]

Hauser's law is disconcerting to politicians who want both 'social justice', by which they mean making the rich poorer, and at the same time, want more tax revenue to spend. Taxes can make the rich poorer, but most economists acknowledge that taxes slow the economy. Taxes reduce incentives for work, investment, and risk taking, all the behaviors that grow GDP. So, taxing the rich only puts the brakes on the economy, and the rich don't suffer when that happens; ordinary citizens suffer.

**If the government wanted more tax revenue, its strategy should be to lower taxes, grow the economy, and take 17% of a larger GDP.** Unfortunately, many politicians don't understand this concept and don't want to understand it. They want to raise tax rates no matter what, which will shrink GDP, and they will get about 17% of a smaller amount.

---

[18] Laffer, Arthur B. 2004. "The Laffer Curve: Past, Present, and Future," The Heritage Foundation for American Leadership. June 1. www.heritage.org/Research/Taxes/bg1765.cfm

[19] Hauser, Kurt W. and David Ranson. 2008. "Hauser's Law," Hoover Digest. 2008 No. 4. Oct. 12. http://www.hoover.org/publications/hoover-digest/article/5728. This essay appeared in the *Wall Street Journal* on May 20, 2008

**Table 4.4 Tax Revenue and Marginal Tax Rates, 1950-2016**

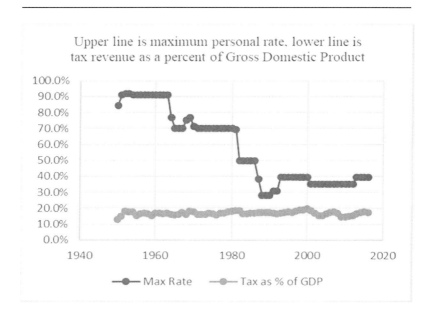

## Tax Avoidance

No one likes to be poked with a stick. No one likes to be put upon. No one likes to think they are being taken advantage of. When taxes reach a certain point, and people conclude the government is confiscating too much of their income, they feel like they are being poked with a stick. While most people are willing to pay taxes, they resent the government wasting money on ineffective programs and wealth redistribution.

What do people do? There are two ways people legally avoid taxes. One is by not working, or working less, not investing, or investing less, not producing, or producing just enough for their own needs and those of their family. For example, a worker might decide that instead of working overtime, or on weekends, he or she might go fishing. A business person might decide not to expand. An investor might decide not to invest in a property, or, if he or she has a property, rather than paying a high tax rate on the sale of that property, they may decide just to keep it. When the most productive, high income people work less, invest less, and produce less, the economy contracts and everyone is worse off.

The other approach is tax migration. People and capital are mobile. If entrepreneurs, investors, or corporate executives feel they are being overtaxed, they might simply leave. The CEO of Cypress Semi-Conductor indicated he is moving his facilities out of California because of high taxes.[20] Over the past decade, 330,000 Massachusetts residents moved to one of the nine states that have no state income tax.[21] Since Connecticut instituted its income tax in 1992, there has been exactly zero growth in the number of new jobs. Over this same period the rest of the country added 22 million jobs.[22]

After New Jersey passed the 'millionaires tax' the president of a local bank indicated that he was moving to Florida, a no-income-tax state, and he was moving the Bank's corporate headquarters to Florida as well.[23] There are indications other New Jersey residents will follow.[24]

In 2007 Maryland passed a 'millionaires tax', a higher tax rate on those making over $1 million a year. Since then, one third of Maryland's millionaires have left the state.[25] General Electric left Connecticut for Boston, Massachusetts, because of higher taxes.[26]

The insert, "Heartland Tax Rebellion" on the next page, provides a look at the divergence in states' thinking about taxes.[27] Appendix 4B is an overview of states with the lowest and highest personal income, and corporate tax rates.

---

[20] Rogers, T. J. "Golden State Drives Out Business," Wall Street Journal August 2-3, 2008.

[21] ___ "Boston Tax Party," Wall Street Journal. August 5, 2008. A18.

[22] ___ "Jodi Corzine, Review and Outlook," Wall Street Journal, August 29-30, 2009. A12.

[23] Yates, Craig. 2005. "Leadership and Banking," Speech to The Business Development Leadership Seminar. President, Farmers and Merchants Bank. Feb.18.

[24] Hester, Tom Jr." Poll finds many hoping to leave New Jersey behind," The Associated Press. October 17, 2007.

[25] ___. "Jodi Corzine, Review and Outlook," Wall Street Journal, August 29-30, 2009. A12.

[26] Kudlow, Larry. 2016. "Taxes Chased GE Out of Connecticut," National Review. January 15. www. nationalreview. com/article/429874/ge-leaves-connecticut-boston-blame-taxes downloaded 2017-07-31.

[27] ___. 2012. "The Heartland Tax Rebellion," Wall Street Journal. Feb. 7. A12.

---

**The Heartland Tax Rebellion**

Some states understand that income tax rates have an impact on prosperity. Kansas is cutting its income tax from 6.45% to 4.9% with plans to phase it out. Oklahoma has announced it will cut its income tax from 5.25% to 3.5% with plans to phase it out. Missouri has a measure on the ballot to abolish the income tax. South Carolina is considering abolishing its corporate income tax.

The Wall Street Journal analyzed changes in population, state product (the state version of gross domestic product) and employment for the ten-year period 2001 to 2010 for the nine highest and lowest personal income tax states and found a dramatic difference between the two groups.

| Growth | Lowest Income Tax | Highest Income Tax |
|---|---|---|
| Population | 13.7% | 5.5% |
| State Product | 58.5% | 42.1% |
| Employment | 5.4% | -1.7% |

---

People and companies are not just migrating out of high tax states. When the United States had a 35% corporate income tax, companies moved to lower tax countries taking jobs, investment capital and tax revenue with them. Reduction of the U.S. corporate tax rate to 21% should reverse that flow.

## Fate of a Capitalist Democracy

There are several constraints on a capitalist democracy. Many people think government is a 'Magic Lantern'. If they rub it, they can get anything they want: free art museums, free healthcare, free food, free housing, free, free, free. Businesses create wealth, but government creates nothing. When the government gives something to someone, it must take something from someone else.

In a democracy, people can vote for the candidate who says he or she will give people the most 'free stuff'. To pay for that 'free stuff', government will have to tax, punish if you will, those who are the most productive. If the benefits of work are taxed away, there is little point in working and producing. The productive can leave, or as in *Atlas*

*Shrugged*[28], simply stop producing. As the number of 'takers' overwhelms the number of 'producers', a capitalist democracy will collapse.

Alex Taylor, a Scottish history professor said: "A democracy cannot exist as a permanent form of government. It can only exist until the voters discover that they can vote themselves money from the public treasury. From that moment on, the majority always votes for the candidates promising them the most money, with the result that a democracy always collapses over loose fiscal policy followed by a dictatorship.

"The average age of the world's great civilizations has been two hundred years. These nations have progressed: (i) from bondage to spiritual faith; (ii) from spiritual faith to great courage; (iii) from courage to liberty; (iv) from liberty to abundance; (iv) from abundance to selfishness; (v) from selfishness to complacency; (vi) from complacency to apathy; (vii) from apathy to dependency' and (viii) from dependency back to bondage."[29]

# Charity

No discussion of tax policy is complete without a discussion of charity. There will always be things that some people feel strongly about funding and others do not. For example, one person might feel strongly that there should be an art museum, or live theatre, in every community. Others feel more money should be devoted to cancer research. Yet others believe more resources should be devoted to the poorest and sickest members of the community. Charity is a good and noble way to fund these activities.

Does American capitalism help or hurt charitable giving? Studies indicate that Americans are among the most charitable people in the world. A cover story in *Philanthropy Magazine* indicated that Americans donated about twice as much of their income to charity as the Dutch, three times as much as the French, five times as much as the Germans and ten times as much as the Italians even after adjusting for differences in income. Private,

---

[28] Ayn Rand. 1957. *Atlas Shrugged*. Reprinted 1999. Plume a Penguin Group Company. New York, New York. *Atlas Shrugged* chronicles an inventor and entrepreneur who rebels against high taxes and over-regulation by refusing to produce more than he needs for himself, and he recruits the leading industrialists of his time to do the same. In effect, he asks the countries' men and women of action to go on strike.

[29] This analysis has been attributed to Alexander Tyler, a Scottish history professor, the French author, Alexis de Tocqueville, former British Prime Minister Benjamin Disraeli (1804-1881) and others. Whoever wrote it, it has an undeniable logic.

charitable donations to foreign countries and people are about $50 billion per year.[30]

Charity is uplifting and enriches donors' self-worth. Charity should be encouraged. But note the difference between charity and taxes; charity is voluntary, taxes are compulsory.

## Paying Taxes

Nobody likes to pay taxes, yet taxes are necessary for a civilized society. No matter how much you dislike paying taxes, **pay them**. If you are unhappy about the amount you must pay, or the way the government is spending **your** money, call them, write them, email them, tweet them, or organize a protest. Campaign against spendthrift politicians, or run for office yourself. But stay on the side of the angels. As long as the tax law is what it is, pay what the law requires.

## Conclusion

Taxes are the price of living in a civilized society. Taxes are necessary for national defense, police, roads, schools and infrastructure.

Capitalism works best when people have the maximum incentive to work save and invest. Taxes reduce incentives. So, there is a natural tension between the two.

The overall level of taxation, who should be taxed, and how much, are among the most important issues in tax policy. In a fair system, everyone would pay an equal share for things like national defense, roads, schools and so forth. But rather than giving everyone the same tax bill, it has been decided that income should be a major determinant of tax. Those in the top 3.3% of income pay about 49.7% of taxes. Those in the bottom 64.8% of income pay only 7.5% of income taxes. Data suggest the rich pay their fair share plus the fair share of most others as well.

Historically, the government gets about 17% of Gross National Product, regardless of the highest marginal tax rate. Since high tax rates slow the economy, taxes should be cut, which will increase economic activity and the government can then harvest 17% of an expanded GDP.

---

[30] Brooks, Arthur C. 2006. "Are Americans Generous?" Philanthropy Magazine. May/June Cover Story.
http://www.philanthropyroundtable.org/topic/excellence_in_philanthropy/are_americans_generous

Unfortunately, many politicians don't understand this, and don't want to understand it.

When taxes get 'too high' people work, save, and invest, less, which slows the economy and reduces job opportunities. The other thing people do when taxes get 'too high' is that they migrate to lower tax jurisdictions. There has been a well-documented migration of people, wealth and jobs from high tax states to low tax states.

A capitalist democracy will fail once citizens and politicians regard the government as a 'magic lantern' which can give everything to everybody. Government does not create wealth; it can only take wealth away from the most productive citizens and businesses to fund programs.

The key concepts are: (i) taxes are necessary for a civilized society; (ii) capitalism produces the most wealth and the most jobs when people have the greatest incentives; (iii) taxes reduce incentives for work, saving and investment; (iv) as with all things in life, balance is necessary between taxation and incentives; and (v) whether one likes taxes or not, one should stay on the side of the angels and pay taxes, due and owing.

## Appendix 4a Speech by President Kennedy on Tax Policy

### President John F. Kennedy Speech to the Economic Club of New York on Tax Cuts 14 December 1962 [Abridged][31]

"Less than a month ago this nation reminded the world that it possessed both the will and the weapons to meet any threat to the security of free men. The gains we have made will not be given up, and the course that we have pursued will not be abandoned. But in the long run, security will not be determined by military or diplomatic moves alone. It will be affected by the decisions of finance ministers as well as by the decisions of Secretaries of State and Secretaries of Defense; by the deployment of fiscal and monetary weapons as well as by military weapons; and above all by the strength of this nation's economy as well as by the strength of our defenses.

America's rise to world leadership in the century since the Civil War has reflected more than anything else our unprecedented economic growth. A prosperous and growing America is important not only to Americans; it is of vital importance to the entire Western World.

---

[31] Kennedy, John F. 1962. "Remarks to the Economic Club of New York," Papers of John F. Kennedy. Presidential Papers. President's Office Files. Speech Files. Dec.14. https://www.jfklibrary.org/Asset-Viewer/Archives/JFKWHA-148.aspx.

There are a number of ways by which the Federal Government can meet its responsibilities to aid economic growth. We can and must improve American education and technical training. We can and must expand civilian research and technology. One of the great bottlenecks for this country's economic growth in this decade will be the shortage of doctorates in mathematics, engineering, and physics.

The final and best means of strengthening demand among consumers and businesses is to reduce the burden on private income and the deterrents to private initiative which are imposed by our present tax system. This administration pledged itself last summer to an across-the-board, top-to-bottom cut in personal and corporate income taxes to be enacted and become effective in 1963.

I am not talking about a 'quickie' or a temporary tax cut; any new tax legislation enacted next year should meet the following three tests. First, it should reduce net taxes by a sufficiently large amount to do the job required. Second, corporate tax rates must also be cut to increase incentives and the availability of investment capital. Third, the new tax bill should improve both the equity and the simplicity of our present tax system. For the present patchwork of special provisions and preferences lightens the tax load of some only at the cost of placing a heavier burden on others. It distorts economic judgments and channels an undue amount of energy into efforts to avoid tax liabilities. It makes certain types of less productive activity more profitable than other more valuable undertakings. All this inhibits our growth and efficiency, as well as considerably complicating the work of both the taxpayer and the Internal Revenue Service.

In short, it is a paradoxical truth that tax rates are too high today and tax revenues are too low and the soundest way to raise the revenues in the long run is to cut the rates now. The experience of a number of European countries and Japan have borne this out. This country's own experience with tax reduction in 1954 has borne this out.

This nation can afford to reduce taxes, but we cannot afford to do nothing. For on the strength of our free economy rests the hope of all free nations. We shall not fail that hope, for free men and free nations must prosper and they must prevail. Thank you."

## Appendix 4b Analysis of State Taxes

State tax rates are one factor in decisions as to where people want to live, start, and expand, a business. Table B-1 Panel A: Personal Income Tax Rates is an analysis of the highest and lowest personal tax income states. Table B-1 Panel B: Corporate Tax Rates is an analysis of the highest and lowest corporate tax rates.[32]

**Table B-1 Panel A: Personal Income Tax Rates**

| Lowest Personal Income Tax | | | | Highest Personal Income Tax | | |
|---|---|---|---|---|---|---|
| State | Personal Income Tax | Corporate Tax | | State | Personal Income Tax | Corporate Tax |
| So. Dakota | None | None | | Hawaii | 11.00% | 6.40% |
| Wyoming | None | None | | Oregon | 9.90% | 7.60% |
| Florida | None | 5.50% | | California | 9.30% | 8.84% |
| Texas | None | * | | Iowa | 8.98% | 12.00% |
| Washington | None | None | | New Jersey | 8.97% | 9.00% |

**Table B-1 Panel B Corporate Tax Rates**

| Lowest Corporate Tax | | | | Highest Corporate Tax | | |
|---|---|---|---|---|---|---|
| State | Personal Income Tax | Corporate Tax | | State | Personal Income Tax | Corporate Tax |
| Nevada | None | None | | Iowa | 8.98% | 12.00% |
| Washington | None | None | | Pennsylvania | 3.07% | 9.99% |
| Wyoming | None | None | | Minnesota | 7.85% | 9.80% |
| So. Dakota | None | None | | Illinois | 5.00% | 9.50% |
| Texas | None | * | | Alaska | None | 9.40% |

* Texas has a 1% franchise tax on the difference between sales and cost of goods sold.

---

[32] ___. 2012 "State Tax Comparisons," Federation of Tax Administrators. 444 N. Capitol St., NW, Suite 348, Washington D.C. www.taxadmin.org/fta/rate/tax_stru.html

# Appendix 4c Regulation

Taxes are not the only drag on entrepreneurship, business expansion, and job creation. Regulation can make it difficult or impossible for companies to get started, grow, and even exist. Just as taxes are necessary for a civilized society, some regulations are necessary. Laws, rules and regulations are necessary to protect people and property from serious injury. No one wants to see child labor, unsafe pharmaceuticals or unsafe aircraft. However, many laws, rules, and regulations go far beyond this common-sense purpose. There are four problems with regulations, but each of them can be fixed if the political will exists.[33]

## The Government has No Sense of Urgency

Many of the things people and businesses want to do require permits or permissions from government. While businesses must move fast to be competitive, government agencies don't seem to understand the adverse impact of delay. In Griffith v. NJDEP, a New Jersey Appellate Court held that a delay in approving permits of seven years was not unreasonable. In Wyatt v. United States, the Supreme Court held that a delay of eight years in approving mining permits was not unreasonable.[34]

The solution is a law which automatically grants permits or permissions if the government does not object within a limited period. For example, if a project involves $10 million or less, the government should have thirty days to object; or if the project involves more than $10 million, but less than $1 billion, the government should have 60 days to object; or 90 days for projects over $1 billion. Any objecting government department or agency should have to detail their objections in writing, cite the specific reason for rejecting the application, and state how the application could be brought into compliance with laws, rules and regulations. If the

---

[33] Vance, David E. 2012. "Regulation Reform," The Independent Review. Fall (Vol. 17, No.2).

[34] Griffith v. State of New Jersey, Department of Environmental Protection, 340 N.J. Super. 596, 775 A.2d 54 (App. Div. 2001). Wyatt, Anne D., Eastern Minerals International, Inc., Van Buren Minerals Corporation, Milton J. Bernos, Jr., Nancy Wyatt Zorn, Mary Anne Wyatt, Wilson W. Wyatt, Jr., and Martin P. Duffy, Executor of Wilson Wyatt, Sr.'s Estate, Plaintiffs-Cross Appellants, v. United States, Defendant-Appellant. 271 F.3d 1090 (2001). Nos. 99-5054, 99-5059. United States Court of Appeals, Federal Circuit. Decided: November 19, 2001.

government does not object to an application within a limited period of time, permits and permissions should be automatically granted.

## The Rational Basis Standard is Too Lax

Courts uphold laws if there is a rational basis between a law and a legitimate government purpose. The rational basis standard is so low, court approval often turns on whether a government agent is a good story-teller. There are many good story-tellers in government.

The solution is to raise the standard. The government should be required not just to tell a good story, but to prove by **clear and convincing evidence** that a law, rule, or regulation will actually prevent serious injury to people or property.

## Statutes and Regulations are Impenetrable

Laws, rules, and regulations have become so long and complicated that few, if any, people understand them. For example, the Affordable Health Care for America Act is 1,990 pages[35] and the Dodd-Frank Wall Street Reform and Consumer Protection Act is 2,300 pages[36]. James Madison in *The Federalist Papers #62* said that ambiguity in the law poisons the blessings of liberty itself: "…if the laws be so voluminous that they cannot be read, or so incoherent that they cannot be understood…" [37]

The solution is to limit all laws, rules, and regulations to some definite length, like the length of the Constitution of the United States, which is about 24 pages. Industries which are inherently dangerous, like nuclear power, pharmaceuticals, and aviation, should be exempt from this limit, but other laws, rules, and regulations should be held to this definite length.

Before any law, rule, or regulation goes into effect, it should be reviewed by a panel of ordinary citizens to determine whether it is

---

[35] Computational Legal Studies. 2009. "Facts About the Length of H.R. 3962, the Affordable Health Care for America Act (AHCAA)," Computational Legal Studies.    http://computationallegalstudies.com/2009/11/08/facts-about-the-length-of-h-r-3962/ Nov. 9.

[36] Wallison, Peter. 2010. "The Dodd-Frank Act: Creative Destruction, Destroyed," The Wall Street Journal. August 31.
http://online.wsj.com/article/SB10001424052748703369704575461714115902100.html

[37] Madison, James. 1788. "The Federalist Papers No. 62," Independent Journal. Feb. 27. http://constitution.org/fed/federa62.htm

understandable. Ordinary citizens would exclude lawyers or specialists skilled in a particular industry.

## Single Government Point of Contact

Multiple government agencies have jurisdiction over individual and business activities. Often agency rules are inconsistent or contradictory. The burden of sorting out overlapping and conflicting laws, rules, and regulations should not fall on individuals or businesses, but on the government.

For any activity, an individual or business should only have to deal with one government agency which will represent the interests of all government agencies. Individuals and businesses should only have to deal with one person within that agency who would have the power to grant permits, adjust claims, or otherwise administer relevant laws, rules, and regulations.

Reforming regulation along the lines discussed above would significantly reduce the burden on individuals and businesses. That will translate into less regulatory cost, less delay, less uncertainty, and a competitive advantage in the world economy.

## Market Failure

The free market doesn't always get things right. On the other hand, the government makes mistakes too. As Matt Ridley said in *The Wall Street Journal*, "Economists are quick to speak of 'market failure', and rightly so, but a greater threat comes from 'government failure.' Because it is a monopoly, government brings inefficiency and stagnation to most things it runs. Government agencies pursue increased budgets rather than customer service. Pressure groups form alliances with agencies to extract more money from taxpayers for their members. Yet despite all this, most clever people still call for government to run more things and assume that if it did so, it would somehow be more perfect, and more selfless, next time."[38]

In the push-pull of business, government, and personal interest, what is the lesson? Government, like salt, is essential for life, but, like salt, government should be used in carefully measured amounts.

---

[38] Ridley, Matt. 2014. "Government Failure Greater than Market Failure," Notable and Quotable, *Wall Street Journal.* Oct.4. A11. http://online.wsj.com/articles/notable-quotable-1412375942?mod=Opinion_newsreel_7. Downloaded 2014-10-06. Quoting Matt Ridley 's book *"The Rational Optimist" (2011).*

---

**Principles of Regulation Reform**

*Permits and Permissions* - should be automatically approved unless the government objects within a limited period.

*Substantial Harm Test* - Laws, rules and regulations should actually prevent serious injury to people or property. The burden should be on the government to prove by clear and convincing evidence that actual harm would be prevented.

*Clear and Concise Language* - All laws, rules and regulations should be written in clear, concise, standard English free of jargon. They should be limited to some definite length, like the length of the Constitution which is about 24 pages. Inherently dangerous industries like nuclear power, pharmaceuticals and aviation would be exempt from this requirement.

*Single Point of Contact* - The burden of sorting out overlapping laws, rules, regulations, and jurisdictions should be borne by the government, not individuals and businesses. For any activity, a single government agency should be appointed to represent the interests of all government agencies, and a single government agent in that agency should have the power to grant permits, adjust claims, or speak for the government on all matters.

---

# Terms and Concepts

**Apportionment** – Some argue that since each person uses about the same amount of government services, a fair system would apportion taxes so that each person pays about the same amount.

**Burden of tax** – The burden of tax falls on those who shoulder the economic burden of taxes.

**Capitalism and Taxes** – Capitalism works best when people have the maximum incentive to work, save, and invest. Taxes reduce incentives. If taxes get too high, people will stop producing, or migrate to lower tax locations.

**Charity** – is a good and noble way to fund things the government does not. Charity is uplifting. Charity is voluntary. Taxes are not.

**Controversial Expenditures** – Governments frequently spend tax dollars on goods and services that go beyond the necessities. Controversial expenditures include income redistribution, politicians' pet projects and salaries and benefits for government employees which exceed those of ordinary taxpayers.

**Consumption tax** – A consumption tax is a tax that would, in theory, replace all other taxes with a national sales tax. The benefits are that it would be easy to manage and would tax the underground economy. The drawbacks are that many industries would lobby for exemptions which would increase that tax rate on all other industries, and few believe that a consumption tax would replace the income tax, but rather would become an additional tax.

**Corporate tax** – Some argue that corporations should bear the total burden of taxes. Unfortunately, that would require tax rates so high that no one would start or run a business.

**Fair Share of Taxes** – 'Tax the rich' is often the mantra of politicians. The top 3.3% of tax payers pay 49.7% of income taxes. The issue is whether that is fair, or too burdensome.

**Fate of Capitalist Democracy** – A capitalist democracy can only last until citizens discover they can vote themselves whatever they want from the public treasury.

**Gain** – This is output divided by input. In transistors, small changes in gate current result in large changes in output current. In taxes, small increases or decreases in tax rates result in large changes in taxable economic output.

**Hauser's Law** – No matter what the top individual tax rate is, the government will get about 17% of GDP in taxes. Since higher taxes slow the economy and reduce GDP, the sensible thing is to cut taxes, grow the economy and harvest 17% of a larger GDP.

**Incidence of tax** – The incidence of tax falls on those who must remit taxes to the government.
**Issues** – Tax issues include what to tax, who to tax, tax rates, the impact of taxes on incentives to work, save, and invest, and how to maximize tax revenue.

**Magic Lantern** – Some people see the government as a magic lantern that they can rub to get anything they want for free. Once the takers overwhelm the producers, the end of a capitalist democracy is near.

**Personal income tax** – Most revenue is raised from the personal income tax.

**Power to tax** - "The power to tax is the power to destroy." Marshall, John. 1819. McCulloch v. Maryland 17 U.S. 327.

**Progressive tax** – Taxes are said to be progressive if those with higher incomes pay higher tax rates.

**Regressive tax** – Taxes are said to be regressive if those with higher incomes pay a lower effective tax rate than those with lower incomes, even though those with higher income tax pay more tax dollars.

**Revenue Maximization** – See Hauser's Law.

**State taxes** – Many states levy corporate and personal income taxes, sales taxes and a few have personal property taxes. Some states realize that taxes affect incentives and they have, or plan to, lower tax rates. Other states ignore the impact of taxes on incentives and continue to raise taxes. There is a migration from high to low tax states.

**Tax Avoidance** – When people feel the government is confiscating too much of their production through taxes they will either a) reduce their output by working, investing or producing less, or b) migrate to a lower tax venue.

**Taxes** – Taxes are part of the cost of living in a civilized society. Taxes pay for common goods and services such as national defense, police, courts, prisons, roads, bridges, public health, and public education. People have a duty to pay taxes required by law.

**Taxes and Consumer Behavior** – Consumer behavior is sensitive to taxation even among the rich. A 10% tax on yachts collapsed the luxury boat market.

# References

Boston Tax Party. 2008. "Boston Tax Party," Wall Street Journal. August 5, 2008. A18.

Brooks, Arthur C. 2006. "Are Americans Generous?" Philanthropy Magazine. May/June Cover Story. http://www.philanthropyroundtable.org/topic/excellence_in_philanthropy/are_americans_generous

Budget Totals. 2011. "Table S-1 Budget Totals," Summary Tables, Budget of the United States of America. http://www.whitehouse.gov/sites/default/files/omb/budget/fy2012/assets/tables.pdf

CBO. 2011. "The US Federal Budget: Infographic" Congressional Budget Office. December 12. www.cbo.gov/publication/42636. Downloaded 2017-12-28

Computational Legal Studies. 2009. "Facts About the Length of H.R. 3962, the Affordable Health Care for America Act (AHCAA)," Computational Legal Studies. http://computationallegalstudies.com/2009/11/08/facts-about-the-length-of-h-r-3962/ Nov. 9.

Facebook. 2012. "Facebook to the Non-Rescue; IPO windfalls and other California budget illusions.", Wall Street Journal. Dow Jones & Co. March 8. A16.

Griffith v. State of New Jersey, Department of Environmental Protection, 340 N.J. Super. 596, 775 A.2d 54 (App. Div. 2001). Wyatt, Anne D., Eastern Minerals International, Inc., Van Buren Minerals Corporation, Milton J. Bernos, Jr., Nancy Wyatt Zorn,

Gross Domestic Product. 2012. "Table 667. Gross Domestic Product in Current and Chained Dollars," *2012 Statistical Abstract,* U.S. Census Bureau. Downloaded 03/04/2012.
www.census.gov/compendia/statab/cats/income_expenditures_poverty _wealth/gross_domestic_product_gdp. html

Hauser, Kurt W. and David Ranson. 2008. "Hauser's Law," Hoover Digest. 2008 No. 4. Oct. 12.
http://www.hoover.org/publications/hoover-digest/article/ 5728. This essay appeared in the *Wall Street Journal* on May 20, 2008

Hester, Tom Jr." Poll finds many hoping to leave New Jersey behind," The Associated Press. October 17, 2007.

Kennedy, John F. 1962. "Remarks to the Economic Club of New York," Papers of John F. Kennedy. Presidential Papers. President's Office Files. Speech Files. Dec.14. https://www.jfklibrary.org/Asset-Viewer/Archives/JFKWHA-148.aspx.

Kudlow, Larry. 2016. "Taxes Chased GE Out of Connecticut," National Review. January 15. www. nationalreview. com/article/429874/ge-leaves-connecticut-boston-blame-taxes downloaded 2017-07-31.

Laffer, Arthur B. 2004. "The Laffer Curve: Past, Present, and Future," The Heritage Foundation for American Leadership. June 1.
www.heritage.org/Research/Taxes/bg1765.cfm

Madison, James. 1788. "The Federalist Papers No. 62," Independent Journal. Feb. 27. http://constitution.org/fed/federa62.htm

Marshall, John. 1819. McCulloch v. Maryland 17 U.S. 327.

Moore, Stephanie. 2015. "The Tax-Cut payoff in Carolina." Wall Street Journal. June 4. A15. See "Reports and Testimony," U.S. Government Accountability Office www.gao.gov

Rand, Ayn. 1957. *Atlas Shrugged.* Reprinted 1999. Plume a Penguin Group Company. New York, New York.

Receipts by Source. 2014. "Table 2.1 - Receipts by Source 1934-2019," Office of Management and Budget.
www.whitehouse.gov/omb/budget/Historicals April 15. downloaded 2014-06-23

Regional Economic Activity Accounts. 2012. "Regional Economic Activity Accounts," US Department of Commerce - Bureau of Economic Analysis http://www.bea.gov/regional/downloadzip.cfm

Review and Outlook. 2009. "Jodi Corzine, Review and Outlook," Wall Street Journal, August 29-30, 2009. A12.

Ridley, Matt. 2014. "Government Failure Greater than Market Failure," Notable and Quotable, *Wall Street Journal.* Oct.4. A11. http://online.wsj.com/articles/notable-quotable-1412375942?mod=Opinion_newsreel_7. Downloaded 2014-10-06. Quoting Matt Ridley 's book *"The Rational Optimist" (2011).*

Rising Tide. 2009. "The Rising Tide," DVD. SLU Productions, LLC. P.O. Box 64, Caldwell, NJ 07006 www.therisingtide.info

Rogers, T. J. "Golden State Drives Out Business," Wall Street Journal August 2-3, 2008.

Selected Income and Tax. 2011. "Table 1.1 All Returns: Selected Income and Tax Items by Size and Accumulated Size of Adjusted Gross Income, Tax Year 2011" Treasury Department. http://www.irs.gov/uac/SOI-Tax-Stats---Individual-Statistical-Tables-by-Size-of-Adjusted-Gross-Income downloaded 2014-06-24

Sherk, James. 2010. "Extended Unemployment Insurance Benefits: The Heritage Foundation 2010 Labor Boot Camp", the Heritage Foundation. No. 2759. Jan.14.

Singer, Penny. 1991. "New Luxury Tax Trimming Boat Sales," New York Times Archives. July 21. http://www.nytimes.com/1991/07/21/nyregion/new-luxury-tax-trimming-boat-sales.html?pagewanted=print&src=pm

State Corporate Income Tax. 2013. "State Corporate Income Tax Rates, 2000-2013," Tax Foundation. http://taxfoundation.org/article/state-corporate-income-tax-rates-2000-2013

State Tax Comparisons. 2012 "State Tax Comparisons," Federation of Tax Administrators. 444 N. Capitol St., NW, Suite 348, Washington D.C. www.taxadmin.org/fta/rate/tax_stru.html

Tax Rebellion. 2012. "The Heartland Tax Rebellion," Wall Street Journal. Dow Jones & Company. Feb. 7. A12.

Taylor, Alexander. 1747-1813. "A democracy cannot exist as a permanent form of government." Taylor was a Scottish lawyer, writer, and professor in Edinburgh, Scotland.

Tracking the Money. 2011. "Tracking the Money," recovery.gov. Oct. 1 www.recovery.gov/pages/default.aspx

Vance, David E. 2012. "Regulation Reform," The Independent Review. Fall (Vol. 17, No.2).

Wallison, Peter. 2010. "The Dodd-Frank Act: Creative Destruction, Destroyed," The Wall Street Journal. August 31.

http://online.wsj.com/article/SB100014240527487033697045754617l
4115902100.html

United States Census. www.census.gov

Wyatt. 2001. Mary Anne Wyatt, Wilson W. Wyatt, Jr., and Martin P.
Duffy, Executor of Wilson Wyatt, Sr.'s Estate, Plaintiffs-Cross
Appellants, v. United States, Defendant-Appellant. 271 F.3d 1090
(2001). Nos. 99-5054, 99-5059. United States Court of Appeals,
Federal Circuit. Decided: November 19, 2001.

Yates, Craig. 2005. "Leadership and Banking," Speech to The Business
Development Leadership Seminar. President, Farmers and Merchants
Bank. Feb.18.

# CHAPTER FIVE

# ETHICS, MANNERS AND CIVILITY

---

After completing this chapter, you should be able to:

5.1 Define ethics and provide a broad overview of ethical standards.

5.2 Identify situations in which ethical thinking is required, and step through a reasoned ethical analysis.

5.3 Define manners and provide the framework for good manners.

5.4 Define civility and lay out a framework for behavior in a civil society.

---

## Introduction

Society works best when everyone conducts their lives in a mutually respectful and cooperative manner. That doesn't mean people should subordinate their interests to those of others, and it doesn't mean that anyone has a right to demand others conduct themselves in a particular way. Society operates best when mutual respect and cooperation are voluntary.

Companies, organizations, clubs, associations and commerce work better when people follow certain rules of conduct. These rules are variously described as ethics, manners, or civility. In some sense, these rules provide both the glue and lubricant for interactions among people. As such, people with well-developed ethics, manners, and civility are highly sought after and rapidly promoted. Understanding and living by society's rules is highly correlated with success.

Ethics are formalized standards of conduct often backed by sanctions. Manners are standards of conduct based on consideration of others.

Civility is a more broad-based philosophy of how to live a good life which embraces ethics and manners and yet goes beyond both.

While most people have an instinctive notion of right and wrong, situations and circumstances can become complicated, and the right answer isn't always obvious. People have analyzed, developed and thought through guidelines for ethics, manners and civility over a very long time. Together, these guidelines facilitate a mutually respectful, cooperative, and cordial society.

## Ethics

Aristotle conceived of ethics as a field studied to improve our lives. Its principal concern is human well-being. Aristotle, along with Socrates and Plato considered ethical values such as justice, courage, temperance, and consideration of others, complex emotional and social skills. To live well, we must understand and appreciate the way friendship, virtue, honor, wealth, and other things, fit together as a whole. The goal of ethics is to live well. But living well is not simply a state or condition of being. Living well consists of those lifelong activities that provide a sense of achievement and fulfillment; in effect to be all that one can be.

Aristotle believed that ethics can only be acquired through the study of ethical principles and the practiced application of those principles in a deliberate manner. Ethics cannot be reduced to a formula because ethical goals sometimes conflict and reasoned choices must be made.  On the other hand, there are certain actions such as spite, shamelessness, envy, adultery, theft and murder that are always wrong regardless of circumstances.

Among the highest goals of ethics are happiness, which means flourishing, virtue, and excellence. The ethical person lives in a reasoned and moderate way avoiding extremes. For example, a person should be brave but not reckless; cautious, but not cowardly. The appropriate level of courage should be between the extremes.[1, 2]

People's concept of ethics has narrowed since Aristotle's day. Now ethics and ethical guidelines are designed to facilitate the relationship among people, companies, and the government. Ethics provide behavioral standards that supplement the requirements of the law. Ethical standards

---

[1] Kraut, Richard. 2010. "Aristotle's Ethics," Stanford Encyclopedia of Philosophy. http://plato.stanford.edu/entries/aristotle-ethics/
[2] Solomon, J. 1984. *The Complete Works of Aristotle*, The Revised Oxford Translation, vol. 2, Jonathan Barnes, ed., Princeton: Princeton University Press.

are often, but not always, backed up by sanctions. Ethics are different from manners. One can have good manners and be unethical or one can have bad manners and behave ethically.

Aristotle's insights are still important today. If we want to be ethical, we must study ethics and ethical principles. We must think through the application of ethical standards in a reasoned way and not resort to mechanical application of rules. Finally, we must practice application of ethical standards to become ethical people.

## Business and Professional Ethics

Most professions have a code of professional ethics or a code of professional conduct. Arguably these professional codes of conduct protect clients. Ethical codes also protect professionals by providing standards of conduct against which a professional's actions may be measured. Absent a code of conduct, courts would have to make up standards on an ad hoc basis to determine whether a professional's actions were reasonable. Professional ethical standards are also used to discipline those who embarrass the profession. In this sense, standards are mandatory.

### *Characteristics of Professionals*

What makes someone a professional? This is an important question because professionals enjoy privileges others don't have, for example, the privilege of practicing law, certifying financial statements or practicing medicine. The public usually has more confidence in someone they perceive as a professional. In addition to ethical standards, other hallmarks of a professional include:

(i)   Completing tasks in a timely and competent manner. Competence includes attention to detail, accuracy, and oral and written communications of the highest standard.

(ii)   Continuous improvement of methods and skills.

(iii)  Setting aside emotions and personal preferences until an assignment is complete.

(iv)  Extending courtesies to clients, fellow professionals, and others.

## *Characteristics of Professional Ethics*

Most ethical standards have common elements, among them are:

(i)   Placing the interests of clients before one's own self-interest.

(ii)  Being honest, objective and truthful.

(iii) Bringing the highest level of competence to any task or activity.

## Accounting Profession

The American Institute of Certified Public Accountants (AICPA) has a Code of Professional Conduct to provide guidance on professional responsibilities.[3] Table 5.1 AICPA Code of Professional Conduct Highlights summarizes a few of their ethical principles.

### Table 5.1 AICPA Code of Professional Conduct Highlights

---

**This is not an authoritative summary or analysis of the AICPA Code of Professional Conduct; only the AICPA can interpret their Code in an authoritative manner. The term 'members' means members of the AICPA, all of whom must be Certified Public Accountants.**

---

### Act in the Public Interest
A distinguishing mark of a profession is acceptance of its responsibility to the public. Members should act in the public interest. The accounting profession's public consists of clients, credit grantors, governments, investors, the business and financial community, and others who rely on the objectivity and integrity of certified public accountants. The public interest is defined as the collective well-being of the community.

### Maintain Integrity
Integrity is an element of character fundamental to professional recognition and it is the basis of public trust in the profession. Integrity requires a member to be honest and candid. Integrity can accommodate inadvertent errors and differences of opinion; it cannot accommodate deceit or subordination of principle. Integrity is what is right and just.

---

[3] American Institute of CPAs (AICPA) Code of Professional Conduct
http://www.aicpa.org/Research/Standards/CodeofConduct/Pages/default.aspx

Integrity requires a member to observe the principles of objectivity, independence, and due care.

**Objectivity**
Objectivity is a distinguishing feature of the profession. The principle of objectivity imposes the obligation to be impartial, intellectually honest, and free of conflicts of interest.

**Independence**
Independence is impaired if a member has, or is committed to acquire, any direct or indirect financial interest in the client during the period of the engagement. Independence may be impaired if a family member has a material interest in the client.

**Due Care**
The quest for excellence is the essence of due care. Due care requires a member to discharge professional responsibilities with competence and diligence. Competence is derived from a synthesis of education and experience. It begins with a mastery of the common body of knowledge required for designation as a certified public accountant. The maintenance of competence requires a commitment to learning and professional improvement that must continue throughout a member's professional life. Due care requires a member to plan and supervise adequately any professional activity for which he or she is responsible.

**Diligence**
Diligence imposes the responsibility to render services promptly and carefully, to be thorough, and to observe applicable technical and ethical standards.

---

Read generally, the AICPA Code of Professional Conduct could apply to almost any profession or business. Everyone should aspire to work in the public interest in the sense that one should do no harm to one's community. Everyone should have integrity, be objective, act with independent judgment, use due care, and be diligent.

## Legal Profession

The American Bar Association (ABA) has developed Model Rules of Professional Conduct.[4] These rules have been adopted by most states. At their core, ABA rules are strikingly similar to the AICPA Code of Professional Conduct. Table 5.2, Highlights of ABA Model Rules of Professional Conduct, provides some sense of the types of ethical standards lawyers are required to follow.

**Table 5.2 Highlights of ABA Model Rules of Professional Conduct**

---

**This is not an authoritative summary or analysis of the ABA Model Rules; only the ABA can interpret their Rules in an authoritative manner.**

---

**Rule 1.1 Competence**
A lawyer shall provide competent representation to a client. Competent representation requires the legal knowledge, skill, thoroughness, and preparation reasonably necessary for representation. (*This standard is important because the law has many sub-specialties and it is impossible to be competent in all of them.*)

**Rule 1.3 Diligence**
A lawyer shall act with reasonable diligence and promptness in representing a client.

**Rule 1.7 Conflict of Interest**
A lawyer shall not represent a client if there is a conflict of interest. A conflict exists if a favorable outcome for one client results in an unfavorable outcome for another client.

**Rule 3.1 Meritorious Claims and Contentions**
A lawyer shall not bring or defend a proceeding, or assert a claim, unless there is a well-founded basis for it in fact and law.

---

[4] "Model Rules of Professional Conduct," American Bar Association.
http://www.americanbar.org/groups/professional_responsibility/publications/model

The ABA Model Rules contain many of the same elements as the AICPA Code; among them are calls for competence, diligence, integrity and avoidance of conflict of interest.

## Other Professions

Most professions have their own code of conduct enforced by professional organizations; a few of which are shown in Table 5.3 Ethical Standards.

**Table 5.3 Ethical Standards**

| Discipline | Standard Issuing Authority | Name or Title of Standard |
|---|---|---|
| Medicine | American Medical Association (AMA) | AMA's Code of Medical Ethics |
| Real Estate | National Association of Realtors® | Code of Ethics and Standards of Practice of the National Association of Realtors® |
| Law | American Bar Association (ABA) | Model Rules of Professional Conduct |
| Accounting | American Institute of Certified Public Accountants (AICPA) | AICPA Code of Professional Conduct |
| Military | United States Army | The Soldier's Code and Army Values |

The Soldier's Code and Army Values are of particular interest to a well-ordered society. Ultimately, the military are the guarantors of the freedoms articulated in the Constitution of the United States. And, soldiers and other military personnel are ambassadors for the United States when they are deployed overseas. Appendix 5a provides the full text of the Soldier's Code and Army Values.

# Business Ethics

Many companies have ethics policies. There are two reasons for such policies. First, to put employees on notice as to the standards against which they will be judged. Second, to provide insulation in the event of litigation resulting from bad employee behavior.

Most companies face the risk of employee lawsuits. Employees may sue for racial or sexual discrimination, failure to pay overtime, or they may file whistle blower suits designed to bring bad behavior to the attention of the authorities. The issue for companies is whether any of the bad acts are the actions of a single out-of-control employee or are acts based on company policy. Courts may find bad acts are the acts of a company if the company knows about them yet fails to take corrective action.

A strong, clear, enforced ethics policy can go a long way towards separating individual bad behavior from the actions of the company. Table 5.4 Model Business Ethics Policy is an example of the kind of standards a company should set.[5]

---

[5] Vance, David E. 2009. *Corporate Restructuring*. Springer Science + Business Media. London, New York. p.15.

**Table 5.4 Model Business Ethics Policy**

1. Neither the company nor its employees will discriminate on the basis of race, creed, ethnicity, gender, handicap, or sexual preference.

2. The company and its employees will deal fairly with customers, suppliers, government agencies, and each other.

3. Employees will treat customers, suppliers, government officials and each other with respect.

   Respect includes respecting personal space. There should be no physical contact at work, or in a professional environment, except for the business handshake.

4. Sexual or racial harassment will not be tolerated. Anything that tends to make someone uncomfortable in the workplace may be considered harassment.

5. Stealing from the company, its customers, or employees, will not be tolerated. It is the policy of the company to **criminally prosecute** anyone who steals.

6. The company will comply with all city, county, state, and federal laws and regulations, including, but not limited to, payment of taxes properly due and owing, labor laws, and environmental regulations.

**Violation of any of the above ethics guidelines is grounds for immediate termination.**

To ensure that everyone understands a company's code of ethics, every new employee should be required to read and sign a copy of the code of ethics, and that signed copy should be placed in his or her personnel file.

A substantial amount employee litigation occurs because supervisors and managers engage in, or tolerate, inappropriate behavior. Supervisors and managers appear to employees, and to those outside the company, as representatives of company values. Therefore, all managers and supervisors should be required to read and sign off on the code of ethics annually. For companies with annual employee reviews this can be part of the review process. Alternatively, a company might allow supervisors and managers to acknowledge that they read the code of ethics annually by signing onto a company website.

## Codes of Conduct and Other Ethical Standards

There are many ethical standards other than professional ethics and business ethics policies. The overarching theme of these other codes is to improve society for everyone by encouraging individuals to subscribe to certain behaviors, habits and norms of conduct. These codes of conduct are voluntary.

A key character in American history, mythology and literature is the cowboy. Cowboys are generally seen as individuals who live by their strength, wits, and own moral code. The cowboy is the American version of the knight errant, righting wrongs, and defending the weak. There are several cowboy codes of conduct.

Gene Autry, was a famous movie cowboy, singer, and businessman. His Cowboy Code of Conduct is posted on the internet[6]. The interesting thing about Gene Autry's Cowboy Code of Conduct is that it is entirely consistent with Aristotle's view of ethics.

Martin Luther King articulated codes of conduct in "The Six Principles of Nonviolence[7]", and the "10 Point Pledge of Nonviolence.[8]" Dr. King's insights are applicable in everyday life. For example, he said: "Nonviolent resistance does not seek to defeat or humiliate the opponent, but to win his friendship and understanding." He also said, "Observe with friend and foes the ordinary rules of courtesy." Courtesy is needed most when people disagree. These ethical principles speak to how people ought to live together in a civilized society.

---

[6] Autry, Gene. 1947. "Cowboy Code of Conduct," Melody Ranch radio show. August 17. Gene Autry Survivor's Trust Copyright 1994
www.geneautry.com/geneautry/geneautry_cowboycode.html
[7] King, Martin Luther, Jr. 1958. *Stride Toward Freedom*. Harper and Row, New York.
[8] King, Martin Luther, Jr. 1963. "10 Point Pledge to Nonviolence," Teaching American History.org
http://teachingamericanhistory.org/library/document/commitment-card/
downloaded 11/26/2017.

# Manners

What are manners? Are manners about using the correct fork? No! Manners are about consideration of others.

A college degree and good grades can get you a good job with a good company. However, the people who advance most rapidly after being hired are the ones who have the best 'soft skills'. Good manners are a much sought after soft skill.

## The Golden Rule

Manners in their most compact form can be summarized by the Golden Rule, "Do unto others as you would have them do unto you." But what does it mean?

---

**The Golden Rule**

Do unto others as you would have them do unto you.

---

The Golden Rule means that if you want respect, you must show respect. If you want people to be friendly to you, you must be friendly to others. If you want people to be honest with you, you must be honest with them. If you want people to include you in activities, you must include others. And it means if you want others to work hard for you, you must work hard for them.

## St. Paul's Letter

The Golden Rule is easy to recite, but sometimes hard to implement. There have been many attempts to expand on, and explain the Golden Rule, some brilliant, others not so good. One of the best is a letter that St. Paul wrote to the Corinthians almost two thousand years ago. It set forth the principles of Brotherly Love.

In ancient Greek, there are three words that translate into the English word 'love'. 'Agape' is love of God, 'Eros' is physical love, and 'Philos' means brotherly love, as in Philadelphia, the City of Brotherly love. St. Paul's letter uses the word 'love' to mean philos, or brotherly love, love of people, love of those around you. Table 5.6 is an abridged version of St. Paul's letter.

**Table 5.6 Letter of St. Paul to the Corinthians**

---

Though I speak with the tongues of men and angels and have not love, I am a sounding brass or a tingling symbol.

And though I have the gift of prophecy, and understand all things, and know all things, and have faith that can move mountains, and have not love, I am nothing.

And though I give all my goods to the poor, and sacrifice myself for others, and have not love, it profits me nothing.

Love suffers long and is kind. Love envies not. Love is not self-serving, and is not puffed up.

Does not behave itself unseemly, seeks not its own, is not easily provoked, thinks no evil, rejoices not in iniquity, but rejoices in truth;

Bears all things; hopes all things, believes all things, endures all things. Love never fails, though knowledge shall vanish.

When I was a child, I spoke like a child, but when I became a man, I put off childish things. Now abides faith, hope and love, but the greatest of these is love.

---

What exactly does all this mean? It means that no matter how gifted a person is, or how much they do, or how much they sacrifice, if they don't genuinely care for people, it means nothing. St. Paul goes on to describe the attributes of brotherly love. For example, one should be patient and kind. One should not be envious, self-serving, or conceited. And, one should think no evil. Some people enjoy seeing others get into trouble. St. Paul said that if you love people, if you have genuine concern for them, you won't wish for people to get in trouble. The letter advocates mutual respect and concern. At the end of the day, these attributes boil down to consideration of others.

## Practicing Manners

Aristotle believed that ethics can only be acquired through study of ethical principles and the practiced application of those principles in a deliberative manner. The same can be said of manners. To have good manners one must practice good manners. Good manners start with an awareness of one's surroundings. Table 5.7 Examples of Manners provides a few ideas as to how one can show good manners.

**Table 5.7 Examples of Manners**

---

**Is someone following you through a door?**
Take a split second to hold the door open until they get there.

**Are you trying to squeeze through a crowd? Or are you stepping in front of someone?**
Take a second to recognize those around you by saying "Excuse me."

**If someone is struggling with a package.**
Ask, "May I help you with that?"

**If you are dealing with someone noticeably older than yourself, say "Yes sir." "No sir." "Yes ma'am." "No ma'am."**
Recognition of others costs nothing but shows respect.

**Has someone done you a favor or given you a gift?**
Say thank you at the time and follow up with a note or an email saying thank you again.

**Has someone invited you to a job interview?**
Send them a note, not an email, thanking them for taking time to meet with you.

**What if you hear about a job that's not for you?**
If you know of anyone who is looking for a job, pass the information along. Such kindnesses are often returned many fold.

**What do we leave behind?**
When using a workspace, conference room, camp site, or classroom, do we leave it cleaner than when we got there? If yes, we are showing good manners and respect for those who follow. If not, we are disrespecting those who follow.

---

The point is that manners should be proactive, and not simply a polite response to circumstances. Try to do three good deeds a day. Good deeds need not be big. Extending the little courtesies will do wonders for your reputation.

# Civility

An expanded view of manners is called civility. Civility is about conducting one's life in a way that makes people want to be around you, want to support you, and want you to succeed. The difference between manners and civility is that manners are expressed as an interaction among two or more people. Civility is about the way one lives one's life, whether or not there are others to interact with.

There is no single list of all the things that comprise manners. Likewise, there is no single list of things that comprise civility. Nevertheless, some authors have tried to condense civility to a set of rules. Such rules are useful to the extent they get people to think about how they conduct their lives. As Socrates said, "The unexamined life is not worth living." Table 5.8 Steven Carter's Rules of Civility is one example.[9]

George Washington had a "Rules of Civility and Decent Behavior in Company and Conversation." While some of the rules are somewhat dated, for example, Rule 13: "Kill no vermin as fleas, lice, ticks, etc. in the sight of others..." Most will serve a person well into the twenty first century and beyond. For example, Rule 1: "Every action done in company, ought to be done with some sign of respect to those that are present."

Another view is embodied in the author's "Rules of Civility and a Good Life."[10] Table 5.9 Selected Rules of Civility and a Good Life presents several excerpts from this work.

---

[9] Carter, Steven. 1999. *Civility*. Harper Perennial; New York.
[10] Vance, David. 2010. "Rules of Civility and a Good Life."

**Table 5.8 Steven Carter's Rules of Civility**

| Pay attention | Be a considerate guest |
|---|---|
| Acknowledge others | Be quiet |
| Think the best | Respect other people's time |
| Listen | Respect other people's space |
| Be inclusive | Avoid personal questions |
| Speak kindly | Think twice before asking for favors |
| Don't speak ill | Refrain from idle complaints |
| Apologize earnestly | Accept and give constructive criticism |
| Assert yourself | Don't shift responsibility or blame |
| Mind your body | Respect even a subtle 'no' |
| Be agreeable | Respect others' opinions |
| Care for your guests | Accept and give praise |

**Table 5.9 Selected Rules of Civility and a Good Life**

**Rule 1** - Smile and be friendly to everyone. It costs nothing, yet lets others know you acknowledge them. It makes you more approachable.

**Rule 102** - Seek opportunity for yourself and others.

**Rule 150** - The meaning of life is people. There can be no happiness without others to share it.

The point of discussing various rules of civility is not to list rules, but to provoke a conversation as to what it means to be civil and what it means to live a good life. These are questions Socrates and Aristotle thought were among the most important in human experience.

## Protestant Work Ethic

The Protestant Work Ethic is a philosophy of living which cuts across conventional definitions of ethics, manners, civility and what it means to live a good life. Those who follow the tenets of the Protestant Work Ethic are often highly successful.[11, 12]

---

[11] Webber, Max. 1905 The Protestant Work Ethic and the Spirit of Capitalism.

One need not be a Protestant or even a Christian to follow the principles of the Protestant Work Ethic. These principles have also been found in Muslim Turkey,[13] Taiwan[14], and elsewhere.

The term, Protestant Work Ethic, was first coined by Max Weber, a German economist and sociologist, in his 1905 book *The Protestant Work Ethic and the Spirit of Capitalism.* The Protestant Work Ethic is characterized by **a respect for work** and the belief that **work itself is noble**, rather than simply a means to an end. It holds that **all occupations have a divine dignity,** even the most menial manual labor.[15] This view provides a "moral sanction to profit-making through hard work, organization, and rational calculation."[16] Respect for hard work contributes to the social order and the well-being of the community. The Protestant Work Ethic holds disdain for those who are idle or lazy.[17] The Protestant Work Ethic echoes an old Chinese proverb: "The easy road leads to a hard life. The hard road leads to an easy life."

The Protestant Work Ethic holds that dedication to one's calling or task gives rise to personal self-worth, good citizenship and prosperity. Pride in one's work leads to a highly productive attitude. High productivity leads to higher income. When coupled with the principles of frugality and thrift, this leads to wealth accumulation. Wealth accumulation provides pools of capital for investment or to start a business. High productivity also attracts the attention of those who can create opportunities for advancement.

The Protestant Work Ethic does not depend on getting a high paying or prestigious job. Accept a humbler station in life and concentrate on mundane tasks and duties. Ironically, this and diligence at work, coupled with the other elements of the Protestant Work Ethic leads to wealth accumulation. Hard work and wealth accumulation are the foundation of entrepreneurship, which leads to greater wealth.

---

[12] Warner, Stephen L. 1999. "The Protestant Work Ethic and Academic Achievement." Working Paper. Information Resources Information Center.

[13] Bilefsky, Dan. 2006. "Protestant Work Ethic in Muslim Turkey," International Herald Tribune, Global Edition of the New York Times. August 15.

[14] Tang, Thomas Li-Ping. 1991. "A Factor Analytic Study of the Protestant Work Ethic." paper presented at the Annual Convention of the Southwestern Psychological Association 37th New Orleans, La. April 11-13.

[15] Webber. 1905.

[16] Yankelovich, D. (1981). New rules: Searching for self-fulfillment in a world turned upside down. New York: Random House. 247.

[17] Anthony, P. D. (1977). *The ideology of work.* Great Britain: Tavistock.

Weber believed this 'work-and-save' ethic gave rise to capitalism. By the eighteenth century, diligence in work, scrupulous use of time, and deferment of pleasure had become a part of the popular philosophy of life in the Western world. [18]

Unfortunately, in the last century, many Westerners have become complacent. They feel entitled to the benefits of work without the need for actually doing work. They feel entitled to prestigious jobs or positions. One of the reasons there is such a disparity in wealth between rich and poor is that those who follow the tenets of the Protestant Work Ethic tend to become significantly richer than those who don't. People who don't follow the principles of the Protestant Work Ethic often wonder why they haven't gotten further in life.

Table 5.10 Characteristics of the Protestant Work Ethic lists some of the elements of this philosophy.

**Table 5.10 Characteristics of the Protestant Work Ethic**

| | |
|---|---|
| Diligence in work | Scrupulous use of time |
| Deferment of pleasure | Self-discipline |
| Thriftiness and frugality | Capital accumulation |
| Modesty in displays of wealth | Economic rationalism |
| Planning | Orderliness |
| Honesty | Cleanliness |

---

[18] Webber, 1905.

---

**Frugality**

Frugality is: the economical use of resources; not wasteful or lavish; wise in the expenditure or application of force, materials, and time. A frugal person is someone who handles his or her money wisely and sensibly, still enjoying life while being mature and responsible.

"Without frugality none can be rich, and with it, very few would be poor."

~ *Samuel Johnson*

**Thrift**

Thrift is being wise and economical in the management of money and other resources. It is a careful use of money, especially by avoiding waste.

"Industry, thrift and self-control are not sought because they create wealth, but because they create character."

~ *Calvin Coolidge*

---

# Conclusion

Society works best when everyone conducts their lives in a mutually respectful and cooperative manner. In Aristotle's day, ethics was an inquiry into how to live the best, most fulfilling, life possible. Today, ethics is conceived of in a narrow, transactional context. Most professions have a code of professional ethics or a code of professional conduct that sets forth expectations for the profession. These ethical codes are usually backed up by sanctions. Many businesses also have codes of conduct or ethical standards for their employees.

There are many codes of conduct beside professional codes. These are entirely voluntary and designed to help people think about what it means to be a good citizen and community member. Among the most famous of these voluntary codes are the various cowboy codes of conduct.

Manners are about consideration of others. Showing good manners is voluntary, but those that advance most in life do so with soft skills. Good manners are one of the most sought after soft skills. The Golden Rule, 'Do unto others as you would have them do unto you', summarizes manners in their most compact form.

Civility is a broad view of how one ought to live one's life, and as such, goes beyond the modern definition of ethics and manners. Civility is a quality that makes people want to be around you, to support you, to want you to succeed. There is a substantial overlap among the modern views of ethics, manners and civility. However, Aristotle would probably subsume them all under his understanding of ethics.

The Protestant Work Ethic is a philosophy of work and living that is highly correlated with success. One need not be a Protestant or even a Christian to follow the tenets of the Protestant Work Ethic. The term Protest Work Ethic was coined by Max Weber in his 1905 book *The Protestant Work Ethic and the Spirit of Capitalism*.

The Protestant Work Ethic is characterized by a respect for work and the belief that work itself is noble, rather than simply a means to an end. It holds that all occupations have a divine dignity even the most menial manual labor. The Protestant Work Ethic also holds disdain for those who are idle or lazy. The Protestant Work Ethic is characterized by diligence in work, scrupulous use of time, deferment of pleasure, self-discipline, thriftiness and frugality, capital accumulation, modesty in displays of wealth, economic rationalism, orderliness, honesty and cleanliness.

In summary, ethics, manners, civility and the Protestant Work Ethic are meant to help people live their best possible lives; this in turn sets the groundwork for a society in which mutual respect and cooperation make life better for everyone.

## Appendix 5a: Military Ethics

### Professional Standards for the United States Army[19]

*Soldier's Code*

1. I am an American soldier – a protector of the greatest nation on earth – sworn to uphold the Constitution of the United States.

2. I will treat others with dignity and respect and expect others to do the same.

3. I will honor my country, the Army, my unit and my fellow soldiers by living the Army Values.

4. No matter what situation I am in, I will never do anything for pleasure, profit or personal safety which will disgrace my uniform, my unit or my country.

---

[19] Card issued to US Army soldiers. Cite as US Army GTA 22-06-002

5. Lastly, I am proud of my country and its flag. I want to look back and say I am proud to have served my country as a soldier.

## Army Values

**Loyalty:** Bear true faith and allegiance to the US Constitution, the Army, your unit, and other soldiers.

**Duty:** Fulfill your obligations.

**Selfless-Service:** Put the welfare of the nation, the Army, and your subordinates before your own.

**Honor:** Live up to all Army values.

**Integrity:** Do what's right, legally and morally.

**Personal Courage:** Face fear, danger, or adversity, both physical and moral.

# Appendix 5b: Professional Appearance

It would be great of people judged us by our inner beauty, but the reality is that we are judged by our appearance. People who dress like bums are likely to be treated like bums, but people who dress professionally are likely to be treated like professionals. People can't control whether they are tall or short, fat or thin, blonde or bald. But they can control how they dress and carry themselves.

Some people want to express their individuality by dressing in edgy, fashion-forward, Goth, or retro styles. Some extend this expression to hair styles and colors, tattoos, and embedded jewelry.

Employers and potential employers recognize these people as individuals. Employers or potential employers may ask themselves whether such 'individuals' are ready to pull their weight as part of a team, or whether they are going to be 'high maintenance' individuals who demand 'individual' and special treatment throughout their working lives. In business, time is precious, and an employer might decide he or she simply doesn't want to be bothered with the extra time and energy it takes to deal with an individual who considers him or herself 'special.'

Dress on the conservative side of fashion. Fashion changes all the time. Much of fashion consists of short-lived fads. On the other hand, some fashion has enduring quality. Professionals should strive to identify enduring fashion and wear it. This sentiment is echoed in Shakespeare's *Hamlet:* "Buy the best clothes you can afford, not flashy, but of good quality, not extreme or outrageous, for clothes oft make the man (or the woman), and those (in France and elsewhere) of the best rank and station dress well."[20]

Always dress one level better than those around you. When others are wearing T-shirts, wear a polo shirt. When others wear polo shirts, wear a dress shirt. When others wear dress shirts, wear a dress shirt and tie. When others wear a dress shirt and tie, wear a dress shirt, tie and sports coat. When others wear sports coats, wear a suit. It's an old expression that one should dress for the job one wants, not the job one has. On the other hand, overdressing can brand you as an outsider. If everyone is wearing polo shirts and you wear a suit, people might think you odd.

Clothes should be well tailored and fit well. It is better to wear something that fits your body style comfortably rather than force yourself into clothes that are too tight. Clothes should be clean and neat, free of wrinkles and, of course, spotless. One of the worst faux pas a man can make is to wear a necktie with a spot on it. Wearing a necktie with a spot on it shows lack of attention to detail, and employers assume that lack of attention applies to a person's work habits generally.

Many companies have instituted 'casual Fridays' in which their normal dress code is relaxed. Casual Fridays can be a trap for the unwary. Companies watch to see who would dress inappropriately if given a chance. The rule that one should dress one level better than those around them should apply on casual Fridays as well as on other days.

Appearance goes beyond dress and extends to personal grooming. Hair and nails should be neatly trimmed. Hair styles and facial hair as well as clothes should be on the conservative side of fashion. Avoid anything that others can smell, such as make-up or cologne.

Students should think about, and work to improve, their personal appearance long before they graduate or start looking for a job. Like any other virtue, professional appearance is a habit of thought and action that must be practiced to be mastered.

No one can force anyone to dress in a particular manner. The goal here is to help people understand how their appearance is likely to be perceived by others. If a person's goal is to get hired, move into a higher income job,

---

[20] Shakespeare, William. 1600. "Polonius' Advice to Laertes," Hamlet, Act I, Scene iii.

or gain the confidence of employers, clients and investors, the importance of professional appearance cannot be overestimated.

## Appendix 5c: Defusing Anger

Not everyone you meet is going to like you. Some may hate you for who you are, how you think, where you stand on an issue, the town you come from, the football team you root for, or the color of your socks. Some people are going to hate you for no discernable reason at all. The question is, what to do about it.

If they disrespect you and you disrespect them back, does anybody profit? A person might feel good the moment they fire a zinger at the other person, but that is only going to bolster the other person's resolve to get back at you in some way.

It is old wisdom to defuse anger and tension by returning good for evil, and kind words for criticism. Some two thousand years ago, St. Matthew said, "Love your enemies, bless those who curse you, do good to those who hate you, and pray for those who spitefully use you and persecute you."[21] We are all in this together. We need to make the best of things.

Defusing anger doesn't mean letting people walk over you or abuse you. It does not mean subordinating your needs and wants to those of someone else. It does not mean looking weak. Weakness invites continued bad behavior. Say something nice about the other person, even though they treat you with disrespect. If you are consistent in this polite and respectful treatment, most people will eventually let go of their irrational animosity and begin a more cooperative relationship.

---

[21] Matthew 5:44-45 New Kings James Version, abridged.

# Terms and Concepts

**American Association of Certified Public Accountants (AICPA)** – a professional association whose members are all Certified Public Accountants who have passed the CPA exam and fulfilled experience and other requirements, like continuing professional education.

**Aristotle** – Greek philosopher (384 BC to 322 BC) set forth many of the tenets of Western Civilization. He built on the work of Socrates, another Greek philosopher (469 BC to 399 BC).

**Brotherly Love** – Brotherly love is love of people. St. Paul said, no matter how smart one is, or what one has achieved, or what one has sacrificed, if one does not like people, it means nothing.

**Business Ethics** – These are company guidelines that notify employees of required standards of conduct. They are also designed to distinguish between the actions of a bad employee and company policy.

**Civility** - Civility is about conducting one's life in a way that makes people want to be around you, want to support you, and want you to succeed. Civility is about the way one lives one's life, whether or not there are others to interact with.

**Code of Professional Conduct** – Also, Model Codes of Conduct are standards of behavior. Those adopted by professional organizations are often accompanied by sanctions for failure to meet standards.

**Coolidge, Calvin** (1872 - 1933) The 13th President of the United States cut the national debt by 25% during his term and lowered taxes four times. "Industry, thrift and self-control are not sought because they create wealth, but because they create character."

**Ethics, Aristotle** - Aristotle conceived of ethics as a field studied to improve our lives. Its principal concern is human wellbeing. He considered how ethical values such as justice, courage, temperance, friendship, virtue, and honor fit together with wealth and other things to create the best possible life.

**Ethics, Modern** – Modern ethics provide behavioral standards that supplement the requirements of the law. Ethical standards are often backed up by sanctions.

**Golden Rule** – The Golden Rule is "Do unto others as you would have them do unto you." In other words, treat others as you want to be treated.

**Johnson, Samuel** – English Poet, Critic, Writer (1709 – 1784) "Without frugality none can be rich, and with it very few would be poor."

**Manners** – Manners is a set of behaviors based on consideration of others. Aristotle said that ethics must be practiced. Manners must be practiced too.

**Plato** – Greek philosopher (about 424BC – 348BC) who believed human wellbeing was the goal of ethical thought and action.

**Professional, Characteristics of** - Completing tasks in a timely and competent manner, continuous improvement of methods and skills, and setting aside personal preferences until an assignment is complete.

**Protestant Work Ethic** – The Protestant Work Ethic is a philosophy of living which respects work for its own sake and not as a means to an end. It is characterized by diligence, scrupulous use of time, deferment of pleasure, self-discipline, thriftiness and frugality, capital accumulation, modesty, economic rationalism, orderliness, honesty, and cleanliness. Following the Protestant Work Ethic is highly correlated with success. One need not be a Christian to follow this philosophy.

**Society** – Society works best when everyone conducts their lives in a mutually respectful and cooperative manner. Ethical standards, manners and rules of civility are designed to articulate how one might achieve that mutual respect and cooperation.

**Socrates** – A Greek philosopher (469 BC to 399 BC). He considered ethical questions, such as how we should interact with those around us. He said, "The unexamined life is not worth living."

**Webber, Max** - A German economist and sociologist who outlined the tenets of the Protestant Work Ethic in his 1905 book *The Protestant Ethic and the Spirit of Capitalism*.

# References

Anthony, P. D. 1977. *The Ideology of Work*. Routledge. Taylor & Francis Group. London. U.K.

Army Values. 2010. Army Values Card issued to US Army soldiers. Cite as US Army GTA 22-06-002.
http://www.armyg1.army.mil/hr/armyValues.asp

Autry, Gene. 1947. "Cowboy Code of Conduct," Melody Ranch radio show. August 17. Gene Autry Survivor's Trust Copyright 1994.
www.geneautry.com/geneautry/geneautry_cowboycode.html

Bilefsky, Dan. 2006. "Protestant Work Ethic in Muslim Turkey," International Herald Tribune, Global Edition of the New York Times. August 15.

Carter, Steven. 1999. *Civility*. Harper Perennial; New York.

Code of Professional Conduct. 2015. American Institute of CPAs (AICPA) Code of Professional Conduct Dec. 15
https://www.aicpa.org/research/standards/codeofconduct.html

King, Martin Luther, Jr. 1963. "10 Point Pledge to Nonviolence," Teaching American History.org
http://teachingamericanhistory.org/library/document/commitment-card/ downloaded 11/26/2017.

—. 1958. *Stride Toward Freedom*. Harper and Row, New York.

Kraut, Richard. 2010. "Aristotle's Ethics," Stanford Encyclopedia of Philosophy. http://plato.stanford.edu/entries/aristotle-ethics/

Matthew 5:44-45 New Kings James Version, abridged.

Model Rules of Professional Conduct. 1983. American Bar Association.
https://www.americanbar.org/groups/professional_responsibility/public
ations/model_rules_of_professional_conduct.html

Shakespeare, William. 1599-1602. "Polonius' Advice to Laertes," Hamlet, Act I, Scene iii.

Solomon, J. 1984. *The Complete Works of Aristotle*, The Revised Oxford Translation, vol. 2, Jonathan Barnes, ed., Princeton: Princeton University Press.

Tang, Thomas Li-Ping. 1991. "A Factor Analytic Study of the Protestant Work Ethic." paper presented at the Annual Convention of the Southwestern Psychological Association 37th New Orleans, La. April 11-13.

Vance, David E. 2010. "Rules of Civility and a Good Life."

—. 2009. *Corporate Restructuring*. Springer Science + Business Media. London, New York. p.15.

Warner, Stephen L. 1999. "The Protestant Work Ethic and Academic Achievement." Working Paper. Information Resources Information Center.

Webber, Max. 1905. The Protestant Work Ethic and the Spirit of Capitalism. Routledge. Taylor & Francis Group. London. U.K. (May 25, 2001)

Yankelovich, D. 1981. New rules: Searching for self-fulfillment in a world turned upside down. New York: Random House. 247.

# CHAPTER SIX

# FINANCIAL ANALYSIS

After completing this chapter, you should be able to:

6.1 Identify the four major types of financial statements and explain what each is designed to do.

6.2 Identify major income statement and balance sheet landmarks.

6.3 Analyze income statements and determine a company's growth, cost structure and efficiency at converting sales to net income.

6.4 Determine a company's efficiency at generating income from assets and sales from assets.

6.5 Determine whether a company has excess assets, accounts receivable, inventory, or plant property and equipment.

6.6 Discuss a company's debt load and determine whether it is appropriate or excessive.

6.7 Discuss and analyze a company's cash flow and explain its importance.

6.8 Explain the factors that make a company relatively strong or weak.

## Introduction

Business is the engine of the economy. It provides goods, services, and jobs. But businesses are not infallible. Some are lean, mean profit machines, others barely keep their head above water, and still others are about to fail. So why do we care?

If we are going to invest in a company, we better know how well it's doing. No one wants to invest in, or lend money to, a company about to fail. And, it's not wise to take a job with a company that's just treading water. And, if you sell to another company on credit, you want to make sure they can pay their bills.

Ask most people to interpret financial statements and you might as well ask them to interpret hieroglyphics or ancient Greek.

This chapter explains how to analyze and interpret financial statements. There is no one indicator, no one number, or no one measure, that can be used to determine whether a company is strong or weak, growing or about to die. However, when several measures are considered together a mosaic emerges which paints a fairly accurate picture of how well a company is doing.

## Financial Statements

Companies are required to measure and report their performance using a set of standards called Generally Accepted Accounting Principles (GAAP). GAAP requires four financial statements: (i) Income Statement, (ii) Balance Sheet, (iii) Statement of Cash Flows, and (iv) Statement of Retained Earnings. Each of these financial statements looks at a company from a different point of view. Taken together, these views, plus notes to financial statements, present a picture of how well a company is doing.

Why do we need all these views? Why not just one financial statement that provides the whole picture? That is a fair question. But ask yourself, would you really understand what a car was if you only saw pictures of the fronts of cars? Realistically, it would be difficult to understand what a car was just by looking at the front. By getting a lot of views, a more complete picture emerges.

## Reading Financial Statements

**Accounting is about collecting information and presenting it in a standardized way.** Financial statements are the output of accounting. The best way to learn to read financial statements is not by studying the accounting used to compile them, but by learning what they can tell us.

Financial statements can tell how a company did compared to plan, compared to prior years, and compared to its competitors. Financial statements can also help set performance targets.

## Income Statement

The income statement is designed to measure how a company did over a specific period, usually a year. Many companies also publish quarterly income statements, and some companies prepare monthly income statements for internal use.

Revenue starts at zero every year and builds up to some total. Likewise, expenses start at zero every year and add up to some total. Total revenue, less total expenses, is used to create an income statement and arrive at net income.

**Revenue is different from sales.** Revenue is what a company is entitled to. A company can get an order for a hundred computers and it may think of that as a sale. However, under GAAP, a company can only count something as revenue when the goods, in this case computers, have been delivered. So, the general rule is that a company can only book revenue when title to goods has transferred to the buyer. If a company has a contract for services, revenue can only be booked after the service has been rendered. To simplify discussion, we will call revenue 'sales', and by sales, we mean the revenue a company has earned.

## Balance Sheet

A balance sheet is a list of a company's assets and a description of how those assets are financed. Assets are all the things a company has. Examples of assets include cash, accounts receivable, inventory, plant property, and equipment and land. Contrary to statements in the popular press, people are not an asset in an accounting sense, because people cannot be owned.

There are only two ways to finance assets; (i) with borrowed money, or (ii) with the owner's capital. Borrowed money includes bank loans, mortgages, accounts payable, which is money owed to trade creditors, and bonds issued by the company. Owner's capital includes investments made in the company's stock plus retained earnings. Retained earnings are all the profits a company has made since it was formed, less the total amount paid out as dividends.

**The accounting equation is: assets equal liabilities plus equity.** Liabilities are debt. Debt is borrowed money. Equity is the same as owner's invested capital, plus retained earnings. The balance sheet is just a snapshot of the details in the accounting equation at a point in time. Balance sheets must be prepared at year end. Many companies also prepare balance sheets quarterly and monthly.

## Statement of Cash Flows

A Statement of Cash Flows is designed to show where cash has come from and where it went over the course of a year. Generally, cash can be generated or used in (i) operations, (ii) investing, or (iii) financing. Cash from operations includes net income plus non-cash expenses, like depreciation, amortization and depletion, less increases in accounts receivable, inventory and other current assets. Cash from operations also includes increases from accounts payable. The gain on sale of fixed assets is subtracted, but a loss on sale of fixed assets is added.

Investing in this context means purchase or sale of all types of assets, not just financial assets like stocks and bonds of other companies. When a company purchases equipment, like trucks or computers, or fixtures, like desks and lights, or factories, it uses cash. Purchase of land and the stocks and bonds of other companies also use cash. On the other hand, when a company sells old machinery and equipment, or land, or stocks and bonds of another company, that generates cash.

Financing activity includes raising cash by borrowing money and issuing stocks or bonds. It also includes using cash to pay back loans, pay off mortgages, redeem the company's bonds, or pay dividends.

The most important part of the Statement of Cash Flows is the reconciliation which begins with last year's ending cash from the Balance Sheet, and adds the change in cash from operations, investing and financing. The result should be equal to the cash on this year's Balance Sheet. The Statement of Cash Flows is a little complicated. Fortunately, a company's health can generally be assessed with minimal information from this financial statement.

### Statement of Retained Earnings

A Statement of Retained Earnings is meant to update the amount of Retained Earnings on the Balance Sheet. It is the Retained Earnings from last year, plus this year's profits, less any dividends paid this year. The total should be the Retained Earnings on this year's Balance Sheet.

## Financial Statement Summary

Generally Accepted Accounting Principles (GAAP) require that financial statements be accompanied by explanatory notes. Without the notes, the financial statements do not meet GAAP standards. Table 6.1 Financial Statement Summary, provides an overview of the four financial statements discussed above.

**Table 6.1 Financial Statement Summary**

| Statement | Purpose | Time Period |
|---|---|---|
| **Income Statements** | Report on company operations; revenue less expenses equals net income. | Cumulative over a period usually a year. |
| **Balance Sheet** | Lists a company's assets and how they are financed. They can be financed with either debt or equity. | Snapshot at a point in time. |
| **Statement of Cash Flows** | Describes where cash comes from and how it is used. | Cumulative change in cash over a year. |
| **Statement of Retained Earnings** | This updates last year's retained earnings on the balance sheet to this year's. | Cumulative change in retained earnings over a year. |

## Lack of Standardization

Accounting is supposed to be about recording, analyzing and presenting relevant business information in a standard way. Standardization is important, so that anyone can read any company's financial statement and understand its condition.

The problem is that there are so many options within GAAP that no two financial statements are exactly alike. The Income Statement is hardest to interpret because of the number of options and exceptions it contains. To facilitate analysis, financial statements should be reformatted into the simpler, standardized form used in this chapter.

### *Income Statement Terms*

One of the things that makes income statements difficult to interpret is that the same thing may be called different names by different companies.

**Income Statement, Statement of Operations,** and **Earnings Statement** all mean the same thing. These are different names for an Income Statement.

**Sales, Net Sales and Revenue** all mean the same thing. They are all earned revenue.

**Credit Sales vs. Cash Sales** When a business (B) sells to another business (B), it almost always sells on credit, so all B to B sales can be considered credit sales. When a business (B) sells to consumers (C) it is almost always a cash sale. Sales paid for by check, debit card and credit card are all cash sales because the seller assumes no credit risk. So, B to C sales can be considered cash sales. Therefore, if we know the type of company, B to B or B to C, we know whether sales are credit or cash sales.

**Cost of Goods Sold (COGS), Cost of Products, Cost of Sales, Cost of Services** all mean the same thing.

**Operating Income and Earnings Before Interest and Taxes (EBIT)** both mean the same thing. It is a subtotal. It is Gross Profit less Total Overhead.

**Overhead** is everything between the subtotal Gross Profit and Operating Income.

**Interest** is interest net. It is interest expense, less interest income.

**Other Income (Expense)** – Suppose a pharmaceuticals company has invested in a strip store. Should the revenue from that investment be mixed ´up with revenue from selling pharmaceuticals? Should strip store expenses be mixed up with pharmaceutical expenses? Of course not. When a company in one industry has a relatively minor investment in another industry, the pre-tax income or loss from that minor investment is listed between the subtotal Operating Income and the subtotal Earnings Before Tax, as Other Income (Expense).

**Taxes, Provision for Tax, and Income Tax Expense** all mean the same thing.

**Earnings Before Taxes (EBT)** can be called various things. The way to locate EBT is to find the Tax line in the Income Statement and look at the line above it. EBT is taxable income.

**Average Shares Outstanding** is given below Net Income. The number of shares outstanding is classified as **Basic** or **Fully Diluted**. The Basic number of shares outstanding the actual number of shares in the hands of shareholders. This is used in Earnings per Share calculations. Fully Diluted Shares is the theoretical number of shares that may be outstanding under certain circumstances. Unless you deal in mergers and acquisitions, this number has limited utility.

*Income Statement Format*

Another group of options concerns the format of the Income Statement. By understanding common Income Statement variations, it is easier to locate critical financial landmarks.

**Sales** are often broken down into sales by territory, or product line, or sometimes by the top ten customers for internal purposes. Usually, this detail is summarized, and only total sales are reported on the Income Statement.

**Cost of Goods Sold (COGS)** is often broken down by territory, or product line, or sometimes by the top ten customers for internal reporting purposes. Usually, this detail is summarized and only total COGS are reported on the Income Statement. When both sales and COGS are broken down, gross margin can be computed by territory, product line or top customers.

**Gross Profit** is a subtotal. It is Sales less COGS. Not every income statement has a Gross Profit subtotal. If an Income statement doesn't have this subtotal, supply one as part of reformatting.

**Selling and Marketing Costs** are called by various names. Sometimes the elements of this cost are listed separately. Selling and Marketing Costs include: commissions, advertising, market research, salespeople's travel, conventions and trade shows. Not every company reports Selling and Marketing Costs. If some means can't be found to separate Selling and Marketing Costs from Overhead, two ratios; Selling Cost %, and Other

Overhead % cannot be calculated. Other Overhead is all Overhead except Selling and Marketing Costs.

**Net Income** is the amount of revenue that is left after all expenses are accounted for.

# Income Statement Reformat

Generally Accepted Accounting Principles allow many options when preparing Income Statements. To facilitate analysis, Income Statements should be reformatted into a standardized form. Table 6.2 Income Statement Format, shows what a reformatted Income Statement might look like.

**Table 6.2 Income Statement Reformat**

| Original Statement | | | Reformatted Statement | |
|---|---|---|---|---|
| Sales | 1,000 | | Sales | 1,000 |
| Cost of Sales | 600 | | COGS | 600 |
| Sales Commissions | 40 | | Gross Profit | 400 |
| Advertising | 55 | | | |
| Market Research | 5 | | Selling & Marketing | 100 |
| Corporate Facilities | 30 | | Other Overhead | 200 |
| Executive Compensation | 20 | | Total Overhead | 300 |
| Corporate Staff | 65 | | | |
| Insurance | 5 | | Operating Income | 100 |
| Other Expense | 80 | | | |
| Operating Income | 100 | | Interest Net | 10 |
| Interest Expense | 11 | | Other Income (Expense) | 2 |
| Interest Income | 1 | | | |
| Other Income (Expense) | 2 | | Earnings Before Tax | 92 |
| Earnings Before Tax | 92 | | Taxes | 18 |
| Taxes | 18 | | Net Income | 74 |
| Net Income | 74 | | | |

The following is the step-by-step process whereby the Original Income Statement was Reformatted.

1. The original Sales and reformatted Sales are the same.

2. Cost of Sales is renamed COGS.

3. A subtotal for Gross Profit is added. Gross Profit is Sales less COGS.

4. Sales Commissions, Advertising and Market Research are summarized into Selling and Marketing.

5. Corporate Facilities, Executive Compensation, Corporate Staff Insurance and Other Expense are summarized into Other Overhead.

6. A subtotal for Total Overhead is added. Total Overhead is Selling and Marketing plus Other Overhead.

7. The subtotal Operating Income is Gross Profit, less Total Overhead.

8. Interest Income is subtracted from Interest Expense to get Interest Net.

9. Other Income (Expense) is carried over.

10. Earnings Before Tax is Operating Income, less Interest Net, plus or minus Other Income or Expense.

11. Taxes are carried over.

12. Net Income is Earnings Before Tax, less Taxes.

It is important to note that reformatting neither creates nor destroys revenue (sales) or expenses. If the reformatting is done properly, Sales, Operating Income, Other Income or Expense, Earnings Before Taxes, Taxes, and Net Income should be the same on both statements.

# Making Money

How do companies make money? They sell goods and services and must pay for the material and labor that go into those goods and services. They must also pay for selling and marketing costs, office space, accountants and financing charges. Finally, if there is anything left, they must pay income taxes. So, there is a long road between making a sale and net income. Consider Bob's Sporting Goods, whose Income Statement is presented in Table 6.3. What can be said about this company?

**Table 6.3 Bob's Sporting Goods Income Statement**

| Income Statement | Amount | Percent of Sales |
|---|---|---|
| Sales (Revenue) | $1,000,000 | 100% |
| Cost of Goods Sold (COGS) | $600,000 | 60% |
| Gross Profit | $400,000 | 40% |
| | | |
| Total Overhead | $400,000 | 40% |
| Operating Income | $0 | 0% |
| | | |
| Less Interest Expense | $0 | 0% |
| Earnings Before Taxes (EBT) | $0 | 0% |
| | | |
| Taxes @ 21% | $0 | 0% |
| Net Income | $0 | 0% |

This company is going to die. It has no net income. Even though it pays no interest or taxes it is still going to die.

Why? A company that is not making money won't be able to borrow money from banks. It won't be able to get credit from suppliers. It won't have money to invest in advertising. It won't be able to develop new products and won't be able to recruit the best people. When a company gets into trouble, its customers begin to leave, and its best people look for better jobs. Zero net income can easily tip over into a loss and at some point, a company may not be able to pay its bills or its employees. It will die.

What would it take to make Bob's Sporting Goods profitable? Income statements often contain a lot of detail and the mistake most people make is to get bogged down in that detail. What if a company focused on just three landmarks in the income statement and improved each of them by 10%?

If sales were grown by 10% it would increase from $1,000,000 to $1,100,000. If overhead were cut by 10% it would decrease from $400,000 to $360,000.

Cutting cost of goods sold as a percent of net income (COGS%) is a bit tricky. Initially, cost of goods sold consumes 60% of every dollar of sales. Think of selling socks for $1.00 per pair when the wholesale cost of each pair is $0.60. The COGS% is 60% ($0.60 cost / $1.00 price). The goal in this example is to cut COGS% by 10%.

Why not just cut COGS in dollars? The answer is that if more socks are sold to generate more sales, more socks must be bought (or made). Assume for a moment that price cannot be raised, so to increase revenue by 10% more socks must be sold. Making or buying fewer socks is not an option if increasing unit sales is the goal. However, it may be possible to make or buy socks for less than their historical cost.

The target is to cut COGS% by 10% which means cutting COGS% from 60% to 54% (60% - 10% x 60%). If the percentages seem confusing, think about the problem in terms of the cost of socks. They initially cost $0.60 a pair and sold for $1.00 a pair. The goal is to cut the cost of socks 10%. The amount of money saved on each pair of socks is $0.06 (10% x $0.60). The new cost of socks to Bob's Sporting Goods is $0.54 ($0.60 - $0.06). This is the same as reducing COGS% to 54%.

Applying these three improvements to the company's income statement gives revenue of $1,100,000. Cost of goods sold is $594,000 (Sales of $1,100,000 x 54% COGS%). Overhead is $360,000. Earnings before taxes are $146,000; and after paying income tax at the 21% rate, the company has net income of $115,340. These changes are summarized in Table 6.4 Bob's Sporting Goods Target Income Statement.

**Table 6.4 Bob's Sporting Goods Target Income Statement**

|                | Current     | % of Sales | Change | Proposed    | % of Sales |
|----------------|-------------|------------|--------|-------------|------------|
| Sales          | $1,000,000  | 100%       | +10%   | $1,100,000  | 100.0%     |
| COGS           | $600,000    | 60%        | -10%   | $594,000    | 54.0%      |
| Gross Profit   | $400,000    | 40%        |        | $506,000    | 46.0%      |
|                |             |            |        |             |            |
| Overhead       | $400,000    | 40%        | -10%   | $360,000    | 32.7%      |
| Operating Inc. | $0          | 0%         |        | $146,000    | 13.3%      |
|                |             |            |        |             |            |
| Less Interest  | $0          | 0%         |        | $0          | 0%         |
| EBT            | $0          | 0%         |        | $146,000    | 13.3%      |
|                |             |            |        |             |            |
| Taxes @ 21%    | $0          | 0%         |        | $30,660     | 2.8%       |
| Net Income     | $0          | 0%         |        | $115,340    | 10.5%      |

By identifying and changing three critical elements, sales, COGS% and overhead, a company can go from the verge of bankruptcy to healthy. The practical importance of this exercise is to focus management's time and attention on the most important levers of profitability.

## Income Statement Analysis

How does one know whether a company is doing well or poorly? How does one know whether a company is headed for trouble or going to become a roaring success? How can one company be compared to another?

Nothing in the world happens suddenly, neither success nor failure. There are always signs as to which way things are going. The trick is to read the signs.

Analyzing income statements is important because it provides information that management can use to improve profitability.

No two companies are the same size. Ratios help compare companies of different sizes. Ratios can be used to look inside a company to determine what is working well and what needs improvement. Ratios can also be used to spot trends, good or bad. There are two principal ways to use ratios:

(i) Compare a company's ratios to those of other companies in the same industry, and

(ii) Compare a company to its own historical performance.

**Ratios are meaningless unless they can be compared to something.**

## Sales Growth

**Grow or die** is the rule in business. Nothing ever stands still. A company whose sales are not growing is on its way to dying. Growing a company's sales is critical for survival.

Sales Growth (SG) is the change in year-to-year sales divided by the prior year's sales, as shown in equation Eq.6.1. By convention, the highest number represents the most current year and the next lowest number is the previous year, so Sales2 is sales for the most current year.

$$SG = \frac{Sales2 - Sales1}{Sales1} \qquad Eq.6.1$$

Example: A company has $11.5M in sales this year and had $10.9M in sales the prior year.

$$SG = \frac{\$11.5M - \$10.9M}{\$10.9M}$$

$$= \frac{\$.6M}{\$10.9M}$$

$$= 5.5\%$$

## Cost of Goods Sold

Cost of Goods Sold Percent (COGS%) is the percentage of every dollar of sales used to buy products for resale, to make a product or to provide a service. Reducing COGS% increases net income. COGS% can be computed using equation Eq.6.2.

$$COGS\% = \frac{COGS}{Sales} \qquad Eq.6.2$$

Example: A company has sales of $11.5M and a cost of goods sold (COGS) of $6.5M. What is COGS%?

$$COGS\% = \frac{\$6.5M}{\$11.5M} = 56.5\%$$

## Gross Margin

Gross Margin is the percentage of every dollar of sales that is left over after a company provides its product or service to its customer. This amount must cover selling and marketing costs, other overhead, financing costs, taxes and **profit**. An adequate gross margin is essential for company survival. If gross margin is too thin, a company won't be able to cover its overhead and financing costs. The larger the gross margin, the better. Equation Eq.6.3 shows how to calculate gross margin.

$$\text{Gross Margin} = \frac{\text{Sales} - \text{COGS}}{\text{Sales}} \qquad \text{Eq.6.3}$$

Example: Sales for a company was $11.5M and its Cost of Goods Sold was $6.5M. Compute its Gross Margin.

$$\text{Gross Margin} = \frac{\$11.5 - \$6.5M}{\$11.5M} = \frac{\$5.0M}{\$11.5M} = 43.5\%$$

Gross margin plus COGS% must always equal 100% as shown in equation Eq.6.4. If they don't add up to 100% there is an error in one or both calculations.

$$100\% = \text{Gross Margin} + \text{COGS}\% \qquad \text{Eq.6.4}$$

## Overhead

Overhead is one of the great killers of companies. Overhead dollars don't produce products. While some Overhead is used for selling and marketing costs, much of overhead is consumed as back office expense.

When the percentage of sales devoted to Overhead (Overhead%) is growing, the company is headed for trouble. If a company's Overhead as a percentage of sales (Overhead%) is greater than that of its competitors, that is another sign of trouble.

**Overhead** is all the **expenses between** the subtotal **Gross Profit** and the subtotal **Operating Income**. Operating Income is sometimes called

Earnings before Interest and Taxes, or EBIT. Overhead% can be computed using equation Eq.6.5.

$$\text{Overhead\%} = \frac{\text{Overhead}}{\text{Sales}} \qquad \text{Eq.6.5}$$

Example: A company with $11.5M of sales has overhead of $3M. What is its Overhead%?

$$\text{Overhead\%} = \frac{\$3M}{\$11.5M} \quad = 26.1\%$$

## Selling and Marketing Costs

A more sophisticated way to analyze Overhead is to separate it into Selling and Marketing Costs, and Other Overhead. Selling and Marketing Costs include commissions, advertising, marketing department costs, exhibits, salespeople's travel expenses, conventions and trade shows. Selling and Marketing Costs can be expected to rise or fall with sales. Other Overhead includes things like corporate office expense and accountants' salaries. These should not necessarily rise with sales.

The ratio of Selling and Marketing Costs to Sales is called Selling Cost% and can be computed using equation Eq.6.6. If Selling Cost% is rising faster than Sales, or falls slower than Sales, a company may be headed for trouble.

Not every company discloses Selling and Marketing costs in its financial statements. For companies that do, Selling Cost% should be computed.

$$\text{Selling Cost\%} = \frac{\text{Selling \& Marketing Costs}}{\text{Sales}} \qquad \text{Eq.6.6}$$

Example: A company has Selling and Marketing costs of $1.2M and Sales of $11.5M. What is its Selling Cost%?

$$\text{Selling Cost\%} = \frac{\$1.2M}{\$11.5M} \quad = 10.4\%$$

## Other Overhead

Having teased out Selling and Marketing Costs from Overhead, the remaining costs are Other Overhead. Other Overhead% is the ratio of Other Overhead to Sales. This is a more sensitive barometer of whether a company is headed in the right direction (lower Other Overhead%) or the wrong direction (higher Other Overhead%). Other Overhead% may be written as OO%, and computed using equation Eq.6.7.

$$OO\% = \frac{\text{Overhead -Selling \& Marketing Costs}}{\text{Sales}} \quad \text{Eq.6.7}$$

Example: A company has $11.5M in Sales, Overhead of $3M and Selling and Marketing Costs of $1.2M.

$$OO\% = \frac{\$3M - \$1.2M}{\$11.5M} = \frac{\$1.8M}{\$11.5M} = 15.7\%$$

## Profit Margin

Many companies are good at sales, but poor at making a profit. **Profit Margin is a measure of the efficiency of a company in converting sales to profit.** If expenses are high relative to sales, Profit Margin will be low. However, if expenses are low compared to sales, Profit Margin will be high.

Ratios mean nothing unless they can be compared to something. Comparing Profit Margin among companies is difficult because companies have different financing strategies. Some companies finance most of their assets with debt, and those companies have large financing costs. Other companies believe debt makes them a servant to lenders, and they operate with no debt. Most companies are in the middle. Companies also have different tax strategies which makes comparisons difficult.

How can the Profit Margin of companies with different financing strategies be compared? The answer is to scrub out financing costs. Consider Eq.6.8; the equation for Profit Margin.

$$\text{Profit Margin} = \frac{\text{Net Income +Interest x (1-Tax Rate)}}{\text{Sales}} \quad \text{Eq.6.8}$$

Interest is added back to Net Income. This moves part way towards putting companies with large and small financing costs on equal footing. However, if a company pays a bank $100,000 in interest, that payment doesn't reduce Net Income by $100,000. Interest Expense is tax deductible. If a company is in the 21% tax bracket, the company's taxes are reduced by $21,000 ($100,000 x 21%). So, the actual cost of interest is $79,000 ($100,000 payment to the bank - $21,000 tax savings). Multiplying Interest Expense by one minus the tax rate automatically makes the necessary adjustment.

Most companies have Interest Expense, which is the interest paid on debt, and many have cash in bank accounts and certificates of deposit that generate Interest Income. This cash could be used to pay down debt and reduce a company's Interest Expense. So, when computing interest, Interest Income should be netted, that is subtracted, from Interest Expense, as shown in equation Eq.6.9.

$$\text{Interest} = \text{Interest Expense} - \text{Interest Income} \qquad \text{Eq.6.9.}$$

Every company has a different tax strategy which results in a different effective tax rate. The best way to compare companies is to take their tax strategy into account. A company's effective tax rate can be estimated using equation Eq.6.10.

$$\text{Tax Rate} = \text{Taxes / Earnings Before Tax} \qquad \text{Eq.6.10}$$

Taxes are found on the Income Statement, above Net Income, and below Earnings Before Taxes, or EBT.

Example: A company has sales of $30 million, Interest Expense of $2.2 million, Interest Income of $0.2 million, Earnings Before Taxes are $3.0 million, Taxes are $0.63 million and Net Income is $2.37 million.

$$\text{Tax Rate} = \$0.63M / \$3.0M \qquad = 21\%$$

$$\text{Interest} = \text{Interest Expense} - \text{Interest Income} \quad \text{Eq.6.9}$$

$$= \$2.2M - \$0.2M = \$2.0M$$

$$\text{Profit Margin} = \frac{\text{Net Income} + \text{Interest} \times (1 - \text{Tax Rate})}{\text{Sales}} \qquad \text{Eq.6.8}$$

$$= \frac{\$2.37M + \$2M \times (1 - 21\%)}{\$30M}$$

$$= \frac{\$2.37M + \$2M \times 79\%}{\$30M} \quad = \frac{\$3.95M}{\$30M} = 13.2\%$$

**Other Income (Expense)**

If a company has a minor investment in a company not related to its principal business, it may list Other Income (expense) under the subtotal Operating Income, and before the Earnings Before Tax subtotal.

Other Income and Expense are not relevant to a company's primary business. Where there is Other Income or Expense, adjust Net Income to back out these effects, as shown in equation Eq.6.11, before using Net Income in ratios.

Eq.6.11

Adjusted Net Income = Net Income
                      -Other Income or Expense x (1-Tax Rate)

Suppose a pharmaceutical company has Operating Income of $10,000, Net Interest Expense of $1,000 and Net Rental Income from a shopping mall of $300. A portion of its Income Statement might look like this.

| | |
|---|---|
| Operating Income | $10,000 |
| Interest Net | ($1,000) |
| Other Income (Expense) | $300 |
| Earnings Before Tax | $9,300 |
| Tax | $2,000 |
| Net Income | $7,300 |

Compute the Tax Rate using equation Eq.6.10.

Tax Rate     = Tax / Earnings Before Tax          Eq.6.10

             = $2,000 / $9,300          = 21.5%

Adjust Net Income to see what it would be without the Other Income (Expense). The Other Income increases Earnings Before Tax by $300, but taxes reduce this effect, so we adjust it my multiplying it by one minus the tax rate.

Adjusted Net Income = $6,300 - $300 x (1 -21.5%)

                    = $6,300 - $300 x .785

                    = $6,300 - $235.5          = $6,535.5

This Adjusted Net Income is used in ratio analysis.

## Income from Continuing Operations

Some companies experience one-time events like a catastrophic loss or sale or closure of a facility. In such cases a subtotal called Income from

Continuing Operations is placed where one would expect to find Net Income. Below this number, Extraordinary Items, or Income or Loss from Discontinued Operations are reported. Then Net Income is reported.

Ratio analysis is used to plan for the future, so such one-time events should be excluded. If a company has a subtotal labeled Income from Continuing Operations, use that figure instead of Net Income in ratios.

### *Discontinued Operations*

Sometimes companies have income from operations they have sold off or closed. This income is stated on an after-tax basis, on a separate line, and labeled Income (or loss) from Discontinued Operations. If a company sells a facility, it may have a gain or loss on the sale. This will be called Gain (or Loss) on Sale of Discontinued Operations. Gain or loss is reported on an after-tax basis. These gains or losses are reported below Income from Continuing Operations and above Net Income.

### *Extraordinary Items*

Sometimes a company experiences an event that is **both unusual and infrequent**, which creates either additional one-time income or more often a one-time loss. These are called Extraordinary Items. The effect of extraordinary items is reported on an after-tax basis. Extraordinary Items are reported below Income from Continuing Operations, and above Net Income.

## Earnings per Share

Corporations are owned by shareholders who want to know how well their investment is doing. Few investors buy whole companies; most buy shares of common stock in a company. Investors want to know how much of a company's earnings can be attributed to a single share of stock. Dividends on Preferred stock are paid first, reducing the amount available for common shareholders.

Earnings per Share (EPS) is Net Income available to common shareholders divided by the number of outstanding shares (OS). This can be computed using equation Eq.6.12.

$$\text{EPS} = \frac{\text{Net Income} - \text{Preferred Dividends}}{\text{OS}} \qquad \text{Eq.6.12}$$

Most of the stock traded on stock exchanges is common stock. Preferred stock is only issued in unusual circumstances, like when a company is starting up or when a company is in trouble. Preferred Dividends can be computed using equation Eq.6.13.

Preferred Dividends = Dividend Rate x Preferred Stock      Eq.6.13

Information on Preferred Stock and Preferred Stock Dividends may be found in the Equity section of the Balance Sheet. The number of outstanding shares (OS) can be found toward the bottom of the Income statement below Net Income. Use Average Outstanding Shares Basic.

Example: A company has net income of $3,000,000, Preferred Stock of $2,000,000, the dividend rate for Preferred Stock is 9%, and the company has 2,000,000 common shares outstanding. What is its EPS?

Preferred Dividends = 9% x $2,000,000

= $180,000

EPS  = ($3,000,000 - $180,000)      = $1.41/share
         2,000,000 shares

## Balance Sheet Analysis

The Balance Sheet lists a company's assets and how they are financed. Assets are the resources a company owns. Examples of assets include cash, accounts receivable, inventory, computers, machinery, equipment, buildings, patents, copyrights, planes, trains, and automobiles. Assets can only be financed by debt or equity. Debt (liabilities) is money owed to others. Equity is the money a company's owner and shareholders have invested in the company plus the company's Retained Earnings. Retained Earnings are all the profits a company has made since inception less any dividends paid.

The Balance Sheet is a representation of the accounting equation shown in equation Eq.6.14. Table 6.5 Bob's Sporting Goods Balance Sheet is an example of this financial statement.

Assets = Liabilities + Owner's Equity      Eq.6.14

**Table 6.5 Bob's Sporting Goods Balance Sheet**

| Assets | (Dollars in Thousands) |
|---|---|
| Cash | 20 |
| Accounts Receivable | 80 |
| Inventory | 290 |
| Plant Property & Equipment | 310 |
| Total Assets | 700 |
| | |
| Liabilities | |
| Accounts Payable | 240 |
| Bank Loans | 260 |
| Total Liabilities | 500 |
| | |
| Equity | |
| Common Stock | 30 |
| Retained Earnings | 170 |
| Total Equity | 200 |
| | |
| Total Liabilities + Equity | 700 |

## Assets

What is the appropriate level of assets? Can a company have too many assets? If a company has too many assets and they are financed by debt, interest expense will be greater than necessary. If a company has too many assets and these assets are financed by owners' equity, there is less money available to pay dividends or to invest in marketing or new product development. Most companies that have been around for a long time have more assets than they need.

The issue is how to determine whether a company has excess assets. Whether a company has too many assets can only be judged by looking at the level of assets in the industry. Two ratios help in this regard; Return on Assets (ROA) and Asset Turnover (AT).

## Return on Assets

**Return on Assets (ROA) is a measure of management's efficiency in using assets to generate net income.** A low ROA could mean either:

(i) management is inefficient, in which case it might be necessary to retrain or replace them; or

(ii) a company has too many assets.

Ratios are only useful if there is something to compare them to. But, every company has its own financing and tax strategy. Equation Eq.6.15 adjusts for different financing and tax strategies, so ROA is comparable across companies. See Profit Margin for a discussion of the rationale for such adjustments. Also, see Profit Margin for a calculation of Interest and the Tax Rate.

$$ROA = \frac{\text{Net Income} + \text{Interest} \,(1\text{-}\,\text{Tax Rate})}{(A2 + A1)/2} \quad \text{Eq.6.15}$$

Where Interest is Net Interest, A2 is total assets at the end of the most current year, and A1 is total assets at the end of the prior year.

Example: A company has Net Income of $2 million, Interest of $1 million, Assets Year 2 of $21 million and Assets Year 1 of $19 million, and a 21% tax rate.

$$ROA = \frac{\$2M + \$1M \times (1 - 21\%)}{(\$21M + \$19M)/2}$$

$$ROA = \frac{\$2M + \$1M \times 79\%}{\$40M \,/\, 2}$$

$$= \frac{\$2M + \$.79M}{\$20M}$$

$$= 14.0\%$$

Return on Assets cannot be used when Net Income is zero, negative, or close to zero. In these circumstances ROA has no meaning.

## Asset Turnover

**Asset Turnover is the efficiency of generating sales with assets**. It can be thought of as the amount of sales that one dollar of assets can generate. Asset Turnover can always be used, because neither sales nor assets can be zero. Asset Turnover (AT) is given by equation Eq.6.16. A higher Asset Turnover is better than a lower Asset Turnover.

$$AT = \frac{Sales}{(A2 + A1) / 2} \qquad \text{Eq.6.16}$$

Example: Suppose a company has Sales of $22 million; Assets last year of $19 million; and Assets this year of $21 million.

$$AT = \frac{\$22M}{(\$21M + \$19M) / 2} = \frac{\$22M}{\$20M} = 1.1$$

This company generates $1.10 in sales for every dollar of Assets.

## Excess Assets

If a company's Return on Assets and Asset Turnover are both lower than its competitors, it probably has excess Assets. Excess Assets should be identified and sold off to raise cash. The three most likely places to find excess Assets are in Accounts Receivable, Inventory and Plant, Property and Equipment.

## Accounts Receivable

Accounts Receivable is a list of customers that owe the company money. Accounts Receivable is one of the first assets to be listed on the Balance Sheet, usually right after cash.

Businesses usually fall into two broad categories, those who sell business to business (B to B), and those that sell to consumers (B to C). Those which sell business to business sell on credit, and few, if any, have cash sales.

Companies that sell to consumers sell for cash. Sales paid for with coins and currency are cash sales; sales paid by check are cash sales; sales paid by debit or credit card are also cash sales from the point of view of the seller. **Companies that sell for cash have no Accounts Receivable. Accounts Receivable ratios are meaningless for those companies.**

When a business sells on credit, it is making a loan to its customers as surely as if it hands customers a check. Some people mistakenly think the objective of business is to make a sale. It is not. The objective is to get paid. The job of the Credit and Collections Department is to make sure everyone who gets credit pays their bills promptly.

**Accounts Receivable Turnover is a measure of the efficiency of the Credit and Collections Department.** See equation Eq.6.17. Accounts Receivable Turnover (AR Turns) can also be used to determine whether the company has too much money invested in accounts receivable. Higher

Accounts Receivable Turns are better than lower Turns, because higher Turns mean quicker collections.

$$\text{AR Turns} = \frac{\text{Credit Sales}}{(\text{AR2} + \text{AR1})/2} \qquad \text{Eq.6.17}$$

Where AR2 is accounts receivable this year and AR1 is accounts receivable in the prior year.

Example: A company has $40 million in credit sales, Accounts Receivable this year was $5.2 million and Accounts Receivable last year was $4.8 million. What is the AR Turns?

$$\text{AR Turns} = \frac{\$40M}{(\$5.2M + \$4.8M)/2} = \frac{\$40M}{\$5M} = 8.0$$

The question is whether AR Turns of 8.0 is good or bad. If a company has AR Turns of 8.0, but the industry average AR Turns is 10.0, the company isn't doing very well. However, if the company has AR Turns of 8.0, but the industry average is 6.0, it is doing great.

## Days Sales Outstanding (DSO)

The problem with Accounts Receivable Turnover is that it's hard to visualize or explain.  Accountants understand it, but it has no intuitive meaning. A measure of credit and collections that is easier to understand is Days Sales Outstanding (DSO) as shown in equation Eq.6.18. It is the average number of days it takes a company to collect from its customers.

$$\text{DSO} = 365 \text{ days} / \text{AR Turns} \qquad \text{Eq.6.18}$$

Example: A company has AR Turns of 8.0. What is its DSO?

$$\text{DSO} = 365 \text{ days} / 8.0 \qquad = 45.6 \text{ Days}$$

The faster a company collects money owed to it, the better, so a lower DSO is better than a higher DSO. Increasing AR Turns and decreasing DSO will reduce the amount of capital needed to finance accounts receivable. Is 45.6 days good enough? That depends on the industry.

## Inventory Turnover

Inventory is goods available for sale in the ordinary course of business. For a baker, bread, cakes and cookies are Inventory. For an auto manufacturer cars, trucks, and other vehicles are Inventory. For a grocery store, the goods on their shelves and in their storeroom are Inventory. Inventory that is ready to sell is 'Finished Goods Inventory'. But cars, for example, start out as sheet metal, glass, tires, paint and upholstery. These are the raw materials that go into making a car and are called 'Raw Materials Inventory'. Raw materials to which some labor has been applied is called 'Work in Process Inventory', or WIP Inventory. Inventory Turnover considers all three types of inventory together.

**Inventory Turnover is a measure of the efficiency of inventory management.** If a retailer buys too much Inventory or stocks Inventory no one wants, its Inventory Turnover will go down. If a company purchases too much raw material, produces finished goods faster than it can sell them, or takes too long to manufacture goods, its Inventory Turnover will go down. For a manufacturing company, Inventory Turnover is also a measure of production efficiency. Service companies have little if any Inventory, so Inventory ratios have little meaning for those companies.

Inventory Turnover (Inventory Turns) may be computed using equation Eq.6.19. The Inventory at the end of the current year is I2 and the Inventory at the end of the prior year is I1. COGS is the Cost of Goods Sold.

$$\text{Inventory Turns} = \frac{\text{COGS}}{(I2 + I1)/2} \qquad \text{Eq.6.19}$$

Example: A company has COGS of $20M, Inventory last year of $1.9M and Inventory this year of $2.1M.

$$= \frac{\$20M}{(\$2.1M + \$1.9M+)/2}$$

$$= \quad \$20M \, / \, \$2M \quad = 10.0$$

Whether Inventory Turns of 10 is good or bad depends on the industry. However, higher is always better.

## Days in Inventory

Inventory Turns is a technical measure of performance, and it's not obvious to everyone exactly what it means. Part of the burden of leadership is to explain goals and performance standards in terms people can understand. Days in Inventory (DII) converts Inventory Turnover into the average number of days between the time a company purchases Inventory and the time it is sold. Days in Inventory can be computed using equation Eq.6.20.

$$DII = 365 / \text{Inventory Turns} \qquad \text{Eq.6.20}$$

Example: A company has Inventory Turns of 10.0 what is DII?

$$DII = 365 / 10.0 \quad = 36.5 \text{ days}$$

A DII of 36.5 days would be fantastic for an aircraft manufacturer, but would be bad for someone selling eggs, cut flowers, or bread. The best way to evaluate whether a DII is good or bad is to compare it to industry averages.

---

**Efficiency Measures**

**Profit Margin** measures the **efficiency** of generating **profits from sales.**

**Return on Assets** measures the **efficiency** generating **profits from assets.**

**Asset Turnover** measures the **efficiency** of generating **sales from assets.**

**Accounts Receivable Turnover** measures the **efficiency** of the **credit and collections** department.

**Inventory Turnover** measures **inventory management efficiency.**

---

## Plant, Property and Equipment Turnover

Most companies have enormous sums of money invested in Plant, Property and Equipment (PP&E). Plant, Property and Equipment includes factories, office buildings, trucks, manufacturing equipment, computers, desks, chairs and phones. A well-run company should concern itself with whether it has too much invested in Plant, Property and Equipment. One way is to compute PP&E Turns as shown in equation Eq.6.21. One can think of PP&E Turns as the number of dollars of sales generated by each dollar of Plant, Property and Equipment. If PP&E Turns are lower than the industry average, that might indicate a company has too much Plant, Property or Equipment.

$$\text{PP\&E Turns} = \frac{\text{Sales}}{(\text{PP\&E2} + \text{PP\&E1})/2} \qquad \text{Eq.6.21}$$

Example: Suppose a company has sales of $30 million and Plant, Property and Equipment of $6.2 million at the end of this year (PP&E2) and $5.8 million at the end of last year (PP&E1).

$$\text{PP\&E Turns} = \frac{\$30M}{(\$6.2M + \$5.8M)/2} = \frac{\$30M}{\$6M} = 5.0$$

PP&E Turns may be thought of as the sales dollars generated by each dollar of Plant Property and Equipment. In this example, the company is generating $5 of sales from each dollar of PP&E.

## Debt Measures

Debt is another great killer of companies. Even the best companies can be crushed by debt if they are not careful. There are many ways to analyze debt; two of the most important are the Debt Equity Ratio and the Debt Ratio.

## Debt Equity Ratio

The Debt Equity Ratio is simply a company's debt, that is to say its liabilities, divided by its equity as shown in equation Eq.6.22.

$$\text{Debt Equity Ratio} = \text{Liabilities/Equity} \qquad \text{Eq.6.22}$$

Example: A company has $20 million of assets financed by $12 million of debt and $8 million of equity.

$$\text{Debt Equity Ratio} = \$12M/\$8M = 1.5$$

The Debt Equity Ratio is cited as 1.5 to 1. Whether a Debt Equity Ratio is good or bad depends on the ratios of a company's best competitors. However, if the Debt Equity Ratio rises above 3.0, most banks and investors will consider that bad, per se. A Debt Equity Ratio of 2.0 or less is usually considered acceptable.

## Debt Ratio

Debt Ratio is the percentage of assets financed by debt. For many people, the Debt Ratio is a more intuitive measure than the Debt Equity Ratio. The Debt Ratio may be computed using equation Eq.6.23.

$$\text{Debt Ratio} = \text{Liabilities/Assets} \qquad \text{Eq.6.23}$$

Example: A company has $20 million of assets financed by $12 million of debt and $8 million of equity.

$$\text{Debt Ratio} = \$12M \,/\, \$20M \qquad = 60\%$$

## Cash

One of the worst things that can happen to a company is running out of cash. If it runs out of cash it can't pay its bills and it can't meet payroll. If it can't meet payroll, its employees will walk away and that could mean the company's collapse. Cash is as important to a company as oxygen is to a person.

Cash flow is how much cash a company generates. Cash flow and Net Income are different. A company can make a profit and still not generate enough cash to keep going. The Statement of Cash Flows tells people where cash comes from and where it went, but few people use the Statement of Cash Flows directly to estimate how much cash a company is generating or using. The measures people generally use are called Cash Flow and Free Cash Flow.

| Cash is as important to a company, as oxygen is to a person. |
|---|

## Cash Flow

Depreciation is the allocation of the cost of an asset to the sales it helps generate. Suppose a $50,000 truck helps a company generate sales over five years. Assume the truck has no trade-in value at the end of five years. One fifth of the cost of the truck is allocated to each year. This means each year the company will record a Depreciation Expense of $10,000. This expense will be included in Cost of Goods Sold and subtracted from revenue to get Gross Profit and ultimately Net Income.

Companies write checks for most expenses. They write checks for payroll, rent, raw materials, water, electricity and insurance. Who do they write a check to for Depreciation Expense? No one. Unlike most expenses, depreciation does not use cash. It is a non-cash expense. It is just an accounting entry. Another non-cash expense is called Amortization. It is like Depreciation, but for intangible items like leasehold improvements, copyrights and patents. Depletion, another non-cash expense, is used to account for consumption of natural resources like timber, coal or oil.

To get a rough idea of how much cash a company generates add Depreciation, Amortization and Depletion to Net Income, as shown in equation Eq.6.24. Depreciation, Amortization and Depletion are found on the Statement of Cash Flows.

Eq.6.24

$$\text{Cash Flow} = \text{Net income} + \text{Depreciation} + \text{Amortization} + \text{Depletion}$$

Example: A company has Net Income of $4.0 million; Depreciation of $1.0 million, Amortization of $0.2 million and Depletion of $1.5 million. What is its Cash Flow?

$$\text{Cash Flow} = \$4.0M + \$1.0M + \$0.2M + 1.5M$$

$$= \$6.7M$$

## Free Cash Flow

Companies must constantly re-invest cash back into their businesses. That means the cash flow estimate of equation Eq.6.24 usually **overestimates** the cash available to invest in new products and advertising, to acquire other companies, and to pay dividends. So, what else affects the cash available to a company?

**Accounts Receivable (AR).** Selling on credit increases Accounts Receivable. Selling on credit is like lending cash to customers. This is a use of cash. Collecting money owed reduces Accounts Receivable. This is a source of cash. When Accounts Receivable increases year over year, that means more money is being lent to customers than is being collected. An increase in Accounts Receivable of $10,000 means that $10,000 more was lent out than collected. The increase in Accounts Receivable represents a net use of cash. However, a year to year reduction in Accounts Receivable is a net source of cash.

**Inventory (I).** Purchasing Inventory uses cash. Selling Inventory generates cash. The question is whether a company is purchasing Inventory faster than it is selling it. An increase in Inventory year over year is a net use of cash. However, a reduction in Inventory is a net source of cash.

**Plant, Property and Equipment (PP&E).** When a company purchases Plant, Property or Equipment it uses cash. When it sells Plant Property or Equipment because it is no longer needed, it generates cash.

**Accounts Payable (AP).** The amount of money a company owes its suppliers is called **Accounts Payable**. Accounts Payable is a liability. When a supplier sells to a company on credit it is lending the company money. That is a source of cash. When a company pays for its supplies, it uses cash. If a company borrows more from suppliers than it pays back, accounts payable increases year over year; that is a net source of cash. However, if Accounts Payable declines year over year, that is a net use of cash.

**Dividends.** Many companies pay **Dividends**. Dividends are payments to shareholders to reward them for investing in the company. Cash expended on Dividends is not available for other corporate purposes. Dividend payments are a use of cash.

**Taxes.** Taxes are an important source and use of cash. The tax expense on an income statement is not the same as taxes paid because GAAP accounting rules and IRS tax regulations are different. Some differences are permanent, for example, the IRS may disallow a deduction for fines, whereas fines are a deductible expense for GAAP. Some differences are temporary, such as those for accelerated depreciation. Temporary differences reverse themselves over time. Temporary differences shift cash flow among years.

When Deferred Taxes increase, the IRS is lending a company money because of a temporary difference. That is a source of cash. When Deferred Taxes decrease, a company is paying down the 'loan' made by the IRS, and this is a use of cash.

**Free Cash Flow.** Free Cash Flow (**FCF**) represents the amount of cash available for any purpose, considering the amount of money reinvested in the company in the form of new Plant Property and Equipment, changes in Accounts Receivable, Inventory, Accounts Payable, Taxes, and Dividends. Free Cash Flow can be estimated using equation Eq.6.25.

Eq.6.25
$$FCF = \text{Net Income} + \text{Depreciation} + \text{Amortization} + \text{Depletion}$$
$$- \text{Increase in AR} - \text{Increase in I}$$
$$+ \text{Increase in AP} + \text{Increase in Deferred Taxes}$$
$$- \text{Additions to PP\&E} + \text{Sales of PP\&E}$$
$$- \text{Dividends}$$

Net Income is found on the Income Statement. Depreciation, Amortization and Depletion, as well as purchase and sale of Plant, Property and Equipment and Dividends are found on the Statement of Cash Flow. Changes in Accounts Receivable, Inventory and Accounts Payable is computed by taking the difference between account balances on this year's Balance Sheet and last year's Balance Sheet.

Example: A company has Net Income of $600, Depreciation of $60, Amortization of $15, Depletion of $5, Plant Property and Equipment purchases of $70, and paid dividends of $150. The company's Balance Sheet is given in Table 6.6 Larry Fine, Inc. Balance Sheet.

**Table 6.6 Larry Fine, Inc. Balance Sheet**

|  | **2014** | **2013** | **Change** | **Impact** |
|---|---|---|---|---|
| Cash | $80 | $50 |  |  |
| Accounts Receivable | $700 | $600 | $100 | Use of Cash |
| Inventory | $820 | $700 | $120 | Use of Cash |
| PP&E | $940 | $950 |  |  |
| *Total Assets* | *$2,540* | *$2,300* |  |  |
|  |  |  |  |  |
| Accounts Payable | $480 | $390 | $90 | Source of Cash |
| Bank Loans | $920 | $900 |  |  |
| Deferred Taxes | $20 | $10 | $10 | Source of Cash |
| *Total Liabilities* | *$1,420* | *$1,300* |  |  |
|  |  |  |  |  |
| *Total Equity* | *$1,120* | *$1,000* |  |  |
|  |  |  |  |  |
| *Total Liabilities & Equity* | *$2,540* | *$2,300* |  |  |

## Cash Flow Calculation

Eq. 6.24

Cash Flow = Net income + Depreciation
+ Amortization + Depletion

= $600 + $60 + $15 + $5

= $680

## Free Cash Flow

1.  Net Income is $600. This is a source of cash.

2.  Depreciation of $60, Amortization of $15 and Depletion of $5 are sources of cash.

3.  Accounts Receivable increased $100 (from $600 to $700) which used cash.

4.  Inventory increased $120 (from $700 to $820) which used cash.

5.  Plant, Property and Equipment purchases of $70 are a use of cash.

6.  Accounts Payable increased by $90 (from $390 to $480); this is a source of cash.

7.  Deferred Taxes increased by $10 (from $10 to $20); this is a source of cash.

8.  Dividend payments of $150 were a use of cash.

Applying these facts to equation Eq.6.25 gives the company's Free Cash Flow.

Free Cash Flow = $600 + $60 + $15 + $5
-$100 -$120 -$70 +$90 +10 -$150

= $340

Based on the data in this example, Cash Flow at $680 was significantly higher than Free Cash Flow at $340. The difference is the amount the company reinvested in its operations.

# More on Ratios

There are many more ratios than those discussed in this chapter. Some ratios are specific to certain industries.[1] Others can be used for profit planning and corporate restructuring.[2] Creative uses for ratios are almost endless.

# Conclusion

Generally Accepted Accounting Principles (GAAP) provide guidelines for collecting, analyzing and presenting financial information on a systematic and consistent basis. GAAP requires four financial statements plus notes to financial statements. These statements include: (i) the Income Statement which presents the results of operations over a period of time; (ii) the Balance Sheet, which is a summary of a company's assets, liabilities and equity at a point in time; (iii) the Statement of Retained Earnings which reconciles Retained Earnings from one year to the next; and (iv) the Statement of Cash Flows, which analyzes where cash came from and how it was used over a period of time.

GAAP provides many alternatives to those preparing financial statements. GAAP also allows different names for the same thing. The result is that no two statements are exactly alike. Income statements have the most variability. Recasting them into a standard format increases comparability across companies.

A company's performance can be significantly improved by focusing on three key levers of profitability: (i) Sales, (ii) COGS%, and (iii) Overhead.

Companies neither succeed nor fail abruptly. There are always signs as to which way a company is headed. The best way to identify trends is through ratios. Ratios only have meaning if they are compared to something else. Ratios allow a company to compare itself to its competitors, even though no two companies are the same size, have the

---

[1] Vance, David E. 2009. Ratios for Analysis, Control and Profit Planning. Global Professional Publishing. Cranbrook, Kent, U.K.
[2] Vance, David E. 2009. Corporate Restructuring. Springer Science +Business Media. New York.

same financing strategy, or the same tax strategy. Ratios can also be used to compare a company to its own historical performance.

Some ratios, like Sales Growth, Profit Margin, and ratios that analyze various costs as a percent of Sales, use Income Statement data, and are useful in analyzing company operations. Earnings per Share estimates the amount of earnings attributed to one share of common stock. Some ratios like Return on Assets and Asset Turnover use both Income Statement and Balance Sheet data to determine whether a company is effectively using its assets or whether it has too many assets. Other ratios, like Accounts Receivable and Inventory Turnover, are useful in measuring departmental effectiveness and setting goals. Some ratios, such as the Debt Equity Ratio and Debt Ratio help evaluate whether a company has excess debt.

Cash is as important to a company as oxygen is to a person. If a company runs out of cash it will miss its payroll and its employees will walk away. It won't be able to purchase raw materials or pay its rent. Cash Flow, the amount of cash generated by a company, may be estimated by adding non-cash expenses like depreciation, amortization and depletion to net income. This estimate has been criticized because companies must constantly reinvest cash to maintain operations. Free Cash Flow adjusts cash flow by considering changes in accounts receivable, inventory, accounts payable and deferred taxes. It also considers purchase and sale of equipment, changes in deferred tax, and payment of dividends.

Companies neither succeed nor fail abruptly. There are always signs as to where they are headed. Taken together, ratios that analyze the income statement and balance sheet present a fairly broad view of a company's direction.

# Terms and Concepts

**Accounting Equation** – Assets = Liabilities + Equity. See Balance Sheet.

**Accounts Payable** – This is a list of the amounts due to trade vendors for goods, materials and supplies purchased on credit. It is a liability.

**Accounts Receivable** – This is a list of the customers that owe the company money for goods and services. Accounts Receivable is an asset.

**Accounts Receivable Turnover** (AR Turns) – measures the efficiency of the credit and collections department.

**Amortization** – this is the allocation of the cost of an intangible asset such as a patent, copyright or leasehold improvement, over the years which it helps generate revenue.

**Asset Turnover** (AT) – measures the efficiency of generating sales from assets. It is the dollars of sales generated by each dollar of assets.

**Balance Sheet** – is a representation of the Accounting Equation Assets = Liabilities + Equity. It lists a company's assets and how they are financed. Assets can only be financed with debt or equity.

**Cash Flow** – Net Income plus Depreciation, Amortization and Depletion. Cash Flow is often less than Free Cash Flow.

**COGS%** - Cost of Goods Sold as a Percent of Sales is the percent of every dollar of sales is used to provide customers with goods or services.

**Cost of Goods Sold** (COGS) - Cost of Products Sold (COPS), Cost of Sales (COS) and Cost of Services (COS) all mean the same thing. These are the costs to provide products or services to customers.

**Days in Inventory** (DII) - This is the average length of time that goods are in inventory.

**Days Sales Outstanding** (DSO) – This is the average length of time it takes to collect outstanding accounts receivable.

**Debt** – is the money owed to others. Liabilities are the same as debt.

**Debt Equity Ratio** –is Debt divided by Equity. A Debt Equity Ratio above 3.0 is generally considered bad.

**Debt Ratio** – This is the percentage of assets financed by debt. It is debt divided by assets.

**Depletion** – This is the allocation of the cost of a natural resource over the years which it helps generate revenue.

**Depreciation** – This is the allocation of the cost of an asset to the years it helps generate revenue.

**Discontinued Operations** – When a company sells or closes a facility, it will no longer contribute to future income. The income or loss for this facility is separated out and reported net of tax, after the subtotal Income from Continuing Operations.

**Earnings before Interest and Taxes** (EBIT) are sometimes called Income from Operations or Operating Income.

**Earnings before Taxes** - is taxable income from on-going operations

**Earnings per Share** – This is the amount of Net Income available to common shareholders. divided by the number of Outstanding Shares.

**Extraordinary Items** – Sometimes a company has a transaction which is both unusual and infrequent. These items are listed separately below the subtotal Income from Continuing Operations. Extraordinary items are listed net of tax.

**Free Cash Flow** – This is the amount of cash available for any purpose. It considers increases and decreases in working capital, purchase and sale of plant, property and equipment, changes in deferred taxes, and dividends, in addition to Net Income plus Depreciation, Amortization and Depletion.

**Generally Accepted Accounting Principles** (GAAP) - are guidelines used to collect, organize and report financial information. GAAP reporting requires four financial statements: (i) Income Statement, (ii) Balance Sheet, (iii) Statement of Cash Flows, and (iv) Statement of Retained Earnings. GAAP also requires Notes to Financial Statements.

**Gross Profit** - is Sales less COGS. Not all income statements show this subtotal. When reformatting financial statements, insert this subtotal.

**Gross Margin** – This is the percentage of every dollar of sales that is left over after buying or making the product or providing a service. A company with a Gross Margin that is too thin will fail.

**Income from Continuing Operations** - This subtotal only exists when a company has Extraordinary Items, or Income or Loss from Discontinued Operations. Where there are Discontinued Operations or Extraordinary Items, Income from Continuing Operations is used in lieu of Net Income in ratios.

**Income Statement** – reports the performance of a company over a period of time, usually a year, but sometimes quarterly. It starts with sales and subtracts expenses to get to Net Income.

**Interest Expense** – This is interest paid to banks and other creditors.

**Interest Income** – Most companies generate small amounts of interest income from money in banks, and other short-term investments.

**Interest Net** - is Interest Expense, less Interest Income.

**Inventory Turnover** – or Inventory Turns, is a measure of the efficiency with which inventory is managed.

**Net Income**, - Earnings and Net Earnings are the same thing. It is the result of a company's operations.

**Other Overhead Percent (OO%)** - This is the percent of every dollar of sales consumed by Other Overhead.

**Other Overhead** – This is Overhead, less Selling and Marketing Costs. Other Overhead includes things like office buildings and accountants' salaries.

**Outstanding Shares** – This is the number of shares of common stock in the hands of investors and the public.

**Overhead** –is all the expenses other than Cost of Goods Sold, Financing Costs and Taxes. Overhead includes all costs between the subtotals Gross Profit and Earnings Before Interest and Taxes (EBIT). Overhead includes things like selling and marketing costs, office buildings and accountants' salaries.

**Overhead Percent (OH%)** - is the percentage of every dollar of sales consumed by Overhead.

**Preferred Dividends** – Preferred stock is stock created by contract. It is generally only issued when a company is first starting, or when a company is in trouble. Preferred stock has a stated face value. Preferred Dividends are a stated percentage of a stock's face value.

**Plant Property and Equipment** (PP&E) – is a category of assets that includes equipment, machinery, furniture, fixtures and buildings.

**PP&E Turns** – This is a ratio which may indicate whether a company has too much invested in Plant, Property and Equipment. It is the number of dollars of sales generated by each dollar of PP&E.

**Preferred Stock** – This is a type of equity. It has a stated face value. Preferred Dividends are a stated percentage of a stock's face value.

**Profit Margin** – This ratio measures the efficiency with which Sales are converted to Net Income.

**Ratios** – Ratios provide a means of comparing a company's performance to its competitors and to its own historical performance. Ratios make comparisons possible by adjusting for differences in size, financing and tax strategy. Ratios are meaningless unless compared to something.

**Retained Earnings** – this is all the Net Income a company has made since its inception, less Dividends.

**Return on Assets** (ROA) – this is a measure of the efficiency of generating net income from assets. Low Return on Assets may mean a company has too many assets or management is not efficiently utilizing assets.

**Sales Growth** – sales growth is important because companies must grow or die.

**Sales, Net Sales and Revenue** – mean the same thing. Under GAAP sales can only be recorded after title to goods passes to customers or services have been rendered.

**Selling and Marketing Expenses** - are expenses for advertising, commissions, market research and salaries for sales and marketing staff. These expenses are sometimes included in Overhead and not broken out separately.

**Selling Cost%** - is the percent of every dollar of sales consumed by Selling and Marketing Costs.

**Statement of Cash Flows** – this is a financial statement which describes the sources and uses of cash over a period of time usually a year.

**Statement of Retained Earnings** – this financial statement reconciles last year's Retained Earnings, plus Net Income, less Dividends to this year's Retained Earnings.

**Taxes**, - Provision for Income Taxes, and Income Tax Expense are the same thing.

# References

Vance, David E. 2009. Corporate Restructuring. Springer Science +Business Media. New York.

—. 2009. Ratios for Analysis, Control and Profit Planning. Global Professional Publishing. Cranbrook, Kent, U.K.

# CHAPTER SEVEN

# CRITICAL THINKING

After completing this chapter, you should be able to:

7.1 Define critical thinking

7.2 Use the principles of critical thinking to determine whether statements are true.

7.3 Identify the root cause of problems

7.4 Identify alternatives and project the consequences of actions and decisions.

7.5 Understand how forces balance to result in certain conditions.

7.6 Explain and apply the scientific method to find new knowledge.

7.7 Apply negotiating strategies in complex situations.

7.8 Critically evaluate statistical information.

## Introduction

Sharon wanted to invest in a start-up company that had the potential to be the next Facebook, Google or Amazon. A company that made long life batteries seemed interesting. Batteries are in everything, so there is a huge market for better batteries.

The entrepreneur gave a glowing account of his new battery, the likelihood of market acceptance, and sales projections. The entrepreneur was affable, enthusiastic and showed the kind of drive needed for success.

Sharon's older sister Samantha asked her to 'think critically' before making an investment. Her sister's question caused Sharon to wonder what it meant to think critically and wonder how 'critical thinking' could help her with something as practical as an investment decision.

Few people think critically. Most thinking is sloppy, imprecise, confused, biased, self-contradictory, and based on inadequate evidence. Most people accept what they hear or read without a great deal of thought or analysis. Statements repeated often enough are accepted as true. Conclusions are accepted without a rigorous analysis of the logic that connects facts and premises to those conclusions. The implications of conclusions or planned actions are rarely considered, with the result that people, businesses and governments careen from problem to problem.

Critical thinking is important to separate the true from the illusory, the logical from the illogical, and the well-founded from that which is built on sand. Critical thinking questions common beliefs and explanations, in a search for what is true, logical and reasonable. Critical thinking is important in negotiating, planning and assessing challenges.

While critical thinking is essential in making well-reasoned decisions, critical thinking will not make you popular. Politicians, bureaucrats, business people, community, and religious leaders want you to believe what they say. And, they want you to obey.

Socrates, who lived in Athens 2,500 years ago, is widely thought of as one of the first critical thinkers. Socrates believed that commonly held beliefs, as well as the assertions of politicians, should be carefully questioned to distinguish that which is logical, consistent and grounded in facts from that which is mere assertion. Often, widely-held beliefs are comfortable, but not grounded in facts and logic.[1] When politicians and community leaders made statements or took positions, Socrates used probing questions to analyze the foundation for such statements and often found they were not based on evidence, or such statements were illogical. This embarrassed the leaders of his day and they put Socrates on trial for disrespecting the gods; convicted him; and sentenced him to death. Critical thinking is not always popular.

Nevertheless, critical thinking is more important than ever, especially for those who aspire to leadership in business, industry, science, politics and society. Among the critical thinking questions Sharon should ask are: (i) How much longer do the entrepreneur's batteries last than competing batteries? (ii) Were experiments conducted comparing the entrepreneur's

---

[1] "A brief history of critical thinking" Foundation for Critical Thinking. www.criticalthinking.org downloaded 2/2/2012.

batteries to those of competitors, and if so, are the results available for review? (iii) Which competing batteries where used as the basis of comparison? (iv) Does the entrepreneur have a patent to protect his or her invention? and (v) Are there any disadvantages to the entrepreneur's batteries, for example, do they cost more to produce, or are they larger or heavier than competing batteries? Other issues Sharon should consider are discussed throughout the chapter.

---

**Epistemology**

Epistemology (pronounced i,pistə'mäləjē) is a study of the origin, nature and theory of knowledge. It is a study of the methods of knowing whether something is true and valid. It distinguishes between justified belief and opinion. Equally important, it includes the study of the limits of knowledge.

---

# Architecture of Critical Thinking

Critical thinking is about looking below the surface. Critical thinking is a structured analysis which emphasizes clarity, precision and logic. It is about deconstructing an idea into its elements and questioning the premises upon which a proposition is based. It is about testing a proposition or idea with facts. It is about keeping an open mind, free of bias and preconceived notions. It is about considering alternatives and thinking about the implications of a proposition.

Critical thinking may be divided into six parts: (i) defining the issues, (ii) determining whether something is true, (iii) performing research necessary to make informed judgments, (iv) understanding the forces which shape outcomes, (v) assuring conclusions are reasonable and follow logically from facts and premises, and (vi) thinking about alternatives and projecting consequences. Most of the literature on critical thinking confines itself to various aspects of truthfulness. Is someone's assertion true? Does it follow logically from stated premises? Have the facts been proven? What assumptions are the assertions based on? Are the premises valid? Does the analysis show bias?

The world is messy, and problems rarely present themselves in a clear, concise manner. Often people perceive something is wrong but they don't know exactly what or why. Critical thinking is required to identify underlying problems so effort can be focused on meaningful solutions.

Leaders must search for alternatives and examine potential consequences. Many leaders and decision makers fail to think ahead and as a result, decisions lead to adverse consequences.

Finally, critical thinking must rest on an understanding of the forces which shape outcomes. Unless an architect understands the strength of steel, the force of gravity and wind loads, he or she won't be able to build a skyscraper.

There are forces in business and public policy which sometimes support and sometimes oppose each other. Things often are as they are, because opposing forces balance at some point. If a leader wants to affect change, and does not understand the forces in play, the change that he or she implements is likely to cause forces to rebalance in an unpredictable manner. This happens so often it has been given a name. It is called the **law of unintended consequences**.

## Define the Issue

One of the first things a critical thinker must do is to clarify the issues on which a decision turns. What is an issue? An issue is a problem. An issue is a decision point. An issue is a place where one set of rules is applied, or another set of rules is applied. If one does not understand the problem, how can one possibly solve it?

Most of the time solving a problem or dispute turns on a single underlying issue. Complex problems might resolve into a handful of issues, but many problems turn on a single issue. For example, when a judge is considering whether to admit testimony, he or she will say it depends on whether it meets the rules of evidence which require probity (relevance), credibility (honesty, integrity and trustworthiness), not be unduly inflammatory and not be duplicative. The rules of evidence are well defined, so the judge and attorneys know what the issues are and can focus on them.

The Sarbanes-Oxley Act of 2002 was passed because of the outrageous conduct of a couple of dozen high-ranking executives, in a half a dozen companies. The issue should have been stopping the bad behavior of executives. But the act, as passed, burdens public companies with quarterly audits of internal controls. In large measure, internal controls limit the activities of staff and middle management, not the executives whose mischief was the reason for the act. Because Sarbanes-Oxley did not focus on the real issue, bad executive behavior, it failed to prevent

Bernie Madoff from running a $50 billion Ponzi scheme,[2] failed to prevent Lehman Brothers from making risky investments in mortgage bonds,[3] and didn't prevent MF Global from making risky bets on European sovereign debt.[4]

There is a political drumbeat to 'get off oil' as an energy source. What is the issue? For a very long time, the United States increased oil imports every year. That made the US economy dependent on world oil markets. Oil embargos, as well as cartel actions to restrict oil production, kept prices high, and these were good reasons to reduce dependence on imported oil. The articulated and rational reason to 'get off oil', was so the economy would not be burdened by limited supply and price shocks.

In the last twenty years, politicians have argued the reason to 'get off oil', was that burning fossil fuels, including vast amounts of oil, causes global warming. The issue shifted from the availability of oil at reasonable prices to making oil expensive as a way of reducing carbon dioxide emissions.

A critical thinker would ask whether politicians and others have found the real issue. If they haven't found the real issue, it is like a doctor treating the wrong disease. There may have been a time when US oil reserves were declining, but innovative technologies for oil exploration and extraction, such as fracking, have made the US self-sufficient in oil production.[5] So insulating the economy from the price of imported oil no longer seems like a valid issue.

What about global warming? Despite the protests of politicians, and some scientists, people are challenging the notion of man-made global

---

[2] Weiss, Debra Cassen. 2008. "Bernard Madoff's Alleged $50B Investor Fraud 'a Debacle for the SEC" Securities Law Section. *ABA Journal*. Dec. 15. http://www.abajournal.com/news/article/bernard_madoffs_alleged_50b_investor_f raud_a_debacle_for_the_sec/

[3] Mollenkamp, Carrick, Susanne Craig, Serena NG and Aaron Luchetti. 2008. "Lehman Files for Bankruptcy, Merrill Sold, AIG Seeks Cash," HYPERLINK "http://online.wsj.com/home-page" The Wall Street Journal. Sept. 16. http://online.wsj.com/article/SB122145492097035549.html.

[4] ___ 2011. "MF Global moved customer funds to BNY Mellon – WSJ," Thomson Reuters News Service. Nov. 10. http://www.reuters.com/article/2011/11/19/idUSL3E7MJ00G20111119.

[5] ___. 2011. "New Oil Finds Around the Globe: Will the U.S. Capitalize on Its Oil Resources?" Institute for Energy Research. 1100 H St NW, Suite 400, Washington, DC 20005. Sept.13. www.instituteforenergyresearch.org/2011/09/13/new-oil-finds-around-the-globe-will-the-u-s-capitalize-on-its-oil-resources/

warming. Some have pointed out that the earth was warmer when the Roman Empire flourished, so maybe warming isn't so bad.[6]

Life would be impossible without carbon dioxide, and higher levels of carbon dioxide have proven to promote plant growth. Current carbon dioxide levels are around 400 ppm. However, some scientific research indicates that plants evolved when carbon dioxide levels were 3,000 ppm.[7] Finally, even though the use of fossil fuels has accelerated in the last dozen years, the rise in the earth's temperature has paused. According to the United Kingdom's official weather service there was no discernible change in the earth's temperature between 1998 and 2011.[8] So is the possibility of a warming earth the real issue in reducing dependence on oil?

So, what could be behind the current drum beat to 'get off oil?' **H. L. Mencken**, an early twentieth century journalist and commentator, said: **"The whole aim of practical politics is to keep the populace alarmed by an endless series of hobgoblins, most of them imaginary, and clamoring to be led to safety by politicians."**[9] Is global warming just another in a series of hobgoblins?

Perhaps the issue is economic. Cheap energy drives economic expansion, which creates jobs, produces goods and services and expands the government's tax base. If the real issue is the cost of oil, perhaps more exploration and production is the correct approach, rather than limits on production.

> "The whole aim of practical politics is to keep the populace alarmed by an endless series of hobgoblins, most of them imaginary, and clamoring to be led to safety by politicians."
>
> ~H. L. Mencken

---

[6] McCormick, Michael, Ulf Buntgen, Mark Crane, Edward Cook, Kyle Harper, et al. 2012. "Climate Change During and after the Roman Empire: Reconstructing the Past from Scientific and Historical Evidence," Journal of Interdisciplinary History. XLIII:2 (Autumn) pp.169-220, 174.

[7] Schmidt, Harrison and William Harper. 2013. "In Defense of Carbon Dioxide," Wall Street Journal. May 9. A.19.

[8] ___ 2012. "Met Office 2012 Annual Global Temperature Forecast," United Kingdom, Met Office (the Met Office is the UK's national weather center). http://www.metoffice.gov.uk/news/releases/archive/2011/2012-global-temperature-forecast.

[9] Mencken, H. L. 1918. *In Defense of Women*. Reprinted by Kessinger Publishing, LLC PO Box 1404 Whitefish MT 59937 USA (September 10, 2010)

**A critical thinker keeps asking questions, until he or she understands the issues in play at a deep level.**

## Determine Whether Something is True

People often base their policies, plans or actions on their belief as to the truth of certain facts. A critical thinker never assumes the validity of facts. Critical thinkers seek and test evidence, and get context.

### *Evidence and Verification*

Most people are willing to accept what they see, hear and read as true. There is an old story about a con-man who asks his mark, "Who are you going to believe, me or your lying eyes?" Getting to the truth of a matter is all important, but how does one know whether something is true?

One way is to ask for evidence: 'Show me'. If a person is asked to produce evidence and they get insulted or belligerent, there probably isn't any evidence. Evidence should be credible. A web posting by an unknown figure is not credible, but a posting by a government agency, university, or a well-known non-profit organization, is probably going to be highly credible. Information in academic, peer-reviewed journals is also considered highly credible.

Sharon should ask for proof the entrepreneur's batteries last longer than other batteries. Proof might include lab notes on battery tests, the testing protocol, including how the test was conducted, and the brand name of the batteries used for comparison. Even better, extended life might be documented by an independent laboratory.

Another way to tell if something is the truth is to consider the circumstances. A person may say something that is true but do it in such a way that it leaves an untrue impression.

One stormy night there was a terrible accident. The electricity to a train crossing signal was out, and a driver crossing the tracks didn't see the train in the dark. No one was killed, but the driver of the car sued the railroad. At the trial, a signalman for the railroad insisted that he had given the driver ample warning by waving his lantern back and forth for nearly a minute. He even demonstrated how he'd done it. The court believed his story, and the suit was dismissed.

"Congratulations," the railroad's lawyer said to the signalman, "You did superbly under cross-examination."

"Thanks," he said, "but plaintiff's lawyer had me worried."

"Why?" the railroad's lawyer asked.

"I was afraid he was going to ask if the lantern was lit!"
Did you assume the lantern was lit? Obviously, the court did.

**A critical thinker assumes nothing.**

Another way to determine whether something is true is to ask whether it is consistent with other facts. A detective might ask a suspect where he or she was at the time of the murder. The suspect might say, "At home watching television." The detective might then ask, "What program did you watch, and what happened?"

Yet another way to determine the truth of a matter is to test it. Four college students were returning from Spring break. They knew they had an exam the first day back at school and none of them had studied for it. They agreed to tell the professor they had a flat tire and couldn't get back to school in time for the exam. The professor agreed to give the students a make-up exam and put each of them in a separate room. The exam had only one question on it. Which tire went flat?

**Critical thinkers never accept things at face value. They are skeptical, ask for proof, and try to validate the proof offered.**

*Check the Facts*

One of a builder's partners embezzled $385,000 from a real estate company. The realtor's lawyer sued the builder and his partners on the theory that the money went into their construction project.

The realtor hired an accountant to 'follow the money', and the accountant prepared an impressive hundred-page analysis which consisted mostly of check numbers, payees and amounts. Each partner hired his own lawyer and most of the partner's lawyers were so impressed with the analysis they were ready to concede that the embezzled money probably ended up in the construction project.

However, the lawyer for one of the partners obtained the canceled checks that were the basis of the accountant's report. He then traced them into the report. During cross-examination, he got the accountant to admit that some of the payees in the report were wrong, some of the amounts were wrong, some of the payments had been misclassified, some of the account numbers were wrong, and there were duplicate checks in the analysis. A half hour after the accountant was cross-examined, the case was dismissed.

**A critical thinker checks the facts.**

## *Context*

Facts in insolation mean nothing. Context is needed to give facts life. If a company is growing 20% per year, is that good or bad? It depends. How fast are other companies in the industry growing? If other companies in the industry are growing 50% per year, a 20% growth rate is poor. On the other hand, newspaper sales are rapidly declining. So, in the newspaper business, a growth rate of 5% per year is spectacular. Context is everything.

A man was riding his horse along the road and his dog was running alongside them. The driver of a big old car, hit the dog, hit the horse and threw the man to the ground. The driver settled for the value of the horse, the value of the dog, and the horseman's medical bills and lost wages. The only issue when the horseman sued the driver was the value of his pain and suffering.

At trial, the driver's attorney asked the horseman, "Is it true that Officer Murphy arrived at the scene moments after the accident? And you said to him, 'I never felt better in my life.'"

"Yes sir."

"Your honor, there was no injury here. I move for a dismissal."

"Your honor," the horseman's attorney spoke up. "May I examine my client?" The judge nodded. "After the accident, what happened?"

"Officer Murphy arrived at the scene and saw my horse was suffering so he took out his service revolver and shot my horse in the head. Then Officer Murphy saw my dog was suffering and he shot my dog in the head."

"Then what happened?"

"Officer Murphy walked over to me, holding his revolver in his hand and said, "How do you feel?" And, I said, "I never felt better in my life."

Context is everything. Facts cannot be evaluated, weighted or understood without context.

**A critical thinker probes for context.**

## Perform Research Needed to Understand the Problem

Few problems can be solved with a handful of facts. Either a person must have substantial experience with a subject or he or she must do research to familiarize themselves with the terms, conditions, and issues relating to a type of problem.

A widespread problem in discussions, negotiations, news, and political analysis is that people use ill-defined terms and ill-defined concepts. Without a penetrating understanding of terms and concepts, it is unlikely that any meaningful discussion or analysis can take place. Concepts can be imprecise as well as terms. Research is also necessary to draw well-reasoned conclusions.

### *Clarify Terms*

The Assistant Attorney General of a state was going to suspend a physician's medical license because of a complaint by another physician. The physician's previous lawyer had tried and failed to resolve the case for two years. Digging through the documentation, the physician's new lawyer found the doctor had been accused of 'pirating patients.' Piracy is defined as unlawfully taking property. The premise underlying this prosecution was that physicians have a property interest in their patients. If physicians have a property interest in people, can they be bought, sold, traded, or leased?

In the legal brief submitted to the State's Attorney General's office, the new attorney said, that if the state's position was that physicians have a property interest in their patients, the public should know about it, and the medical profession should be regulated like any other trade, rather than receiving the special deference it now enjoys. Several weeks later, the Attorney General's office sent back a letter that said, "Never mind. Case dismissed."

**A critical thinker clarifies terms and asks how facts and premises lead to conclusions.**

### *Challenge Authority*

Challenge the right of someone to implement a rule or set a standard against which conduct is being measured. Often, people, governments and businesses assert rights they do not have. Research helps determine whether people, businesses or governments have the authority they say they do.

It is common for landlords to put a clause in leases that says, "If the tenant goes bankrupt, the landlord has the right to terminate the lease." Even though a lease is an enforceable contract, bankruptcy law overrides lease terms and will allow a bankrupt tenant to continue its leasehold as long as the tenant pays the rent. When bankrupt tenants fail to challenge the landlord's authority, they end up with the cost and inconvenience of a move for no good reason.

A lot of real estate law revolves around townships trying to regulate businesses without a proper legal basis for doing so. A builder tried unsuccessfully to get building permits in a rural town for twenty-five years. The town wanted to keep its rural character, and township officials resisted development. On the other hand, builders have a right to use their land as they please, within the bounds of the law.

The last lawyer on the case met with the township solicitor and the solicitor gave the lawyer four pages of things he wanted the builder to do before the town would issue permits. The list was one of many the builder had tried to comply with over the years, and this was merely a delaying tactic. The lawyer sued the town to get the client the building permits.

At a meeting in the judge's chambers, the lawyer said the builder would comply with any statute or ordinance in effect when he first made his permit application twenty-five years ago. The judge said that was reasonable, and the town solicitor confessed that twenty-five years ago, there were virtually no requirements. The builder got his permits.

The builder's lawyer challenged the premise that the rural township had the authority to make unlimited demands. By challenging authority, the builder got his permits.

**Critical thinkers do enough research so that they can challenge authority.**

> "The first responsibility of every citizen is to question authority."
>
> ~ Benjamin Franklin

## Balancing Forces

*Ask Why*

One of the most powerful things a critical thinker can do, is to ask **why?** Things are what they are, because opposing forces balance. Inertia causes things to move in a straight line. So why doesn't the earth fly off into space? The sun's gravity keeps pulling the earth in. Inertia and gravity balance.

Banks need money to make loans. They get money by paying interest on deposits. If they pay a high rate of interest they will get more deposits than they need. If they pay too low a rate they will not get enough deposits. Banks set their interest rate at a point where there is a balance between encouraging people to save so they have money to lend, but not having more money than needed for loans.

Politicians say the country is addicted to oil. But is the cost and efficiency of gasoline powered cars versus electric cars a factor? Is the convenience or inconvenience of public transportation a factor? Is the desire for people to live in the suburbs, rather than in the city, a factor? These forces balance to make gasoline powered vehicles the dominant form of transportation. If, on the other hand, batteries were three times more efficient, and cost one third as much, that balance might shift in favor of electric cars.

A Nash Equilibrium is a more formal and mathematically rigorous statement of the principle that forces balance. John Forbes Nash won a Nobel Prize for developing the Nash equilibrium.[10] See the emphasis box on the next page for a concrete example of a Nash equilibrium.

**A critical thinker finds the forces in play and how they balance.**

## Reasonable Conclusions

### *Do Premises Support Conclusions?*

Most propositions are built on a series of premises. A premise is a logical starting point for an argument. Some premises can be traced back to verifiable facts, figures, rules, laws or principles. Other premises are little more than assumptions about how things work. Sometimes something has been heard so often people believe it is true. One element of critical thinking is to look at the premises underlying a proposition.

A large insurance company wanted to buy a software company. The acquisitions department asked a manager to be on the due diligence team. Due diligence is the process of analyzing a company before it is purchased, to make sure the seller's representations are accurate.

The insurance company had four thousand programmers, so the manager asked why the acquisition department thought it was a good idea to buy the software company. The head of the acquisition team said the insurance company's programmers were slow and didn't develop good quality software.

---

[10]    2007. "Nash Equilibrium," International Encyclopedia of the Social Sciences. 2nd. Ed. Pp540-542.

The manager asked, "Why not hire the software company's best programmers? Even if their salaries were doubled, it would cost a lot less than buying the company." The head of acquisitions said their programmers wouldn't want to work for a large company. Set aside for a moment the fact that if the insurance company bought the software company, its programmers would still be working for a large company with all the restrictions that entails.

---

### Nash Equilibrium and the Balance of Forces

A Nash equilibrium is a sophisticated analysis of balancing forces. The Nash equilibrium is the strategy each player would take if he, she, or it, knew the strategies of all other players. It involves the probabilities of various strategies and their expected payoffs.

For example, suppose there are five pizza parlors in town. Pizzas are all more or less alike. Business people want to charge the highest price they can without losing business. Suppose the average price of a large pie is $15. If one or two parlors raised their price to $20, they would lose business, as customers switched to lower price sellers. If a pizza parlor lowered its price to $10 it could gain more customers, but the lower price would erode profits.

Now suppose one pizza parlor was in the center of town, in a trendy shopping area, and they could charge $18 without losing any customers. Suppose one pizza parlor was five miles out of town and could only charge $12 per pizza without losing customers and the others maintained their $15 price. The five pizza parlors are in a Nash equilibrium because each is optimizing its strategy taking into account the actions of all the other players.

If other players change their strategy, or if the payoffs change, a new Nash equilibrium might be established. The Nash equilibrium is part of Game Theory, which is a method of developing and testing strategies.

---

The next question the manager asked was, "Why are they up for sale?" The head of acquisitions said they were for sale because they were having cash flow problems. The manager asked why they were having cash flow problems. The head of acquisitions said the software company's customers weren't paying their bills.

The manager asked why customers weren't paying their bills. The head of acquisitions said customers stopped paying their bills because the software company's software wasn't working properly. So, the manager asked again, "Why do you want to buy this software company?"

Hunter's hunt; fisherman fish; flyers fly, and the acquisitions department buys companies. The department had already convinced senior management to buy the software company and assumed the due diligence team was simply going to rubber stamp their decision. But critical thinking in the form of probing questions challenged the rational for the acquisition and it was called off which saved the insurance company tens of millions of dollars.

**A critical thinker checks whether premises support conclusions.**

*Search for a clear link between cause and effect.*

Deconstructing an argument begins with clarifying terms and separating the relevant from the irrelevant. Parents say, "Eat your dinner. There are children starving in xyz country." How will more food get to the children in xyz country if you eat your dinner? Whether you eat your dinner or not is irrelevant to starving children in another country.

Politicians say, "People can't afford gas to get to work. We need a greater investment in wind and solar power." Is there any prospect that wind or solar power will get you to work in the next twenty or thirty years? And even if a solar-wind car is built, will it be affordable or will it cost more than existing cars plus gas? Isn't solar-wind energy irrelevant for getting to work in the foreseeable future? For a hundred years people have been saying, "Electric cars are the cars of the future... and they always will be." But, electric cars are now proving to be practical and not a future dream. A critical thinker keeps an open mind.

Politicians and pundits say, millions are out of work, we need to increase taxes on the rich. But how exactly will taxing the rich create jobs? What is the step by step process that connects higher taxes with more jobs?

Many statements made by politicians, business leaders and commentators involve 'magical thinking.' Magical thinking is defined as a belief in forms of causation with no known physical basis. There was a time when a rabbit's foot key chain was considered a good luck charm.

But since there is no physical link between a rabbit's foot and a good outcome, good luck charms are an example of magical thinking.[11]

Young children engage in magical thinking all the time. For example, they may ask Santa Claus for a pony, or believe in fairy tales like Jack and the Beanstalk. By the time most children reach their teen years, they develop a more pragmatic, cause and effect sense of reality. Yet a handful of people reach adulthood, and even become successful politicians and commentators, and still believe in magical thinking. For example, they think they can promote job creation by vilifying businesses, or lower gas prices by increasing the tax on oil companies.

**Critical thinkers demand a clear link between cause and effect.**

## Consider the Widest Possible Set of Options

### *Change the Framework of the Discussion*

Often, people get so caught up in looking at a problem a certain way, they reach a dead end. This is a problem when negotiating contracts. One party may have a set of objectives that seems at odds with the other party's objectives. A critical thinker might ask, "Is there another way to view this issue?"

A physician wanted his attorney to negotiate a contract with a hospital that gave him eight weeks' vacation. The hospital only wanted to give the physician four weeks. The hospital administrator explained that no one else in the hospital got eight weeks' vacation and that if he gave one physician eight weeks' vacation, every physician would demand eight weeks. The hospital wanted the physician's expertise and was willing to pay for it. The physician's goal and the hospital administrator's goal seemed at odds.

The physician's attorney crafted a contract where the hospital agreed to pay a certain sum of money for 44 weeks of work. The money was to be paid evenly throughout the year. The contract did not give the physician any vacation time.

Were the hospital administrator's goals met? Yes. He contracted for the physician's services without setting the precedent of giving him eight weeks' vacation. Were the physician's objectives met? Yes. He got the money he wanted and didn't have to work eight weeks per year.

---

[11] Kurie, Peter. 2010. "Inventions, Innovations, Ideas," Princeton Report on Knowledge. Vol.3 No.2 Oct.27.
http://www.princeton.edu/prok/issues/3-2/inventions.xml

**A critical thinker considers the widest possible range of possibilities.**

*Ask, what if I do the opposite?*

A critical thinker keeps his or her mind open to all possibilities. What if A happened before B? What if C costs more than D? Keeping an open mind to all the possibilities helps reduce the likelihood of introducing bias into an analysis and helps anticipate consequences and may lead to better options.

A critical thinker also considers all possible courses of action before deciding what to do. One possible course of action is to do the opposite of what is expected.

Before the United States entered World War II, Britain was desperately fighting a defensive air campaign. They knew that once Germany achieved air dominance, the invasion of England was weeks or days away. Every plane, and every pilot, was important, but planes and pilots were in short supply.

One way to increase the odds of survival for a British fighter plane was to armor it. But armor plate is heavy and slows planes down. In air-to-air combat, speed is life, so loading up planes with armor seemed counter-productive.

Many of the planes returning from combat had been badly shot up. The British carefully recorded the location of every bullet hole in every plane. Before long a map appeared. It was a map of all the places a plane could be shot without bringing it down. Armor plate was then re-arranged so it only protected those locations where a bullet would bring down a plane.

The British did the opposite. Rather than looking for places to put armor plate, they looked for places it wasn't needed.

There is a natural tendency to cut costs when a company is in trouble. Layoffs and advertising cuts are common. Circuit City laid off its knowledgeable higher paid sales staff in favor of less-knowledgeable staff who weren't as good at providing customers with technical advice. Circuit City customers went to Best Buy, where experienced employees could give advice. Circuit City went bankrupt.[12] Best Buy did the opposite of Circuit City and spent more on sales staff and sales staff training. Best Buy is thriving.

---

[12] Galuszka, Peter, 2008. "Eight Reasons Why Circuit City Went Bankrupt," CBS News Interactive. Nov.13 www.cbsnews.com/8301-505125_162-28241493/eight-reasons-why-circuit-city-went-bankrupt/

Even though the opposite is not always the right answer, **a critical thinker always considers the opposite.**

## Consider the Consequences

### *Think About Secondary Impacts and Ripple Effects*

Few people consider the implications of what they want to do or project the consequences of their actions. The law of unintended consequences says that while one might do something with the best intentions, there are often negative side effects that should have been anticipated.

Congress decided to 'stick it' to the rich by putting a 10% surtax on the sale of yachts. Sales at Viking Yachts dropped to practically zero, and it laid off 1,332 people (95% of its workforce). The rich believed a special tax on yachts unfairly targeted them, simply because they were rich. Their response to this perceived injustice was to stop buying US-built yachts. Who really suffered when the government decided to 'stick it to the rich', the 'rich', or the workers?

**A critical thinker would consider all the consequences of a policy.**

### *What if we ran with a proposal all the way?*

Sometimes the way to test an idea for reasonableness and unintended consequences is to think about what would happen if the idea were pushed to extremes. The French limit the work week to 35 hours. They believe that companies' have a fixed block of work to do. If that work is sliced into 40-hour work weeks a company will need a certain number of people. But, if they slice the work into 35-hour work weeks, companies will need to hire more people, thereby creating more jobs. If a 35-hour work week, is good, why not have a 30-hour work week? Why not a 25-hour work week?

A critical thinker would ask questions like, where do jobs come from? Why do companies hire workers? Is it true that there is a well-defined amount of work that needs to be completed? Is spreading work across more people more cost effective for an employer or less cost effective? Is the decision to hire based on the relationship between the valued added by an employee and the employee's cost? If the work week is reduced, the amount of value an employee contributes is reduced. Will reducing an employee's value encourage a company to hire more people, or discourage it from hiring?"

Some years ago, Nobel Prize-winning economist Milton Friedman visited Asia and saw thousands of people digging a canal with shovels. Dr. Friedman asked why they didn't use bulldozers. His host said the project would employ more people if hand shovels where used. Then Dr. Friedman asked, "Why not use spoons?"[13]

**A critical thinker tests the consequences of ideas by pushing them to extremes.**

*If some will be harmed, will any be helped?*

A critical thinker looks at the benefits and burdens of all parties when making a decision or instituting a policy. There is a certain group of people who don't like Wal-Mart and fight to keep Wal-Marts out of towns. The argument is that Wal-Mart, with its enormous purchasing power, makes it impossible for small, independent retailers to compete. Small retailers will be harmed, but will anyone be helped?

Consumers generally benefit from Wal-Mart's low prices. Price competition engendered by Wal-Mart resulted in market-wide price reductions estimated at $263 billion in 2004.[14] Those who want to keep Wal-Marts out of towns want to pick economic winners and losers. They are choosing small businesses as winners, and consumers as losers. Is that fair? Or is it politics as usual?

**A critical thinker considers the benefits and burdens to all parties.**

## Disagree Without Being Disagreeable

Critical thinking is **not** about being disagreeable. It's about analysis. It's about digging below the surface; it's about clarifying terms; validating facts and premises; keeping an open mind; considering alternatives; determining whether conclusions flow logically from facts and premises;

---

[13] Roberts, Russell. 2011. "Obama vs. ATMs: Why Technology Doesn't Destroy Jobs," The Wall Street Journal. Opinion.
http://online.wsj.com/article/SB10001424052702304070104576399704275939640.html
[14] "The Price Impact of Wal-Mart: An Update Through 2006." GLOBAL INSIGHT, Inc.
http://www.globalinsight.com/MultiClientStudy/MultiClientStudyDetail2438.htm

and considering implications. Aristotle is reputed to have said, "It is the mark of an educated mind to be able to entertain a thought without accepting it." Consider the following guidelines when analyzing another person's position.

(i)     Listen carefully to the other person's position. Unless you understand what they are saying, your analysis will be incomplete.

(ii)    You don't need to tell people their argument or position is stupid, misinformed, or naïve. Ask probing questions and share facts they might not have. Let them see the flaws in their argument.

(iii)   At the end of the day, it's all right to disagree. Not everyone has to agree with everyone else. Reserve your right to disagree and walk away.

(iv)    When the other side is being disagreeable, treat them with kindness.

A physician wanted to sell his medical practice to a hospital and hired a lawyer to help with the negotiation. The physician was adamant about getting $750,000 for his practice and vowed not to take a penny less. While waiting for the hospital's administrator, the physician got more and more upset at the thought the hospital was going to try to buy his practice on the cheap. As the administrator walked through the door, the physician practically leapt over a table to get his hands around the administrator's throat and choke him into submission. Fortunately, the physician's lawyer grabbed him with both hands and said, "Let's hear what the man has to say."

The administrator said, "I've conferred with the hospital board, and our best and final offer is $1.2 million. Take it or leave it." Listening always pays. This time it paid an additional $450,000.

**Critical thinking is not about being disagreeable. Listen to what others have to say. Reserve your right to disagree and be polite.**

---

**Elements of Critical Thinking**

Define the issue

Search for the truth

Perform research

Search for the forces balancing to reach equilibrium

Analyze whether conclusions are reasonable

Consider the consequences

Disagree without being disagreeable

---

## Scientific Method

The scientific method is a specialized application of critical thinking. Its goal is to explain, in a logical, rational and verifiable manner, how things work. With knowledge of how things work, it is possible to make predictions as to likely outcomes of various choices. Should one build a bridge out of steel or concrete? This very practical question depends on knowledge of how steel behaves, how concrete behaves, the body the bridge must cross and the cost of alternatives.

The scientific method is an orderly search for explanatory theories. **Theories are only good if they are predictive.** An idea or hypothesis as to how something works does not rise to the level of a theory until it is tested time and again. And here we run into an oddity of the scientific method. No number of experiments can prove a theory correct, but one experiment in which the theory fails to predict an outcome, can prove the theory invalid or at least incomplete. This is a very high standard, but an important one. This standard makes the scientific method self-correcting.

Isaac Newton formulated a law of gravity that explains almost everything. It explains how objects fall, how the path of bullets and cannon balls curve in flight, and it explains the motion of the moon and planets. Almost. Mercury, the planet closest to the sun does not behave exactly as predicted by Newton. While Newton's law of gravity is useful for most things, it doesn't explain everything.

Albert Einstein developed the general theory of relativity which, in most everyday situations, provides the same answers as Newton's law of gravity. But, in extreme situations such a planet orbiting close to a star like Mercury, general relativity explains behavior more accurately. The predictions of general relativity have been tested thousands of times and the predictions have always been accurate. That is still not proof it will always work. If it fails to make an accurate prediction one time, there will be a search for an ever more refined theory of gravity.

The scientific method generally proceeds through several steps: (i) observation, (ii) hypothesis, (iii) experimentation, (iv) data collection, and (v) conclusion.

## Observation

Observation is collecting information. Observation goes beyond mere watching and measuring, to researching available information, asking questions to clarify what observations mean, and understanding the context in which observations are being made. Observation includes sharing information with others and getting their input.

Observation usually ignites a spark of interest in a thing, event or circumstance. For example, a doctor might notice that bald men taking a certain blood pressure medicine start re-growing their hair. This might spark an interest in how baldness might be cured using blood pressure medicine.

## Hypothesis

With enough observations and information, one might begin to formulate a hypothesis. A **hypothesis** is an idea about how things work. A hypothesis might mature into a theory if sufficient experimental evidence supports the hypothesis.

## Experiment

To determine the validity of a hypothesis, an investigator creates an experiment. Suppose you were running a pharmaceutical company and were trying to decide whether to invest $50 million in a new drug to cure the xyz disease. Suppose a certain percentage of people with the disease got well without any treatment. The company's scientists might set up an experiment to test the hypothesis that the new drug cures the disease more often than the disease is cured without treatment. Such an experiment would involve a **double-blind study** in which one group of people are given the drug, and another group of people are given a placebo. A placebo is something that looks like a drug but has no active ingredients. A double-blind study is one in which neither the patents nor physicians know whether patients are getting the medicine being tested or placebos. If the cure rate with the medicine being tested is higher than with placebos, the next question is whether this is a random occurrence. Statistics, based on sample size and cure rates, could be used to determine whether there is a **statistically significant difference** in cure rates between those taking the medicine and those taking the placebo. Statistical significance implies the odds of a result occurring by random chance are low.

Other kinds of experiments are done to test other kinds of hypotheses. Suppose for example, observation shows that a certain kind of chemical reaction stores and releases more electrons for a longer time than other chemical reactions. An engineer might construct a hypothesis as to why that is and devise an experiment to test this hypothesis.

One of the hallmarks of an accepted theory, is that the results of an experiment can be replicated by anyone who follows the experimental design. If one investigator gets a certain result, but other investigators cannot, the theory will lose credibility and eventually be rejected. This is part of the self-correcting mechanism built into the scientific method.

## Data Collection

The nature and quantity of data collected is important. Measurement errors, collecting the wrong kind of data, or insufficient data can invalidate an experiment. For example, when testing a drug, data collection is meaningless if not all the people in the study showed the same initial symptoms, or if people were at dissimilar stages of a disease, or if progress was measured differently for different people.

When experimenting as to whether one battery design is superior to another, it is important to know whether the experiment tested voltage, current or power. There might be a difference in battery life, if batteries were used to power electronic devices, as compared to electric car motors. The total power produced might vary with the frequency and depth of charging, or with the temperature at which batteries were operated or stored. Collecting the right data is an important part of the scientific method.

## Conclusion about the Hypothesis

Conclusions should follow logically from the results of the experiment. Conclusions should consider limits in the experimental design and the context of the experiment. Additional experiments may strengthen the conviction that the hypothesis is correct, and, with enough experimental evidence, a hypothesis might mature into a theory. A theory is a generally accepted formulation as to how things work.

A theory is only good if it can predict outcomes. Experience or subsequent experiments might identify flaws, limitations or inadequacies in a theory. In which case, it would have to be revised or refuted entirely.

## Revisions, and Iterations

The scientific method is about discovering new knowledge. Such discovery never moves in a straight line. A hypothesis may lead to an experiment with unexpected results. That may cause investigators to observe more, or different, data and formulate a new hypothesis. A new hypothesis may lead to a new experiment, collecting different data. If the results are still unexpected, investigators may begin the process again.

---

### Scientific Method

The Scientific Method is a systematic method of accumulating knowledge in a way that conclusions can be verified. Steps in this method include:

Observation,

Hypothesis,

Experimentation,

Data collection,

Conclusion.

Revise Hypotheses, and Try Again

Scientific theories are only useful if they are predictive. No amount of testing can prove a theory. However, one adverse result can disprove a theory or at least indicate it is incomplete.

---

# Critical Thinking in Writing

Critical thinking can lead to better writing. A writer might start with a statement, and then ask him or herself what a reader would like to know about it. For example, a proposition might be:

**High tax states spend more on higher education than low tax states.**

Critical thinking does not mean it's your job as a writer to support or defend a proposition. Critical thinking involves evaluating the proposition and letting the facts and logic take you where they will. A good writer might start out on one side of a proposition and be convinced by facts and logic that he or she should be on the other side.

What would a reader want to know if he or she were reading an article regarding this proposition? One might ask: How is a high tax state defined? Does it mean high sales taxes? High income taxes? Is it the average tax burden for each resident of the state? One might also ask: How is higher education defined? Is it high school and up? Community college and up?

Are total expenditures a useful measure? California might spend twenty times as much as Montana but might have forty times the population. If I said a state spends a certain amount per resident on higher education, does that mean anything without context? Would a table ranking states on per resident educational expenditures be useful?

A critically thinking reader might also want to know what the payoff is in spending more on higher education. Does it simply enrich educational institutions, or does it result in higher incomes for residents?

Starting with a proposition, one should think about all the questions that flow from that proposition. What are its implied premises? What do they mean? How can they be tested? What facts are available? What forces are balanced against each other?

These questions should provide the basis for research. It is much easier to research a subject when one knows what one is looking for. Given the facts, the questions, the premises and the proposition, one can begin to write.

Perhaps the proposition is a valid one, then you can write about how everything flows together to support the proposition. Perhaps your research will lead you to believe the proposition is false, or at least wildly inaccurate. That's OK. You will still have the research to write a logical, fact-filled paper.

# Conclusion

Critical thinking is important to separate the true from the illusory, the logical from the illogical, and the well-founded from that which is built on sand. Critical thinking questions common beliefs and explanations in a search for that which is true, logical and reasonable. Critical thinking is important in identifying the real issue, and it is important in negotiating, and planning.

Critical thinking involves: (i) defining the issues (ii) determining whether something is true, (iii) performing research necessary to make informed judgments, (iv) understanding the forces which shape outcomes, (v) assuring conclusions are reasonable and follow logically from facts and premises, and (vi) thinking about alternatives and projecting consequences.

Critical thinking is not about being disagreeable. It is about analysis. A critical thinker doesn't need to tell others their argument or position is stupid, misinformed, or naïve. When the other side is being disagreeable, treat them with kindness.

Critical thinking is essential in negotiations where success or failure often revolves around a thorough understanding of the issues. What are the objectives of each party? What do they really want? Often what they really want, and what they say they want, are different. A critical thinker must ask probing questions to identify a party's underlying goals and objectives. Finding out what the parties want goes directly to defining the issue or issues on which a negotiation or analysis turns.

The scientific method is a specialized application of critical thinking. Its goal is to explain, in a logical, rational and verifiable manner, how things work. With a knowledge of how things work, it is possible to make predictions as to likely outcomes of various choices. The scientific method generally proceeds through several steps: (i) observation, (ii) hypothesis, (iii) experimentation, (iv) data collection, and (v) conclusion. Often experimental results are unexpected, and a new hypothesis must be constructed. This new hypothesis might require additional experimentation, data collection and a new conclusion.

Critical thinking can lead to better writing. A writer might start with a statement and then ask him or herself what a reader would like to know about the proposition to make a fair and balanced analysis. Such questions provide the basis for research about a topic. It is much easier to research a subject when one knows what one is looking for. Given the facts, the questions, the premises and the proposition, one will then have the information needed to write a logical, fact-filled paper.

# Appendix 7a Negotiation

Negotiations arise when two or more parties each have something they want and are trying to minimize what they must give up to get it. While critical thinking is essential in negotiation, not all parties to a negotiation think critically. Some are driven by emotion and some fail to understand that to get something they must give something. Many have not thought through the implications of what they are demanding; some argue for the sake of argument. Negotiation is a high art, but the following principles combined with elements of critical thinking can result in a deal which creates value for all parties.

## Best Alternative to a Negotiated Agreement (BATNA)

Critical thinkers know that things come to rest where forces balance. The same is true in negotiation. Negotiators analyze forces in terms of the Best Alternative to a Negotiated Agreement (BATNA).

Suppose Kathy wants to buy a five-year-old Mercedes Benz Roadster from Bob's Autoworld, and Bob's price is $50,000. Kathy is willing to pay up to $47,000 and makes an opening bid of $45,000. Bob laughs at her and says he will give her $1,000 off the list price.

If Kathy knows a comparable Roadster is for sale somewhere else for $47,000, buying the other Roadster is her BATNA. There is no reason to buy from Bob if he won't come down in price. But suppose Kathy's research found that the next best price on a comparable Roadster was $51,000? Then her alternatives are: (i) accept Bob's $49,000 price, or (ii) walk away and look for an older car, or a different brand.

What are Bob's alternatives? Bob is probably weighing the profit he can make from Kathy with the risk he will have to hold the car for another buyer, a buyer who may not offer more than Kathy. If Bob has done his homework, he may know that comparable five-year-old Roadsters sell for $48,000. His BATNA is to walk away from Kathy's offer of $45,000 and hold out for a more typical offer. Each of the parties has a BATNA.

Now, Kathy's BATNA looks more attractive than Bob's because she is certain she can get what she wants for $47,000 elsewhere. Bob is playing the odds he can sell for $48,000.

Over the course of the negotiation, each party's BATNA can change. Suppose Kathy gets a call saying the $47,000 Roadster has been sold. Her new BATNA is the $51,000 Roadster she knows is for sale. Bob's BATNA hasn't changed. But, if he knows Kathy's BATNA is the $51,000 Roadster, he has no reason to drop his price below $49,000.

Kathy's initial move might have been to say, "Bob, I can buy your Roadster for $47,000 or I can buy the one down the street for the same price. What do you want to do?"

Bob's BATNA is to wait for a buyer willing to pay the average price of $48,000, a buyer who might not appear for days, weeks or months. Bob might say, "I'll sell you this Roadster and throw in a 3-year warranty for $48,000." Now it's much less clear whether Kathy's BATNA is better than Bob's offer.

## Negotiating Points

Poor negotiators get hung up on price. Good negotiators look beyond price to other points that may change their BATNA or the other parties' BATNA.

Larry is a 21-year-old college student who has been working at Wal-Mart for six months. Kathy is a 31-year-old accountant who has been in her job for ten years. Bob's Autoworld has been having difficulty selling the Mercedes because most of its customers are looking for cars under $20,000. Larry and Kathy do not know each other, but they appear at Bob's Autoworld on the same day, and each wants to buy the Roadster. Bob's price for the car is $50,000; Kathy offers $47,000; Larry offers $49,000. Bob wants to accept Larry's offer of $49,000 and his BATNA is Kathy's offer of $47,000.

Kathy wants to change Bob's BATNA. She asks, "Bob, how is Larry going to finance his purchase? He's just a college student." Bob asks whether Larry's parents will cosign a loan note, and Larry says no.

How has Bob's BATNA changed? Even though car dealers say they offer financing, what they do is to get a buyer to sign a loan note, and then the dealer sells the note to a finance company at a discount. Without some assurance the buyer is willing and able to pay, no finance company will buy the note. Of course, Bob could lend the purchase price to Larry personally, but that is very risky since Larry doesn't have a track record at a well-paying job. Without a co-signer, Bob's best option is to try to sell the Roadster for its fair market value of $48,000. This entails waiting to see whether some other buyer appears. His BATNA is still to sell to Kathy for $47,000.

Kathy knows that Bob will have to discount any loan note used to finance the sale. Kathy estimates the loan note will have to be discounted by 5% to be attractive to a finance company. Kathy makes an all-cash offer of $46,550 which is the $49,000 Bob offered to sell the car for, less the 5% discount it will cost Bob when he sells the loan note to a finance company. Now Bob's BATNA is to wait for someone who hasn't done their homework and who is willing to purchase the car at above the fair market value of $48,000. The prospect of waiting indefinitely for a less-educated buyer is unappealing and Bob takes the deal.

## Preparation

Often parties can't reach a mutually satisfying agreement because one or more of the parties fails to understand the situation. If the matter is technical, make sure you understand the technology in play; if it is economic, understand the economics; if it is political, understand people's goals and motives. All these factors affect negotiations. If the matter is legal, make sure you understand the law, the facts, and how courts have applied the law to the facts in similar situations. Make sure you understand the consequences of any potential deal. Know your facts, be clear about your goals, and know the other party's goals.

Research what others have done in similar situations. For example, many personal injury suits are settled by looking at what juries have awarded for similar injuries in the past. Negotiations might also be informed by historical contract terms, financial ratios, or trade practices.

Bob's research provides information on average selling price. Kathy's research includes the selling price of comparable cars and knowledge of auto financing.[15]

## Goals

Unless you and your client understand exactly what you, he, she, or it wants, negotiations will go nowhere. Suppose a client says, "the list price of this car is $60,000. Negotiate a better deal for me." Unless the client defines 'a better deal' there is little chance of success. If you negotiate 2% off list price, they may say, "I'm disappointed. I wanted 5% off." But, if you had originally negotiated 5% off list price the client may say, "I'm disappointed. I wanted 7% off." It's common for clients not to know exactly what they want; they only know they want 'more'. Unless the parties have well defined goals, negotiations are likely to go around and around with no resolution and a lot of time wasted.

Managing client expectations is a key to setting goals. When negotiating for a new car, one might go to TrueCar[16] which provides the

---

[15] Beagrie, Scott. 2003. "How to Negotiate, Personnel *Today.* Martin Couzins, Ed. 11/4. Pp21-22.

average price customers paid. There are a number of services that analyze jury awards. Such services can help manage client expectations as well as negotiations with insurance companies. When negotiating to buy a company, things get much more complicated. See Chapter 14: Company Valuations.

One element of goal setting is called the **negotiating range**. One should go into any negotiation with both an initial offer, and the best offer one is willing to make before walking away. The initial offer must have some reasonable basis, otherwise the other party will think you are not serious and will stop negotiating. On the other hand, there must be some well-defined point at which one is willing to walk away; otherwise one loses all negotiating power. This is true in purchasing real estate, cars, trucks and businesses. The walk-away point is the BATNA.[17]

## Other Party's Goals

One of the hardest things in the world is to see things from someone else's point of view. In negotiation, success or failure often revolves around a thorough understanding of the objectives of the other party. Often what parties really want and what they say they want, are different. A critical thinker must ask probing questions to identify a party's underlying goals and objectives. Sometimes people think they are talking about the same thing, but just talk past each other. And while some people are good at asking probing questions, few are good at listening to what the other party says. Finding out what the other party wants goes directly to defining the issue or issues on which a negotiation turns. This is analogous to defining the issues in critical thinking.[18]

It is both polite and strategically advantageous to let the other party speak first. Sometimes what they are asking for is something you can give, and what they are willing to offer will satisfy you, or your client's goals. When the other side offers something in your negotiating range, accept it. Many a deal has been lost because one party gave the other what it needed, only to have that party move the goalpost.[19]

---

[16] TrueCar. 2018. TrueCar Inc. Santa Monica, CA www.truecar.com

[17] Rooney, Ben. 2002. "How to Negotiate," *Management Today*. June 1. http://www.managementtoday.co.uk/news/407272/NEGOTIATE/?DCMP=ILC-SEARCH

[18] Malhotra, Deepak and Max H. Bazerman. 2007. "Investigative Negotiation," *Harvard Business Review*. Sept. pp73-78.

[19] Rooney, Ben. 2002. "How to Negotiate," *Management Today*. June 1.

A common question to ask is: "What do you need to get out of this deal?" The answer is likely to include a lot of posturing and big numbers, but the answer may also include useful information.

An American company wanted an exclusive contract to buy all the output of a European company. That output was two hundred thousand pounds a year. The American company didn't want its competition to have this secret ingredient. The European manufacturer said it wouldn't sign any exclusive deal. The American company was about to offer a higher price and guaranteed minimum purchases, when its negotiator asked why the European company resisted the exclusive contract. It turned out a friend of the President of the European company was buying a thousand pounds of the material for his company each year and the President didn't want to jeopardize his friendship. The negotiator offered a carve-out for sales to that one specific company and negotiated an exclusive contract to purchase the rest of the company's output. Price isn't everything.[20]

## Give Something to Get Something

Negotiation is a two-way street. Once it is clear what the other party wants or needs, a good negotiator will try to give it to him or her, without impairing his or her own position. In the end, it might be prudent to make minor concessions, or give up peripheral matters to achieve one's main goal. It's rare when all parties get everything they want. An excellent strategy for determining what is most important to the other party is to offer alternatives. "I will give 10 X and Y, or I will give one X and two Y."[21] Offering alternatives also make you look reasonable.

## Consider Negotiation Design

Change the design of the game. Make moves away from the table. Involve other stakeholders - governments, protest groups, lobbies, and financial institutions - to make the other party's BATNA unappealing and more costly.

---

http://www.managementtoday.co.uk/news/407272/NEGOTIATE/?DCMP=ILC-SEARCH
[20] Rooney, Ben. 2002. "How to Negotiate," *Management Today*. June 1.
http://www.managementtoday.co.uk/news/407272/NEGOTIATE/?DCMP=ILC-SEARCH
[21] Rooney, Ben. 2002. "How to Negotiate," *Management Today*. June 1.
http://www.managementtoday.co.uk/news/407272/NEGOTIATE/?DCMP=ILC-SEARCH

Find a way to raise the other party's stake in a negotiated agreement. Involving other parties can improve your BATNA and worsen the other party's. This is at the heart of negotiation design.[22]

---

**Change the BATNA**

Enhance your BATNA and make the other party's BATNA worse. Insurance companies often deny claims because they have superior bargaining power compared to the average policy holder. If a policy holder does nothing but complain, they may not get the result that they want. The insurance company's BATNA is to pay nothing and put up with a complaining policy holder.

However, if a policy holder hires a lawyer, the lawyer will know when insurance companies are required to pay claims as a matter of law. That will make the insurance company's BATNA considerably

---

## Confidence Building

Sometimes parties have a bad history among themselves, so trust is lacking. In such circumstances, it might be necessary to do some confidence building before the main negotiating issues can be addressed.[23]

Allison Company has a contract to supply Baker Company with 10,000 motors. There were 50 defective motors in the first batch of 500. Baker might say, "We need a reliable supplier, so we are going to terminate the contract." Baker claimed Allison breached the contract, so it is null and void. Baker's BATNA is to purchase motors elsewhere and accept the risk that Allison will sue for breach of contract.

Allison wants to hold Baker to the contract. Allison's BATNA might be to sue Baker, but litigation is expensive and uncertain. If Allison were smart, it might say, "Agree to accept another 1,000 motors from us, and if the defect rate is greater than 0.1%, we will cancel the contract."

Allison is trying to do some confidence building. It is also providing Baker with a means for exiting the contract without litigation and setting the kind of high performance standard Baker needs in a supplier. Allison is creating a less risky, less costly BATNA for Baker.

---

[22] Lax, David A. and James K. Sebenius. 2003. "3-D Negotiation: Playing the Whole Game," Harvard Business Review. Nov. pp.65-74.
[23] Malhotra, Deepak and Max H. Bazerman. 2007. "Investigative Negotiation," *Harvard Business Review*. Sept. pp73-78.

## Think About Implementation

Often contract disputes arise because contracts are so complicated the parties have a completely different understanding of their duties. Contracts should be as short and simple as possible. After all, the Constitution of the United States is only about twenty-four pages long. Million-dollar contracts have been reduced to one page. The contract should specify what each party is supposed to do, when they are supposed to do it, provide price, quantity, specifications, and any quality control standards that are relevant.

There is an unfortunate tendency for negotiators to press every advantage. But, a signed agreement won't work in practice unless it creates value for everyone.[24] If a contract is too one-sided, with all the advantages flowing to one party, the contract is bound to fail. The party with little to gain will be resentful, will foot drag, and may be disruptive. An agreement must create value for all parties, otherwise it will collapse. An agreement that fails in implementation is far more expensive than one which allows the other party a reasonable profit.

## Relationship Building

Be agreeable. Contract negotiations often break down, not because the goals of the parties cannot be reconciled, but because one or more of the parties becomes rude, impatient, or overly emotional. Calm, orderly, polite discussion is the best way to reach agreement.

Sometimes people act loud or belligerent because they need 'ego income'. It costs little to praise someone for their style, preparation or something else. Ego-stroking goes a long way towards establishing the conditions for a successful negotiation.[25] Sometimes infinite patience is needed. When the other side is loud and boisterous, speak more softly. When the other side is being unreasonable, treat them with kindness.

---

[24] Ertel, Danny. 2004. "Getting Past Yes," *Harvard Business Review*. Nov. pp.61-68.
[25] Schuler, A. J. 2004. "How to Negotiate Effectively," *Healthcare Executive*. Mar/Apr. p.39 adapted from "Negotiate to Win," by A. J. Schuler. wwwSchulerSolutions.com.

## Critical Thinking

How have elements of critical thinking emerged in negotiations? The first element of critical thinking is defining terms and issues. We must know our goals and expectations, so we can determine the negotiating range and BATNA. We must determine the truth of what the other parties are telling us. Can they really perform? Will they perform? Research is necessary to make informed judgments. For example, is a five-year-old Mercedes Roadster worth $50,000? We must perform research to understand the forces in play during the negotiation. For example, is Bob's Autoworld having a tough time selling a particular car? Does Bob's face any costs in financing the sale? Do the offer price and terms follow logically from facts and premises? What alternatives are presented throughout the negotiation, and what are the consequences of each move? As can be seen, critical thinking is very important to a successful negotiation.

## Appendix 7b: Challenge Statistics

Benjamin Disraeli (1804–1881) a British Prime Minster, was reputed to have said, "There are four kinds of lies: lies, damn lies, budgets and statistics." A critical thinker never takes data at face value. Data, like other information, must be vetted for truthfulness, consistency and context.

## Completeness

Part of critical thinking involves checking data for completeness. This can be a problem in business, politics, and in medical and academic research. Without complete data there is no way to appropriately analyze information.

Table 7B.1 Average Excess Global Temperature reports the excess temperature over the recent average of 14 degrees Centigrade.[26] A Centigrade degree is about 1.8 degrees Fahrenheit. Data is listed as NA in several of the years.

---

[26] __. 2012 "Met Office 2012 annual global temperature forecast," Met Office, United Kingdom. Oct. 13.
http://www.metoffice.gov.uk/news/releases/archive/2011/2012-global-temperature-forecast

**A critical thinker would examine data for completeness and question why data were omitted.**
The original data in Table 7B.1 was sorted by temperature. This recast version is sorted by date. Suppose that one looked at the excess temperature in 1997 of 0.36 and looked at the excess temperature in 2011 of 0.36 fifteen years later. Does that mean that there is no discernable change in the earth's temperature? It is not the business of this text to support or defend propositions like climate change, but only to get people to think critically about the data.

**Table 7B.1 Average Excess Global Temperature**

The column Excess is how much the average annual temperature exceeded the recent average global temperature of 14 degrees Centigrade. HadCRUT3 is temperatures measured by Met Office and the University of East Anglia; NOAA NCDC is temperature as measured by the U.S. National Oceanographic and Atmospheric Center/National Climatic Data Center; NASA GISS is temperature as measured by NASA Goddard Institute of Space Studies; World Average is the average of all three reporting entities.

| HadCRUT3 | | NOAA NCDC | | NASA GISS | | World Average | |
|------|--------|------|--------|------|--------|------|--------|
| Year | Excess | Year | Excess | Year | Excess | Year | Excess |
| 1997 | 0.36 | NA | NA | NA | NA | NA | NA |
| 1998 | 0.52 | 1998 | 0.50 | 1998 | 0.49 | 1998 | 0.51 |
| 1999 | NA | NA | NA | NA | NA | NA | NA |
| 2000 | NA | NA | NA | NA | NA | NA | NA |
| 2001 | 0.40 | 2001 | 0.42 | 2001 | 0.40 | 2001 | 0.41 |
| 2002 | 0.46 | 2002 | 0.48 | 2002 | 0.49 | 2002 | 0.47 |
| 2003 | 0.46 | 2003 | 0.49 | 2003 | 0.48 | 2003 | 0.47 |
| 2004 | 0.43 | 2004 | 0.45 | 2004 | 0.41 | 2004 | 0.43 |
| 2005 | 0.47 | 2005 | 0.52 | 2005 | 0.55 | 2005 | 0.52 |
| 2006 | 0.43 | 2006 | 0.46 | 2006 | 0.48 | 2006 | 0.45 |
| 2007 | 0.40 | 2007 | 0.45 | 2007 | 0.51 | 2007 | 0.45 |
| 2008 | NA | 2008 | 0.38 | 2008 | 0.37 | 2008 | 0.36 |
| 2009 | 0.44 | 2009 | 0.46 | 2009 | 0.50 | 2009 | 0.47 |
| 2010 | 0.50 | 2010 | 0.52 | 2010 | 0.56 | 2010 | 0.53 |
| 2011 | 0.36 | 2011 | 0.41 | 2011 | 0.45 | 2011 | 0.41 |

# Trend Analysis

Selectively including or excluding data, sometimes called 'cherry picking' can alter fundamental results. Suppose one looked at the World Average of .41 starting in 2001 and continued to the .53-degree average in 2010. One might conclude that the earth was warming 0.013 degrees a year ((.53-.41)/9 years), or about 1.33 degrees per century (0.013 x 100). On the other hand, comparing the 1998 world average of .51 degrees to the 2011 world average of 0.41 degrees, one might conclude the earth was cooling 0.008 degrees per year ((.51-.41)/13 years), and would cool by .8 degrees over the next century (.008 x 100).

Many people cherry pick data to suit their purposes. When a business is reporting its sales growth, it may pick a starting year that was particularly bad, giving the appearance of a high growth rate. Suppose a company had $20 million in sales in 2012, $10 million in sales in 2013, and $15 million in sales in 2014. If the business picked 2013 for the base year, it might say sales grew 50%. But if it picked 2012 as the base year it might say sales have declined an average of about 12.5% per year since 2012.

**A critical thinker questions how data are analyzed because the method of analysis can change the apparent result.**

# Scaling

The data in Table 7B.1 at different scales presents a different analysis, as shown in Table 7B.2 Global Temperature Data.

Excess is the excess temperature over the recent average of 14.0 degrees Centigrade. The freezing point of water is zero degrees Centigrade. A Centigrade degree is about 1.8 Fahrenheit degrees. Kelvin is a temperature scale used by physicists. It starts at absolute zero. The freezing point of water is 273.15 degrees Kelvin. A Centigrade degree is the same size as a Kelvin degree. The difference is where they start counting.

**Table 7B.2 Global Temperature Data**

| Year | Excess | Centigrade | Kelvin |
|------|--------|------------|--------|
| 1997 | 0.36 | 14.36 | 287.51 |
| 1998 | 0.52 | 14.52 | 287.67 |
| 2001 | 0.40 | 14.40 | 287.55 |
| 2002 | 0.46 | 14.46 | 287.61 |
| 2003 | 0.46 | 14.46 | 287.61 |
| 2004 | 0.43 | 14.43 | 287.58 |
| 2005 | 0.47 | 14.47 | 287.62 |
| 2006 | 0.43 | 14.43 | 287.58 |
| 2007 | 0.40 | 14.40 | 287.55 |
| 2009 | 0.44 | 14.44 | 287.59 |
| 2010 | 0.50 | 14.50 | 287.65 |
| 2011 | 0.36 | 14.36 | 287.51 |

The Excess temperature jumped 44.4% from 1997 to 1998 ((0.52 − 0.36)/0.36), and declined 28.0% ((0.50 − 0.36)/0.36 from 2010 to 2011. However, the story looks dramatically different when the same calculation is made in Centigrade degrees. In Centigrade the temperature rose only 1.11% ((14.52 − 14.36)/14.36) between 1997 and 1998 and declined only 0.97% ((14.50 − 14.36)/14.50) from 2010 to 2011.

Consider the same information presented in Kelvin degrees. The temperature increase from 1997 to 1998 in Kelvin is 0.06% ((287.67 − 287.51) / 287.51) and the temperature decline over the period 2010 to 2011 is 0.05% ((287.65 − 287.51) / 287.65).

An increase of 44.4% or a decrease of 28% is dramatic. But, how many people are interested in a rise of 0.06% or decrease of 0.05%? If one were measuring the width of a room, is it possible to measure within 0.06% of the actual size? Are increases and decreases of this magnitude swamped by statistical background noise, or measurement error? A critical thinker considers the scale on which data are being reported and examines information in context.

# Ex Post Facto Data Manipulation

When reported data does not fit a particular story and then are later 'corrected', a critical thinker should be skeptical, and thoroughly analyze the basis for such 'corrections'. If a corporate controller handed an income statement to a Chief Executive Officer, and the CEO asked the controller to 'correct' revenue and expenses to show a greater profit, such 'corrections' could lead to civil and criminal liability.

# Averages

Averages are useful, but don't always tell the whole story. The average population of the largest 1,000 cities in America is 127,600. Of course, the average doesn't tell us that the population of New York is equal to the total population of the 211 smallest cities in the top 1,000. When the largest 1% of cities is removed from consideration, average city population drops to 104,147. From a decision-making point of view, will policies for cities with a million people work for cities with 100,000 people, or 35,000 people?

Averages can be deceiving. Companies may hide information on underperforming stores or products by citing average sales, or average sales growth across all stores or products.

Medians provide additional information. The median is the point at which half the observations are larger and half smaller. The median city in the top 1,000 cities has a population of about 65,000. The point is that a critical thinker will carefully analyze data to get a more complete understanding of what it means. Reporting city population by quartile (quarter) provides a truer understanding of city size. For example, one might consider the cutoff for the top 25% of data points, in this case cities with about 104,000 of population, and the cutoff for the lowest 25%, in this case cities with a population of 47,000. Together with the median city population of 65,000, it is easy to see most cities in America are pretty small compared to New York, Chicago, Los Angeles or Philadelphia, all of which have a population of far more than a million.

Averages are most useful when the data being averaged are similar. For example, the average residential electric bill, the average daily sales for a particular store, or the average height of students.

# Outliers

Inclusion or exclusion of outliers can significantly alter results. Outliers can come about because of measurement errors, inclusion of data on something which is different in kind from other items being measured, or by random chance. In the above example, New York, Los Angeles, Chicago, Houston, Phoenix and Philadelphia, which represent less than 1% of the data, might be considered outliers and eliminated from an analysis of typical cities. Their size makes them different in kind.

On the other hand, sometimes outliers are more interesting, and more valuable, to study than average items. If one wanted to study urban problems, one might want to study cities that were so big they were different in kind from the averages. To study longevity, focus on people who have outlived the averages.

# Robustness

A mathematical or statistical finding is said to be robust if the finding doesn't change much with the addition or deletion of a few data points. A study of 14,033 materiality decisions indicated that the mean threshold of materiality was 8.52%. Materiality is the change in net income needed to change someone's opinion about a company. Removing 1,341 data points only changed the result to 8.38%. Such a small change in the result indicates the finding is robust.[27] Some mathematical techniques give wildly different results if a few data points are added or taken away.

Whether there is global warming, global cooling or no discernible trend changes based on whether a few data points are added or deleted. As a rule, robustness increases with the amount of data. Beware of any conclusion based on a limited number of data points.

# Budgets

Budgets are often flights of fancy, anticipating revenue that may never come. Government entities often project revenue which is unrealistic to justify excess spending. They may also underestimate costs. For example, they may base pension contributions on returns which are unrealistic. Suppose a city looks out thirty years and estimates that it will have to pay its teachers, firemen and police $1,000,000 in pension payments.

---

[27] Vance, David E. 2011. "A Meta-Analysis of Empirical Materiality Studies," *Journal of Applied Business Research*. Sept/Oct Vol.27. No.5 pp53-72.

Money contributed to the pension fund now, plus accumulated interest, must equal that promised $1,000,000. If a city assumes it can get 9% interest per year, it will only have to contribute about $75,371 out of its current funds. With compound interest at 9% per year, over 30 years $75,371 will grow to $1,000,000. However, if the city assumes it can only get 5% interest, it will have to contribute $231,380 to the pension fund. If the city assumes 3% interest, the contribution jumps to $411,990. Actual pension calculations are much more complex, but this example illustrates that unrealistic budget assumptions can dramatically impact government's ability to meet its obligations. Many state and local governments have significant unfunded pension obligations.

Businesses make unrealistic assumptions as well governments. An entrepreneur might forecast sales growth for which there is no firm foundation. An established company might ignore changes in labor, material or energy costs, changes in regulations, or even rates of return on invested capital. Budgets are often wrong, not because the future is unknown, but because of the refusal to make realistic assumptions. A critical thinker challenges the assumptions that budgets are based on; tries to verify their relevance and truthfulness; and determine whether conclusions flow logically from premises.

Is it possible to lean on statistics too heavily? Should a critical thinker consider human nature as well? Consider the view of John Cowperthwaite in the emphasis box below.[28]

---

[28] Ferguson, Andrew. 2014. "No Statistics, No Mischief: A Modest Proposal for the New Fed Chairman," about Sir John Cowperthwaite, Hong Kong's financial secretary, 1961-71, in the Jan. 27 issue of the Weekly Standard. Reprinted "Notable and Quotable," Wall Street Journal. January 22. A.13.

---

**You Don't Need Statistics to Understand Economics**

John Cowperthwaite was Hong Kong's financial secretary from 1961 to 1971, a time of unprecedented economic growth. He was a student of human nature, not an economist. Rather than relying on numbers to manage Hong Kong's economy he relied on old truths about how the world works. If you tax something you get less of it; as a rule, an individual manages his or her own affairs better than his or her neighbor can; it's rude to be bossy; the number of problems that resolve themselves if you wait long enough is far larger than the number of problems solved by mucking around with them; and the cure is often worse than the disease.

In the long run, the aggregate decisions of business people, exercising individual judgment in a free economy, even if mistaken, is likely to do less harm than the centralized decisions of government; and certainly, the harm is likely to be counteracted faster. Cowperthwaite knew this was true, and he didn't have to work out a

---

## Computer Modeling

Some business, and many government policies, are based on the results of computer models. Computer models are sets of equations, run one after another, with output from one iteration feed into the next iteration. For example, a model of the Oregon salmon population might use, as an input, the number of salmon in a starting year. There is a certain logic to this because the number of salmon next year is, in part, based the number of salmon available to breed this year.

If a population of salmon were estimated to grow 10% per year, one million salmon this year would produce a salmon population of 10.8 million in 25 years. If the estimated growth rate was 5% per year, the salmon population would only grow to 3.4 million in 25 years. But if a 15% growth rate were used, the model would estimate 32.9 million salmon in 25 years. Slight changes in assumptions result in vastly different outcomes.

Experience tells us that populations of salmon, and other wildlife grows to some point, then collapses and grows again. Studies have demonstrated this pattern in lemmings, a small rodent.[29] Models have a

---

[29]. Reid, D.G., R.A. Ims, N.M. Schmidt, G. Gauthier, D. Ehrich. 2012. "Lemmings (*Lemmus* and *Dicrostonyx spp.*)," *Artic Report Card: Update for 2012.* Nov. 7.

tough time predicting the subtle forces at work, causing population growth and decline. While numbers such as $\pi$ are known with great precision, model coefficients for growth rates, the effect of predation, and other environmental factors, aren't known with precision, so estimates are used. Such estimates may be wildly inaccurate, which means model results will be wildly inaccurate. Selection of model coefficients may be influenced by outside pressure, or by the result the modeler wants to report.

Robert Caprara, a consultant to the Environmental Protection Agency in the early 1980s, was asked to build a model of the estimated benefits from improving waste water treatment. The model included every river and stream in the country, as well as every existing sewage treatment facility. The model showed that by the late 1980s, population growth and people shifting from septic tanks to municipal sewage would totally offset the benefits of improved treatment. Caprara reported this to the EPA and they asked him to take another look at the data. He did this several times with no change in the result. Finally, he asked, the EPA what number it wanted the model to produce. The EPA official he was working with said $2 billion. By adjusting model coefficients up and down was able to get the model to show a $2 billion benefit. Was the modeler being pressured to lie?[30]

A critical thinker asks whether a computer modeler or model sponsor has a **hidden agenda**. A critical thinker also asks **how model results** were **validated**.

## Critical Thinking

Critical thinkers challenge statistical data in the same way they challenge other information. They try to verify its truthfulness and completeness. They analyze it in context. They also inquire as to the forces which balance to shape outcomes and ask whether conclusions flow logically from the data.

---

[30]. Caprara, Robert J. 2014. "Confessions of a Computer Modeler," Wall Street Journal. July 9. A13.

# Terms and Concepts

**Assume** – Most people's minds fill in missing pieces of information to present a coherent mental picture. A critical thinker will resist this natural temptation and probe for verifiable details. They never assume.

**Context** – The circumstances around an event or piece of information are important to give it context. Without context, information has little meaning. "Meet me at 124." Without context, this information is meaningless. "Meet me at 124 Burton Avenue, Edge City at 2:00 PM, June 4th," gives context to information.

**Credible** – Information is credible if it is believable. Credibility is increased if it can be reproduced scientifically, or if multiple witnesses saw the same thing. Information is more credible if it is consistent with other information and it is the type of information commonly used.

**Critical Thinking, Definition of,** - Critical thinking is about looking below the surface. Critical thinking emphases clarity, precision and logic. It is about deconstructing an idea into its elements, questioning the premises upon which a proposition is based. It is about questioning the basis for a proposition or idea and testing that proposition or idea with facts; it is about keeping an open mind, free of bias and preconceived notions. It is about considering alternatives, and thinking about the implications of a proposition.

**Critical Thinking, Elements of,** Elements of critical thinking include: (i) defining the issues, (ii) determining whether something is the truth, (iii) performing research necessary to make informed judgments, (iv) understanding the forces which shape outcomes, (v) assuring conclusions are reasonable and follow logically from facts and premises, and (vi) thinking about alternatives and projecting consequences.

**Epistemology** - is a study of the theory of knowledge, methods of knowing whether something is true, how to distinguish between justified belief and opinion, and the limits of knowledge.

**Evidence** – Critical thinkers seek evidence to confirm information offered is true.

**Experiment** – As used in the scientific method, an experiment is a structured test to see whether a hypothesis holds true. In the scientific method, one cannot prove a hypothesis, but one can disprove it.

**Forces, Balancing** – Things are what they are because forces balance at equilibrium points. For example, banks pay just enough interest to attract the deposits they need, but no more.

**Franklin, Benjamin** – "The first responsibility of every citizen is to question authority."

**Game Theory** - is a way of testing strategy and forecasting behavior under a variety of circumstances. A Nash equilibrium is an important example of Game Theory.

**Hypothesis** – A hypothesis is an idea about how something works.

**Issue** - An issue is a problem; a decision point; a place where one set of rules is applied, or another set of rules is applied.

**Law** – In the context of the scientific method, a theory that has been tested many times, and not disproven and which has been very successful at predicting things, may gradually become accepted as a law; as for example, the law of gravity.

**Mencken, H. L.,** Mencken was an early twentieth century journalist and satirist. He said, "The aim of practical politics is to keep the populace alarmed by an endless series of hobgoblins, most of them imaginary, and clamoring to be led to safety by politicians."[31]

**Nash Equilibrium** – A Nash equilibrium exists when several players know each other's strategy and pick the strategy that best suits them under the circumstances. A Nash equilibrium is part of Game Theory which is a way of testing strategy and forecasting behavior under a variety of circumstances.

---

[31] Mencken, H. L. 1918. *In Defense of Women*. Reprinted by Kessinger Publishing, LLC PO Box 1404 Whitefish MT 59937 USA (September 10, 2010)

**Observation** – As used in the context of the scientific method, observation means gathering as much information as possible, in addition to watching and measuring.

**Premise** – A premise is a starting point for a discussion. It may be a fact, principle, or law.

**Theory** – A hypothesis which is tested many times through experiment and has never been proven untrue, may achieve the status of a theory. A theory is a generally accepted notion as to how something works. Theories only have value if they are predictive.

**Sarbanes-Oxley Act of 2002**, - This law was passed because of the outrageous conduct of a couple of dozen high-ranking executives in a half a dozen companies.

**Scientific method** – The scientific method is a self-correcting method for determining how things work. Generally, it proceeds through several steps: (i) observation, (ii) hypothesis, (iii) experimentation, (iv) data collection, and (v) conclusion. Experiments might have unexpected outcomes, which means an investigator might have to begin again at observation, create a new hypothesis and perform a new experiment. The scientific method is an iterative process.

**Unintended Consequences, The Law of,** - Governments, businesses and people often fail to consider all the consequences of their policies, procedures and actions. As a result, policies sometimes fail to achieve stated goals and sometimes create situations worse than the problem the policy was meant to solve.

# References

Beagrie, Scott. 2003. "How to Negotiate, Personnel *Today.* Martin Couzins, Ed. 11/4. Pp21-22.

Caprara, Robert J. 2014. "Confessions of a Computer Modeler," Wall Street Journal. July 9. A13.

Critical Thinking. 2012. "A brief history of critical thinking" Foundation for Critical Thinking. www.criticalthinking.org downloaded 2/2/2012.

Ertel, Danny. 2004. "Getting Past Yes," *Harvard Business Review.* Nov. pp.61-68.

Ferguson, Andrew. 2014. "No Statistics, No Mischief: A Modest Proposal for the New Fed Chairman," about Sir John Cowperthwaite, Hong Kong's financial secretary, 1961-71, in the Jan. 27 issue of the Weekly Standard. Reprinted "Notable and Quotable," Wall Street Journal. January 22. A.13.

Galuszka, Peter, 2008. "Eight Reasons Why Circuit City Went Bankrupt," CBS News Interactive. Nov.13 www.cbsnews.com/8301-505125_162-28241493/eight-reasons-why-circuit-city-went-bankrupt/

Global Temperature. 2012. "Met Office 2012 Annual Global Temperature Forecast," United Kingdom, Met Office (the Met Office is the UK's national weather center). http://www.metoffice.gov.uk/news/releases/archive/2011/2012-global-temperature-forecast.

Kurie, Peter. 2010. "Inventions, Innovations, Ideas," Princeton Report on Knowledge. Vol.3 No.2 Oct.27. http://www.princeton.edu/prok/issues/3-2/inventions.xml

Lax, David A. and James K. Sebenius. 2003. "3-D Negotiation: Playing the Whole Game," Harvard Business Review. Nov. pp.65-74.

Malhotra, Deepak and Max H. Bazerman. 2007. "Investigative Negotiation," *Harvard Business Review*. Sept. pp73-78.

McCormick, Michael, Ulf Buntgen, Mark Crane, Edward Cook, Kyle Harper, et al. 2012. "Climate Change During and after the Roman Empire: Reconstructing the Past from Scientific and Historical Evidence," Journal of Interdisciplinary History. XLIII:2 (Autumn) pp.169-220, 174.

Mencken, H. L. 1918. *In Defense of Women*. Reprinted by Kessinger Publishing, LLC PO Box 1404 Whitefish MT 59937 USA (September 10, 2010)

MF Global. 2011. "MF Global moved customer funds to BNY Mellon – WSJ," Thomson Reuters News Service. Nov. 10. http://www.reuters.com/article/2011/11/19/idUSL3E7MJ00G20111119.

Mollenkamp, Carrick, Susanne Craig, Serena NG and Aaron Luchetti. 2008. "Lehman Files for Bankruptcy, Merrill Sold, AIG Seeks Cash," HYPERLINK "http://online.wsj.com/home-page" The Wall Street Journal. Sept. 16. http://online.wsj.com/article/SB122145492097035549.html.

Nash Equilbrium. 2007. "Nash Equilibrium," International Encyclopedia of the Social Sciences. 2nd. Ed. Pp540-542.

Oil Finds. 2011. "New Oil Finds Around the Globe: Will the U.S. Capitalize on Its Oil Resources?" Institute for Energy Research. 1100 H St NW, Suite 400, Washington, DC 20005. Sept.13.

www.instituteforenergyresearch.org/2011/09/13/new-oil-finds-around-
the-globe-will-the-u-s-capitalize-on-its-oil-resources/

Reid, D.G., R.A. Ims, N.M. Schmidt, G. Gauthier, D. Ehrich. 2012.
"Lemmings (*Lemmus* and *Dicrostonyx spp.*)," *Artic Report Card:
Update for 2012*. Nov. 7.

Roberts, Russell. 2011. "Obama vs. ATMs: Why Technology Doesn't
Destroy Jobs," The Wall Street Journal. Opinion.
http://online.wsj.com/article/SB100014240527023040701045763997o
4275939640.html

Rooney, Ben. 2002. "How to Negotiate," *Management Today*. June 1.
http://www.managementtoday.co.uk/news/407272/NEGOTIATE/?DC
MP=ILC-SEARCH

Schmidt, Harrison. and William Harper. 2013. "In Defense of Carbon
Dioxide," Wall Street Journal. May 9. A.19.

Schuler, A. J. 2004. "How to Negotiate Effectively," *Healthcare
Executive*. Mar/Apr. p.39 adapted from "Negotiate to Win," by A. J.
Schuler. wwwSchulerSolutions.com.

TrueCar. 2018. TrueCar Inc. Santa Monica, CA www.truecar.com

Vance, David E. 2011. "A Meta-Analysis of Empirical Materiality
Studies," *Journal of Applied Business Research*. Sept/Oct Vol.27. No.5
pp53-72.

Wal-mart. 2006. "The Price Impact of Wal-Mart: An Update Through
2006." GLOBAL INSIGHT, Inc.
http://www.globalinsight.com/MultiClientStudy/MultiClientStudyDeta
il2438.htm

Weiss, Debra Cassen. 2008. "Bernard Madoff's Alleged $50B Investor
Fraud 'a Debacle for the SEC" Securities Law Section. *ABA Journal*.
Dec. 15.
http://www.abajournal.com/news/article/bernard_madoffs_alleged_50b
_investor_fraud_a_debacle_for_the_sec/

# CHAPTER EIGHT

# SUPPLY, DEMAND AND MARKET STRATEGY

---

After completing this chapter, you should be able to:

8.1 Describe how supply and demand combine to set the market clearing price.

8.2 Interpret the price signals given by surpluses and shortages.

8.3 Implement a strategy to increase price above the initial market clearing price without creating a surplus.

8.4 Formulate a market segmentation strategy that enables a company to charge nearly the maximum amount consumers will pay.

8.5 Apply the concept of price elasticity of demand to pricing strategy.

---

## Introduction

Alan has been hired as a consultant by an entrepreneur who wants to start an electric car company. The entrepreneur is an engineer and doesn't have a clear idea about to how much demand there is for electric cars, or the amount he can charge for them. Without this basic information, the entrepreneur is finding it difficult to write a sensible business plan. Alan studied economics at one time and recalled it had a lot to say about supply, demand, and price.

Economics provides a robust tool box of ideas, concepts and techniques that a CEO or entrepreneur can apply every day. Economics can help predict what will happen if alternative strategies are followed; it can provide a structured means of analyzing and interpreting data; and it can give guidance as to the data is needed to answer certain kinds of strategic questions. Economics can also provide clues as to how to shape the business environment to achieve a company's goals. The study of economics can give someone a **competitive edge.**

## Sales

Sales are one of the most important things a business can focus on. Nothing happens until a sale is made. There is no need to produce goods or services unless they can be sold. There is no reason to build plants or buy equipment unless sales are made. There is no reason to hire people unless sales are made. There is no income unless sales are made. Without sales, a company will fail.

Sales are dependent on many variables, but one of the most important is price. Gasoline at $20 per gallon will not sell. Gasoline at $1 per gallon will sell out. A Ferrari priced at $20 million will not sell. New Ferraris priced at $20,000 will sell out.

If the price of a good-quality item is low enough, one can sell as many as one wants. However, no matter how good something is, or how badly people want it, if the price is too high, no one will buy it. This creates a dilemma for companies. If price is too low, the company could be giving away sales dollars that people are willing to pay. If price is too high, sales volume will drop. What is the answer?

## Demand

A company introducing a new product should know what people are willing to pay for it. **Demand is the quantity of something people are willing to buy at any given price.** Consider the demand for electric cars. Suppose a survey was conducted of all car buyers in an area, for example Southern New Jersey. Each person could be asked whether they would buy an electric car and at what price. As a practical matter, it is unlikely everyone could be surveyed. Suppose half a million people live in South Jersey, it might be enough to survey 1,000 people to estimate demand for this market. Table 8.1 Demand for Electric Cars is an example of what survey results might look like.

A key concept in analyzing demand is that all variables other than price are kept constant. For example, if demand is being analyzed for electric cars, all people surveyed should be asked about cars with the same range and features. Suppose, for purposes of this analysis, the survey asked about people's interest in purchasing an electric car with a 300-mile range that could be recharged in an hour without any special electrical equipment.

## Table 8.1 Demand for Electric Cars

**Demand data is only relevant for a limited and well-defined market. This data is illustrative and not based on actual surveys.**

| Price | Number of Buyers |
|-------|------------------|
| $10,000 | 900 |
| $20,000 | 520 |
| $30,000 | 320 |
| $40,000 | 180 |
| $50,000 | 90 |
| $60,000 | 50 |
| $80,000 | 30 |

The lower the price, the greater the sales. The higher the price, the lower the sales. This is known as **The Law of Demand**. Table 8.2 Demand Curve for Electric Cars is just a graph of demand data.

**Table 8.2 Demand Curve for Electric Cars**

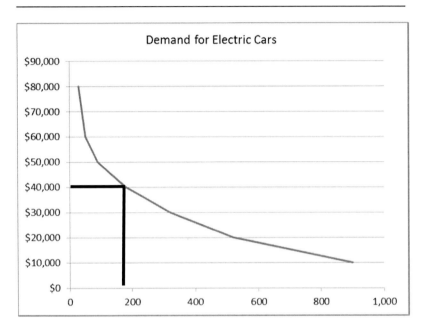

To read the graph, find the price on the left, and then move horizontally across the graph to the demand curve. At the point where price intersects the demand curve, read straight down to get the number of cars consumers will buy at that price. Suppose electric cars are priced at $40,000, based on this demand curve 180 people would buy them.

# Supply

Consumers can demand all they want, but if no one is willing to produce, consumers will have to continue wanting. So, how do consumers induce suppliers to produce? The answer is simple; they offer a price attractive to suppliers. The higher the price consumers offer, the more producers are willing to produce.

**Supply is the quantity that all producers are willing to produce at a given price.** As price rises, companies are willing to produce more by paying overtime and expanding their plants. High prices attract new companies to an industry, and they add to supply. To estimate supply, one might survey car manufacturers to see what price would induce them to produce. See Table 8.3 Survey of Electric Car Supply.

**Table 8.3 Survey of Electric Car Supply**

**Supply is the cumulative supply of all those who are likely to supply to a particular marketplace. This table is illustrative and not based on actual survey data.**

| Price | ---------Production by Car Company------- | | | | | |
|-------|---------|------|------|------|-------|-------|
|       | Electra | AMP  | Zap  | Ford | Chevy | Total |
| $10,000 | 0   | 5    | 5    | 0    | 0     | 10    |
| $20,000 | 5   | 10   | 10   | 0    | 0     | 25    |
| $30,000 | 20  | 40   | 40   | 0    | 0     | 100   |
| $40,000 | 40  | 70   | 70   | 0    | 40    | 220   |
| $50,000 | 60  | 100  | 110  | 0    | 70    | 340   |
| $60,000 | 90  | 150  | 180  | 0    | 120   | 540   |
| $80,000 | 120 | 250  | 300  | 100  | 230   | 1000  |

The supply curve is a graph with price on the vertical axis and quantity on the horizontal axis, as shown in Table 8.4 Supply Curve for Electric Cars.

**Table 8.4 Supply Curve for Electric Cars**

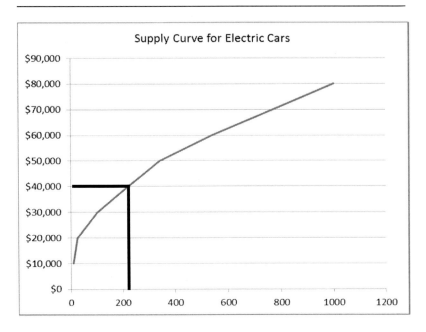

To estimate the number of cars that suppliers, in total, will supply to the market at any given price, select a price on the left side, then read across to the supply curve, and then read down. For example, to find how many cars suppliers will produce at $40,000, find $40,000 on the vertical axis, read across to the supply curve, then down to the horizontal axis to find quantity. In this instance, suppliers are willing to supply about 220 electric cars at $40,000 each.

## Market Clearing Price

The market clearing price is the price at which customers are willing to buy the same quantity that suppliers are willing to supply. Graphically, the market clearing price is the price at which the demand and supply curves intersect as shown in Table 8.5 Supply, Demand and the Market Clearing Price.

**Table 8.5 Supply, Demand and the Market Clearing Price**

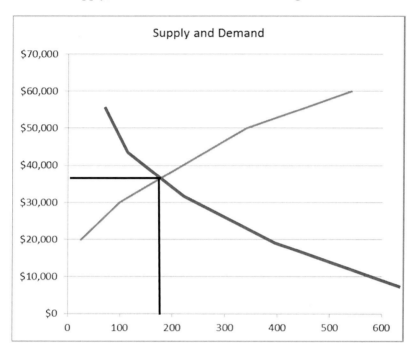

At the market clearing price, all customer demand will be satisfied, and there will be no excess production. The market clearing price in this case is about $38,000. The quantity sold at this price, is about 195 units.

How can Alan and his client use this information? For one thing, his research indicates that if the price is below $40,000, manufacturers like Ford and Chevy won't bother to enter the market because there is not enough profit to justify their investment.

There are fixed and variable costs in every product, and the fixed costs per unit of production go down as the number of units increases. For example, fixed factory costs might be $600,000 per year. Suppose the variable costs that go into a product (parts and labor) are $10,000 and only ten units per year are manufactured, the cost per unit will be $70,000 ($10,000 variable costs + ($600,000/10 units per year)). But, if that same factory produces and sells 30 units, the cost per unit drops to $30,000 ($10,000 + ($600,000/30 units)). If the factory produces 60 units per year, the cost per unit drops to $20,000.

Alan and his client should think about whether there will be enough sales volume to keep fixed costs per unit low enough for the company to make a profit.

---

**Economics as a Tool Kit**

Economics provide CEOs and entrepreneurs with a toolkit that can help them develop and implement strategy.

It can show them how to estimate what the public is willing to pay for a good or service.

It can help assess competition at various price levels.

It can estimate the market clearing price.

It can estimate the volume at the market clearing price so decisions can be made as to whether there will be enough sales volume to cover fixed and variable costs.

---

## Price Signals

Despite a knowledge of supply and demand, companies struggle with pricing decisions all the time. What if supply and demand surveys are inaccurate? For example, suppose the survey accidently oversampled people who were early adopters, that is, people likely to try new products, or it oversampled those with high incomes, then the survey would be inaccurate. Is there any way to assure pricing decisions are rational?

If a company sets a price which it too high, it will produce more than customers are willing to buy. This means the company could be stuck with unsold inventory. On the other hand, If the price is too low, a) customers will demand more than the company wants to make resulting in shortages, and b) the company will be giving away sales dollars it could otherwise harvest. Shortages encourage others to enter a market which increases competition.

### Surplus

If a company sets its price above the market clearing price, producers will produce more than consumers want to consume. Suppose the electric car company set its price at $45,000, as shown in Table 8.6 Price and

Surplus. Start at $45,000 and follow the price line to the right. It will intercept the demand curve where quantity is about 125 units. Then continue following it to the right until it intercepts the supply curve, where quantity is about 275 units. In this example, supply will exceed demand by 150 units. A surplus provides actionable intelligence. The presence of a surplus tells a company that its price is too high.

**Table 8.6 Price and Surplus**

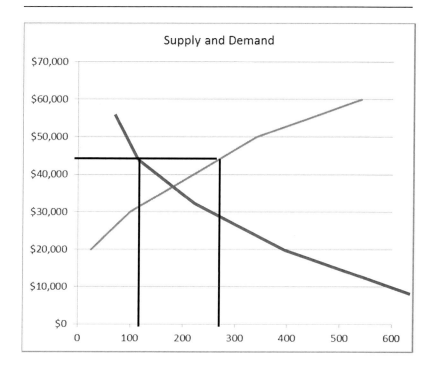

## Shortage

A shortage occurs when a company sets its price below the market clearing price. See Table 8.7 Price and Shortage. Suppose the electric car company set its price at $30,000. Start at $30,000 and follow the price line to the right. It will intercept the supply curve at a quantity of about 100 cars. Following the price line further to the right, it intercepts the demand curve at about 305 cars. This means that consumers are going to want 205

more cars than producers are willing to produce at that price. This creates
a shortage.

**Table 8.7 Price and Shortage**

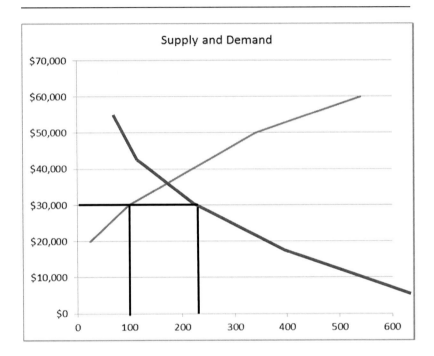

A shortage is a signal that a company should raise its price. If a
company's price is below the market clearing price, raising price to the
market clearing price will enable it to harvest more of the dollars
customers are willing to spend.

Failure to raise price won't just cause loss of income. It will create a
black market in the company's goods. A black market is an unauthorized
channel of distribution. Suppose a company sets the price of its electric
cars at $30,000 when the market clearing price is $38,000. Some people
who don't really want electric cars will buy them anyway at $30,000 and
resell them closer to the market clearing price, harvesting the difference
for themselves.

---

### Economics Provides Price Signals

Economics can be used to verify whether a company has set its price too high or too low.

If the price of a good or service is too high, there will be surpluses. Producers will produce more than consumers demand.

If the price of a good or service is too low, consumers will demand more than producers are willing to produce. There will be shortages.

Surpluses and shortages provide on-going signals regarding price.

---

## Strategy

If the laws of supply and demand control price, and setting price two high or low has adverse consequences, what can a company do? Are companies leaves blowing in the wind? No. Economics provides several strategies for improving a company's competitive position.

### Shifting the Demand Curve

Companies should try to shift the demand curve for their products to the right. If the demand curve shifts right, that means consumers are willing to buy more at any given price; the market clearing price will increase and more units will be sold.[1] Table 8.8 Shifting the Demand Curve to the Right shows the effect of shifting the demand curve from D0 to D1. In this example, the market clearing price rises from about $38,000 to about $44,000, and the quantity sold at the market clearing price increases from about 195 units to about 270 units. The issue for Alan, and his entrepreneur client, is how to shift the demand curve to the right.

---

[1] Vance, David E. 2003. Financial Analysis and Decision Making. McGraw-Hill. New York. pp.280-281

**Table 8.8 Shifting the Demand Curve to the Right**

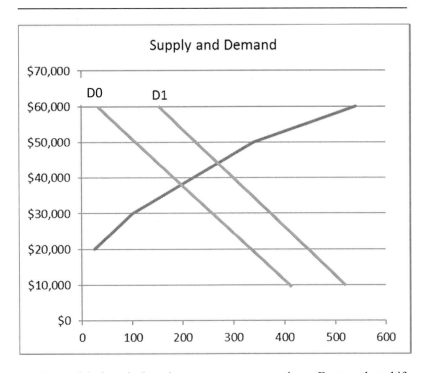

Demand is largely based on customer perceptions. Factors that shift perceptions shift the demand curve. Four factors that shift the demand curve are: (i) tastes and preferences, (ii) income and its distribution, (iii) number and ages of customers, and (iv) expectations about prices and availability.[2, 3]

***Taste and Preferences***

One way to shift the demand curve using taste and preferences is to consider styling and performance. For electric cars, style, range and other features will push the demand curve to the right. Electric cars have been

---

[2] Byrns, Ralph T. and Gerald W. Stone. 1995. Economics, 6th Ed. HarperCollins College Publishers. New York. pp.63-69.
[3] McConnell, Campbell R. and Stanley L. Brue. 2002. Economics, 15th Ed. McGraw-Hill Irwin. New York. Pp.45-46.

around for over a hundred years. They were not generally accepted by the public as an alternative until Tesla introduced cars with a two-hundred-mile range and dramatically improved styling.

### Income and its Distribution

When people have more money or feel richer, they increase their demand for the best goods. As the stock market rises, people feel wealthier and tend to spend more for homes and other luxury goods. For example, people who work for successful start-up companies, and who get substantial stock bonuses might demand more sports cars.

### Number and Ages of Buyers

As demographics change, the cumulative demand for goods will change. For example, young people starting their families demand baby clothes, baby carriages, formula and disposable diapers. Older people, with good incomes and accumulated savings, demand more luxury goods such as premium cars, cruises, and better homes.

### Expectations about Prices and Availability

If something is scarce, or its price is expected to rise, people's demand will increase ahead of the price rise. If the price of gasoline is expected to rise and stay up, that may increase the demand for electric cars.

Of the four factors cited above, the only one that a company can influence is taste and preferences. This can be done by producing a better product in terms of style, ease of use, performance, warranties or other non-price factors. Advertising affects tastes and preferences by changing the perception of a product's style, quality and desirability. For example, advertising might demonstrate that the Tesla's acceleration compares favorably with the best sports cars, and so forth.

## Consumer Surplus

Looking at Table 8.10 Consumer Surplus, one might notice that there are people on the demand curve above the equilibrium price of about $38,000. Consumer C1 appears willing to pay about $2,500 above the market clearing price. Consumer C2 is willing to pay about $8,000 above the market clearing price, and consumer C3 is willing to pay about $11,500 above the market clearing price. This means that consumer C1 would be willing to pay $40,500 ($38,000 + $2,500) for an electric car if he or she thought that was the asking price. Whereas consumer C3 would be willing to pay $49,500 for an electric car if he or she thought that was the asking price.

The difference between the market clearing price and the price a specific consumer is willing to pay is called **consumer surplus**.[4] It's the extra value a consumer gets if he or she only pays the market clearing price.[5]

**Table 8.10 Consumer Surplus**

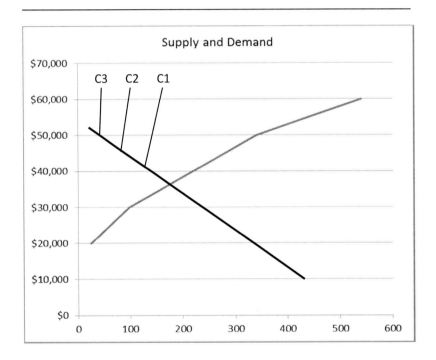

[4] Vance, David E. 2003. Financial Analysis and Decision Making. McGraw-Hill. New York. pp.282-283.
[5] McConnell, Campbell R. and Stanley L. Brue. 2002. Economics, 15th Ed. McGraw-Hill Irwin. New York. p.459.

## Market Segmentation

When a company charges a customer less than he or she is willing to pay, the company forfeits that amount of pre-tax profit. So, for example, if a company charges consumer C1 $38,000, instead of the $40,500 he or she is willing to pay, the company is giving away $2,500 of pre-tax profit. Wouldn't it be great if a company could charge everyone the maximum amount they were willing to pay?

In fact, companies try to charge consumers the maximum amount they are willing to pay through market segmentation. Companies attempt to separate consumers into different demand curves, based on their willingness to pay as shown in Table 8.11 Market Segmentation. The market clearing price for consumers on demand curve D1 is about $38,000. Whereas, the market clearing price for consumers on demand curve D2 is about $40,500. Finally, the market clearing price for consumers on demand curve D3 is about $46,000.

**Table 8.11 Market Segmentation**

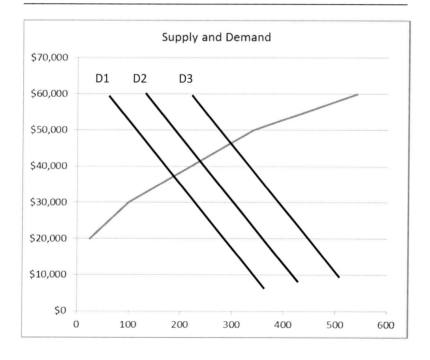

The trick, or strategy if you will, is to keep consumers on the D3 demand curve from jumping to the D1 demand curve and getting a lower price.[6]

One way to do this is to add features to the product on D3 not available on products on D2 or D1. For example, cars on D3 might be completely autonomous and self-driving. Cars on D2 might have automatic breaking and leather seats, but no self-driving features. Cars on D1 might be basic.[7]

Sometimes, consumers self-segregate based on brand perceptions. This is common in retailing. People who shop at Neiman Marcus and Saks believe they deserve the best and are willing to pay for it. Therefore, they are willing to pay very high prices. For example, it would not be unusual to see a $4,000 purse in one of these stores.

On the other hand, many people want quality merchandise, fair prices and a pleasant shopping experience, and they may shop at, for example, Macy's. They feel good about themselves for purchasing quality merchandise.

Finally, there are many people who shop at Wal-Mart. Wal-Mart offers rock bottom prices on goods, many of which are produced by name brand manufacturers. The people who shop at Wal-Mart may think anyone who pays more than they must for merchandise is stupid. Thrift is a forgotten virtue, except perhaps, by people who shop at Wal-Mart and similar stores.

---

**Economics Informs Marketing Strategy**

If supply and demand sets price and quantity, what can a company do?

By shifting the demand curve to the right, a company can raise the market clearing price for its goods and services as well as the quantity demanded.

By segregating people onto different demand curves, a company can get them to pay almost the maximum amount they are willing to pay.

---

[6] McConnell, Campbell R. and Stanley L. Brue. 2002. Economics, 15th Ed. McGraw-Hill Irwin. New York. p.477.

[7] Vance, David E. 2003. Financial Analysis and Decision Making. McGraw-Hill. New York. pp.283-285.

In retailing, people self-segregate onto different demand curves based on their self-image and value perception. Similar strategies are used in the automotive world, as, for example, Toyota and Lexus are both made by the same company, Ford and Lincoln are both made by the same company, and Nissan and Infinity are both made by the same company. People self-segregate by selecting a higher or a lower priced brand of vehicle based on their budget, value perception, and self-image.

## Price Elasticity of Demand

Cutting price doesn't always reduce revenue and raising price doesn't always increase revenue. That is because of a phenomenon called the price elasticity of demand.[8] The price elasticity of demand is one more instance in which economics provides a method for creating a competitive advantage.

### Elastic Demand

The law of demand says that, when price is cut, consumers will purchase more of a good. If the price demand is elastic, total revenue will rise. Suppose Tim is selling a thousand toasters a month at a price of $20. His revenue will be $20,000 per month ($20 x 1,000). If Tim cuts his price to $18, one might expect his revenue to decline to $18,000 ($18 x 1,000). But the law of demand says cutting price ought to increase the number of toasters sold. Now suppose Tim cut the price of toasters to $18 and sells 1,200 per month. His total revenue will be $21,600 ($18 x 1,200), an increase of $1,600. So, it is possible to cut price and increase revenue.

As a company cuts price to increase revenue, it should constantly monitor the impact of pricing decisions on gross margin. Recall that gross margin is the percentage of every dollar of sales left over after accounting for the cost of a good. If gross margin gets too thin, there will not be enough money left over for overhead, financing costs and taxes.

Suppose Tim raises the price of toasters knowing their price is elastic. As price increases customers will demand less of a good. If Tim set the price of his toasters at $22, he might only sell 800 of them giving total revenue of $17,600 ($22 x 800). Raising the price on an item with an elastic price demand will decrease total revenue.

---

[8] McConnell, Campbell R. and Stanley L. Brue. 2002. Economics, 15th Ed. McGraw-Hill Irwin. New York. pp.374-383.

Does cutting price always increase revenue? No. Cutting price only increases revenue when price demand is elastic. Price is said to be elastic when cutting price increases revenue. Price demand is most elastic when there are many substitutes for a good, such as generic aspirin, jeans, or T-shirts.

## Inelastic Demand

When price is price is inelastic, cutting price reduces total revenue. Suppose Silvia sold Corvette Stingrays, with a price of $90,000, and usually sold twelve a month, her revenue would be $1,080,000 ($90,000 x 12). Now suppose she cut her price to $81,000 and sold 13 cars, her total revenue would be $1,053,000 ($81,000 x 13). Her total revenue would decline by $27,000 ($1,080,000 - $1,053,000) even though she sold more cars. The price of Stingrays is said to be inelastic because cutting price increases unit sales, but not enough to make up for the reduced price on the cars she would have sold anyway.

When there are no close substitutes for a good, price tends to be inelastic. The price for prescription drugs that have no generic equivalent tends to be inelastic. Luxury cars such as Stingray, Maserati, Lamborghini and Ferrari tend to have inelastic prices as well.

What might happen if Silvia raised the price of a Stingray? Suppose she raised the price to $99,000. She still might only sell 11 cars for total revenue of $1,089,000 ($99,000 x 11). This is a slight increase in total revenue, but her cost is dramatically reduced if she must only provide 11 Stingrays to customers rather than 12.

## Strategy

When a product's price demand is elastic, companies should lower price, sell more units and gain market share. But, companies should not lower price so much that gross margin becomes unacceptably low.

When a product's price demand is inelastic, companies should consider raising price a little, accept fewer unit sales, but because price is inelastic, total revenue will increase. Profits should increase both because total revenue increases and the cost of goods sold will decrease, because fewer units must be provided to customers.

Many new products start out with an inelastic price demand. At those times, companies should maximize price and thereby maximize revenue. However, as new products are more widely distributed, and substitutes enter the market, price demand becomes elastic. Companies should watch for this transition and be ready to change their pricing strategy accordingly. Thirty years ago, a personal computer could cost half as much as a new Ford Mustang. Today a much more powerful computer can be had for a few hundred dollars. This same price change has occurred for DVD recorders, flat screen televisions and many other goods.

## Conclusion

Economics provides tools that CEOs and entrepreneurs can use to gain a competitive advantage. Setting the right price is an ongoing issue for most companies. Set the price too high and the company will lose sales. Set the price too low and a company will give away pre-tax profit it could otherwise harvest.

Demand is the quantity of a good or service consumers will purchase at any given price. Demand can be estimated through surveys, or by making test sales at various prices. The law of demand says that as price increases, the quantity demanded decreases.

Supply is the cumulative quantity of goods that all suppliers are willing to supply at a given price. The law of supply says that as price rises, suppliers will provide a greater quantity of goods and services to the market.

The market clearing price is the price at which consumers will purchase exactly as much as suppliers will supply. At the market clearing price, there are neither shortages nor surpluses.

A surplus is a signal that price should be reduced. If there are chronic shortages, that is a signal that price should be increased.

If supply and demand set the optimum price, does this mean that companies are helpless to control price? No.

If a company can shift the demand curve for its goods or services to the right, more will be purchased at every price. Shifting the demand curve to the right will increase the market clearing price, and the quantity demanded.

Several factors can shift the demand curve, but tastes and preferences are the factors a seller can influence the most. Tastes and preferences can be affected by providing better quality goods, goods that are easier to use, require less labor, are more efficient, have better warranties or a better style. In addition to changing the characteristics of the product itself, companies can use advertising to shift the perception of a product's value through images, and ideas.

Consumer surplus is the difference between what a specific customer will pay for a good or service and the market clearing price. In a perfect world, a company would charge each consumer the maximum amount he, she or it was willing to pay. This situation can be approximated by segregating consumers onto different demand curves. The market clearing price for each demand curve becomes a rough approximation of the maximum amount consumers will pay. Sometimes consumers self-segregate by shopping in distinct types of stores, or by selecting certain brands or by shopping in different channels of distribution.

Economics provides CEOs and entrepreneurs with a wide array of strategy tools. Some of those tools revolve around an analysis of supply and demand data.

# Terms and Concepts

**Consumer surplus** – The difference between the maximum amount the consumer will pay and the market clearing price is called consumer surplus.

**Demand** – is the quantity consumers will purchase at any given price.

**Demand curve** – The demand curve is a graph of demand. Generally, price is plotted on the y-axis, and quantity is plotted on the x-axis.

**Demand curve, shifting** –When a company wants to raise price without creating a surplus, it attempts to shift the demand curve to the right. Shifting the demand curve to the right means more will be demanded at every price. Shifting the demand curve to the right will increase the market clearing price and the quantity demanded. Factors that shift the demand curve include: (i) taste and preferences, (ii) income and its distribution, (iii) the number and age of buyers, and (iv) expectation about prices and availability.

**Demand, Law of** – The higher the price, the lower the quantity demanded.

**Elastic Demand** – Where price is elastic, lowering price will cause so many more units to be sold that total revenue will rise. Price is elastic for goods with many close substitutes.

**Inelastic Demand** – Where price is inelastic, raising price will cause fewer units to be sold, but the increased price on every unit that would be sold anyway increases total revenue. Goods for which there are no close substitutes have inelastic demand.

**Market clearing price** – The market clearing price is the price at which the quantity demanded by consumers exactly matches the quantity supplied by suppliers. At the market clearing price, there are neither surpluses nor shortages.

**Market segmentation** – To maximize the price that can be charged to consumers, companies try to segregate consumers into different demand curves, each of which has its own market clearing price.

**Price signals** – A surplus is a signal that price has been set too high. A shortage is a signal that the price has been set too low.

**Shortage** – When a company sets a price lower than the market clearing price, customers will demand more than suppliers are willing to supply and there will be shortages.

**Strategy** – Use supply and demand curves to estimate the market clearing price and quantity. Raise price when there are shortages. Lower price when there are surpluses. Shift the demand curve to the right through tastes and preferences. Segregate customers onto different demand curves so that each will pay almost the maximum price they are willing to pay. When price is inelastic, raise price a little to increase revenue and reduce cost of goods sold. When price is elastic, lower price to sell more units and raise revenue, but don't lower price so much that gross margin erodes.

**Supply** – is the cumulative quantity of goods that all suppliers will supply at a given price.

**Surplus** – When price is set above the market clearing price, suppliers will produce more than consumers are willing to purchase. The excess is called a surplus.

**Supply, Law of** – The law of supply is that the higher the price, the more suppliers will cumulatively supply to the market.

# References

Byrns, Ralph T. and Gerald W. Stone. 1995. Economics, 6th Ed. HarperCollins College Publishers. New York.

McConnell, Campbell R. and Stanley L. Brue. 2002. Economics, 15th Ed. McGraw-Hill Irwin. New York. p.459.

Vance, David E. 2003. Financial Analysis and Decision Making. McGraw-Hill. New York.

# CHAPTER NINE

# ECONOMICS OF CONSUMER BEHAVIOR

---

When you complete this chapter, you should be able to:

9.1 Describe and analyze the factors that cause the demand curve to slope down and to the right.

9.2 Explain how the law of diminishing marginal utility impacts consumer choice.

9.3 Use utility maximizing rules to drive increased sales.

9.4 Estimate consumer satisfaction in dollars.

9.5 Understand how value creation drives employment.

---

## Introduction

What makes a consumer buy one brand of toothpaste rather than another? What makes them buy one phone versus another? Why do consumers buy the cars or clothes they do? Wouldn't it be great if there was an instruction manual on consumer choice? If there were, companies could use that manual to get their goods and services selected in preference to competitor's goods and services. There is no perfect answer to any of these questions. However, economic theory provides some interesting insights into consumer choice.

One of the most important jobs in marketing is to figure out how to get customers to choose a company's products or services. Customers have an enormous array of choices. Go to any supermarket and count the brands of hairspray, cookies, breakfast cereals, cheese, and laundry soap. Customers also have limited budgets. They can't buy everything. They must pick and choose. So, understanding decision mechanisms is critically important.

# Law of Demand

Price is a key factor in consumer decision making. With a demand curve, one can forecast the quantity demanded at every price. Cutting price increases sales. But, **cutting price** without cutting cost is going to **shrink gross margin**. If gross margin shrinks too much there won't be enough left to run the company and make a profit. Some competitors are willing to cut price until no one makes a profit. What marketers really want to influence is **selection** without cutting price. Three factors influence the demand curve, and therefore the quantity customers purchase and the price they pay. These are: (i) the Income Effect, (ii) the Substitution Effect, and (iii) Marginal Utility.

## Income Effect

If the price of something declines, consumers face a real increase in purchasing power.[1] Increases in purchasing power tend to increase purchases. In 2001, many people had 8% mortgages. Interest on a $300,000 mortgage was about $24,000 per year. About this time, the economy tipped toward recession.

The Federal Reserve cut interest rates so that most people could refinance at about 5%. That meant the interest on a $300,000 mortgage dropped to $15,000. The reduction in interest from $24,000 to $15,000 increased the amount of money available for other purposes by $9,000 per year. Cutting the price of money (the interest rate), increased consumers' real purchasing power which averted a recession.

Raising prices reduces a consumer's purchasing power, for example increasing gas prices reduces the amount consumers have for other things like going out to dinner or purchasing a larger car.[2]

## Substitution Effect

When prices rise, customers seek to substitute other goods for the good whose price is rising. When price drops, customers use more of the good whose price has dropped. A person might prefer to drive from his or her home in New Jersey to their office in Philadelphia. However, as the price

---

[1] McConnell, Campbell R. and Stanley L. Brue. 2002. Economics, 15th Ed. McGraw-Hill Irwin. New York. pp.41.
[2] Byrns, Ralph T. and Gerald W. Stone. 1995. Economics, 6th Ed. HarperCollins College Publishers. New York. pp.474-475.

of gasoline rises, they might decide to take the train, which is a lower-cost substitute.

If the price of a train ticket stays at $5 per day and the price of gasoline drops from $4 to $1 per gallon, many of those taking the train might begin driving again. Both the **income effect** and the **substitution effect** help explain why the demand curve slopes down and to the right.[3, 4]

## Diminishing Marginal Utility

The law of diminishing marginal utility states that as more of a good is consumed, its marginal utility declines. Stated another way, one ice cream cone is good. A second ice cream cone is all right. A third ice cream cone might make you sick. More is not always better.

### Utility

In economics, the term **utility** is a measure of satisfaction. It is not the same as usefulness. A unit of 'satisfaction' will be called a 'util', for want of a better term. This theoretical measure is a convenient way to discuss customer satisfaction. The amount of utility in a good (or service) is highly subjective.[5, 6] The amount of satisfaction in one util might be completely different for different people.

Total Utility is the total amount of satisfaction. Marginal Utility is the change in total utility by adding one more unit of whatever is generating the satisfaction. Consider Table 9.1 Utility of Hot Dogs. This table represents the utility or satisfaction in consuming hot dogs, for a very hungry person.

[3] McConnell, Campbell R. and Stanley L. Brue. 2002. Economics, 15th Ed. McGraw-Hill Irwin. New York. pp.41-42

[4] Byrns, Ralph T. and Gerald W. Stone. 1995. Economics, 6th Ed. HarperCollins College Publishers. New York. pp.60, 473-474.

[5] Byrns, Ralph T. and Gerald W. Stone. 1995. Economics, 6th Ed. HarperCollins College Publishers. New York. 467-470.

[6] McConnell, Campbell R. and Stanley L. Brue. 2002. Economics, 15th Ed. McGraw-Hill Irwin. New York. pp.41, 395-397.

**Table 9.1 Utility of Hot Dogs**

| Number of Hot Dogs | Total Utils | Marginal Utility |
|--------------------|-------------|------------------|
| 0 | 0 | |
| 1 | 20 | 20 |
| 2 | 35 | 15 |
| 3 | 45 | 10 |
| 4 | 50 | 5 |
| 5 | 50 | 0 |
| 6 | 45 | -5 |

Table 9.1 shows that when no hot dogs are consumed, there is no satisfaction, but when the first hot dog is consumed, 20 utils of satisfaction are obtained. The difference between no hot dogs and the first hot dog is a marginal utility, or incremental change in utility of 20. When hot dog number two is consumed, the total satisfaction measured in utils rises to 35, and the marginal utility or incremental change in total utility is 15.

Consumption of hot dog number four only increases total utility a little and marginal utility is now down to 5. Consuming a fifth hot dog does not increase the consumer's overall satisfaction and consuming a sixth hot dog reduces total satisfaction.

## Graphing Utility

Table 9.2 Satisfaction versus Consumption is a graph of the data in Table 9.1. Total Utility rises fast at first, and then more slowly until it hits a maximum, then declines as additional units are consumed.

Satisfaction is thought to drive consumer decision-making, so an understanding of when and where a consumer derives the maximum satisfaction, aids in trying to influence consumer choice.

**Table 9.2 Satisfaction versus Consumption**

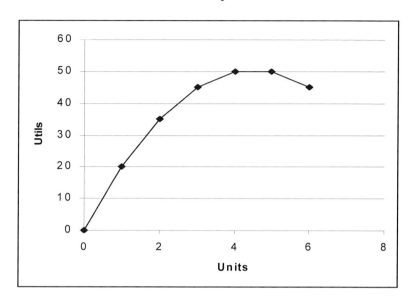

---

### Diminishing Marginal Utility

Utility is a measure of the satisfaction from consuming something.

As more is consumed, the marginal utility diminishes until it reaches a maximum. Above that point, total and marginal utility decline. **More of something is not always better.**

---

## Utility Maximizing Rule

Consumers are believed to make purchasing decisions based on a kind of consumer logic. This logic will not cause everyone to make the same purchasing decisions. Consumer logic is **not** hard and fast like Boolean algebra, mathematics or a computer program. Rather consumer logic is more like a recurring pattern. Four principles of consumer logic seem to impact purchasing behavior:[7]

---

[7] McConnell, Campbell R. and Stanley L. Brue. 2002. Economics, 15th Ed. McGraw-Hill Irwin. New York. pp.397-401.

(i) Consumers are rational. They allocate their money to **maximize total utility**.

(ii) Consumers have clear-cut preferences linked to their **perceived satisfaction** from goods and services.

(iii) Consumers have **limited budgets** and are therefore constrained as to the type and quantity of goods they can purchase.

(iv) No consumer has enough purchasing power to change the equilibrium of supply and demand.

Given these four principles, economists have developed a utility maximizing rule. To maximize satisfaction, a consumer will allocate his or her money so that the **last dollar spent** on each product **yields the same amount of marginal utility**.[8, 9] Given two products to choose from, a consumer will allocate his or her purchases according to equation Eq.9.1. What consumers are comparing are Marginal Utils per dollar.

$$\frac{\text{Marginal Utility of X}}{\text{Unit Price of X}} = \frac{\text{Marginal Utility of Y}}{\text{Unit Price of Y}} \qquad \text{Eq.9.1}$$

Table 9.3 Utility Maximization of Products X and Y provides a concrete example of utility maximizing in action.

---

[8] Byrns, Ralph T. and Gerald W. Stone. 1995. Economics, 6th Ed. HarperCollins College Publishers. New York. pp.470-473.
[9] McConnell, Campbell R. and Stanley L. Brue. 2002. Economics, 15th Ed. McGraw-Hill Irwin. New York. pp.398-401.

**Table 9.3 Utility Maximization of Products X and Y**

Assume that one unit of X costs $1 and one unit of Y costs $2. Consumers will select either an X or Y to maximize the marginal utility of each purchase. Assume a consumer's total budget is $11.

| Units | Product X - Marginal Utils | Utils / $ | Product Y - Marginal Utils | Utils / $ |
|---|---|---|---|---|
| 1 | 20 | 20 | 60 | 30 |
| 2 | 16 | 16 | 40 | 20 |
| 3 | 12 | 12 | 20 | 10 |
| 4 | 10 | 10 | 10 | 5 |
| 5 | 6 | 6 | 8 | 4 |
| 6 | 2 | 2 | 6 | 3 |
| 7 | 0 | 0 | 2 | 1 |

Given the data in Table 9.3, a rational consumer would purchase a Y first, because satisfaction, measured in utils per dollar, is greatest for the first unit of Y purchased. This purchase will use $2 of the $11 budget. The first Y will yield 30 utils per dollar of satisfaction.

In the next purchasing round, the consumer should be indifferent as to whether he or she purchased another Y, or purchased an X, because each provides 20 utils per dollar. Suppose the consumer purchases an X and then purchases Y. At this point $5 of the budget has been spent.

The next logical choice is to purchase an X, because it provides 16 utils per dollar of satisfaction which is more than the 10 utils per dollar he or she could get purchasing a Y.

The rest of the budget would be spent in the following order: purchase the third X, purchase the third Y or the fourth X, then purchase the X or Y not purchased in the prior round, then purchase the fifth X. That would use up the consumer's total budget of $11.

## Utility Maximizing Rule Generalized

Companies competing for customer dollars, are not just competing against one alternative product, but against all other products or services a customer could spend money on. For each choice, consumers select the good or service that provides them with the maximum marginal utility per dollar. Spread across all the goods and services a consumer buys, the marginal utility per dollar for each type of good tends to be equal to that of all others. For example, one could spend all one's money on a Maserati and sleep in the woods. Or one could spend all one's money on a mini-mansion or luxury condo and take the bus to work. But consumers tend to balance the satisfaction, in terms of the marginal utility per dollar, across all possible purchases. Generalizing equation Eq.9.1 above, we get equation Eq.9.2.

$$\frac{\text{Marginal Utility of Xi}}{\text{Unit Price of Xi}} = \frac{\text{Marginal Utility of Xj}}{\text{Unit Price of Xj}} \qquad \text{Eq.9.2}$$

In equation (9.2) Xi and Xj are any of an indefinite number of competing products. How can this theory be used to gain a competitive advantage?

## Valuing Utils

Utils are subjective units of measure, so no two people will place the exact same dollar value on a util of satisfaction. How might one estimate the value of a util in dollars? It turns out that the dollar value of a util is approximately equal to the price of the last unit purchased. Stated differently, a consumer will keep purchasing units of a good or service until the utility in dollars of the next unit is less than the purchase price.[10, 11]

Suppose a hiker walked ten miles across a desert and finds a store. What would that person pay for a bottle of water? They might be willing to pay $10. After drinking that first bottle of water, he or she may only be willing to pay $5 for the second bottle, $3 for the third bottle and $2 for the fourth bottle.

Suppose this person entered a store where every bottle of water was priced at $4. He or she would certainly purchase the first bottle, because the first bottle of water is going to provide at least $10 worth of satisfaction, even though the price is only $4. This person would also purchase the second bottle because its satisfaction to this person is worth $5 even though the price is only $4. The first and second bottle seem like bargains. The question is whether he or she would purchase the third bottle. If the satisfaction a person receives is less than the $4 price of a bottle of water, the consumer won't buy it.

---

[10] McConnell, Campbell R. and Stanley L. Brue. 2002. Economics, 15th Ed. McGraw-Hill Irwin. New York. pp.395-397.
[11] Byrns, Ralph T. and Gerald W. Stone. 1995. Economics, 6th Ed. HarperCollins College Publishers. New York. 467-468.

The price of the last unit purchased is an estimate of the dollar value of the utils in that unit. In the case of the hiker, the dollar value of the utils in the last bottle of water purchased is at least $4. We also know the dollar value of the utils in the third bottle of water is less than $4 because the hiker didn't purchase it.

What can be said about the value of the utils in the first bottle of water? There is no precise way to estimate the value of this unit. The only thing that is known is that its utility in dollars is more than the value of the last bottle purchased. Utils of satisfaction decline, as more is consumed.

A retailer could vary the price of goods up and down and use sales data to construct an estimate of how the average person would measure the satisfaction of units in dollars. For example, one could price bars of soap at $3 each, $2, $1, and $.50, and see how many were purchased.

## Mechanics of Choice

Consumers want to maximize satisfaction from purchases. So, when confronted with a list of options, their next choice will probably be the good or service that provides the greatest utils per dollar. Consider Table 9.4 Product Utility.

**Table 9.4 Product Utility**

| Product or Service | Utils | Cost | Utils/$ |
|---|---|---|---|
| Movie Tickets | 50 | $12 | 4.2 |
| Tablet Computer | 1,000 | $249 | 4.0 |
| Running Shoes | 400 | $49 | 8.2 |
| Opera Tickets | 10 | $80 | 0.1 |
| DVD Movie | 80 | $19 | 4.2 |
| Maserati Gran Turismo | 150,000 | $135,000 | 1.1 |

For this customer, running shoes have more utils per dollar than competing choices, so running shoes would be the next purchase. After running shoes, the next purchase would probably be a toss-up between movie tickets and a DVD movie.

What are the strategic implications of the Utility Maximizing Rule? If a company increases the utils per dollar of its product, it can increase the probability that its product will get selected, rather than someone else's product. Suppose a company improved its tablet computer to the point at which it provided 1,100 utils of satisfaction to a user without raising its price. Its utils per dollar would rise to 4.4. That would make it the second product selected from among the products in Table 9.4, rather than the fourth. Since consumers have limited funds, it is important to move up in the selection process before consumers run out of money.

## Strategy

If consumer decisions are based on utils per dollar, and we don't want to reduce price, the only alternative is to increase the utils of satisfaction. How can a company do this? Satisfaction is driven by:

| | |
|---|---|
| Prestige | Availability |
| Ease of purchase | Ease of use |
| Reliability | Packaging |
| Life-span | Preparation time |
| Maintenance | Operating costs |
| Taxes | and other factors. |

The value of time should be carefully considered as a factor that can increase or decrease satisfaction. The time a consumer needs to do things, perform tasks, and so forth, has an implicit cost. Many goods require the consumer to use time to purchase, prepare, consume or use them. The implicit cost of that time should be considered in estimating marginal utility per dollar. For example, condensed soup is easier to prepare and use than soup made from raw ingredients. It has more utils, because it requires less preparation time. Soup which just has to be heated is easier to prepare than condensed soup and has higher utils because of this increased ease. Soup in pop top cans is easier to use than soup requiring a can opener, and so forth. The battle for increased utils is fought on many fronts.

## Conclusion

Price is set by supply and demand. Looking deeply into the factors that shape demand provides insights as to how one might shift the demand curve to the right and increase the quantity demanded at every price. Three of the factors that influence the demand curve are: (i) the income effect, (ii) the substitution effect, and (iii) marginal utility. The income effect means that if the price of a good goes down, consumers will have more money to spend. They often spend some of that money on the good whose price has been lowered. The substitution effect says that, as the price of a good rises, people will purchase less of a good and will find substitutes for it. If the price of an alternative good goes down, consumers will substitute the low priced good for other goods they have been buying.

Marginal utility is the idea that consumers get the most satisfaction from the first unit of a good purchased, and a little less satisfaction from each subsequent unit of the same good. At some point, incremental satisfaction might turn negative implying more is not always better.

Marginal utility is measured in a theoretical unit of satisfaction called a util. Utils provide a convenient means of discussing consumer preference. Satisfaction is subjective. Therefore, it is difficult to value a util in dollars.

Consumers are rational. They allocate their money to maximize total utility. They have clear preferences linked to their perceived satisfaction from goods and services. Consumers have limited budgets and are therefore constrained as to the type and quantity of goods they can purchase.

When faced with an array of choices, consumers tend to pick the product or service which provides the greatest utils per dollar. There are two ways to increase utils per dollar, lower price or increase utils. When price is reduced, gross margin and profit per unit are also reduced. On the other hand, utils may be increased, at little or no cost, by making goods easier to purchase and use, improving the packaging, increasing their life span, reducing operating costs or increasing their prestige.

## Appendix 9a: Value Added and Employment

The economics of choice isn't limited to consumers. Businesses use economics to shape choices all the time. For example, why do some companies have fifty employees, some five hundred and some five thousand? Why will one job applicant be hired and another not? Why do companies hire and fire workers? What must be done to get a job?

Society works best when everyone contributes. So, employment is an important component of a civil society. This raises the question of why businesses hire people, and why businesses terminate them.

The answer is value creation. If a business believes an individual will create substantially more value than he or she will cost, the company will hire them. Critical thinkers recognize this as a balancing of forces. When a company selects from among several candidates for a job, the company will hire the candidate it believes will add the most value for his or her cost. This can be summarized by equation Eq.9A.1

$$\text{Value Created} \gg \text{Cost} \qquad \text{Eq.9A.1}$$

In this equation, the symbol '>>' means much, much greater. Value Created must be much, much greater than the cost incurred.

## Value Creation

In public accounting, staff auditors and managers are expected to bill at least three times their salary. Attorneys working the fields of tax, corporate law or insurance defense are expected to bill at least three times their salary. Consultants are also expected to bill at least three times their salary.

For those in sales, value added is expressed as sales targets. It's less clear how to measure the value of the typical non-sales employee. Does the employee do what is asked of them? Do they do it promptly? Accurately? Professionally? Are they willing to do a job better and more thoroughly than asked? How much do they contribute to the company's mission? Do they continually improve their methods to the benefit of the company? Do they identify cost saving approaches? Are they instrumental in developing new, better and more profitable products? Answers to these questions are subjective. Nevertheless, employers constantly scrutinize the value that each employee creates to make sure it is much, much greater than an employee's cost.

## Employee Cost

Cost is the other side of equation Eq.9A.1. Cost includes: salary or wages; the employer's share of social security (currently 6.2%) and Medicare (currently 1.45%); workers compensation insurance (which can range from 0.3% to 5.0% of wages); federal and state unemployment insurance which can range from a few hundred to a thousand dollars per employee; health benefits, which are often more than $7,000 per person; and costs for pensions or some other retirement plan. The effect of vacation and paid holidays is to reduce the number of days an employee can create value. It is not, per se, an additional cost. The total cost to the employer for an employee making $50,000 per year with modest benefits could easily be 30% to 40% more than the person's base salary. The total cost for low wage employees is proportionately more, because costs like health insurance are fixed and costs like unemployment insurance are usually only assessed on the first $30,000 or so of wages. As a result, the cost of an employee making $25,000 per year could be 40% to 50% more than their base pay.[12]

Some companies require ten to twenty times value added before they will hire. Why do companies demand such high multipliers? For one thing, businesses are not charities. If there is insufficient return on invested dollars, there is no point in maintaining business operations. Companies are liquidated, and capital returned to investors so they can find more profitable investments.

Second, employee costs are not the only cost borne by businesses. There are costs for capital equipment and other investments to improve productivity, such as computers and software. All companies require some investment in plant, property and equipment (PPE), and many require additional assets in the form of accounts receivable and inventory. Employees must produce enough of a return on those assets, so that banks will lend to companies and investors will get a return on invested capital.

---

[12] Assume a worker earns $50,000 per year and has healthcare. This employee would cost his or her employer about $15,425 in addition to the employee's base salary. The employer's share of social security is $3,100 (6.2% x $50,000), the employer's share of Medicare is $725 (1.45% x $50,000). Workers compensation insurance, insurance for workers that get hurt on the job, is $1,000 (2% x $50,000). Assume unemployment insurance is based on the first $20,000 of wages and the combined Federal and state rate is 5.5%. Unemployment insurance cost is $1,100. Assume health insurance is about $7,000 per person. Also assume the employer contributes 5% of an employee's pay into a 401(k) or some similar retirement plan. That is an additional $2,500. A more generous health or retirement benefit increases the cost per employee. For example, a company might provide medical benefits to an employee's spouse or children.

Assume a worker earning $25,000 per year has the same benefits as the worker earning $50,000. The cost of this worker is about $36,763 which is the salary plus $11,763 of taxes and benefits. The employer's share of social security is about $1,550 (6.2% X $25,000). Medicare is about $363. (1.45% x 25,000). Workers compensation is about $500 (2% x 25,000). Unemployment insurance is about $1,100 (5.5% x 20,000). Health insurance is about $7,000. Assume the employer contributes $1,250 (5% x $25,000) toward the employee's retirement plan.

For all these costs, the typical employer will get about 1,920 hours of labor (52 weeks x 40 hours/week – two weeks' vacation x 40 hours/week – 10 holidays days x 8 hours/day). Within that envelope of time, the employee must generate enough value to justify his or her salary and other costs.

## Regulations

Regulations create economic friction and while employees may create value, some of that value is consumed complying with laws, rules and regulations. A Small Business Administration study found the cost of federal regulations was $1.75 trillion per year. That works out to $15,586 per person.[13]

Finally, non-employee related business taxes eat into business returns. The higher the taxes on capital assets, inventory, and income, the lower the returns for investors. Since there will be no businesses without returns, higher taxes mean employees must create more value to justify their employment.

## Not Enough Value Created

What happens when employees fail to create enough value? If a single individual fails to create enough value, he or she is likely to be dismissed. If most of a company's employees fail to create enough value, the company will collapse with the result that all jobs will be lost.

## Job Security, Innovation and Productivity

The best way to assure continued employment is to innovate and improve productivity. Productivity can be increased through better planning, fewer defects, improved market response, innovative products and services, and automation. Productivity increases when a company gets greater output from the same inputs or the same output with fewer inputs. Inputs may be labor, time, energy or materials. Constantly improving productivity should mean value created rises faster than employee cost, and that goes a long way toward employment security. Seen in that light, employment security isn't just the responsibility of a company, but also of its employees.

## Balancing Forces and Unintended Consequences

Critical thinkers understand that employment is the result of the balance between competing forces. When value creation is much, much

---

[13] Crain, Nicole and Mark Crain. 2010. "The Impact of Regulatory Costs on Small Firms," Small Business Administration, Office of Advocacy. Contract SBAHQ-08-M-0466. Sept. www.sba.gov/advo

greater than employee cost, employment goes up. When value creation is low, employment goes down.

There are many well intentioned laws that tax employment, set minimum wages, burden employers with regulations, and limit the productivity of employees. These laws increase cost and limit value creation. Union contracts also increase costs. What's the point of having a union if employees can't get more out of a company? When value creation drops below some threshold multiplier of cost, companies will stop hiring and will lay off existing employees.

---

### Lateness, Absenteeism and Excuses

Work habits are one indication of whether an employee is creating value. The habits one develops in school are the habits that one is likely to take to the workplace. Students completing assignments in a professional manner and submitting them on time are likely to complete work in a professional manner and on time as employees.

Students casual about attending class are likely to be casual about going to work. Students who are chronically late to class are likely to be chronically late to work.

When someone is chronically late, they are screaming, "**I don't want to be here!**" Employer's notice this. Employers want people who are glad they have a job and look forward to coming to work. Employees who are chronically late go to the top of a company's cut list.

Some people make endless excuses for absenteeism and lateness. In the real world, no one cares about excuses. Either a person is ready, willing and able to create value by doing their job or they are not. If they are not, they go to the top of the cut list.

While this may seem harsh, it is worse for people to leave school with unrealistic expectations about work.

# Terms and Concepts

**Consumer selection** – Consumers tend to purchase the good or service that provides the greatest number of utils per dollar.

**Income effect** – As the price of a good or service declines, consumers face a real increase in purchasing power. This increase in purchasing power may drive consumers to purchase more.

**Law of diminishing marginal utility** – The marginal utility of a good declines as more of it is consumed. Utility is a measure of satisfaction. Consuming the first unit of something usually provides the greatest satisfaction, the second unit provides a little less satisfaction, and so forth. Eventually, marginal satisfaction becomes negative. More is not always better.

**Substitution effect** – The substitution effect says that, as the price of a good rises, consumers will substitute other goods for the good in question. As the price of a good declines, consumers will substitute the lower priced good for other goods.

**Util** – A util is a theoretical measure of satisfaction. It is subjective, which means it is difficult to quantify in dollars. However, the amount paid for the last unit of a good purchased is a rough estimate of the dollar value of the utils in that unit of a good.

**Utility** – In economics, utility means satisfaction. It does not mean usefulness. Utility is highly subjective.

**Utility maximizing rule** – To maximize satisfaction, a consumer will allocate his or her money, so the last dollar spent on each product yields about the same amount of marginal utility.

**Value Added** – Employees must create much more value than their cost to get hired and keep their jobs.

# References

Byrns, Ralph T. and Gerald W. Stone. 1995. Economics, 6th Ed. HarperCollins College Publishers. New York.
McConnell, Campbell R. and Stanley L. Brue. 2002. Economics, 15th Ed. McGraw-Hill Irwin. New York.

# CHAPTER TEN

# MARKETING

---

When you complete this chapter, you should be able to:

10.1 Distinguish between sales and marketing.

10.2 Articulate the purpose and goals of marketing.

10.3 Know the purpose of market segmentation and how to segment a market.

10.4 Discuss the meaning of Product, Place, Promotion and Price in the context of marketing.

10.5 Define and explain the buying window.

10.6 Explain the goals of advertising and how they might be effectively met.

10.7 Measure advertising effectiveness.

10.8 Explain some of the key elements in closing a sale.

---

## Introduction

Nothing happens until a sale is made. Without sales, there is no reason to produce a product, buy raw material, buy equipment, or to hire people. The sale is the spark which ignites the big bang. Everything in the business universe derives from sales. But, making a sale is no trivial feat. It is often the hardest thing companies do. No company can force a customer to purchase its goods or services; customers must *want* to purchase.

**A sale is closing the deal**; getting the customer to agree to buy; billing and getting paid for something. **Marketing is about increasing the odds of making a sale.** Sales don't happen through random chance. There are well defined approaches to making a sale.

Companies compensate successful salespeople very well, because they directly contribute to company profits. Marketing, and market research, on the other hand, is often seen as an expense. The connection between marketing and profits is not as clear as those between sales and profits, so those in marketing are not usually compensated as well as those in sales. Nevertheless, most universities teach marketing, not sales.

---

**Sales** – is about closing the deal, delivering goods or services and getting paid.

**Marketing** – is about improving the odds of making a sale.

---

## Marketing and Sale Probability

To increase the odds of making a sale, companies must understand customers at a deep level. Rudyard Kipling, a twentieth century novelist, poet, and philosopher[1] said,

> "I had six honest serving men,
> They taught me all I knew.
> Their names were what and where and when,
> And why and how and who."

When a company understands the who, what, where, why, when and how of a customer, it is in a better position to implement an effective sales and marketing strategy.

### Value Added

When a company wants to sell anything, it must think about how it adds value for the customer. Does it add value by increasing a person's self-esteem? Does the company's product solve a problem? For example,

---

[1] Ricketts, Harry. 2001. Rudyard Kipling: A Life. Da Capo Press. Boston. Rudyard Kipling (1865-1936) was born in Bombay and educated in England. He was a reporter, short story writer, novelist and poet. In 1907, he won the Nobel Prize for Literature.

does it reduce costs, save time or improve the customer's experience? If so, how much? The amount of value added is a crucial factor in customer decision making. A company may add more value for some customers than for others, and that fact is important when deciding who to target.

Consider the value added by a company that makes yacht propellers. Hampton Company manufactures yachts and has its own foundry to cast and machine propellers. Suppose it costs Hampton $1,800 to manufacture each propeller itself. If Laurel Machining could sell Hampton a comparable propeller for $1,700, how much value would it add? The value added by Laurel isn't that much, only about 5.6% (($1,800 - $1,700)/$1,800). Now suppose Cape May Yachts buys propellers from Baltimore Tool & Die which cost $3,000 each. For Cape May Yachts, the value added by Laurel Machining is $1,300, which is Baltimore's cost of $3,000 less Laurel Machining's price of $1,700 or about 43.3% (($3,000 - $1,700)/$3,000).

The point is, that some customers value a company's product far more than others. To increase the probability of making a sale, companies should determine which customers benefit most from its goods and services. Those are the customers most likely to purchase.

Are there other ways a company can add value for a customer other than by offering a lower price? Of course. Companies can make ordering easier by having websites, catalogues, and a phone ordering system that doesn't make a customer press '1' a half a dozen times or wait endlessly for a representative. A company can add value through prompt delivery, or by offering free delivery.

A company can add value by offering delivery and set-up even if there is an up-charge for these services. A company can offer to haul away old appliances or equipment for free. A company can offer warranties and service contracts. Service contracts represent a significant source of revenue for many companies. Again, the point is that companies should try to identify customers who value their goods and services the most and sell to them.

A company selling thousands of propellers a year to boat or outboard engine manufacturers might not want to deal with small orders. This creates an opening in the market for a new company. Marinas and marine supply companies may need to order propellers one at a time to fulfill specific customer orders. A company trying to break into the propeller market might be willing to sell propellers one at a time, over the internet with two-day delivery to meet this need.

## Target Marketing

Target marketing is about finding those customers who are most likely to purchase a good or service. But what's the point of defining a market more and more narrowly? Shouldn't a company want to sell to as many customers as possible?

Rather than trying to sell to as many customers as possible, wouldn't a better question be: Who can the company sell to most profitably? It costs money to print and mail brochures, it takes time, which is the same as money, to make phone calls, and it takes time and money to make personal sales calls on customers. If there was one group of customers where a hundred sales calls resulted in two sales, and another group of customers where a hundred sales calls yielded twenty sales, which group would you want to spend your time calling? Target marketing helps companies zero in on the customers most likely to buy.

Assume you already have a company with a product. Then you must ask questions like:

(i)   What product characteristics do customers value most?
(ii)  Do different customers value different characteristics?

Suppose a person had a company that made propellers. He or she could stand on a street corner and ask every passer-by, "Want to buy a propeller?" That would take a lot of time and effort, and the payoff in terms of sales would probably be small. Or a person could call everyone in the phone book to ask whether they wanted to buy a propeller. Again, this would take a lot of time, energy and money, and the results would probably not be that great. So, let's step back and do a little thinking about the product and who is likely to purchase it. One of the first decisions should be, what kind of propellers will be sold.

Product characteristics are driven by customer needs; customer needs drive what a company makes. Customer needs continually reshape product size, shape, design and features.

## Segmentation

One way to increase the odds of making a sale is to analyze the characteristics of those who currently purchase propellers. Table 10.1 Market Segmentation is an analysis of who buys boat propellers, the characteristics of the propellers purchased, and the annual volume.

**Table 10.1 Market Segmentation**

| Customer: Use | Propeller Size | Characteristics | Volume |
|---|---|---|---|
| **Government:** | | | |
| Warships | 6'- 20' | Custom designed | 30/yr. |
| Small Craft | 1'- 3' | Standardized | 1,000/yr. |
| **Private Industry:** | | | |
| Cruise ships | 10'- 20' | Custom designed | 70/yr. |
| Luxury Yachts | 5'- 6' | Semi-custom | 200/yr. |
| Yachts | 2'- 4' | Standard | 3,000/yr. |
| Small Craft | 1'- 3' | Standard | 12,000/yr. |
| Outboard Engines | 10"- 16" | Standard | 40,000/yr. |
| Marine supply | 10"- 6' | Mostly standard | 9,000/yr. |
| Marinas | 10"- 2' | Standard | 1,200/yr. |

If a company doesn't have any special expertise in government contracting, it might focus on companies in private industry. If it makes standardized propellers in the range of 10" to 4', cruise ships and luxury yachts can be eliminated because they need propellers larger than the company can make. So, we've gone from offering propellers to everybody, to focusing on a narrower range of customers.

## Analysis of Competition

A target marketing analysis isn't complete unless it considers the competition. Suppose a company wants to open an online book store and develops a comprehensive analysis of who purchases books online. Unless it considers the impact of competitors like amazon.com and Barnes and Noble, it is likely to waste a lot of time, money, and energy.

Returning to the propeller company, suppose 95% of propellers bought by outboard engine manufacturers are purchased from two Chinese manufacturers. It might be difficult to dislodge enough sales from current suppliers to make this a worthwhile target market. But suppose the market for propellers sold to yacht and small craft manufacturers, marinas and marine supply stores was spread across thirty different manufacturers, no one of which had more than 20% of the market. Then it is more likely these customers would consider a new source of supply.

---

**Improving the Odds of Making a Sale**

**Value Added** – A company must be able to add value for the customer. This can be done by solving a problem in a better way, or it can add value by enhancing a customer's self-esteem.

**Market Segmentation** – Market segmentation is dividing a market into groups and finding the group that is most likely to purchase a good or service.

**Competitive Analysis** – Competitive analysis is necessary to avoid segments where the odds of making a sale are low because of intense competition.

---

## Classic Marketing Strategy

Classically, marketing is discussed in terms of **product, place, promotion** and **price**. Product is finding the right product to sell. Place is figuring out where to sell the product. Promotion is informing customers about the product, where to get it, and how it solves their problem or enhances their self-esteem. Price is about offering goods and services at a price that the customer perceives as adding value. Product, place, promotion and price are referred to as the four 'Ps'. While these four concepts provide a conceptual framework for thinking about marketing, it is not the only framework, and what affects one of the 'Ps' often affects others.[2]

## Product

Should a company sell products that people want, or should it sell products it knows how to make and sell? Maybe a little of both. A company won't be successful if it doesn't know how to produce products that represent real value. On the other hand, it might be highly skilled at making things nobody needs or wants. A good marketing plan must start with an understanding of what customers wants.

The complement of this strategy is finding customers the company wants to deal with and analyzing the problems faced by those specific

---

[2] McCarthy, E. Jerome. 1975. Basic Marketing, 5th Ed. Richard D. Irwin, Inc. Homewood, Ill. pp.74-80.

customers. This is the approach used by the pharmaceuticals, genetic engineering, and medical device companies.

A pharmaceutical company might begin by examining the leading Causes of Death from Disease as shown in Table 10.2.[3] It then might want to estimate the number of customers in a market segment because significant sales volume is usually necessary to justify the cost of research, development and regulatory approval.

**Table 10.2 Causes of Death from Disease**

| Cause of Death | Annual Deaths | Deaths per 100,000 |
|---|---|---|
| Diseases of heart | 598,607 | 195.0 |
| Malignant neoplasms (cancers) | 568,668 | 185.2 |
| Chronic lower respiratory diseases | 137,082 | 44.7 |
| Cerebrovascular diseases | 128,603 | 41.9 |
| Alzheimer's disease | 78,889 | 25.7 |
| Diabetes mellitus | 68,504 | 22.3 |
| Influenza and pneumonia | 53,582 | 17.5 |
| Kidney diseases | 48,714 | 15.9 |
| Septicemia (blood infections) | 35,587 | 11.6 |
| Chronic liver disease and cirrhosis | 30,444 | 9.9 |
| Hypertensive renal disease | 25,651 | 8.4 |
| Parkinson's disease | 20,552 | 6.7 |

Within each of these disease categories there may be further breakdowns that are useful in guiding research, so drugs are developed for the largest, most profitable markets.

## Place

Place usually means the channel of distribution. The channel of distribution is how the product moves from the manufacturer or originator to the ultimate consumer.

---

[3] Kochanek, Kenneth, Jiaquan Xu, Sherry Murphy, Arialdi Minino & Hsiang-Ching Kung. 2011. "Table B Deaths and Death Rates for 2009," National Vital Statistics Reports. Vol.59 No.4. U.S. Department of Health and Human Services, Centers for Disease Control and Prevention, National Center for Health Statistics. March 16.

Campbell Soup doesn't sell directly to consumers. It sells to supermarkets who sell to customers. There are two steps in its primary channel of distribution. It must make two sales. One sale is to the supermarket which will carry Campbell's brand soup. The other sale is to consumers who will ultimately buy Campbell Soup. Smaller grocery stores might have to buy soup from wholesalers who buy from manufacturers. That puts three steps in their distribution channel. Every step in a distribution channel has costs and benefits.

In the case of a pharmaceuticals company, it must sell the benefits of its product to doctors who write prescriptions. The patient then must purchase the drug from a pharmacy which adds another step in the channel of distribution.

## Promotion

Promotion is communication with the customer. Communication has traditionally been thought of as advertising, but customer communication is far broader than advertising. Every time a customer touches a company or its products, a communication takes place.

### *Customer Service as Communication*

Assume a company advertises three dress shirts for $100, and a customer orders them from the company's website. If the customer gets shirts that are the wrong size or color, that is a customer communication, a bad one. How many of the customer's friends and acquaintances will hear about this bad experience?

How many dollars of advertising will it take to persuade the customer to do business with that company again? The point is that every customer contact is a communication. Communications can be good or bad. The goodwill developed through ten good contacts can be wiped out by a single bad one.

You might say the issue here is customer service not communication. **Customer service is all about communication.** Customer service communicates whether a company is competent to deliver desired goods and services in a timely manner. **Customer service** is not about making a sale. It **is about making the next sale** and the sale after that, and winning a life-long customer, and getting referrals.

*Advertising*

Effective advertising breaks down into several parts: (i) goals, (ii) means, and (iii) measurement.

**Goals**

The message conveyed by an advertisement is often unclear or does nothing to help a company meet its promotional goals. Consider the advertisement in Table 10.3 Auto Advertisement. Any idea what brand is being advertised, or where to buy it?[4]

**Table 10.3 Auto Advertisement**

Wall Street Journal, November 12, 2009 B3

THE WORLD'S FIRST
*ACTIVE PEDESTRIAN DETECTION SYSTEM*

Vehicle Shown and described with optional equipment. *The Active Pedestrian Detection System, part of the Advanced Pre-Collision System, is designed to help reduce the impact speed and damages in certain frontal collisions only. It is not a collision-avoidance system and is not substitutable for safe and attentive driving. System effectiveness depends on many factors, such as speed, driver input and road conditions. Please see your Owner's Manual for further information

Unless a company has a clear idea of the goals of advertising, the most entertaining, prize winning advertisements will be a waste of money. What should the goals of advertising be?

---

[4] Active Pedestrian Detection System. 2009. "The World's First Active Pedestrian Detection System™. Wall Street Journal. Nov. 12. B3.

**(i) Let the customer know who you are and where to find you.**
This might include providing your name, address, phone number and web address. It should also tell the potential customer what you do. "We sell antique auto parts for less."

**(ii) Educate the customer as to your product's features.**
"Our antique auto parts are manufactured from original drawings and come with a 5-year warranty. Our customers can also download installation manuals from our free online library."

**(iii)  Increase the value perception of your product.**
A Porsche Boxster and a VW Beetle use the same amount of steel, glass and aluminum, but the Boxster is 'perceived' to be a higher status item, so people are willing to pay more for the same weight of materials. Perception is often driven by images. Celebrity endorsements, product placements and advertising that re-enforce a positive self-image, contribute to perceived value.

**Methods**

Table 10.4 Promotional Methods lists some of the ways companies communicate with potential customers.

**Table 10.4 Promotional Methods**

| Radio | Newspapers | Bill Boards |
|---|---|---|
| Broadcast Television | Direct Mail | Flyers |
| Cable Television | Telemarketing | Coupons |
| Magazines | Web marketing | Store displays |
| End cap displays | Posters | Caps and T-shirts |
| Demonstrations | Sports sponsorships | Give-aways |
| Contests | Endorsements | Product placements |
| Social Media | Email | Tweets |

Radio, television, magazines, newspapers and the web keep detailed statistics on how many people they reach, their age, sex, and sometimes income. Often, they can track leads and sales.

What is the most effective means of advertising a restaurant in Cherry Hill, New Jersey, a town ten-miles east of Philadelphia? Is television the most effective means? Television is expensive in terms of total dollars and some say that if a company can't afford at least 50 commercials, it won't be able to make its message stick. On the other hand, television provides low-cost customer contacts, because tens of thousands of people will see every prime time commercial.

But is it likely that people from all over the Philadelphia viewing area will drive to a restaurant in Cherry Hill? Will people in Media, a town twenty-miles west of Philadelphia do it? And if a few people from Media drive to Cherry Hill, thirty miles away to try a restaurant, are they likely to become regular customers? Probably not. That means most of the low-cost customer contacts are being wasted.

If a business is local, it might be better off focusing on a more targeted promotion such as local newspapers, direct mail, flyers or coupons. But, if a company has stores throughout a viewing area, television might be cost effective.

**Measurement**

Measuring the effectiveness of advertising is an important topic and is discussed separately later in the chapter.

## Price

The right price is a function of supply and demand. Competition impacts supply. Value added, perceived status and many other factors drive demand. Setting the right 'price point' is critical to both maximizing sales and profits. Marketing analysis helps determine the appropriate 'price point' for a good or service. See the prior chapter for more details on price strategy.

---

### Classic Marketing Strategy – The Four Ps

**Product** – Product is selecting the product that helps a customer solve a problem or increase his or her self-esteem.

**Place** – Place is the channel of distribution between the manufacturer or service provider and the ultimate customer.

**Promotion** – Promotion is communication with the customer.

**Price** – Price is the price at which a customer will perceive the product or service adds value.

---

# Buying Window

The who, what, where, why and how of customers have been discussed. Now it's time to discuss when. If a randomly selected group of fifty people were asked whether they were ready to buy a new car, odds are that somewhere between zero and two would be ready. But, if each person in that group were asked every day for the next ten years whether they were ready to buy a new car, most people would eventually say 'Yes'.

The buying window is the interval of time between when a person is ready to consider information about a purchase and the time they purchase. No matter how good the product, or how great the price, offers to sell will be ignored until a customer is ready to consider a purchase. No matter how great the product or how low the price, a customer will ignore offers after they have purchased a product that meets their needs. A good marketing strategy should help a company identify when a customer's buying window is open so that it can make offers during that interval.[5]

The best way to identify a customer's buying window is to study customers' buying patterns. For example, many people have new cars maintained by their dealership. Some new cars are sold with free 10,000-mile check-ups, or the first five oil changes for free. A dealership can use data collected during these visits to estimate the number of miles a customer drives per year. Dealers might have statistics that show cars need new brakes every 50,000 miles, tires every 60,000 miles, new generators every 80,000 miles and batteries every five years. Given this, a dealership might estimate when a car is going to reach 50,000 miles and send information indicating that a car might need replacement brakes. They might also send a coupon giving a discount on such a replacement.

Likewise, a dealership might estimate when a car needs new tires, a new generator or a new battery and send coupons for those services at appropriate times. And, every time a customer returns to the dealership for service, that is an opportunity for the customer to inspect the latest models.

---

[5] Vance, David E. 2009. Corporate Restructuring. Springer. Berlin. pp.140-142.

---

### Customer Intelligence System and the Buying Window

The buying window is the interval of time between when a customer is ready to consider a purchase and when a purchase has been made.

A customer intelligence system should anticipate customer behavior and put appropriate offers in front of customers when their buying window is open.

---

Heating companies often send out offers for furnace maintenance around the time of the first frost. Travel companies might track when people book vacations and send brochures and coupons to customers a few weeks before that date. The Customer Intelligence System Travel Agency Case Study is an example of how such a system might work.

## Customer Intelligence System Travel Agency Case Study

### What the Company Does:

Suppose a travel agency collects customer information to better understand customer travel needs and accommodate them. Information might include:

(i)    travel purpose: business or pleasure travel;
(ii)   the type of traveler, family, couples only, or single;
(iii)  when during the year customers usually book travel;
(iv)   when during the year customers travel;
(v)    customer budget; and
(vi)   the types of vacations customers book.

This information can be used to model customer behavior and put appropriate offers in front of people when they are making travel decisions. A customer intelligence analysis might unfold like this:

1. Extract pleasure travelers from the travel company's database. Business travelers travel when business demands, so it is hard to predict when they will travel.

2. Compute the average budget of each pleasure traveler for the last three years, if data is available.

3.  Sort customers by the month in which they booked travel.

4.  Separate them into traveler type: family, couples only, or single.

5.  Identify the types of vacations the traveler has taken before: cruise, theme park, wilderness adventure, foreign travel.

6.  One month before the time a traveler usually books, send brochures for vacations that match the traveler, based on: a) budget, b) traveler type, and c) vacation preference.

7.  Send a $200 coupon with the travel offer to entice the traveler to promptly book with the travel agency.

8.  Send a follow-up note two weeks after the original offer.

9.  For customers that spend more than $5,000 per year, make a follow-up call.

**What the Customer Sees**

John and Martha Grimes, owners of a garden center, look forward to taking a cruise every fall after their peak business season. They have been booking with Alice's Travel each August.

This year they were thinking about booking with another agency. However, in July, they got a package from Alice's Travel listing several interesting cruises and a coupon good for $200 if they booked within 30 days. The Grimes' booked with Alice's Travel again this year.

# Advertising Measurement

John Wanamaker (1838–1922) was born in Philadelphia, and was a much respected and admired merchant, civic and political figure. He is considered the father of modern advertising. Wanamaker said, "Half the money I spend on advertising is wasted; the trouble is I don't know which half." [6] How can a company know whether its money is being wasted?

---

[6] Appel, Joseph Herbert. *The Business Biography of John Wanamaker, Founder and Builder, America's Merchant Pioneer From 1861-1922: with glimpses of Rodman Wanamaker and Thomas B.* Wanamaker. New York: The Macmillan Company, 1930. The phrase "Half of all advertising dollars is wasted" is also sometimes credited to Lord Leverhulme (1851-1925).

For some companies, advertising is effective, and for others it seems like a waste of money. How can a company know what to do?

## Experiment

Every company and market is different. Sometimes a company must run a series of experiments to determine what works best.

Suppose a company advertises in a newspaper or magazine and the advertisement includes a coupon with a code that identifies where it was run. For example, the coupon could have a code number for advertisements in the Sunday Philadelphia Inquirer, a different number for the Wednesday Philadelphia Inquirer, another number for the Courier Post and so forth. By tracking coupon redemption, a company can estimate the effectiveness of using each type of media. Table 10.5 Media Test is an example of how one might systematically analyze the effectiveness of various advertising media.

**Table 10.5 Media Test**

| Media | Date | Cost | Coupon No. | Sales | Cost / Sale |
|-------|------|------|-----------|-------|-------------|
| Inquirer, Sunday | Nov. 6 | $2,000 | 7501 | 50 | $40.00 |
| Inquirer, Wednesday | Nov. 16 | $1,200 | 7503 | 40 | $30.00 |
| Courier Post | Nov. 2 | $450 | 7507 | 35 | $12.86 |
| Voorhees Trend | Nov.28 | $125 | 7509 | 25 | $5.00 |
| South Jersey (SJ) Magazine | Nov.10 | $300 | 7513 | 25 | $12.00 |

Analyzing the data in Table 10.5, the most cost-effective way to market this company is through the Voorhees Trend, because it has the lowest cost- per-sale.

How might the effectiveness of a television ad campaign be measured? The commercial might include a promotion code that entitles customers to a discount. Or the commercial might provide a phone number to place orders.

# Quantitative Analysis

Several metrics are useful when evaluating a marketing campaign.

**(i) Cost** - What is the cost of a method in absolute dollars? Television, for example, usually requires a substantial commitment, typically fifty or more commercials.[7]

**(ii) How targeted is the promotion method** – Is your message spread too widely, or just widely enough?

**(iii) Cost per Customer Contact** – What is the cost of reaching one of your target customers? The equation for cost per contact is shown in equation Eq.10.1. Suppose a direct mail marketing campaign for kitchen remodeling cost $5,000 and contacted 2,000 people. What is the cost per contact?

$$\text{Cost per Contact} = \text{Cost / Number of Contacts} \quad \text{Eq.10.1}$$

$$= \$5,000 / 2,000 \quad = \$2.50$$

**(iv) Cost per Lead** – A lead is defined as someone who has shown at least a minimum level of interest in a company's products or services. That interest may be in the form of a phone call, store visit, email, or some other form of contact. Everyone who inquired about free estimates would be a lead. Cost per Lead may be computed using equation Eq.10.2. Suppose the campaign cost $5,000 and 125 people inquired about free estimates. What is the Cost per Lead?

$$\text{Cost per Lead} = \text{Cost / Number of Leads} \quad \text{Eq.10.2}$$

$$= \$5,000 / 125 \quad = \$40.00$$

**(v) Cost-per-Sale** - Sales are the end goal of promotional campaigns. Metrics, like cost per contact and cost per lead, are means to the ultimate end of sales. Cost-per-Sale may be computed using equation Eq.10.3. Suppose the campaign cost $5,000 and 40 people made a purchase.

---

[7] Levinson, Jay Conrad. 2007. Guerrilla Marketing 4th Ed. Houghton Mifflin. New York.

$$\text{Cost-per-Sale} = \text{Cost / Number of Sales} \quad \text{Eq.10.3}$$

$$= \$5,000 / 40 \quad = \$125$$

Whether the cost per contact, cost per lead, or cost-per-sale, is good or bad depends on whether there is a more effective means of promotion, and whether there is enough gross profit in a product to cover the cost-per-sale.

## Contribution

In addition to measuring costs for contacts, leads and sales, a company should consider how much an advertising campaign contributes to profit after the costs of the promotional campaign are subtracted. This amount is called the contribution, and it can be calculated using equation Eq.10.4.

$$
\begin{aligned}
\text{Contribution} = {}& \text{increase in sales} \quad\quad\quad\quad\quad\quad \text{Eq.10.4} \\
& - \text{full absorption cost of goods or services} \\
& - \text{campaign costs} \\
& - \text{sales commissions, if any.}
\end{aligned}
$$

Suppose a campaign costs $5,000, the cost of goods sold as a percentage of sales (COGS%) is 65% of sales. Sales commissions for following up on leads and closing sales is 10%. Assume kitchen remodels average $6,000 and 40 sales are made.

The increase in sales is $240,000 ($6,000 x 40).

Cost of goods sold is $156,000 ($240,000 x 65%).

Sales commissions are $24,000 ($240,000 x 10%).

$$
\begin{aligned}
\text{Net Contribution} = {}& \$240,000 \text{ sales} \\
& - \$156,000 \text{ cost of goods sold} \\
& - \$5,000 \text{ campaign costs} \\
& - \$24,000 \text{ commissions.}
\end{aligned}
$$

$$= \$55,000$$

Generally, if a marketing campaign has a significant, positive contribution, it is considered effective and might be repeated again sometime. However, if a marketing campaign's contribution is small or negative, it shouldn't be repeated.

## Repeat Sales

Repeat sales are the best way to build a business. The first sale to a customer is expensive and time consuming, because the company must find the new customer and convince him, her, or it, to try its product or service. But, if a customer has had a good experience with a company and its products or services, the next sale should be easier and less expensive.

Suppose a pizza parlor spent $500 advertising in a local paper, and the ad included a $5 coupon. If 400 coupons were redeemed, the pizza parlor would know that at least 400 people saw the ad.

If the average sale without a coupon was $20, that would mean that $6,000 of sales were directly attributed to the ad (400 x ($20 average sale - $5 coupon)). If the gross margin on pizza were 55%, that is $0.55 of each dollar of sales was left over after the cost of making the pizza, the campaign would increase contribution by $2,800 ($6,000 x 55% - $500 advertising).

If 20% of those using a coupon made two more purchases without further advertising or coupons, that would increase sales by $3,200 (400 x 20% x 2 x $20) and increase gross profit by an additional $1,760 ($3,200 x 55%). This is the **Residual Advertising Effect.**

Residual effects might be measured by giving those who used the first $5 coupon, a $2 coupon for their next visit. Ask whether customers would like to be placed on a company's email or mailing list to get additional coupons. Customer loyalty cards are another way to track repeat sales. The ways a company can track customers is only limited by one's imagination.

---

### Measurement

Measure the results of advertising expenditures because half of all advertising dollars are wasted.

Measure **cost per** customer **contact.**

Measure **cost per lead.**

Measure **cost-per-sale.**

Measure the **contribution of** an advertising **campaign.**

# Making the Sale

Customer intelligence systems are sometimes called lead generation systems. These systems are especially important in business to business sales, where personal relationships with customers can make the difference between a sale and no sale. Salespeople must have an orderly way to access customer information such as: Customer name, address, phone number, email address, and other intelligence about the customer.

## Follow-up

Sales people also need a system to track follow-up calls, meetings and post-sale contacts to make sure appropriate goods and services were timely delivered and that the customer was satisfied. Many software packages are available to collect, organize and manage customer contacts and customer intelligence.

Some have estimated that between a quarter and a third of sales are lost because of inadequate follow-up. Follow-up can mean:

(i)    promptly returning phone calls;
(ii)   promptly returning emails;
(iii)  providing estimates when promised;
(iv)   keeping appointments and being on time or canceling with plenty of notice.
(v)    promptly responding to complaints, and listening quietly and sympathetically;
(vi)   compiling and acting on customer intelligence.

Most important, follow-up should be pro-active not reactive.

## Customer Preferences

Customer intelligence systems often capture:

(i)    The kind of goods and services purchased in the past.
(ii)   The names of purchasing agents and their bosses.
(iii)  The names of the real deciders in the company. For equipment, this might be the engineering department not the purchasing department.

(iv) A description of what the company does, and who its customers are.

(v) A list of goods or services customers have inquired about, whether they bought anything or not.

(vi) Preferences the company has, as to color, size, and features.

(vii) Customer complaints. This is important in overcoming objections.

(viii) When customers are likely to purchase.

## Closing the Sale

We've identified the products customers want; we've narrowly targeted the customers most likely to buy; we've placed products in the channels of distribution where customers shop; communicated the features of the product, and explained how it solves a customer's problem or will enhance a customer's self-esteem, set a fair price point, and have estimated when the customer's buying window is open. Yet, the customer still hasn't purchased. Why? A good salesperson would run through a checklist of things in his or her mind.

## The Ask

The number one reason sales aren't made is that no one asks for the sale. Expressions like, "Can I write up that order?", or "How many would you like?", or "When do you need delivery?", or, "What color would you like?" These questions are examples of an ask.

## Overcoming Objections

If a potential customer says 'No', it's important to ask why. Don't ask why in a way that puts the customer on the defensive. Ask as though you are merely curious. Overcoming objections is an important art form in making sales.

Sometimes it's important to step back and confirm that you understand the problem the customer is trying to solve, or what the customer is doing to feel better about him or herself. Once you know a customer's objectives, you are in a better position to overcome objections.

Suppose a person has been looking at a Corvette ZR1 with 638 horsepower because it will make them feel good about themselves. But, when you ask if you can write up the order they say 'no', and with a little probing you find cost is the reason. ZR1s are expensive; a new one might cost $115,000. A good salesperson would offer alternatives. A Corvette Coupe with 430 horsepower costs around $50,000. Unless one is set on drag racing, the extra 200 horsepower might not be that useful. Or, if a customer insists on a supercar, a salesman might point him or her to a used Corvette ZR6 with 505 horsepower which can be had for around $50,000.

Objections come in many forms and some may seem trivial, but to close the sale, it's important to be patient and explore them. If the customer says, "It's the wrong color," the salesperson should say, "I can order one in any color you like." If the customer says, "It doesn't get good gas mileage," the salesperson might say, "You could buy a Volkswagen and save $10 a week in gas. But you know, life's too short to worry about $10 a week. Besides, you deserve it."

## Safety

Sometimes customers won't tell you why they aren't buying. But that doesn't mean there isn't a reason. Sometimes it's as simple as the fact that customers want safety. They don't want to regret their choice. There are several ways to make a customer feel safe. Flagship customers are one way. Flagship customers are customers with an excellent reputation of their own. If these well-known and important customers think enough of a company to purchase its products and services, that provides some assurance that the company's products and services are good. References, endorsements, warranties and money-back guarantees, all help provide a sense of safety.

It takes practice to get good at closing sales. For any given product or service there are dozens of possible objections. When talking to a customer, they might come up with an objection you can't overcome. But every time you pitch a sale to a customer, you should learn something that can be used to close the next sale.

---

**Closing the Sale**

**Customer Objectives** – Make sure you understand the problem the customer is trying to solve or how the customer is trying to raise their self-esteem.

**Ask for the sale** – The main reason people fail to close a sale is that they don't ask for the sale.

**Overcome Objections** – Provide the customer with alternatives.

**Make the customer feel safe** – Customers don't want to regret a purchase decision.

---

# Conclusion

Making a sale is the most important thing a company does. Nothing happens until a sale is made. A sale is getting the customer to agree to purchase something and getting paid. Marketing is about increasing the probability of making a sale.

No company can force a customer to buy. A customer will only buy if the seller can create value for a customer, for example by reducing cost, increasing efficiency or by enhancing a customer's self-esteem.

Target marketing increases sales efficiency by identifying groups of customers that are the most likely to purchase. An essential element of target marketing is analyzing the competitive environment. New or smaller companies are rarely able to compete directly with large established companies. Companies should seek markets which are easier to penetrate.

Classic marketing analysis revolves around the four Ps: (i) product, (ii) place, (iii) promotion, and (iv) price. Product is about selecting a product that adds value for the customer. Place is the channel of distribution from the originator to the consumer. Promotion is about communication with the customer. Price must add value for the customer and make the sale profitable for the business.

The 'buying window' is the interval of time between when a customer is prepared to consider information about a product or service, and when a purchase is made. Information and offers made before and after the 'buying window' is open, will be ignored. The trick from the marketing point of view is to know when a customer's 'buying window' is open and make offers during that period.

The goals of advertising are: (i) to let the customer know where to find a company and what the company does, (ii) to educate the customer as to how the company's product or service will solve the customer's problem or enhance the customer's self-esteem and (iii) to increase a customer's value perception of the product.

It is said that half of all advertising dollars are wasted, so it's important to measure the results of every advertising campaign and judge its effectiveness. Measurement might include cost per contact, cost per lead, cost-per-sale, and the contribution of the advertising campaign.

The number one reason that salespeople fail to close a sale is that they don't ask for the sale. If a customer doesn't purchase after the ask, a sales person should step back and re-evaluate the needs and wants of the customer to determine which products or services add value from the customer's perspective. A salesperson should probe why a customer isn't purchasing and attempt to overcome objections. Offering alternatives is one method. A salesperson should make the customer feel safe through endorsements, flagship customers, warranties, and a liberal return policy. Marketing can increase the probability of a sale, and well-established selling techniques can help close a sale, so a company can survive and grow.

# Appendix 10a: Market Research

It is one thing to say a company should analyze the market and target those companies most likely to buy. It's quite another thing to do it. How does one get started? Where does one look?

It turns out that there are a lot of resources available to identify target markets. A company should start by asking who buys its products now, or who it thinks would buy its products if they knew about them. Current and potential customers probably fall into broad categories. Find new customers by looking for companies similar to existing customers. Companies in the same industries as existing customers might be potential customers.

## Business to Business Market Research

There are many sources of information for business-to-business sales. Every good library has access to databases or directories that list every business in the country. One example is the Reference USA database.

Such databases list things like the industry a company is in, its sales, number of employees, and its location. All US companies are classified by business type and assigned a Standard Industrial Classification (SIC) code. Once a company finds a customer's SIC code, it can search for all other companies with the same SIC code.

Companies that are publicly traded have registered their securities with the Securities and Exchange Commission (SEC). Financial statements and other information about publicly traded companies are posted on the SEC's website: www.sec.gov.[8] This website allows one to search companies by SIC. Another place to find new customers is finance.yahoo.com. For each company listed, this website also lists its competitors. The competitors of your customers are potential future customers. If customers are in trade associations, it might be useful to get a list of trade association members. Each of their members might be a potential customer. Occasionally, one can find lists of companies in a particular industry through internet searches and that information can be used to construct customer lists.

## Business to Consumer Market Research

There are many ways to do consumer market research. Focus groups can be used to test product acceptance and customer price sensitivity. Lists containing names, addresses, and phone numbers for direct marketing campaigns can be purchased. MapQuest and zip codes can be used to determine how far customers are from a company's facility.

The census department publishes average income by town, so customer income can be estimated. See www.census.gov. Information on consumer preferences can sometimes be gleaned by analyzing magazine subscription lists. For example, people who subscribe to Golf Digest are probably interested in golf equipment, sportswear and vacations. Those who subscribe to Road and Track are probably interested in cars, or more

---

[8] To find a company on the SEC website, go to www.sec.gov. Click on Filings, then Company Filings Search. In the search box fill in the name of the company you want. Click on the CIK code on the left of the screen. Each company files many reports with the SEC. In the "filing type" box input 10-K. The 10-K includes a company's annual financial statement and other information about a company. An alternative to searching for companies one at a time is to click on the red SIC code which is on the left side of the screen. Find new customers by looking for companies with the same SIC code as existing customers. Then analyze each company's 10-K.

specifically performance cars and accessories. Many magazines sell customer lists, so research can be narrowed by customer interest.

Some of the most powerful customer research tools are web-based. For example, Google Analytics can track website access, page views, dwell time and the links a user clicks on. This can be useful in identifying the types of goods and services a particular individual is interested in, so that offers can be made proactively. There are dozens of other web-based tools, some of which monitor sentiment and trends by analyzing tweets and other online activity.

# Terms and Concepts

**Buying Window** – The buying window is the interval of time between when a customer is willing to consider a purchase and when they have made a purchase.

**Competitive Analysis** – A good marketing strategy considers the competition and looks for segments where competition is weakest.

**Contribution** – Contribution is the net contribution of an advertising campaign. It is the increase in sales less the increase in Cost of Goods Sold, less Advertising Costs, less Commissions, if any.

**Cost per Customer Contact** – This is the cost of reaching one customer. Cost per Customer Contact = Advertising Costs/Number Contacted.

**Cost per Lead** – A lead can be defined as someone who has shown at least a minimum level of interest in a company's products or services. That interest may be in the form of a phone call, store visit, email, or some other form of contact with the company.
Cost per Lead = Advertising Costs / Number of Leads.

**Cost-per-Sale** – Cost-per-sale is the advertising cost of making one sale.
Cost-per-Sale = Advertising Cost / Number of Sales.

**Four Ps** – Classic marketing strategy analyzes the world through the four Ps: Product, Place, Promotion, and Price.

**Kipling, Rudyard** - A twentieth century novelist, poet and philosopher who said to understand a problem one should know who, what, where, why, when and how.

**Law of Demand** – The law of demand says that, when price falls, customers will buy more of that good; and when price rises, people will buy less of that good.

**Marketing** – Marketing is about increasing the odds of making a sale.

**Measurement, Advertising** – Before money is spent on advertising, a company should determine how it will measure the effectiveness of an advertising campaign.

**Objections, Over-coming** – Many customers decline to make a purchase even though a product or service solves their problem or makes them feel good about themselves. A good salesperson would gently probe for reasons a person did not make a purchase and overcome objections. Empathy, flexibility and offering alternatives that may get a customer to purchase.

**Place** – Place, in marketing, means the channel of distribution by which products are moved from the producer to the ultimate customer.

**Price** – Price is a substantial factor in what people buy, and how much. See the Law of Demand, and the Chapter on Supply and Demand.

**Product** – Product is the type of product that is appropriate for a particular customer. Products must create value for customers.

**Promotion** – Promotion is communication with the customer. Every contact with a customer is a communication.

**Residual Advertising Effects** – An advertising campaign should change a customer's buying habits so that some change persists after the advertising campaign is over.

**Sales** – Sales is closing the deal, getting the customer to agree to buy, billing, and getting paid for something.

**Segmentation** – Also called market segmentation, is grouping potential customers into categories with similar characteristics. Segmentation is a tool for target marketing.

**Target Marketing** – Is the process of finding customers most likely to purchase.

**Value Added** – A company should carefully think about how its products and services add value for a customer. Does it solve a problem or make the customer feel good about him or herself?

**Wanamaker, John** – He said, "Half of all advertising is wasted, but I don't know which half."

# References

Active Pedestrian Detection System. 2009. "The World's First Active Pedestrian Detection System™. Wall Street Journal. Nov. 12. B3.

Appel, Joseph Herbert. *The Business Biography of John Wanamaker, Founder and Builder, America's Merchant Pioneer From 1861-1922: with glimpses of Rodman Wanamaker and Thomas B. Wanamaker.* New York: The Macmillan Company, 1930. The phrase "Half of all advertising dollars is wasted" is also sometimes credited to Lord Leverhulme (1851-1925).

Company Filings. 2018. Securities and Exchange Commission. www.sec.gov.

Kochanek, Kenneth, Jiaquan Xu, Sherry Murphy, Arialdi Minino & Hsiang-Ching Kung. 2011. "Table B Deaths and Death Rates for 2009," National Vital Statistics Reports. Vol.59 No.4. U.S. Department of Health and Human Services, Centers for Disease Control and Prevention, National Center for Health Statistics. Mar.16.

Levinson, Jay Conrad. 2007. Guerrilla Marketing 4th Ed. Houghton Mifflin. New York.

Marketing Mix and the 4Ps. 2018. "The Marketing Mix and the 4Ps: Product Price Place and Promotion." Learn Marketing.Net    3/17 http://learnmarketing.net/marketingmix.htm

McCarthy, E. Jerome. 1975. Basic Marketing, 5th Ed. Richard D. Irwin, Inc. Homewood, Ill. pp.74-80.

Ricketts, Harry. 2001. Rudyard Kipling: A Life. Da Capo Press. Boston. Rudyard Kipling (1865-1936) was born in Bombay and educated in England. He was a reporter, short story writer, novelist and poet. In 1907, he won the Nobel Prize for Literature.

Vance, David E. 2009. Corporate Restructuring. Springer. Berlin. pp.140-142.

# CHAPTER ELEVEN

# BUSINESS INTELLIGENCE AND ANALYTICS

After completing this chapter, you should be able to:

11.1 Define business intelligence and analytics and discuss how it might be used.

11.2 Explain the theory behind data mining.

11.3 Design and complete a data mining project.

11.4 Write a client report on data mining.

11.5 Understand some of the elements of successful consulting

## Introduction

Business intelligence provides a company with a competitive advantage. It can increase sales by better identifying target markets and proactively making offers. It can reduce costs by identifying unprofitable products, customers, and stores, and by identifying inefficient processes. It can reduce losses by avoiding loans to poor credit risks and avoid selling insurance to those who are accident prone.

Business Intelligence and Analytics (BI&A) combines critical thinking with computer, statistical, and management science, to discover new information. Most companies are awash in computer generated data, but few exploit it to their best advantage.

Management should develop objectively verifiable, fact-based strategies. Analytics can help avoid subjectivity and provide consistency.[1] On the other hand, some management decisions must be made before data is available. For example, there was no data on smart phones before Apple

---

[1] Banerjee, Arindam, Tathagata Bandyopadhyay, and Prichi Acharya. 2013. "Data Analytics: Hyped Up Aspirations or True Potential?" *Vikalpa*. Vol.38 No.4 pp.1-11.

launched its iPhone. Likewise, Ford had little data on the prospects for its all-aluminum pick-up truck before the first truck was sold. The decision as to when to use fact-based decision making, and when to make a leap of faith is the essence of executive judgment. However, where data exists, it should be used to inform decision making. Some of the kinds of questions BI&A can, and should answer are:[2]

| Descriptive Analytics | What happened? |
| Diagnostic Analytics | Why did it happen? |
| Prescriptive Analytics | What should be done about it? |
| Predictive Analytics | What is likely to happen next? |

Companies that embrace BI&A generate 16% more revenue through human and physical assets than companies that are not BI&A intensive; outperform industry averages by 6% to 9% on measures like revenue per employee and fixed asset turnover; and are 9% to 26% more profitable than industry averages on measures like operating margin and profit margin.[3] McKinsey and Company, a top ranked consulting firm, estimates big data and analytics could boost retail operating margins as much as 60%.[4]

## Evolution of Business Intelligence and Analytics

The science of Business Intelligence and Analytics (BI&A) is evolving. BI&A 1.0 consisted of internal company data and a few purchased databases. This information supported standardized reports, scorecards, dashboards, and simple graphics to help management better understand information. Statistical analysis, data mining, and queries that facilitated ad hoc report generation, were common tools.[5]

---

[2] Banerjee, Arindam, Tathagata Bandyopadhyay, and Prichi Acharya. 2013. "Data Analytics: Hyped Up Aspirations or True Potential?" *Vikalpa*. Vol.38 No.4 pp.1-11.
[3] Westerman, George, Didier Bonnet and Andrew McAfee. 2014. "The Advantages of Digital Maturity," *MIT Sloan Management Review* http://sloanreview.mit.edu/article/the-advantages-of-digital-maturity/ Nov. 20, downloaded 2014-12-11
[4] Freeland, Chrystia. 2012. "In Big Data, Potential for Big Division," *New York Times*. Jan.12. www.nytimes.com/2012/01/13/us/13iht-letter13.html downloaded 2014-11-18.
[5] Chen, Hsinchun, Robert H. L. Chiang and Veda C. Storey. 2012. "Business Intelligence and Analytics: From Big Data to Big Impact," MIS Quarterly. Dec. Vol.36 No.4 pp. 1165-1188.

The internet launched BI&A 2.0. Web based information such as IP specific user search terms, information collected via cookies, user generated content, social media, crowdsourcing, click streams, traffic volume, photos, and video, provided a vast new sea of data for analysis. Google Analytics, for example, analyzes browsing and purchase patterns. Because much of this data is unstructured, text mining and other software to extract actionable intelligence, will have to be developed. [6]

Large scale adoption of mobile devices such as smart phones and tablets, with their downloadable app software, is leading to the development of BI&A 3.0. Many mobile devices provide real-time location information, as well as meta-data, like number called, call length, websites browsed, and dwell time. BI&A 3.0 also includes sensor-based information, barcodes, and information from internet-connected devices, such as vehicles, heating and cooling systems, appliances, security systems, and machinery. Methods of visualizing information and creating real-time dialogues with large populations of users and devices are likely to be features of BI&A 3.0. New, undreamed of applications for this information may appear, and the software tools needed to interpret this information have yet to be developed.

## Big Data

Big data is a term used to apply to the ever-expanding ocean of data available for analysis. Big data is defined by the four V's: (i) volume, (ii) velocity, (iii) variety, and (iv) veracity. [7]

Almost every interaction in the world involves something computerized, and computers leave digital footprints. Many processes and internal operations create event logs which can be used to gain operational insights. All of this creates an enormous volume of data which must be stored, classified, and retrieved as needed.

Some data must be analyzed in near-real-time to be useful. For example, sentiment can change in weeks, days or even hours. If data is not promptly analyzed and used, it loses value. Sentiment and trending information enable companies to anticipate changes in financial markets and to get ahead of consumer demand for goods and services.

---

[6] Chen, Hsinchun, Robert H. L. Chiang and Veda C. Storey. 2012. "Business Intelligence and Analytics: From Big Data to Big Impact," *MIS Quarterly*. Dec. Vol.36 No.4 pp. 1165-1188.
[7] Goes, Paulo B., "Big Data and IS Research," *MIS Quarterly*. Vol.38 No.3 pp.iv

One of the challenges of big data is integration of information from a variety of sources. Not all data have a common element like a social security number or an IP address, so pulling data together from various sources is no trivial feat. There are other problems as well. Much of big data is imperfect and incomplete, so analytical software must compensate for these anomalies.

Veracity includes truthfulness and reliability. Just because data is digitized, doesn't mean it's reliable. Veracity includes sifting the signal from the noise, deception detection, and relevance ranking.[8] News streams, blogs, Tweets, social media and images are largely unstructured. Most of this unstructured data is probably noise. Social bots are programs designed to actively deceive people by praising or criticizing products, people and policies. A recent report estimated as many as 48 million Twitter accounts are bots, and they are responsible for as many as one in four tweets. Bots are designed to look like real people, and as such, can influence real users. A different study estimated that ten percent of social media posts used to study consumer behavior are actually bots.[9] Caution when analyzing data is advised.

Big data analytics is mostly grounded in text recognition, data mining and statistical analysis. Data mining looks for frequent events, relationships among pieces of data, and exceptions, and it slices data into subsets with common characteristics. An interesting use of data mining is cluster analysis which identifies marketing or influence 'hot spots'. Clusters can occur in a market space, at a geographic location, among people, or in time.

Search term and contact information might be mined to identify thought leaders. It is believed that if a thought leader can be persuaded to try a product, others in their circle of influence will try it too. Statistical analysis can be used to measure the strength of relationships and forecast future events from past data.

## Marketing Applications

Data mining can be used to identify groups or sub-groups that are likely to purchase a particular item. Applications in e-commerce include recommender systems, in which a person searching the web for an item

---

[8] Goes, Paulo B., "Big Data and IS Research," *MIS Quarterly*. Vol.38 No.3 pp.iv
[9] McEvoy, Fiona J. 2017. "Social bots are ruining the internet for the rest of us," YouTheData.com originally printed in *Medium*.
venturebeat.com/2017/12/05/social-bots-are-ruining-the-internet-for-the-rest-of-us/

can be shown similar items that others have purchased. For example, a person searching for a particular genre of book might be shown the same genre of book by a different author. A person purchasing a computer might be shown computer accessories. A person purchasing a dress might be shown matching accessories, or dresses of the same style.

An advance on recommender systems is the Next Best Offer (NBO) system which uses detailed information about an individual such as age, gender, location, historical online activity, and information about how similar shoppers have behaved, to anticipate needs and place offers in front of people when they are ready to buy. Some systems email coupons; others make offers in real time when a person is online. A good NBO system can increase a website's conversion rate by 70%. Conversion means converting a looker to a buyer. However, it is important not to overdo offers. Research indicates that an excess number of offers, or poorly focused offers, can create ill will and reduce, rather than increase, sales.[10]

Sentiment analysis analyzes news groups and social media, to forecast fashion trends, to tell whether people are apprehensive about the economy, in which case they may be offered lower priced goods, or to tell whether they feel good about the economy, in which case they may be offered premium goods. Some systems use location and other demographic information to adjust the price of goods offered, to maximize both the likelihood of a sale, and the price at which a sale is made. In a study of sixteen travel and retail websites, seven adjusted prices based on a consumer's browsing history.[11]

Analytics can also be used to anticipate product demand and make sure stores are appropriately stocked. For example, Wal-Mart wanted to know what types of items were sold when a hurricane was forecast. People bought obvious things like milk, bread, flashlights and batteries. But analysis also showed the demand for strawberry pop-tarts increased seven-fold. It also found one of the top selling pre-hurricane items was beer.[12]

---

[10] Davenport, Thomas H., Leandro Dalle Mule, and John Lucker. 2011. "Know What Your Customers Want Before They Do," *Harvard Business Review*. Dec. hbr.org/2011/12/know-what-your-customers-want-before-they-do/ar/1 downloaded 2014-12-04.

[11] Ehrenberg, Rachel. 2014. "Online Retailers Personalize Search Results to Try to Maximize Profits," SN Science News Magazine. Nov.29 p.7 Also see www.sciencenews.org.

[12] Wladawsky-Berger. 2013. "Data-Driven Decision Making: Promises and Limits," CIO Journal, Wall Street Journal. Sept.27.

## Operations Applications

Data mining can be used to look for exceptions and transactions that are exceptionally good or bad. For example, it can be used to analyze products, customers, contracts and stores for profitability.

The 80–20 Rule says that 80% of sales come from 20% of customers; 80% of profits come from 20% of customers; 80% of sales come from 20% of products and so forth. Why does the 80-20 rule work? No one knows. However, experience indicates it works for most data sets.

Turning this around, 80% of unprofitable transactions, products, or customers come from 20% of the relevant population. Often a company underperforms, not because of any inherent weakness in the company, but because some of its transactions, customers, or products, are unprofitable. If unprofitable activities can be identified and eliminated, company-wide performance can be substantially improved.

For example, analytics might identify individuals who are unlikely to repay loans, or who are likely to default on credit cards. Avoiding defaults can significantly increase operating income. Credit scores are one example of companies using aggregated data to reduce risk.

Mathematical tests such as Benford's Law can be applied to detect fraud. Benford's Law predicts the frequency of naturally occurring business numbers. It predicts that about 30.1% of digits should be a one; about 18% of digits should be a two, and so forth with each higher digit having fewer and fewer occurrences. About 5% of digits should be nines. When numbers vary from this pattern, it is likely to be because of fraud. One retailer's refunds varied from this pattern because a dozen employees were issuing fraudulent refunds. Enron, a company notorious for falsifying its books, also violated Benford's Law.[13]

Products can be analyzed for profitability and products with low, zero, or negative gross margins eliminated. Likewise, divisions, stores, and customers, can be analyzed and those that are unprofitable can be eliminated.

Freight hauling is a very competitive business with low margins. As a result, most freight companies are deep in debt, running old equipment and making minimal profits. Analytics might be used to evaluate delivery records for routes where the cost in terms of driver time, fuel, and tolls, is greater than delivery fees. When unprofitable routes are found, a company

---

blogs.wsj.com/cio/2013/09/27/data-driven-decision-making-promises-and-limitations/

[13] McGinty, Jo Craven. 2014. "To Find Fraud, Just Do the Math," *Wall Street Journal*. Dec.6-7. A2.

might discontinue them, or re-price them, to adequately cover costs and profits. In fact, a Mid-western freight company did exactly that, and now has a profit margin of nearly 15%, almost three times the industry average.[14]

One large insurance company was spending ten million dollars per year buying computer storage equipment. Analytics was used to compare file histories to the company's file retention policy. About 40% of files were temporary or test files, retained for more than a year past the time they should have been deleted. When excess files were deleted, the company found it had plenty of storage, and the company canceled new equipment orders, saving several million dollars a year.

Workers Compensation Insurance is based on state-controlled prices. To maximize profits, a company must price policies exactly right. Premiums are based on the payroll that clients report to insurance companies. Unfortunately, companies often under-report payrolls. Auditing every company's payroll is expensive and could wipe out Workers Compensation profits.

One insurance company had been randomly auditing a small percentage of its clients, with mixed results. Analytics identified clients that were likely to under-report payrolls. By focusing on likely offenders, the insurance company increased premiums by $1.2 million without increasing audit costs. There are many other examples of analytics improving operations.

Competitive advantage implies finding and using insights that others have not yet found or used. This requires creativity. It is also a moving target. Those who innovate and find new uses for data will be in high demand. It is estimated that the United States will face a shortage of 140,000 to 190,000 people skilled in Business Intelligence and Analytics in 2018.[15] The number of people needed with skills in data analytics will grow, because they can create significant value at relatively low cost.

## Data Mining Applied to Marketing

There are many levels of sophistication in data analytics and some marketers have taken it to a high art complete with complex statistical

---

[14] Bailey, Jeff. 2001. "For One Trucking Entrepreneur, Success Is in the Details: CEO Makes Heartland Express Envy of the Industry with Printouts and Short-Haul Trips," Wall Street Journal, November 27, 2001, p. B4.
[15] Chen, Hsinchun, Robert H. L. Chiang and Veda C. Storey. 2012. "Business Intelligence and Analytics: From Big Data to Big Impact," MIS Quarterly. Dec. Vol.36 No.4 pp. 1165-1188.

analysis. Sometimes companies set up experiments and mine the results for insights into consumer behavior. If you want to know how a large population will react, study a small sample of it.

Companies can buy name and address lists, and mail offers to hundreds of thousands of people at a time. The issue is whether sending an offer to everyone on a list is the most effective thing to do. Sending offers to everyone is somewhat like calling everyone in the phone book to see whether they would like to buy a product.

To make the process more efficient, one might mail offers to a sample of people and see who responds. Correlation analysis can be used to identify those variables that predict who is most likely to make a purchase. For example, correlation analysis might indicate that distance from a store is an important variable. So, instead of mailing offers to everyone, offers could be limited to those within five miles, reducing costs and increasing the probability that each offer will result in a sale.

## Newline Computer Case Study

Newline sells computers through direct marketing. It purchased a mailing list containing 400,000 names and addresses. It will cost Newline $5 to send a glossy brochure to each person on the list for a total cost of $2,000,000 ($5 x 400,000). See equation Eq.11.1. The problem with sending brochures to everyone, is that Newline won't know whether the payoff is worth the investment until the money has been spent.

$$\text{Cost of Offers} = \text{Cost per Offer x Number of Offers} \quad \text{Eq.11.1}$$

$$= \$5 \times 400{,}000 \quad = \$2{,}000{,}000$$

Newline decided to do an experiment to determine (i) whether anyone will purchase a computer after receiving a brochure, and (ii) who is likely to purchase a computer. By analyzing the characteristics of those who purchased a computer in response to the sample mailing, Newline should be able to focus its marketing effort more narrowly. For example, if the experiment finds that men are twice as likely to purchase a computer by mail as women, maybe Newline should only send brochures to men. The experiment works like this:

(i)     Get as much information as is practical about the people on the mailing list. For example, it may be possible to classify people as men or women based on their name. Some mailing lists contain age, or perhaps age can be obtained from the internet. Town or city can be used to estimate the distance from a store, if one sells through stores. Town or city can also be used to estimate income, because the United States Census Bureau reports the average income of every town and city in America. See www.census.gov.

(ii) Randomly select some names from the list. Suppose Newline selects 1,000 names.

(iii) Send brochures to the randomly selected individuals.

(iv) List the names and other information about those in the sample on an Excel spreadsheet.

(v) Add a column to the spreadsheet labeled "Sale." Fill this column with zeroes.

(vi) Add a column to the spreadsheet labeled "Count." Fill this column with ones.

(vii) Keep careful records of the people in the sample who purchase a computer. When someone in the sample purchases a computer, change the zero in the "Sale" column to the number "1."

(viii) Use correlation analysis to identify the characteristics of those most likely to purchase. For example, age, income, gender or distance from a store might be correlated with sales.

(ix) Conduct experiments using the data in the Excel file to better define the target market. If, for example, age was positively correlated with sales, that would mean that older people are more likely to purchase than younger people. Select a cutoff, say 30 years old, and determine whether those over 30 were more likely to buy than the average person in the file. A second experiment might consider whether those over 40 are more likely to buy than those over 30. Other experiments are possible.

(x) Once a target market has been defined from this experiment, send offers to those on the mailing list with the target characteristics.

---

**Sampling's Big Idea**

If you want to know how a large population will react, study a small sample of it.

Suppose you have a list of 100,000 golfers of which 60,000 are men and 40,000 are women and you want to know whether they would like to buy leather golf gloves.

Select a random sample from the list of perhaps 500 and send them offers. If you find that women are three times as likely to buy leather golf gloves as men, then a considerable amount of money could be saved by only sending offers to women.

---

Table 11.1 Newline Mailing List is an example of what an Excel spreadsheet, tracking purchases made by those who were in the sample, might look like.

**Table 11.1 Newline Mailing List**

---

**SALE = 1 means the individual has made a purchase, SALE = 0 means no sale;**

| Customer No. | Sale | Gender 0=F, 1=M | Age | Region | Count |
|---|---|---|---|---|---|
| 12355 | 0 | 0 | 37 | 1 | 1 |
| 12357 | 0 | 1 | 48 | 4 | 1 |
| 12358 | 1 | 0 | 32 | 2 | 1 |
| 12359 | 0 | 1 | 65 | 2 | 1 |
| 12360 | 0 | 0 | 22 | 4 | 1 |
| 12360 | 1 | 1 | 42 | 1 | 1 |
|  | . |  |  |  | . |
|  | . |  |  |  | . |
| *Totals* | *34* |  |  |  | *1,000* |

## Response Rate

The response rate is the number of sales divided by the number of offers presented to potential customers, as shown in equation Eq.11.2. In the example above, 1,000 offers were mailed, and 34 computers were sold.

Response Rate = Number of Sales / Number of Offers   Eq.11.2

= 34 / 1,000        = 3.4%

Assume for a moment that the 1,000 people who got brochures were a representative sample of all 400,000 people on its list. **If the response rate for the sample was 3.4%, then the response rate for the entire mailing list should be about 3.4%.** The estimated number of sales for the whole mailing list is the response rate, times the number of offers mailed. See equation Eq.11.3.

Estimated Sales = Response Rate x Number of Offers   Eq.11.3

= 3.4% x 400,000        = 13,600

## Correlation Analysis

Correlation analysis is a statistical technique that shows how one variable moves in relation to another. Consider variables A and B. If A increases by 10% and B increases by 7%, they have a correlation coefficient of 0.7. One can say these two variables are highly correlated. High correlation means two variables move in the same direction, and about the same amount. Suppose A increases by 10% and B only increases by 4%. Their correlation coefficient is 0.4. They are still correlated, though less strongly. When the correlation coefficient nears zero, we say variables are not correlated. Changes in A are not reflected in changes in B.

When a correlation coefficient is negative, it means variables move in opposite directions. If A increases 10% and B decreases 5%, their correlation coefficient is -0.5. Negative correlations can provide useful information. For example, there is usually a negative correlation between price and the number of units sold. As price goes up, the number of units sold goes down.

In data mining, even slight correlations can yield useful information. See Table 11.2 Interpretation of Correlation Coefficients.

**Table 11.2 Interpretation of Correlation Coefficients**

| Correlation Coefficient | If A increases by 10% B increases by... | Meaning |
|---|---|---|
| 1.00 | 1.00 x 10% =10% | Perfect correlation |
| 0.70 | 0.70 x 10% = 7% | Strong correlation |
| 0.40 | 0.40 x 10% = 4% | Correlated |
| 0.10 | 0.10 x 10% = 1% | Slight correlation |
| 0.05 | 0.05 x 10% = 0.5% | Very slight correlation |
| 0.00 | 0.00 x 10% = 0% | No correlation |
| -0.50 | -0.50 x 10% = -5% | Negative correlation |

Suppose Newline Computer is able to determine the gender, age, and region for customers in its sample. It will want to know whether sales are related to any of these variables and if so, how strongly. Newline might consider focusing its marketing effort on those most likely to buy. If a correlation analysis were performed on the data from Table 11.1 Newline Mailing List, the output would look like Table 11.3 Newline Correlation Analysis. A correlation analysis function is built into Excel.

**Table 11.3 Newline Correlation Analysis**

|        | *SALE* | *GENDER* | *AGE* | *REGION* |
|--------|--------|----------|-------|----------|
| SALE   | 1.000  |          |       |          |
| GENDER | -0.099 | 1.000    |       |          |
| AGE    | 0.165  | -0.007   | 1.000 |          |
| REGION | 0.005  | -0.014   | 0.037 | 1.000    |

Find the column headed *SALE*. The numbers under this heading are the correlation coefficients of interest. They indicate how 'related' other variables are to the number of sales.

The highest correlation coefficient, 0.165, is for AGE. That means for this population and product, age is the most closely related to sales. Since the correlation is positive, that means increasing age increases the likelihood of a sale. A 40-year-old is more likely to buy a Newline computer than a 35-year-old, and a 35-year-old is more likely to buy than a 25-year-old. As with any statistical analysis, results should be tempered by common sense. A 90-year-old is not more likely to purchase a computer than someone who is 40. So, there is probably some upper limit on age.

When evaluating correlation coefficients, think in terms of the **absolute value** of the coefficient. In terms of absolute value, GENDER has a larger correlation coefficient than REGION. Therefore, GENDER is more important than REGION in terms of Newline Computer sales. The correlation coefficient for GENDER is -0.099. To understand what this means, we must know something about GENDER coding. In this database 0 is for female and 1 is for male. Every database is different, so you must read the instructions that come with the database. For this database, a negative correlation coefficient would mean **not** male, or female. So, women are slightly more likely to purchase than men.

The correlation coefficient for REGION is 0.005. This is so close to zero we can say there is no correlation between REGION and SALE.

## Using Correlation Analysis

In the Newline Computer example, age is most highly correlated with sales, even though the correlation is slight. The issue is whether we can use this information to improve the response rate:

(i)     Sort the sample file, Table 11.1, by age, oldest to youngest.

(ii)    Select an AGE cutoff. This selection is based on your judgment as a professional. If decisions like which age cutoff to select could be reduced to simple rules, there would be no reason to pay consultants big fees for data analysis. Let's select 35 as a cutoff. This age cut-off is an experiment. It is meant to see what would happen if Newline only mailed to people 35 and older.

(iii)   Insert blank lines between those on the file 35 and over and those less than 35. Sum (add up) the number of people over 35 by adding up the COUNT column. Sum the number of sales to people over 35 by adding up the SALE column.

(iv)    Suppose there are 803 people over 35 and suppose there are 33 sales to people over 35.

(v)     Compute the response rate for the 35 and over group using equation Eq.11.2.

Response Rate = Number of Sales / Number of Offers  Eq.11.2

Response Rate 35+ = 33 / 803          = 4.1%

This an improvement over the base response rate of 3.4% one would expect if brochures were sent to everyone in the database.

This improved response rate will help Newline focus effort where the payoff is greatest. The next step is to estimate the percentage of people on the database that are 35 and over. The percentage of the database in a group is the number of people in the sample with the group's characteristics divided by the sample size as shown in equation Eq.11.4.

Percentage in Group  = Number in Group / Sample Size      Eq.11.4

= 803 / 1,000     = 80.3%

If 80.3% of the sample are people over 35, then 80.3% of those on the whole database of 400,000 are probably over 35. If Newline decided to focus on those 35 and older, it could reduce the number of offers it makes as shown in equation Eq.11.5.

Number of Offers  = Database Size x Percentage in Group  Eq.11.5

= 400,000 x 80.3%       = 321,200

If Newline only sends out 321,200 offers, its mailing cost would be reduced to $1,606,000 (321,200 x $5). This represents a saving of $394,000 as compared to Newline's original plan to send brochures to everyone at a cost of $2,000,000.

Equation Eq.11.3 can be used to estimate the number of sales if offers are targeted to those 35 and over.

Number of Sales = Response Rate x Number of Offers  Eq.11.3

= 4.1% x 321,200        = 13,161

Can Newline do better? Suppose Newline selects a cutoff of 40 instead of 35. What would be the result? Sum (add up) the count of those 40 and above. Sum the sales to those 40 and above. Suppose there are 360 people 40 and above, and 23 sales were made to them. What is the response rate for this group?

Response Rate 40+  = 23 / 360          = 5.0%

This response rate is better than for the 35 and over group, and much, much better than the response rate for sending a brochure to everyone. The percentage of people in the over 40 group is about 36.0% (360 number in group/1,000 sample size). If Newline focused on the 40 and over group, it would send out about 144,000 offers (400,000 in the database x 36.0% percentage in group). The cost of this more focused campaign would only be $720,000 (144,000 offers x $5).

Is it possible to improve on a response rate of 5.0%? Perhaps. Try an experiment in which the age cutoff is 42. Again, we must use common sense in defining cutoffs. If we selected 65 or 70 as a cutoff we might find only one or two sales, hardly enough to justify a marketing campaign.

Suppose with a cutoff of 42 and older, there are 18 sales on 216 offers. The response rate would be 8.3% (18 sales/216 offers). The percentage of the sample 42 and older is 21.6% (216 number in group/1,000 sample size). About 86,000 offers would have to be mailed to reach everyone in this group (400,000 number in the database x 21.6% percentage in group). The cost of making those offers would be about $432,000 (86,400 offers x $5). The estimated number of sales to this group would be about 7,171 (86,400 offers x 8.3% response rate). Focusing the marketing effort on people 42 and over, and only sending out 86,400 offers at a cost of $432,000, entails considerably less risk than mailing out 400,000 offers at a cost of $2,000,000.

## Trade Offs

There is a trade-off between focusing marketing efforts narrowly, which reduces the number of offers and mailing costs on the one hand, and getting as many people as possible to purchase on the other hand. For example, sending brochures to everyone would cost $2,000,000 (400,000 offers x $5) versus sending offers only to those 42 and over, which would only cost $432,000 (86,400 offers x $5). But narrowly targeting offers reduces the number of sales. Expected sales on sending brochures to everyone would be about 13,600 (400,000 on database x 3.4% response rate), whereas only sending offers to those 42 and over would result in about 7,171 sales (86,400 x 8.3%). How can one decide which is best? One way is to analyze cost-per-sale.

## Cost-per-Sale

Cost-per-sale is a way to measure the efficiency of a marketing campaign. Cost-per-sale should be considered for telemarketing, radio, television, internet, or other kinds of marketing campaigns If the cost-per-sale is too high, sales costs will destroy profits. Cost-per-sale can be calculated using equation Eq.11.6.

$$\text{Cost-per-sale} = \text{Costs/Number of Sales} \qquad \text{Eq.11.6}$$

Mailing to everyone would cost $2,000,000, and 13,600 sales are expected.

$$\text{Cost-per-sale} = \$2,000,000/13,600 \qquad = \$147.06$$

A high cost-per-sale might extinguish any hope of a reasonable profit. Mailing to only to those over 42 would cost $432,000 and is expected to generate about 7,171 sales.

$$\text{Cost-per-sale } 42+ = \$432,000/7,171 = \$64.43$$

On a cost-per-sale basis, a highly focused marketing campaign is more efficient, and requires less invested capital than sending offers to everyone. But can Newline improve on this even more?

## Other Variables

For Newline Computer, AGE is most highly correlated with SALE. For other companies, proximity to the store or factory might be the most highly correlated variable. Income is also strongly correlated with sales in some situations. For example, higher income is probably highly correlated with Mercedes sales. Higher income might be negatively correlated with Dollar Store sales.

Newline computer only has two variables other than AGE. One is REGION, for which the correlation coefficient is so close to zero that REGION is not correlated and can be ignored. The other variable is GENDER.

To conduct a GENDER experiment, we must restore the sample file of 1,000 records, Table 11.1, to its original state. That is we must remove any subtotals or blank lines. Then sort it by GENDER. Recall that in this database, women are represented by 0, and men are represented by 1. In other databases, it might be different, so be sure to read the instructions which come with each database.

Sort the sample file so that all the women's records in the sample sort to the top. In this case, sort the GENDER column in ascending order. Sum (add up) the SALE column and the COUNT column for the section of the file containing women's records. Suppose there are 19 Sales and 314 women. Use equation Eq.11.2 to estimate the response rate.

$$\text{Response Rate} = \text{Responses/Number in Group} \qquad \text{Eq.11.2}$$

$$= 19 / 314 \qquad = 6.1\%$$

This is much better than the original response rate of 3.4% when sending offers to everyone. It's even better than the 5.0% response rate when sending to all who are 40 and over. On the other hand, it is not as good as the response rate for those 42 and over. Given that the 42 and over response rate is higher, should GENDER be ignored? Or can another experiment be performed to improve target marketing?

## Combining Criteria

Criteria can be combined to focus marketing effort ever more tightly on those most likely to purchase. Two criteria seem important to Newline Computer; AGE and GENDER. It should be no surprise that men and women shop differently. Maybe Newline can use this difference to improve its marketing strategy.

We have already separated out women's records, GENDER = 0, from our sample. Now let's sort women's records by AGE so that the oldest women are at the top of the list and the youngest at the bottom. We can now run another set of age experiments focused on women over 40. Suppose there are 12 sales for 119 women 40 and over. The response rate for this group is 10.1% (12 sales/119 in group).

Women over 40 are 11.9% of the sample (119 number in group/1,000 sample size). The percentage of women over 40 in the sample is a good estimate of the number of women over 40 on the entire database. This implies there about 47,600 women 40 and over in the whole database (400,000 x 11.9%). Offers to this group would cost $238,000 (47,600 x $5). The number of sales to this group should be about 4,808 (47,600 offers x 10.1% response rate). The cost-per-sale would be about $45.50 ($238,000/4,808). This would make women 40 and over the best group to target.

## Incremental Approach

In the Newline sample, there is a higher sales response rate for women than for men. So, what should we do with the men? Should we ignore men? The overall response rate for men is only 2.8% (15 sales/686 men). A better approach is to determine whether there is a subset of men whose response rate is nearly as good as that for women 40 and over.

Restore the sample file, Table 11.1, to its original state. Sort the sample file by GENDER, highest to lowest. This would put men at the top of the sample file. Then sort the men by AGE, oldest to youngest. Select an experimental age cutoff, say 50. Sum the number of men over 50 and the number of sales to these men. Suppose there are 3 sales to 17 men of 50 and older. The response rate would be 17.6% (3/17).

At this point, common sense and caution are advised. When a group is too small, it is difficult to reliably generalize results to a much larger population. For data mining, the number in a group should be at least 100.

Select a cutoff of men age 42 and over. Suppose there were 137 men over 42, and there were 8 sales to them. The response rate would be 5.8% (8 sales/137 in group). The percentage of the sample consisting of men of 42 and over is about 13.7% (137 in group/1,000 sample size). This implies there are about 54,800 men 42 and over on the database (13.7% percentage in group x 400,000 database). Offers to this group would cost $274,000 (54,800 offers x $5). Estimated sales would be 3,178 (54,800 offers x 5.8% response rate). Cost-per-sale would be $86.22 ($274,000/3,178). This would make men over 42 the second-best target market.

---

### Cautions When Using Analytics

Don't abandon common sense. Correlation analysis and other analytical tools just point the way. Don't take them to extremes.

There is a trade-off between a highly focused marketing campaign with high response rates and low costs per sale on the one hand, and low total sales on the other hand.

Response rate, cost-per-sale, and the total amount invested in a marketing campaign, help decide how tightly to focus a campaign.

If a sample, or a group within a sample, is too small, it is hard to draw reliable conclusions about the whole database. Groups less than 100 are probably not reliable.

Some databases have three, four, or more variables correlated with sales. For those, it is possible to narrowly define several highly efficient target markets. This conserves cash and reduces risk. Companies pay well for people who can help them sell more and do it at a lower cost.

---

**Key Concepts**

Send offers to a sample of a database to understand who is most likely to purchase and who is less likely to purchase.

Use correlation analysis to identify the factors that improve the likelihood of a sale.

Conduct 'experiments' with information gathered from the sample to further target the market. For example, use different age cutoffs, income cutoffs, etc.

Response Rate = Responses/Number of Offers

%Group = Number in Group/Sample Size    If 22% of the sample is in a certain group, then 22% of the entire mailing list is likely to be in that group.

Number of Offers = %Group x Size of Database

Cost of Offers = Number of Offers x Offer Cost

Estimated Unit Sales = Response Rate x Number of Offers

Cost per Offer = Cost of Offers/Unit Sales

Prepare a client memo explaining the research methodology and findings, and pointing out the trade-off between an economical, narrowly focused campaign and the estimated number of sales.

---

## Conclusion

Business Intelligence and Analytics (BI&A) can give a company a competitive advantage, by better targeting markets, and helping a company make timely offers of appropriate goods and services. It can identify unprofitable products, services, customers. It can also identify inefficient operations.

Analytics refers to the methods used to generate new knowledge from data. Analytics involves creative and critical thinking, computer science, statistics and management science.

Big data refers to the ocean of data generated internally by companies, data from the web, from user-generated content, on news groups, blogs, websites, social media, and from mobile devices and their apps. Big data also includes operations logs, sensor, and barcode data. Internet-connected devices, such as vehicles, appliances, and machinery, also contribute to big data.

Big data is characterized by the four Vs; (i) volume, (ii) velocity, (iii) variety, and (iii) veracity. Storing, classifying and retrieving enormous amounts of data can be challenging. Some data, like sentiment or location data is perishable, and must be promptly analyzed and used or it loses value. Integrating data from a variety of sources is difficult, because data may be in different formats, may be incomplete, and may not have common identifying elements. Just because data is digitized doesn't mean it is truthful and reliable. Much of big data is noise that must be filtered out.

The 80-20 rule says that 80 percent of sales and profits come from 20 percent of products, customers and transactions. Likewise, 80 percent of losses come from 20% of products, customers and transactions. Analytics can help a company identify winners and losers.

Data mining can be used to gain marketing insights. Consider the application of data mining to direct mail marketing. Many companies sell name and address lists. However, mailing offers to everyone on a list is generally not efficient. A company may send offers to a random sample of people on a list and see who responds. The results can be analyzed using correlation analysis, to determine which factors increase the probability of sales. Common factors include age, sex, income, and distance from a store or service provider. Other factors can also be added, such as whether potential customers subscribe to certain magazines, are members of special interest groups like campers' groups, Greenpeace or the American Farmers Association.

Focusing offers more narrowly, reduces the cost of making offers, increases the response rate and lowers the cost-per-sale. On the other hand, a narrow focus and fewer offers means the total number of expected sales is reduced. In marketing, as in life, balance is everything.

Some estimate that hundreds of thousands of Business Intelligence and Analytic jobs will open in the next few years, because those with BI&A skills can create a lot of value at relatively little cost.

# Appendix 11a Consulting

## Creating Value

There is a lot of money to be made in consulting. Companies pay for consultants who can add or create value for a client. Good consultants are always thinking about how to increase and measure value. Most consultants strive to create three or more dollars of value for every dollar of fees. Better consultants may add four, five or ten times the value they take in fees.

However, a consultant can create considerable value for a client and yet not get paid. Common reasons consultants don't get paid are: (i) they give away their insights; (ii) they fail to get an agreement on the basis for compensation before starting work; (iii) they don't adequately explain the value created; or (iv) they don't properly manage client expectations.

Clients are reluctant to pay a consultant if what a consultant is doing seems obvious. Here we run into a paradox of client expectations. Once a consultant explains how to do something, it may seem obvious. But if it was obvious, the client would have already done the work himself or herself. At some level, a good consultant creates an air of mystery about an engagement; something the client can almost understand, but is just outside their grasp. In the Newline Computer Case Study, part of that mystery is supplied by correlation analysis. Few clients are experienced with statistics so using statistics to guide actions seems mysterious and non-obvious. Another element of mystery is supplied by the equations used to analyze results.

Managing expectations is all important. Never say you will do something, achieve a goal or produce a result, unless you are absolutely, positively, sure you can do it. Do what you say; and say what you will do. Clients often attempt to get you to agree to impossible goals before they will hire you. Never over-promise. Be realistic about what can be achieved. Always complete tasks within deadlines. Always document and measure work performed. Two key documents go a long way toward eliminating these problems, an engagement letter and a consulting report.

## Engagement Letter

An engagement letter sets out the scope and limitations of a consulting engagement and the basis for compensation. An engagement letter is important because clients' memories of what was agreed to is short. An engagement letter is also important, because both the client and consultant should clearly understand client expectations. An engagement letter is a contract and should be signed by the client. If they are reluctant to sign, then either they don't agree with the scope of the engagement; don't agree on your compensation; or are already thinking about a way to avoid paying you.

Consultants may be compensated in different ways. One type of contract calls for a fixed fee. For example, a consultant might agree to write a program to schedule fuel oil deliveries, or create a website with certain capabilities, for a certain price. When a consultant accepts a fixed price contract, it is important to clearly specify exactly what the consultant is supposed to deliver; otherwise the client is likely to ask for revisions, improvements and upgrades without end.

Another type of contract is one in which the consultant is paid an hourly rate for work performed. To get paid under this type of contract, consultants must keep detailed records of hours applied and work performed. It is rarely enough to say, "September 18th - 7 hours, September 19th - 4 hours. More detail about what was done on the 18th or 19th is needed. Since hourly contracts may extend over some period of time, it is important to bill clients frequently. No client wants to be surprised by a large bill at the end of an engagement. Billing should be at least monthly; weekly billing is not unusual.

A few consulting agreements contain performance incentives. These clauses may be triggered by completing a job early or creating more value than expected. Incentive agreements are usually in addition to either a fixed or hourly fee. When a contract has performance incentives, it is critical to clearly specify what must be done to merit a performance payment.

A few clients want penalties inserted into an engagement letter. For example, "If the website is not up, running and responding to customer queries by September 10th, the consultant agrees to a penalty of $100 per day until the website is working." If the contract is billed on an hourly basis, there is likely to be language in the contract that prohibits the consultant from continuing to bill. Penalty clauses are more common for fixed fee contracts.

Another reason consultants don't get paid is because they are so eager to pitch their services that they tell the client what they are going to do, and how they are going to do it, before they are hired. Once the client knows what to do, they are likely to do it themselves. A consultant must walk a fine line, between assuring a client that he or she can achieve client goals and giving the client a road map that they can use to get there themselves.

Finally, some consultants don't get paid because their clients run out of money. It's important to find out whether the client is able and willing to pay before commencing an engagement.

## Consulting Report

Clear, concise communication is important when dealing with a client. Most engagements end with a report. The report should briefly recount the scope of work, any limitations on the scope, what was done, how it was done, and how it added value for the client. No matter how hard you work, or how smart you are, you will not get credit for your work or value added if you cannot clearly and concisely explain what you did, and how you added value. If a report isn't clear, concise, well written, and brilliant, clients will ask themselves what they are paying for. Client communications must follow certain formalisms in addition to being technically correct.

A report to a client could be in one of several forms. One form is a bound report transmitted with a cover letter. A bound report is appropriate when the report is more than six pages long. A memo report is somewhat less formal and is probably acceptable if the report is five pages or fewer.

Whether a report is in the form of a memo or a bound report, it should contain several elements. Among them are:

(i) The scope and goals of the consulting engagement.

(ii) A brief description of the conditions that existed when the engagement began. This provides a baseline against which to measure value added.

(ii) A description of the data and methods used during the consulting engagement.

(iv) Findings and recommendations. Findings and recommendations should be prioritized from the most important to the least important.

(v) A quantitative analysis of value added.

## Memo Report

A memo report is less formal than a bound report, but should include most of the same elements as a bound report. Table 11A.1 Newline Memo Report, provides an example of a memo format report.

**Table 11A.1 New Line Memo Report**

---

Date:              November 11, 2019

To:                Robert Murdock, Vice President, New Line Computers

From:              Patrick Dempsey / Dempsey Marketing

Subject:           Direct Marketing Campaign

The mailing list you provided contained 400,000 names and addresses. We selected 1,000 names at random from the list and conducted a sample mailing. From this sample, 34 people purchased a Newline computer giving a response rate of 3.4% (34/1,000). The estimated number of sales on making offers to the whole database is about 13,600 units (3.4% x 400,000).

Reaching all 400,000 individuals on the database would cost about $2,000,000 assuming each offer costs $5 to print and mail. The cost-per-sale on making offers to everyone is estimated at $147.06 per unit ($2,000,000 / 13,600 units).

We found computer purchases were slightly correlated with age. Since the correlation is positive, that implies older individuals are more likely to buy from a direct mail solicitation than younger individuals.

Sales were very slightly, negatively correlated with gender. In this database, men are represented with a 1 and women with a 0. The negative gender correlation on this database can be read as 'not men', meaning women. Therefore, women were very slightly more likely to purchase than men. Region was not correlated with sales. See Correlation Analysis Attached.

Since there is a slight purchasing difference between men and women, we recommend a different marketing strategy for each. Combining gender and age criteria will create the most targeted marketing campaign.

The best strategy is to target the highest response rate groups first; harvest profits from them, and then decide whether to target lower response rate groups.

Targeting women over 40 provides the highest response rate and lowest cost-per-sale. There were 119 women over 40 in the sample mailing, and they purchased 12 computers, giving a response rate of 10.1%. Women over 40 represent 11.9% of the sample mailing (119/1,000). Since this is a random sample of the larger database of 400,000, we estimate there are about 47,600 women over 40 on the database (11.9% x 400,000). The cost of offers to this group will be about $238,000 (47,600 offers x $5). The estimated number of sales to this group is about 4,808 (10.1% x 47,600). The cost-per-sale should be about $45.50 ($238,000/4,808). This represents a significant improvement over the cost-per-sale of $147.06 ($2,000,000/13,600) if offers had been made to all 400,000 people on the mailing list. Targeting this group reduces the initial capital required, from $2,000,000 to $238,000.

The next best strategy is to target men over 42. There were 137 men over 42 in the sample mailing, and they made 8 purchases for a response rate of 5.8%. Men over 42 were about 13.7% of the sample (137/1,000). There should be about 54,800 men over 42 on the database (13.7% x 400,000). The cost to make offers to these men will be about $274,000 (54,800 x $5). Estimated sales will be about 3,178 (5.8% x 54,800). The estimated cost-per-sale will be about $86.22 ($274,000/3,178).

The third best strategy is to target women 35 to 39. There were 122 of these individuals in the sample, and they purchased 6 computers for a response rate of 4.9% (6/122). About 12.2% (122/1,000) of the sample were woman ages 35 to 39. And, there are about 48,800 of them in the database (12.2% x 400,000). The cost to reach this group would be about $244,000 (48,800 x $5). Estimated sales to this group would be about 2,391 (4.9% x 48,800). The cost-per-sale would be about $102.05 ($244,000/2,391).

Narrowly targeting customers reduces the cost of offers and the cost-per-sale. On the other hand, narrowly targeting customers reduces total sales.

Please advise as to how targeted you would like us to be in terms of cutoffs.

## *Letter Report*

A letter format report is an alternative to a memo format report. Usually letter format reports are fairly brief, often less than three pages. The following is a common format for a letter report.

A letter usually has a letterhead that identifies the author of the letter, and underneath that the author's address, phone number and email address. Below this is a date.

The name, title, company name, and address of the person to whom the report is addressed usually follows, left justified. The recipient's phone number and email address are often below this.

Below the recipients' address, there is usually a subject line. The subject line should briefly tell the reader what the letter is about. Table 11A.2 Letter Format Report, provides an outline of a letter report for the Newline Computer case.

**Table 11A.2 Letter Format Report**

---

### DEMPSEY MARKETING
214 Federal Street, Suite 301, Camden, New Jersey 08103
856-555-1234  ▪  marketing@dempsey.net

November 11, 2019

Robert Murdock, Vice President,
New Line Computers
10260 Route 70
Cherry Hill, New Jersey 08042
856-770-1234
rmurdock@newline.net

Subject:  Direct Mail Marketing Campaign

Dear Mr. Murdock,

-----     the body of the letter goes here ----
Sincerely,

Patrick Dempsey

---

## *Bound Report Form*

A bound report is typically only used for longer reports, more than six pages of content, and where there are many exhibits or attachments. Bound reports are often transmitted with a very brief cover letter or cover memo.

Bound reports should have a cover. The title of the report should be bold, in a larger than normal font, and centered, on the cover. The author of the report, his or her company and the date of the report should either be directly under the title, or in the lower right-hand corner of the report.

A bound report should have an Executive Summary, which gives the highlights of the report and tells the reader why they are reading it. An Executive Summary should be less than a third of a page; a quarter page is better.

Bound reports should have descriptive section headings to help people find information in the report. If the report is more than ten pages including exhibits and attachments, it should have a table of contents.

Reports which contain a lot of statistical or financial data can often be made more clear and concise if numeric details are removed from the text and placed in tables, either near related text or at the end of the report, as appendices or exhibits. Tables should be numbered and have a title, for example, Table 1 Educational Expenditures by State. Columns should be labeled. If it is not obvious from the column title what the data means, it may be necessary to place a brief explanatory note between the table title and the body of the table.

Appendices and exhibits should be referenced in the text, identified by a capital letter and have a title. For example, in the body of the report, it might say: "Sales have grown 11% per year over the period 2010 to 2018, see Appendix F Income Statements."

# Terms and Concepts

**Business Intelligence and Analytics** – combines creative and critical thinking with computer, statistical and management science, to discover new information.

**Correlation Analysis** – Correlation analysis is a statistical technique which measures how related two variables are. Variables correlated 1.0 are perfectly correlated; variables correlated 0.7 are strongly correlated; variables correlated 0.1 are slightly correlated; variables correlated 0.0 are not correlated; and variables correlated -0.5 are negatively correlated.

**Cost-per-sale** – This is a measure of the efficiency of a marketing campaign. Cost-per-sale = Offer Cost/Number of Sales.

**Criteria, combining** – Marketing programs can combine criteria to more tightly focus campaigns. For example, a campaign could focus on males, under 50 with incomes more than $75,000.

**Customer Intelligence System** – This is a system which helps companies place relevant offers in front of customers when their buying window is open.

**Data Analytics** – This is the use of computer, statistical, and management insight to discover new knowledge.

**Direct Mail Marketing** – Direct mail marketing is based on large databases of names and addresses. Sending offers to everyone on such a database is costly. Companies can send offers to a sample to see who responds. Response information is used to focus marketing efforts on those most likely to make a purchase.

**Information Technology** – Information technology includes computers, databases, and the software needed to make them useful.

**Response Rate** – This is the percentage of sales, divided by the number of offers. Response Rate = Responses/Offers.

**Number of Offers** – Narrowly limiting offers to those most likely to buy reduces initial cost, cost-per-sale, and improves the response rate. Number of offers = %Group x Number on Database.

**Percentage in Group** – Within a sample, a certain group of individuals may have common characteristics. It is useful to know the percentage of the sample with group characteristics because the same percentage of the database is likely to have those same characteristics. %Group = Number in Group/Sample Size.

**Reports** – A consulting report should state: (i) the scope and goals of the consulting engagement; (ii) a brief description of the conditions that existed when the engagement began; (ii) the data and methods used during the consulting engagement; (iv) findings and recommendations; and (v) a quantitative analysis of value added.

**Sales, Estimated Number of** – The number of direct marketing sales can be estimated by multiplying the Response Rate, times the Number of Offers made. Sales = Response Rate x Number of Offers.

**Sampling** - Sampling's big idea is that if you want to know how a large population will react, study a small sample of it.

**Trade Offs** – As the market is more and more narrowly defined, the response rate should rise, and the cost-per-sale decline. The number of sales will also decline. The total cost of a marketing campaign and the cost-per-sale are factors in deciding how narrowly focused a campaign should be.

**Variables, Common** – Common direct marketing variables include age, gender, income, location, distance, and other associations, such as club memberships or magazine subscriptions.

# References

Bailey, Jeff. 2001. "For One Trucking Entrepreneur, Success Is in the Details: CEO Makes Heartland Express Envy of the Industry with Printouts and Short-Haul Trips," Wall Street Journal, November 27, 2001, p. B4.

Banerjee, Arindam, Tathagata Bandyopadhyay, and Prichi Acharya. 2013. "Data Analytics: Hyped Up Aspirations or True Potential?" *Vikalpa.* Vol.38 No.4 pp.1-11.

Chen, Hsinchun, Robert H. L. Chiang and Veda C. Storey. 2012. "Business Intelligence and Analytics: From Big Data to Big Impact," MIS Quarterly. Dec. Vol.36 No.4 pp. 1165-1188.

Davenport, Thomas H., Leandro Dalle Mule, and John Lucker. 2011. "Know What Your Customers Want Before They Do," *Harvard Business Review.* Dec. hbr.org/2011/12/know-what-your-customers-want-before-they-do/ar/1 downloaded 2014-12-04.

Ehrenberg, Rachel. 2014. "Online Retailers Personalize Search Results to Try to Maximize Profits," SN Science News Magazine. Nov.29 p.7 Also see www.sciencenews.org.

Freeland, Chrystia. 2012. "In Big Data, Potential for Big Division," *New York Times.* Jan.12. www.nytimes.com/2012/01/13/us/13iht-letter13.html downloaded 2014-11-18.

Goes, Paulo B., "Big Data and IS Research," *MIS Quarterly.* Vol.38 No.3 pp.iv

McEvoy, Fiona J. 2017. "Social bots are ruining the internet for the rest of us," YouTheData.com originally printed in *Medium.* venturebeat.com/2017/12/05/social-bots-are-ruining-the-internet-for-the-rest-of-us/

McGinty, Jo Craven. 2014. "To Find Fraud, Just Do the Math," *Wall Street Journal.* Dec.6-7. A2.

Westerman, George, Didier Bonnet and Andrew McAfee. 2014. "The Advantages of Digital Maturity," *MIT Sloan Management Review* http://sloanreview.mit.edu/article/the-advantages-of-digital-maturity/ Nov. 20, downloaded 2014-12-11

Wladawsky-Berger. 2013. "Data-Driven Decision Making: Promises and Limits," CIO Journal, Wall Street Journal. Sept.27. blogs.wsj.com/cio/2013/09/27/data-driven-decision-making-promises-and-limitations/

# CHAPTER TWELVE

# CONTRACTS AND THE LAW

---

When you complete this chapter, you should be able to:

12.1 Explain what a legal theory is and how it can be used.

12.2 List the elements of a contract and determine whether a contract has been formed.

12.3 Use contract defenses.

12.4 Explain the types of relief available for breach of contract.

12.5 Evaluate alternative dispute resolution methods and know when to use each.

---

## Introduction

How can anybody be sure that people will follow through on promises? How does anybody know who they can trust? These are important questions for businesses where thousands or millions of dollars are at stake, not to mention company reputation, customer relations, shareholder interests, loans, and perhaps the survival of a company itself.

It would be great if everyone kept their word all the time. It would be great if everyone was reliable. While most people are reliable, some are not. Contract law evolved to make sure people understand their obligations, to encourage people to do what they promised, and to provide remedies when people fail to keep their promises.

This chapter discusses the development of the law, how legal theories provide a framework for analysis, the elements of a contract, how an offer to contract is made and how it can be terminated. Contract defenses are analyzed and applied. Rules of contract interpretation and remedies for breach of contract are also discussed.

There are several ways to resolve contract disputes other than through litigation. The pros and cons of each alternative dispute resolution method are explored.

## Development of the Law

Prior to the Norman conquest of England in 1066, justice was dispensed by feudal lords on an ad hoc basis. After the Norman invasion, a succession of kings recognized the need for a consistent and systematic method of dispensing justice. By 1154 **common law** began to emerge. The decisions of local judges and magistrates were written down and shared. The law began to define forms of injury and rules for each of them. For example, there were actions for crimes, intentional injury, and collection of debts.

A feature of **common law** is its reliance on precedents. Courts use decision rules, developed and applied in prior cases, to decide the outcome of new cases. Interpreting and applying the law in a consistent manner provides stability and predictability to the legal system. It also helps citizens understand their rights and duties under the law. The term *Stare Decisis*, which means 'let the decision stand'. It is the legal principle that prior decision rules should be followed.[1]

**Common law** did not always take the direction England's leaders thought best and, from time to time, Parliament passed statutes that superseded common law. For example, in the seventeenth century, oral contracts were enforced by courts. This left room for unscrupulous individuals to lie about contract terms. "The Statute of Frauds" (1677) said that certain kinds of contracts were so important they must be in writing. Examples of such contracts include those for land or for purchase or sale of goods over a certain amount.[2] Another example is "The Statute of Anne" (1710), which made it illegal to reproduce books or other written

---

[1] Smith, Len Young and Roberson, G. Gale. 1971. *Business Law*. West Publishing, St. Paul. pp.6-7.

[2] Edwards, Carolyn M. 1978. "The Statute of Frauds of the Uniform Commerce Code and the Doctrine of Estoppel," Marquette Law Review. Vol.62 pp.205-225. Original source: 29 Car. 2 (1677).

material without the consent of the author. In effect, this statute granted copyright protection.[3]

Colonial America followed English common law and statutes. After the Revolution, English law was still the basic law in America. However, it slowly evolved in a different direction from English law. The United States adopted the Constitution in 1787, which set forth the organization of the federal government, the federal government's relationship to state governments, the powers of the federal government, and restraints on governmental powers. States also have constitutions, and several state constitutions pre-date the Constitution of the United States.

The Constitution of the United States is the supreme law of the land. Congress can pass any law if it doesn't conflict with the Constitution. State legislatures can pass any law as long as it does not conflict with the state's constitution or the Constitution of the United States.

Federal and state judges interpret federal and state law, and write opinions as to how the law is to be interpreted and applied. Judges' opinions are collectively called **case law**. Judges are generally bound to follow the decisions of prior authoritative courts in applying the law.

## Legal Theories

The law is not an exact science. It is distillation of the best thinking of how things should work in a just, moral and orderly society. Justice Oliver Wendell Holmes, a Supreme Court Justice from 1902 to 1932 said, "The life of the law is not logic. It has been experience."[4]  As experience changes, the law changes. Experience also means that in business law, customs and trade practices influence how judges interpret and apply the law.

The basic building block of legal analysis is the theory. A legal theory is like a box with rules in it. There are many legal theories, and so, many boxes. The first step in legal analysis is to find the theory that is appropriate for the facts and circumstances of a case. The rules related to one legal theory might favor a particular individual, and the rules related to another legal theory might not. Winning or losing can turn on the legal theory used.

---

[3]    2008. "The Statute of Anne; April 10, 1710," Lillian Goldman Law Library, Yale. http://avalon.law.yale.edu/18th_century/anne_1710.asp Original source: 8 Anne, c. 19 (1710)
[4] LaPiana, William. 1994. *Logic and Experience*. Oxford University Press. Oxford, England.

Can one pick and choose whatever legal theory one wants, or is there some criteria for who gets to use the rules associated with a theory? The criteria are based on something called an element. An element is a fact, or circumstance that qualifies one to use a legal theory.[5] For example, the elements of negligence are: (i) duty, (ii) breach, (iii) proximate cause and (iv) damages. If any of these elements are missing, the theory of negligence cannot be used.[6]

---

**Legal Theory**

The law is organized around **legal theories**.

A legal theory is like a box with **decision rules** in it.

One qualifies to use a particular legal theory by showing that the facts and circumstances of a case constitute the **elements** of the theory.

---

There is a lot of space between the boxes (theories). That means there will be times when no legal theory quite fits the facts and circumstances. In such a case, a judge will dismiss a lawsuit for **failure to state a cause of action**. To protect one's rights it is important to find and qualify to use an appropriate legal theory. Table 12.1 Legal Theories are a few of the legal theories courts recognize.

**Table 12.1 Legal Theories**

| | | |
|---|---|---|
| Assault | Battery | Trespass |
| Negligence | Contract | Strict Liability |
| Secured Interest | Commercial Paper | Mortgages |
| Bankruptcy | Workers Compensation | Agency |
| Surety | Bailment | Leases |

---

[5] Field, Richard H., Benjamin Kaplan, Kevin M. Clermont. 1978. Civil Procedure. 4th Ed. The Foundation Press. Mineola, New York. p.372-374.
[6] Prosser, William L. 1983. Law of Torts. West Publishing Company. St. Paul, Minn. p.143-144.

---

### Example of No Legal Theory

Bob and Alice have worked together for a couple of years. Alice throws a party and invites everyone except Bob. Bob is so insulted, he gets drunk and drives his pick-up truck into a ditch, wrecking the truck, injuring himself and his hound dog *Blue*.

Bob sues Alice for the insult and his injuries. Bob's first step is to tell the court the legal theory under which he wants the court to act. It is not enough that there was a real injury to his truck, his hound dog and himself.

The court might agree that Alice should have invited Bob to the party. But, since no legal theory requires anyone to invite anyone else to a party, the court will dismiss the case.

---

# Contract

## Importance of Contracts

Enforcement of contracts is important so that individuals and businesses can rely on promises that have been made. Suppose it is winter in Minnesota, and Leon's Tractor Company has a contract with Bob's Fuel Company to deliver heating oil. If Bob's Fuel doesn't deliver heating oil, it will have breached the contract and a court may award Leon damages.

It would be great to think that Leon could rely on Bob's good sense to deliver oil. The fact that a court will enforce their contract adds another level of assurance for Leon. It also provides an extra incentive to Bob's Fuel to do what it promised.

**Contract enforcement is a key element of capitalism and a property-oriented economic system**. Without contracts and a mechanism to enforce them, parties would not have the confidence to exchange valuable property interests.

## Elements of a Contract

Contract law is primarily state law. Each state is entitled to write its own contract law. The Uniform Commercial Code (UCC) is a model law that has been adopted by most states to make contract law uniform from state to state. Nevertheless, several states have made minor changes to the UCC.

UCC Article 2 covers contracts for goods. The law enforces the reasonable expectations of the parties. Contracts may be **written or oral**.

How do we know whether we fit into contract theory? The **elements** of contract law are:[7]

   (i)   Offer,
   (ii)  Acceptance,
   (iii) Consideration,
   (iv) Capacity, and
   (v)  Lawful purpose.

## *Offer*

An Offer is a specific promise and a demand. Suppose I say, "I will give you $10,000 for your Buick." The promise, is that I will give you $10,000. The demand, is for your Buick.

Distinguish between an offer, and an invitation to another to make an offer. "Would you give me $10,000 for this Buick?" This is an invitation for the other person to make an offer.

**Indefiniteness may make an offer invalid.** "I will pay a reasonable amount for your house," is too indefinite. Every piece of real estate is unique and has a unique price. However, some missing terms may be supplied by the Uniform Commercial Code (UCC) Article 2. For example, I will pay you the published price for fuel oil on January $12^{th}$ of next year, plus $.25 per gallon for delivery on that date. This is specific enough as to price under the UCC. However, this offer is indefinite as to quantity, which will make the offer invalid.

## *Acceptance*

**Acceptance must be overt.** Silence is not acceptance. Larry says, "Bob, I will give you $10,000 for your Buick and, unless I hear from you, I will assume you accept." Larry doesn't hear from Bob. Does Larry have a contract? No. Bob's silence cannot be construed as acceptance.[8]

For acceptance to be valid, there must be a **mutual understanding** as to the subject matter and terms of the contract. Larry says, "Bob, I will give you $20,000 for your car." Bob says, "OK." Bob has two cars, a year-old Buick and a five-year-old Ferrari. Bob thought Larry wanted to buy

---

[7] Smith, Len Young and Roberson, G. Gale. 1971. Business Law. West Publishing, St. Paul. p.50-51, 60-61.
[8] Ibid. pp.63-64.

the Buick. Larry offered to buy the Ferrari. There is no mutual understanding and no contract.

### Consideration

Consideration may be thought of as payment. Payment may be in the form of money, property, performance of an act, or forbearance from doing something one is entitled to do.

Consideration must be bargained for. Prior consideration is not consideration. Agreement to do something one is already obligated to do is not consideration. An agreement *not* to do something one has no intention of doing is not consideration. Consideration may be nominal, like a dollar. Promises to make gifts are not binding, because there is no bargained-for consideration to support the promise.

However, under UCC 2-209(1) if a buyer of more than $500 of goods promises to pay more than the agreed price, the buyer is bound, though he or she receives no new consideration. This provision is thought to smooth commercial relations.

Suppose Serge contracts to buy heating oil from Alice's Oil Company at $3.50 per gallon for a year. During the year, the wholesale cost of heating oil to Alice spikes to $5.00. Clearly, she will lose money on each delivery. Serge wants to maintain a relationship with Alice and doesn't want her to go out of business, so Serge might say, "Alice, I will pay your wholesale cost plus 3% for the next year." There is no new consideration for this promise to pay more than $3.50 per gallon. But if Serge buys more than $500 of heating oil from Alice, he will be bound to the new terms under UCC 2-209(1).

Under UCC 2-205, if a **merchant** offers goods at a certain price for a certain period, the merchant is bound by those terms, though the potential buyer has given no consideration. This is called a '**firm offer**'.

Bob's Autoworld says, "We will sell any 2017 Corvette on our lot for $40,000." Larry stops by with a $40,000 check and picks out a 2017 7.0-liter Corvette Z06. Bob's declines to sell the Z06 for $40,000 and asks for $50,000. Larry sues. Bob's defends saying there was no consideration for his promise to sell at $40,000. What would be the result?

Bob's Autoworld is a merchant subject to UCC 2-205. It has made a firm offer which Larry accepted. As a merchant, Bob could have qualified his offer by saying the offer only applied to Corvettes with engines smaller than 6.0 liters, or he could have limited his offer to Corvettes in a specific part of his lot, or he could have limited his offer to a list of specific Corvettes, but he didn't, and courts will construe ambiguity against the party that created the ambiguity, or the party that was in the best position to avoid the ambiguity.

## *Capacity*

Capacity refers to whether parties are legally capable of entering into a contract. Usually minors, those under 18, lack the legal capacity to enter a binding contract. The exception is that minors can contract for the necessities of life, such as food, shelter or medical care. A 5.0-liter Mustang is not a necessity of life. A person under 18 can disavow their contract obligations, but an adult contracting with a person under 18 is usually bound to the contract if the minor performs their end of the bargain.

Those declared incompetent by a court, lack legal capacity. Drunks lack capacity only when they are so drunk they don't know what they are doing. It is a question for the court as to whether a person was so drunk they lacked the capacity to contract.

## *Lawful Purpose*

Courts will not enforce contracts with an unlawful purpose. Instead, a court will leave the parties where it found them. Contracts that restrain trade, that are illegal, or immoral, do not have a lawful purpose.[9]

Larry says, "Put $100 on Greenstaple, the fifth race at Aqueduct." Sam places the bet for Larry and Larry loses. Larry doesn't pay. Sam sues Larry for the $100. What would be the result?

Betting on horse races is only legal under certain limited circumstances. If Sam is a bookie taking illegal bets, the court will not require Larry to pay. However, if Sam works in a casino that has been authorized to take bets on horse races, Larry will have to pay.

Suppose it is January 1, 1933 and Salvatore signs a contract wherein he will trade a warehouse for 400 ounces of gold. Settlement is to take place June 30, 1933. What would be the result?

This contract will be declared illegal. On April 5, 1933 President Franklin Roosevelt signed an Executive Order declaring possession of gold illegal after May 1, 1933. Since the subject matter of the contract, gold, was made illegal, the contract would not be enforced. This order was rescinded years later, and it is now legal to own gold in the United States.

---

[9] Smith, Len Young and Roberson, G. Gale. 1971. *Business Law*. West Publishing, St. Paul. Pp.153-155.

If an otherwise valid contract has both legal and illegal clauses, the courts will enforce the legal part of the contract and not enforce the illegal part.

---

**Elements of a Contract**

**Offer** – This is a specific and well-defined promise and a demand. The demand may take the form of a promise or an act.

**Acceptance** – This is agreement to the offer. Silence is not acceptance.

**Consideration** – Consideration must be bargained for, and may include a promise, act, or agreement *not* to do something one has the right to do. Prior consideration is no consideration.

**Capacity** – Generally, mentally competent adults have capacity.

**Lawful Purpose** – Courts will not enforce contracts with an unlawful purpose.

---

# Offer Termination

There are several ways to terminate an offer. Once an offer is terminated, an offeree (the person to whom an offer is made) cannot unilaterally revive the offer. The point is, that if a good offer is made, the offeree should promptly accept it. Once an offer is terminated, there can be no contract, because an offer is an essential element of a contract.[10]

### Revocation

An offer can be terminated by revocation, up until the time it is accepted.

At lunch, Larry says to Bob, "I will buy your Corvette for $30,000."

Bob says, "I'll think about it," and starts calling around to see if anyone will pay him more than $30,000.

At 2 o'clock Larry says to Bob, "I withdraw my offer."

At 5 o'clock Bob says, "I accept. Give me a check for $30,000."

What would be the result? The offer was terminated before acceptance so there is no contract.

---

[10] Smith, Len Young and Roberson, G. Gale. 1971. *Business Law*. West Publishing, St. Paul. pp.55-59.

### Termination at a Set Time

Offers can **terminate at a set time**. This is common in real estate. "I offer to buy your house for $200,000. The offer is good for 72 hours." The reason for terminating an offer at a certain point in time, is so that the offeror can make an offer to another to try to form a contract.

### Termination by the Passage of Time

Offers automatically terminate after a '**reasonable**' period. Larry sends Bob an email that says, "I want to offer you the job of president of my electronics company, at a salary of $500,000 per year." Two months later, Bob sends Larry an email, "I accept your offer." What would be the result?

The offer has probably terminated automatically. A company cannot operate for long without a president.

### Termination by Rejection

An offer is terminated by **rejection**. Larry says, "I will sell you my Corvette for $30,000." Bob says, "No." The offer is terminated by Bob's rejection.

### Termination by Counter Offer

A counter offer is created when the offeree takes elements of the original offer and constructs his or her own offer. A **counter offer serves as a rejection**. Larry says, "I will sell you my Corvette for $40,000."

Bob says, "I'll buy your Corvette for $30,000." Bob's counter offer is a rejection of Larry's original offer.

### Additional Terms Not a Rejection

As **between merchants**, under the UCC, if the terms of the counter offer do not conflict with, or alter the principal terms of the original offer, the original offer is not rejected. Additional terms may be accepted or rejected by the offeror.

Winchell emails Rachel and says, "I will buy 500 of your toasters for $10 each." Rachael emails back, "Agreed, but I can't ship until December 15th." What would be the result?

Rachel did not reject Winchell's offer, she merely suggested additional terms. Winchell can accept or reject the additional terms. If he accepts, the contract is complete. Or, he may reject the term regarding delivery and rescind the offer.

### Termination by Destruction of Subject Matter

An offer may be **terminated by** the **destruction of the subject matter**. Larry says, "I will sell you my Lamborghini for $90,000," but before Larry delivers the car, it is run over by a dump truck. The offer is automatically terminated.

### Termination by Offeror Incapacity

An offer may be terminated by the offeror's **death** or **insanity**. Jake offers to sell his house to Quinn for $200,000. Before title to the home is transferred, Jake dies. The offer is terminated, which means Jake's heirs are not obligated to sell the house.

### Termination by Illegality

An offer is terminated if the subject matter becomes illegal. In October of 1919, the Volstead Act made the sale of alcohol illegal; President Franklin Roosevelt's Executive Order banning ownership of gold made use of gold in contracts illegal; drugs may start out legal and be reclassified as controlled substances, which make sales under certain circumstances illegal. On the other hand, fifty years ago gambling was generally illegal, until states found out they could raise substantial tax revenue from gambling activities, and so they have made some gambling legal.

---

**Offer Termination**

Offers may be terminated by:

1. **Revocation.**

2. Termination at a **set time.**

3. Termination by the **passage of** a reasonable **time.**

4. **Rejection.**

5. A **counter offer**, which acts as a rejection.

6. **Destruction** of the subject matter.

7. **Death or insanity** of the offeror.

8. **Illegality.**

Once an offer has been terminated, the offeree cannot unilaterally revive the offer.

---

*Effect of Offer Termination*

An offer is an essential element of a contract. When an offer is terminated, what is left cannot be called a contract, because of the missing element. Courts will not enforce actions for breach of contract when any essential element is missing.

# Types of Contracts

Different rules apply to different types of contracts. Elements are used to determine which legal theory and rules are used.[11], [12]

A **bilateral** contract is one in which a promise is exchanged for a promise: "I will pay you $10,000 for your Buick"; I promise to pay $10,000, and you promise to deliver the Buick.

---

[11] Smith, Len Young and Roberson, G. Gale. 1971. Business Law. West Publishing, St. Paul. pp.47-54.
[12] Roszkowski, Mark E. 1989. Business Law 2nd Ed. HarperCollins Publishers. pp157-161.

A **unilateral** contract can only be accepted by an act, not a promise; "I will pay you $50 if you mow my lawn." This is an offer. The only way to accept this offer is through **performance**. That is, the only way to accept this offer is to mow the lawn.

An **express** contract is one in which the parties spell out the terms. For example, "I will pay you $10,000 for your Buick," is an express contract.

An **implied** contract can be created by the actions of the parties. No words are necessary. Suppose Randy has a lumber yard and he has an understanding with a builder that she can bring her trucks into the lumber yard before it opens, load up material, and then pay for the materials that afternoon. This is an example of an implied contract.

As soon as the builder loads her trucks, there is an implied promise to pay Randy's price for the lumber. Implied contracts are enforced to prevent unjust enrichment.

A **valid contract** and an **enforceable contract** have all the elements needed for a court to uphold the validity of a contract and apply the appropriate contract rules.

Not every contract is enforceable. An **unenforceable, or void, contract** lacks one or more elements of a contract. Courts may also decline to enforce a contract where there is a valid contract defense.

An **executory contract** is one in which neither party has performed. Suppose Winchell emails Rachel and says, "I will buy 500 of your toasters for $10 each." Rachael emails back, "Agreed." They have a valid and enforceable contract. However, at this stage neither party has done what they promised to do. Executory contracts are important in bankruptcy, because a debtor can reject executory contracts without penalty.

An **executed contract** is one in which both parties have performed. Once both parties have performed they are discharged, and under no further obligation.

A **voidable contract** is one in which one of the parties may withdraw without penalty. For example, minors may enter into a contract, but then later reject the contract, unless the contract is for a necessity of life. A debtor in bankruptcy may withdraw from an executory contract.

---

**Types of Contracts**

**Bilateral** – a promise for a promise.

**Unilateral** – a promise for an act.

**Express** – terms spelled out.

**Implied** – obligations arise from actions.

**Enforceable or Valid** – contain all the elements to form a contract.

**Unenforceable or Void** – lack a contract element or have a defect.

**Executory** – contracts neither party has performed.

**Executed** – contracts both parties have performed.

**Voidable** – one party can withdraw without a penalty.

---

# Contract Interpretation

## Statute of Frauds

The **Statute of Frauds** is a law that says some contacts are so important they must be written to avoid misunderstandings. This statute is intended to avoid a situation in which one party says there was an oral contract (and lies about it), and the other party says there was no contract. The Statute of Frauds is also intended to document the details of what the parties agreed to.[13, 14]

### *Land or an Interest in Land*

Written contracts are required for the **sale of land** or an interest in land. An easement is an example of an interest in land. An easement is the right to cross the land of another. An electric company might get an easement to string power lines across a farmer's field. A life estate, that is the right to use a piece of property until one dies, is another example of an interest in land.

---

[13]Hall, Kermit L. Ed. David S. Clark, Joel Grossman, James W. Ely Jr., N.E.H. Hull, Eds. 2002. The Oxford Guide to American Law. Oxford University Press. 161, 671, 767

[14] Roszkowski, Mark E. 1989. Business Law 2nd Ed. HarperCollins Publishers. pp.270-272, 280, 682

### Secure Debts of Another

Written contracts are required to **secure the debts of another.** Suppose you want to buy a Jaguar, but your credit isn't good enough. The bank will want someone else to guarantee that they will repay the loan if you don't. Such a guarantee must be in writing to be enforceable.

---

**Securing the Debts of Another**

Never co-sign a loan. Never guarantee the debts of another. Never agree to make payments for another person.

Do not co-sign for a mother, father, brother, sister, boyfriend, girlfriend, buddy, or best friend.

If someone needs your help, and you can afford to give them money with no thought of repayment, do it, but never co-sign.

**In law school, they teach that a co-signer is a fool with a pencil.**

---

### Services Taking More than a Year to Perform

Written contracts are required for **services that cannot be performed in one year**. Suppose an oil company wants you to drill for oil in Alaska. They agree to move you there, help you find a home, and move you back, but to make it worth their while, they require that you drill for two years. Such a contract must be in writing.

### Sale of Goods over a Certain Amount

Written contracts are required for the **sale of goods** for **more than $500** (higher in some states). Oral offers to buy or sell a Lamborghini would not be valid under the Statue of Frauds, but email offers would be valid.

### What constitutes a writing?

A 'writing' is the reduction of an agreement in fixed form. Paper and pen can be used to form a writing, but pencil is also acceptable. The definition of a writing is very broad. An oil painting could be a writing if it contained all the elements of a contract. An exchange of letters can form a writing, as could an exchange of emails, tweets or Facebook postings. Video and audio recordings can be a writing for purposes of the Statute of Frauds. As technology advances, other valid forms of writings will emerge.[15]

## Parole Evidence Rule

The Parole Evidence Rule says that a **signed**, written **contract is the final word on what the parties agreed to.** Discussions or negotiations prior to signing the contract cannot be introduced to determine what the parties agreed to. Anything that went before was simply negotiation. However, behavior or statements made after the contract was formed, that clarifies terms, may be admissible. The court will then have to weigh and balance what the evidence means. Most courts are reluctant to enforce terms not within the four corners of the contract.

## Hierarchy of Contract Terms

Sometimes pre-printed contracts are used, and the parties type additional or different terms on the contracts, or they hand write additional, or different, terms on the contracts. **Handwritten terms control typed terms, and typed terms control pre-printed terms.**

## Contract Defenses

There are several defenses against contracts. A defense allows a party to escape a contract without penalty.[16]

## Fraud and Misrepresentation

Fraud and misrepresentation are defenses in contract law because the central premise of contract law is that the parties have voluntarily consented to enter a transaction. Consent is only possible where both parties are truthful. Consent based on false or misleading information is no consent.

---

[15] Roszkowski, Mark E. 1989. Business Law 2nd Ed. HarperCollins Publishers. pp 280-282.
[16] Smith, Len Young and Roberson, G. Gale. 1971. Business Law. West Publishing, St. Paul. pp.60-108.

Suppose Larry emailed, "I will sell you my truck for $20,000. It's good as new and only has 20,000 miles on it."

Bob emailed, "OK." However, before paying the money, he found the truck really had 120,000 miles on it. He refused to go through with the purchase, and Larry sued. What would be the result?

Bob can defend against the contract based on fraud and material misrepresentation. The court will not enforce the contract.

## Material Omission

Fraud and misrepresentation imply that one party to a contract did something to mislead the other party. What if a party says nothing, and allows the other party to assume facts not stated? What if the other party fails to ask a critical question that might change his or her mind about the deal? Can inaction be the basis for a contract defense? Yes. If one party has material information about a deal and fails to disclose it, the other party may assert the defense of a material omission. The reasoning is the same as for the defenses of fraud and misrepresentation. Contracts imply a voluntary consent to engage in a transaction. Consent is only possible when both parties are truthful. An omission can be untruthful if the omission causes one of the parties to make a decision they otherwise might not have made.

Suppose Larry emailed, "I will sell you my Jaguar for $40,000." Assume for the moment that a Jaguar of this vintage in good condition typically sells for $35,000 to $50,000. Bob emails, "OK." Before completing the contract, Bob sees Larry driving the Jaguar and a trail of blue smoke follows the car.

Bob asks, "How much oil does that car burn?" Larry says, "One or two quarts a week." Assuming Jaguars of similar vintage rarely burn oil, Bob will be able to defend against the contract because Larry failed to disclose how badly the car was burning oil. That failure constitutes a **material omission.**

Suppose Larry emailed, "I will sell you my Jaguar for $4,000." Assume for the moment that Jaguars of this vintage in good condition typically sell for $35,000 to $50,000. Bob emails, "OK." Before completing the contract, Bob sees Larry driving the Jaguar and a trail of blue smoke follows the car. What would be the result?

If a car, or another asset, is being sold for far less than fair market value, the purchaser is put on notice that there is some material defect in the item. In this case, the court would probably say the exceptionally low price put the buyer on notice of a defect, and the court will probably hold Bob to the contract.

## Mutual Mistake and Unilateral Mistake

Both mutual mistake and unilateral mistake can act as defenses against a contract. The parties to a contract must be talking about the same subject matter and terms for there to be agreement. Larry says, "Bob, I will give you $20,000 for your car." Bob says, "OK." Bob has two cars a year-old Buick and a two-year-old Corvette. Bob thought Larry wanted to buy the Buick. Larry offered to buy the Corvette. There is no mutual understanding and no contract.

Suppose Bob emails Larry and says I will give you $20,000 for your red Corvette. Larry has two red Corvettes, one a 1987 with 210,000 miles on it and one two years old with 15,000 miles on it. Larry accepts by letter and encloses the title to the 1987 Corvette. Is there an enforceable contract? If Bob didn't know about the older car there probably isn't an enforceable contract because of unilateral mistake. This can be distinguished from mutual mistake, wherein both parties have made a mistake about the subject matter of the contract. In any event, both mutual and unilateral mistake are contract defenses.

# Alternative Dispute Resolution

Sometimes, one of the parties to a contract fails to perform their part of the bargain. Other times, disputes arise over the quality or completeness of performance. How can such disputes be resolved? Does every dispute have to land in court? Law suits (litigation) are expensive, time consuming and the results are uncertain. **Alternative dispute resolution** is about resolving disputes outside the court system. Means of resolving disputes, from the quickest and least expensive to the slowest and most expensive, are (i) negotiation, (ii) mediation, (iii) arbitration, and (iv) litigation.[17]

## Negotiation

Negotiation is the simplest way to resolve a dispute. Talk to the other party and try to negotiate a settlement. Often what appears to be a breach

---

[17] Roszkowski, Mark E. 1989. Business Law 2$^{nd}$ Ed. HarperCollins Publishers. pp.31-36.

of contract is simply a misunderstanding, or the failure of one party to follow-up on something they should have done.

Negotiations are most successful when conducted in a friendly, courteous, cooperative manner. Negotiations can rapidly break down when one party becomes rude, abrupt, demanding or accusatory.

Negotiations should start by identifying the things both parties agree on. Then the discussion can be narrowed to the items in dispute. The next step in negotiation is for each side to quietly lay out what they think the other party must do. A good negotiator knows he or she will have to give up something to get something. When both parties are reasonable, an acceptable resolution can almost always be negotiated.

## Mediation

Sometimes, the parties are too close to a situation to see reasonable alternatives. Sometimes, one or both parties become rude or demanding, and that causes the other party to resist compromise.

In mediation, the two parties agree on a third party to help them work through the issues on which they disagree. Often a mediator can see both sides more clearly than the parties. Mediators have less at stake emotionally and can suggest solutions that both parties can agree on. Mediation can be very effective, especially if both parties know and respect the mediator. Mediation is non-binding. Mediators can only make suggestions. They cannot force the parties to do anything.

## Arbitration

Arbitration is a non-judicial (that is outside the court) but binding way to resolve disputes. Before arbitration begins, both parties sign a contract agreeing to be bound by the decision of an arbitrator. Courts generally enforce arbitration agreements and decisions made by an arbitrator. Arbitration is usually much quicker and much less expensive than a lawsuit.

The arbitrator is someone mutually agreed to by the parties to hear the facts and decide the matter. Sometimes there are three arbitrators, often only one. The decision of the arbitrator is binding and cannot be appealed unless the arbitrator was incompetent or dishonest. The parties can agree on, and select, an arbitrator themselves. However, when they cannot agree on an arbitrator, the American Arbitration Association can provide an arbitrator. All arbitrators charge a fee for their services. An advantage of arbitration through the American Arbitration Association is that they have published administrative rules that facilitate resolution and preserve the rights of the parties. Their website is www.adr.org.

Many contracts contain an arbitration clause that says, "in the event of a dispute, this matter must be settled through arbitration." Such a clause prevents a party from suing. All stock brokerage agreements contain arbitration clauses. A broker will not open an account for an individual who refuses to sign an arbitration agreement. In the future, doctors, lawyers, accountants and cable companies may require customers to sign arbitration agreements before they provide services.

## Litigation

Unless prohibited from suing by an arbitration clause, one can sue the party alleged to have breached a contract. Litigation begins when the plaintiff, the party bringing the suit, files a **complaint** with the court. The complaint outlines the legal theory under which the action is being brought and states the facts and circumstances needed to constitute the elements of the theory.

Prior to trial, there is an extended period when each party to the dispute tries to get all relevant facts out in the open. This process, and the facts uncovered, are called discovery. Each party has the obligation to provide information, documents, and testimony, requested by the other party. If a party does not timely provide such information, a judge may sanction that party, dismiss his or her case, or suppress some of their evidence. The following are the most common forms of discovery.[18]

### *Depositions*

Depositions are sworn testimony, usually in an attorney's office. Witnesses will be subpoenaed. A subpoena is a court order to appear, and answer questions under oath. This testimony may be introduced, or read, at trial.

### *Interrogatories*

Interrogatories are written questions submitted to the parties which must be answered in writing under oath. Answers may be entered into evidence at trial.

---

[18] Roszkowski, Mark E. 1989. Business Law 2$^{nd}$ Ed. HarperCollins Publishers. pp.37-52.

### Document Production

Document production is asking for, and receiving, documents from the opposing party. Document production might ask for copies of contracts, service agreements, internal policies and procedures, and copies of checks and financial statements.

### Admissions

Where both parties agree on certain facts, this agreement is documented with a signed admission. The purpose of admissions is to limit the number of items that must be proven at trial. For example, one might ask the opposing party to admit that the signature on the contract was their signature. Or they might be asked to admit that they did not follow their usual procedure in delivering goods or services.

### Pre-trial Memo

The purpose of the pre-trial memo is to give the parties a chance to argue how the law should be applied to the facts of the case. Judges are under no obligation to follow the conclusions of pre-trial memos. However, judges usually follow precedents, and the pre-trial memo might influence which precedents the court sees as relevant.

### Settlement

Once all the facts are out in the open, judges usually have a private meeting with the lawyers to try to get the parties to settle. The judge reviews the facts and the law with the lawyers, and points out that there is substantial risk in going to trial. For example, juries may not see facts the way the attorneys do, or witnesses may change their testimony. Some estimate as many as 90% of cases settle before trial. Settlement eliminates the risk of an unexpected outcome at trial.

If the parties settle, they will sign a document called an **Accord and Satisfaction,** which is a binding agreement to settle a dispute. It forever bars additional legal action. The Accord and Satisfaction sets out the terms of the settlement.

### Evidence

Evidence must be (i) probative, (ii) credible, (iii) not prejudicial, and (iv) not duplicative. Evidence is probative if it tends to prove or disprove an element of a legal theory, defense or damages. Evidence is credible if it is the type of evidence that prior courts have relied on. Fingerprints and DNA are considered highly reliable. But a voice analysis of a scream, or an indentation in a pillow, might not be a reliable way to identify someone. Some evidence is prejudicial, in that it is unnecessarily gruesome, or designed to inflame the jury, rather than to prove an element of a theory or defense. Judges have discretion to limit the amount of evidence admitted at trial in the interest of administrative economy, and to avoid prejudicing the jury by the bulk of duplicative evidence.

### Expert Reports and Testimony

Expert reports and testimony can only be used where the subject matter is beyond the understanding of an ordinary citizen. An expert must be 'qualified' as to the subject matter that he or she is testifying on. Opposing counsel gets to ask the expert about his or her qualifications, and either accepts the expert as qualified or makes a motion (request) that the court prohibit his or her testimony. Experts are only allowed to testify where there is a substantial body of literature indicating that the type of evidence being relied on is generally accepted in the technical or scientific field at issue.

### Burden of Proof

Contract litigation is civil litigation. In civil litigation, the plaintiff has the burden of proving, by a preponderance of the evidence, that the other party was at fault, or that the other party failed to complete the contract. The preponderance of the evidence means 'more likely than not'. It means there is a more than 50% chance that the defendant was at fault.

### Trial

Juries are triers of facts. They decide who is telling the truth and what weight to put on evidence. For example, one witness might testify she saw Joe damaging property. Another witness may testify that she was eating dinner with Joe at the time of the incident. The jury's job is to determine who is telling the truth.

In a bench trial, there is no jury. The judge decides the facts. Usually both parties must agree to a bench trial. The advantages of a bench trial are, (i) they are usually quicker, (ii) can be spread out a few days a week over several weeks to facilitate scheduling, and (iii) technical matters are sometimes easier to explain to a judge than to a jury.

Judges apply the law. They decide whether all the elements of a legal theory are present, and they determine which decision rules should be applied, and how. They decide what evidence to admit, and whether expert testimony will be allowed.

### Opinion and Holding

Sometimes, but not always, a judge or arbitrator will write an analysis of how he or she arrived at their conclusion. This is called an opinion. At the end of the opinion there is often a distilled essence of the legal rule that the case turned on. This legal rule is called a holding.

---

**Methods of Dispute Resolution**

**Negotiation** – The simplest, quickest, and most cost-effective way to resolve disputes is through negotiation. Often disputes can be resolved by talking.

**Mediation** – Sometimes the parties are too close to the dispute to see a path to a negotiated settlement. A mediator can help the parties see alternatives.

**Arbitration** – The parties sign a contract to abide by the decision of an arbitrator. Arbitration is quicker and more cost-effective than litigation.

**Litigation** – The parties may sue each other to resolve a dispute, but this method is slow, costly, and the outcome may be uncertain.

---

# Relief

Suppose a party wins an arbitration or lawsuit, what can they get? After a lawsuit or arbitration is over, the judge or the arbitrator will decide what the winner gets and what the loser must give up. This is called an order for relief. Such orders are binding as a matter of law.[19]

---

[19] Smith, Len Young and Roberson, G. Gale. 1971. *Business Law*. West Publishing, St. Paul. pp.272-293.

## *Dismissal*

If the judge or arbitrator enters an order of dismissal, the claim against the defendant is terminated. A dismissal may be based on lack of evidence, an adverse jury finding, or some legal defect in the case, such as failure to prove an element of a legal theory.

## *Compensatory Damages*

Compensatory damages are a payment in cash that is supposed to compensate a party for the cost of the other party's breach of contract. This is the most common kind of damages. Compensatory damages are designed so the injured party cannot profit from their injury, but will not suffer a monetary loss either.

## *Liquidated Damages*

Sometimes it is hard to prove the exact dollar value of damages. So, some contracts stipulate that, in the event of a breach of contract, damages will be a certain amount, like $10,000. These are called liquidated damages.

## *Consequential Damages*

Consequential damages are damages which go to the impact of a breach of contract. In the case of Hadley v. Baxendale,[20] a factory was shut down while its main drive shaft was sent to another town for repair. Rather than promptly fixing the drive shaft and returning it, the repair shop left it sitting around for an extended period. Hadley sued for the lost profits while the factory was closed and won consequential damages.

## *Nominal Damages*

Nominal damages are small dollar damages, like $1, awarded to prove a point or vindicate a principle.

---

[20] *Hadley v. Baxendale*, 9 Exch. 341, 156 Eng. Rep. 145 (1854).

## *Specific Performance*

A court may order a person to do something. This is called specific performance. Courts are reluctant to do this, preferring to award money damages. Suppose a comedian breaches a contract to perform at a casino on a certain date and the court orders him or her to perform. How can the court possibly force the comedian to be funny, or measure whether he or she gave their best performance?

## *Injunction*

An injunction is a court order *not* to do something, for a stated period, in a stated location. For example, suppose an employee signs a non-compete agreement when she goes to work for a company. A company's rival hires her away. Her original employer might ask the court for an injunction to prevent her from working for the competitor for two years and within 50 miles of his or her facility.

## *Punitive Damages*

Punitive damages are damages over and above other damages and are meant to punish a person or company for willful, wanton and reckless acts. Suppose a company knows that their 'organic' cookies contain mercury, a known neurotoxin, but they sell them anyway. A jury might find that such conduct is willful, wanton and reckless and might award punitive damages. The willful, wanton and reckless standard is very high, so punitive damages are very rare. When punitive damages are awarded, courts are likely to limit them to less than ten times actual damages.

# Findings

Often the finder of fact, either a jury or a judge sitting in a bench trial, will have to draw a conclusion about certain facts. These conclusions are called findings. Findings help shape the outcome of litigation and the remedies that may be granted.

## *Complete Performance*

A court may find that both parties have performed, and both are discharged from future obligations.

## *Material Breach*

A court may find that one of the parties has failed to live up to his or her contract obligations in an important way. In that event, the court can award damages that can range from nominal damages to compensatory damages.

## *Substantial Performance*

A court may find that one party has done almost all of what they were obligated to do, but performance is incomplete or substandard in some way. **If a party substantially completes a contact, they are entitled to most, but not all, of the consideration (usually money) promised for their work.** This amount is often the subject of litigation. However, the aggrieved party may be entitled to compensatory damages equal to the cost of completing the contract.[21]

Suppose a builder is under contract to build a four-bedroom, two-and-a-half-bath home, and completes a home with four bedrooms, a bath-and-a-half, and a small empty room. The builder would be entitled to the contract price of the house, less the cost to the homeowner of hiring another contractor to finish the job. If the contract price for the home was $300,000 and it cost the home owner $30,000 to hire another contractor to finish the job, the builder would be entitled to $270,000 ($300,000 - $30,000).

## *Willful, Wanton and Reckless*

On rare occasions, a judge may ask a jury whether a defendant's conduct was willful, wanton, and reckless. Such a finding is generally necessary for a court to award punitive damages.

# Conclusion

The law has developed over a long period of time to provide people and companies with certainty as to their privileges and obligations. Contract law protects property interests, and the reasonable expectations of the parties to a contract.

---

[21] Vernon, David H. 1980. Contracts: Theory and Practice. Matthew Bender. New York. p.10-57. Citing Danville Bridge Company v. Pomeroy and Colony, 15 Pa. 151 (1850).

Case law is a record of how judges decided prior cases. Judges apply decision rules consistent with case law. This is called precedent. Precedent makes the law more predictable. Statutes override case law, and often change the direction of subsequent case law.

The law is organized around legal theories. A legal theory is like a box with rules in it. One box of rules may favor one party, and another box of rules might favor the opposing party. Winning or losing in court often depends on selecting the appropriate legal theory. One is entitled to use a legal theory if one has all the elements of that theory. An element is a fact, circumstance, or principle that qualifies one to use a legal theory.

The elements of a contract are (i) offer, (ii) acceptance, (iii) consideration, (iv) capacity, and (v) lawful purpose. An offer in a bilateral contact is a promise for a promise. An offer in a unilateral contract is a promise for an act. Offers may be terminated by revocation prior to acceptance, at a certain time, by destruction of the subject matter, or the passage of time. Offers may also be terminated by rejection or a counter offer. Acceptance must be overt. Silence is not acceptance. Consideration can be a promise, giving something, performing an act or refraining from doing something one is entitled to do. Capacity refers to the legal capacity to contract. Generally, everyone has legal capacity, except minors and the incompetent. Minors have the capacity to contract for the necessities of life. Drunks only lack capacity when they are so drunk they do not know what they are doing. Most contracts are considered lawful unless there is some law against them.

There are several alternatives for resolving disputes other than through a lawsuit. Negotiation is the simplest, least expensive, and often the quickest way to resolve a dispute. Disputes often arise because of misunderstandings that can be resolved through discussion. However, sometimes the parties are too close to a situation to consider all alternatives. In such a case, they may bring in a mediator who is a person the parties respect and believe can fairly help them resolve their dispute. Arbitration is a dispute resolution mechanism in which the parties sign a contract agreeing to abide by the decision of an arbitrator.

Lawsuits can be tried in front of a judge and jury, or in front of a judge alone, in which case it is called a bench trial. A law suit starts when the aggrieved party files a complaint with the court. The next phase of litigation is discovery, wherein the parties get to ask each other questions under oath and compel each other to produce documents. The purpose of discovery is to bring all facts into the open. Once this is done, the judge usually tries to get the parties to settle the case. Most cases settle. If there is no settlement, the case can go to trial.

Depending on what the jury finds, and the judge rules, the winning party may get compensatory, nominal, liquidated, or punitive damages. Punitive damages are very rare. A court may also order specific performance of an act or it may enjoin, that is prohibit, certain actions. Where the jury or judge finds a material breach, the court is likely to order compensatory damages. However, where the jury or judge finds substantial performance, the court will order the plaintiff to pay the contract price, less the cost to complete the project.

Property and contract law are necessary for orderly and predictable business operations, and economic growth. For business people to succeed, they must know their rights and obligations under the law.

# Terms and Concepts

**Acceptance** – Acceptance is agreement to an offer. Acceptance must be overt. Silence is not acceptance.

**Accord and Satisfaction** – This is a binding agreement to settle a case. It forbids the parties from suing on the same facts again.

**Admissions** – Where the parties agree on facts, they will admit to those facts during discovery, so that they need not be proved at trial.

**Alternative Dispute Resolution** – There are many ways to resolve disputes other than through litigation. From the least expensive and time-consuming, to the most expensive and time consuming, these are (i) negotiation, (ii) mediation, (iii) binding arbitration, and (iv) litigation.

**Ambiguity** – Where mutual mistake is the result of some ambiguity created by one of the parties, the courts are likely to rule against the party which created the ambiguity or had the best opportunity to correct it.

**Arbitration** - is a non-judicial (that is outside the court), but binding way to resolve disputes. Before arbitration begins, both parties sign a contract agreeing to be bound by the decision of an arbitrator. Courts will enforce such arbitration agreements. Arbitration is usually much quicker and much less expensive than a lawsuit.

**Arbitrator** – An arbitrator is the person who supervises an arbitration proceeding, acts as the finder of fact, and applies the law.

**Bench Trial** – This is a trial in which the judge acts as the finder of fact rather than the jury. Generally, all parties must consent to a bench trial rather than a jury trial.

**Burden of Proof** - In civil litigation, the plaintiff has the burden of proving, by a preponderance of the evidence, that the other party was at fault. The preponderance of the evidence means more likely than not. It means there is a more than 50% chance that the defendant was at fault.

**Capacity** – This is the legal capacity to contract. Generally, everyone has legal capacity except minors and those who are incompetent. Minors have the capacity to contract for the necessities of life. Drunks have capacity, unless they are so drunk they did not know what they are doing.

**Common Law** – The decision of judges is written down and shared, so that similar cases will be resolved using similar decision rules. Following the decision-making process of others is called precedent.

**Complete performance** – If the defendant has rendered complete performance, a contract case will be dismissed.

**Compensatory dama**ges - are a payment in cash that is supposed to compensate a party for the cost of the other party's breach of contract.

**Consequential damages** - are damages which go to the impact of a breach of contract. In the case of Hadley v. Baxendale, a factory was shut down while its main drive shaft was sent to another town for repair. Rather than promptly repairing the drive shaft, the repair shop delayed, which cost the factory profits. The lost profits were the consequential damages.

**Consideration** –May be thought of as payment. Consideration can be giving something, promising to give something or promising to refrain from something one has a right to do. Past consideration is no consideration.

**Contract** – The elements of a contract are (i) offer, (ii) acceptance, (iii) consideration, (iv) capacity, and (v) lawful purpose.

**Contract, Bilateral** – A bilateral contract is a promise for a promise.

**Contract Defenses** – A party may escape a valid contract without penalty if it successfully asserts a defense. Common contract defenses are: fraud, misrepresentation, material omission, mistake, destruction of the subject matter, illegality of the subject matter, or incompetence of a party.

**Contract, Enforceable** – Enforceable contracts have all the elements necessary to form a contract.

**Contact, Executory** – Neither party has performed.

**Contract, Express** – An express contract is one in which the terms are spelled out, either orally or in writing.

**Contract, Implied** – An implied contract is a contract which arises from the actions of the parties. Implied contracts are enforced to prevent unjust enrichment.

**Contract Terms, Hierarchy** – Typed terms control pre-printed terms, and hand-written terms control typed terms.

**Contract, Unilateral** – A unilateral contract can only be accepted by an act. "I will pay you $20 if you wash my car." This contract may only be accepted by the act of washing the car.

**Contract, Void** – This is a contract lacking some element of contract formation.

**Contract, Voidable** – Minors lacking capacity may void a contract except for the necessities of life. In bankruptcy, a debtor may void an executory contract.

**Defendant** – The defendant is the party being sued.

**Deposition** – A deposition is a statement taken under oath in an attorney's office. The statement is usually taken in response to questions from a lawyer for one of the parties. Testimony may be used as evidence at trial.

**Discovery** – Prior to trial, the parties try to get all the facts out in the open. Discovery includes depositions, interrogatories, document production, and admissions.

**Dismissal** – A court order of dismissal ends litigation against the defendant. A court may enter a dismissal if the plaintiff fails to allege a valid legal theory; or fails to prove the elements of a theory; or if the judge concludes there is insufficient competent evidence for the jury to find for the plaintiff.

**Element** – An element is a fact or circumstance required to use a legal theory.

**Experience, the Life of the Law** – Oliver Wendell Holmes said: "The life of the law is not logic. It has been experience." As experience changes, the law changes. Experience also means that customs and trade practices influence how judges interpret and apply the law.

**Failure to State a Cause of Action** – If a lawsuit does not specify the legal theory which is the basis of an action, or if a suit fails to allege all the elements of a legal theory, it may be dismissed for failure to state a cause of action.

**Findings** – After trial, the jury, or the judge in a bench trial, may be asked to find specific facts. These facts will shape the court's order of relief. A jury may find complete performance, material breach, substantial performance, or willful, wanton, and reckless, conduct.

**Fraud, Statue of** – see Statute of Frauds.

**Fraud and Misrepresentation** – Contracts are based on voluntary agreement. Where one party has been deceitful as to the subject matter or terms of a contract, there can be no real agreement, and this essential element of contract disappears.

**Firm offer** – Under UCC 2-205, a merchant which makes an offer to sell goods is bound to the terms of that offer for a reasonable period, though the offeree has not given any consideration.

**Hadley v. Baxendale** – is the case that established the principle that one could sue for consequential damages. Consequential damages go to the impact of an injury, such as lost profits.

**Injunction** – Courts may issue an order prohibiting a party from doing something.

**Interrogatories** - are written questions submitted to the parties which must be answered in writing under oath. Answers may be entered into evidence at trial.

**Lawful purpose** – Contracts are presumed to have a lawful purpose unless prohibited by law.

**Legal Theory** – The law is organized around legal theories. A legal theory is like a box with decision rules in it. Whether one wins or loses a case often turns on the legal theory used. To use a legal theory, a case must have all the necessary elements. Cases or matters for which there is no legal theory will be dismissed.

**Liquidated damages** - Sometimes it is hard to prove the exact dollar value of damages. So, some contracts stipulate that in the event of a breach of contract, damages will be a certain amount.

**Litigation** – Litigation is the process of suing a party in court. Litigation begins when the plaintiff files a complaint. A period of fact-finding called discovery follows the complaint. Sometimes lawyers submit a pre-trial memo. The judge tries to get the parties to settle; and if there is no settlement, a trial commences. Litigation is time-consuming, expensive and the outcome can be uncertain.

**Material breach** – A material breach means the defendant has failed to complete their part of the contract in a substantial way. This entitles the other party to some form of relief, usually compensatory damages.

**Material Omission** –A material omission occurs when one party to a contract fails to disclose information that the other party needs to make a fair and reasoned evaluation of the proposed deal.

**Mediation** – A mediator is a neutral party brought in to listen to the positions of both sides, defuse tension, and propose alternatives.

**Misrepresentation** – see Fraud and Misrepresentation.

**Mistake** – Both mutual mistake and unilateral mistake act as contract defenses. The most common mistake occurs where the parties believe the contract involves different subject matter. Where there is mistake there is no mutual assent.

**Negotiation** – This is the process whereby the parties each attempt to get what they need out of a bargain, while giving up as little as possible.

**Negotiation, Dispute Resolution** – Many disputes are the result of simple misunderstandings as to the time, terms, quantity, or some other aspect of performance. The simplest and easiest way to resolve such disputes is to talk to the other party and explain the issues.

**Nominal damages** – are small dollar damages to prove a legal point.

**Offer** – An offer is a promise and a demand.

**Offer Termination** – Offers can be terminated by revocation, rejection, a counter offer, or at a specified time. An offer will terminate after a reasonable period. As between merchants, under the UCC, an offeree may propose additional terms. Additional terms are not a counter offer unless they conflict with the original terms. Destruction of the subject matter terminates an offer. The incapacity of the offeror terminates an offer. Illegality terminates an offer.

**Oral contracts** – Oral contracts are valid. However, the Statute of Frauds says some contracts are so important they must be in writing.

**Parole Evidence Rule** – The Parole Evidence Rule says that a contract represents the final word as to what the parties agreed to. Anything the parties said prior to signing a contract is deemed mere negotiations.

**Plaintiff** – The plaintiff is the party who initiates a lawsuit.

**Precedent** – Decision rules applied in prior cases should be applied to similar new cases. Precedent adds predictability to the law.

**Performance** – This is fulfilling a promise made in a contract.

**Pre-trial memo** – Parties may submit a pre-trial memo, which argues which law and precedents the court should apply to the facts of the case.

**Punitive damages** – Where the defendant's conduct is willful, wanton and reckless, the court may award the plaintiff punitive damages; that is damages to punish the defendant. Punitive damages are extremely rare.

**Relief** – What courts will grant the winner in litigation.

**Settlement** – Prior to trial a judge usually tries to get the parties to settle.

**Specific performance** – Courts may order a party to do something. Courts are reluctant to order specific performance because it is hard to monitor compliance. Courts would rather award money damages.

**Stare Decisis** - means 'let the decision stand'. It is the legal principle that prior legal opinions should be followed.

**Statute of Frauds** – Some contracts are so important the law requires them to be in writing, for example: contracts for the sale of goods over $500 (more in some states); for the sale of land or an interest in land; for services which cannot be performed in a year; and for the debts of another.

**Substantial performance** – means the defendant has done almost everything they were supposed to do, but not quite. If substantial performance is found, the defendant will be entitled to the contract price, less the cost to the plaintiff to hire someone to complete the contract.

**Trial** – Trial is conducted in a court room and may be conducted with a jury or, if all parties agree, without a jury.

**UCC Article 2** – This article provides rules for sale of goods.

**Uniform Commercial Code** – Contract law is state law. The Uniform Commercial Code (UCC) is a model contract law which has been enacted in most states.

**Willful, wanton, and reckless** – This is conduct which is in some way outrageous. It goes far beyond mere negligence or lack of attention. Such a finding is rarely made in a contract matter. If it is made at all, it is in connection with a physical or mental injury.

**Writing** – Writing is the reduction of an agreement to fixed form. Such as contracts, letters, email, tweets, blog posts, video or audio recordings, or any other medium which may be used to record a fixed impression of contract terms.

# References

American Arbitration Association. 2018. www.adr.org.

Danville Bridge Company v. Pomeroy and Colony, 15 Pa. 151 (1850).

Edwards, Carolyn M. 1978. "The Statute of Frauds of the Uniform Commerce Code and the Doctrine of Estoppel," Marquette Law Review. Vol.62 pp.205-225. Original source: 29 Car. 2 (1677).

Field, Richard H., Benjamin Kaplan, Kevin M. Clermont. 1978. Civil Procedure. 4th Ed. The Foundation Press. Mineola, New York. p.372-374.

Hadley v. Baxendale, 9 Exch. 341, 156 Eng. Rep. 145 (1854).

Hall, Kermit L. Ed. David S. Clark, Joel Grossman, James W. Ely Jr.,
    N.E.H. Hull, Eds. 2002. The Oxford Guide to American Law. Oxford
    University Press. 161, 671,767
LaPiana, William. 1994. Logic and Experience. Oxford University Press.
    Oxford, England.
Prosser, William L. 1983. Law of Torts. West Publishing Company. St.
    Paul, Minn. p.143-144.
Roszkowski, Mark E. 1989. Business Law 2nd Ed. HarperCollins
    Publishers.
Smith, Len Young and Roberson, G. Gale. 1971. *Business Law*. West
    Publishing, St. Paul.
Statute of Anne. 2008. "The Statute of Anne; April 10, 1710," Lillian
    Goldman Law Library, Yale.
    http://avalon.law.yale.edu/18th_century/anne_1710.asp          Original
    source: 8 Anne, c. 19 (1710)
Vernon, David H. 1980. Contracts: Theory and Practice. Matthew Bender.
    New York.

# CHAPTER THIRTEEN

# FINANCE AND THE TIME VALUE OF MONEY

---

After completing this chapter, you should be able to:

13.1 Compute the future value of an investment made now.

13.2 Compute the present value of a sum of money to be received in the future.

13.3 Compute the value accumulated by saving a regular amount at regular intervals, plus interest.

13.4 Compute the present value of a sum of payments to be received over a period of years.

13.5 Compute loan payments.

13.6 Analyze loan payments and prepare a loan amortization table.

---

## Introduction

Accounting is about what happened in the past. It is historical in nature. Finance is about what is going to happen in the future. An individual or company that can make better predictions about the future, can make better decisions.

One set of predictions concerns the time value of money. The value of money changes, and usually decreases over time due to several factors. One factor is inflation. Fifty years ago, gasoline cost $0.179 per gallon; recently it cost $2.799 per gallon. The price of most everything else, bread, clothes, cars, and the other necessities of life, has risen as well.

Money in hand today is worth more than money to be received in the future, because money in hand today can be invested and grow. There is also the risk that money promised in the future might not materialize. That risk makes the promise of money to be received in the future worth less than money in hand today.

Common problems related to the time value of money include: (i) the future value of an amount invested at interest today; (ii) the value in today's dollars of money promised in the future; (iii) the value of saving regular amounts plus accumulated interest; (iv) the value in today's dollars of a stream of even payments to be received over several years; (v) loan payments; and (vi) a loan amortization schedule which splits each loan payment into principal and interest.

## Future Value

Future Value asks the question, "If a person invested a sum of money at a certain interest rate for a certain number of years, how much would that person have in the future?"

### Interest

Equation Eq.13.1 provides the calculation for the interest accrued in one year.

$$\text{Interest} = \text{Principal x Interest Rate} \qquad \text{Eq.13.1}$$

### Compound Interest

Compound interest is a term which means that interest is paid on the interest earned in prior periods. Suppose one invested $1,000 at 6% interest for five years. Table 13.1 Compound Interest illustrates how compounding increases the value of invested capital.

**Table 13.1 Compound Interest**

| Year | Principal 1/1 | ------Interest 12/31------ | Total 12/31 |
|------|---------------|----------------------------|-------------|
| 1 | $1,000.00 | $1,000.00 x 6% = $60.00 | $1,060.00 |
| 2 | $1,060.00 | $1,060.00 x 6% = $63.60 | $1,123.60 |
| 3 | $1,123.60 | $1,123.60 x 6% = $67.42 | $1,191.02 |
| 4 | $1,191.02 | $1,191.02 x 6% = $71.46 | $1,262.48 |
| 5 | $1,262.48 | $1,262.48 x 6% = $75.75 | $1,338.23 |

The interest earned in Year 1 is $60.00 (6% x $1,000.00). This increases the value of the investment to $1,060.00 ($1,000 initial investment + $60.00 interest). The second-year interest of $63.60 is based on the value of the investment at the end of the first year $1,060.00. In other words, the second year's interest is based on the initial investment plus accumulated interest.

Computing interest one year at a time is tedious. Is there an easier way? Yes. Equation Eq.13.2 is the Future Value formula.[1, 2]

$$FV = PV \times (1 + i)^n \qquad \text{Eq.13.2}$$

In this equation, FV is the Future Value, the amount to be received when the investment matures. PV is the Present Value of the money invested. Dollars invested today are present value dollars. The interest rate is denoted by i, and n is the number of years of compounding. Suppose $1,000 is invested at 6% interest for five years. Using equation Eq.13.2 the problem would be set up as follows:

$$FV = \$1,000 \times (1 + 6\%)^5$$
$$= \$1,000 \times 1.06^5$$
$$= \$1,000 \times 1.3382256$$
$$= \$1,338.23$$

## More Than One Period per Year

Often, interest is compounded more than once per year. Some certificates of deposit compute interest quarterly. That means the second quarter's interest is based on the original investment, plus any interest earned in the first quarter.

To use equation Eq.13.2 for more than one period in a year, the period interest rate 'i' and the number of periods 'n' must be adjusted as shown in equations Eq.13.3 and Eq.13.4.

i = Annual Percentage Rate/Number of periods per year    Eq.13.3

n = Number of years x Number of periods per year          Eq.13.4

---

[1] Vance, David E. 2003. Financial Analysis and Decision Making. McGraw-Hill Companies. New York. pp.88-91.
[2] Mayo, Herbert B. 1998. Financial Institutions, Investments and Management. The Dryden Press. Harcourt Brace College Publishers. Fort Worth. pp.12-17.

Suppose a bank offers a $1,000 certificate of deposit with an annual percentage rate of 6%, the certificate matures in five years, and the bank compounds interest monthly. Adjust the period interest rate 'i' and the number of periods 'n'.

i = 6% annual percentage rate/12 periods per year = 0.5%

n = 5 years x 12 periods per year = 60

Using the new i and n in equation Eq.13.2 gives the following result.

$$FV \quad = \$1,000 \times (1+0.5\%)^{60}$$

$$= \$1,000 \times 1.34885$$

$$= \$1,348.85$$

The difference of $10.62 between annual compounding and monthly compounding might not seem like much. However, as the dollars invested increases, the length of time increases, the interest rate increases, and the number of times per year interest is compounded increases, the difference can be significant. For example, suppose $100,000 were invested for ten years at an annual percentage rate of 12% per year. Annual compounding would yield a total of $310,584.82, whereas daily compounding would yield $331,946.22 or about $21,361.40 more. Compounding matters.

## Present Value

What if someone promised to pay a certain sum of money in the future; what would that promise be worth in today's dollars? Future dollars are worth less than dollars in hand today for three reasons:

(i)     Money in hand today can be invested to grow.
(ii)    The value of money erodes over time because of inflation.
(iii)   There is some risk that an amount promised in the future will never be received.

These three factors give rise to a variable called the **discount rate**. The discount rate is like sandpaper wearing away the value of money promised in the future. The higher the discount rate, the coarser the sandpaper. The longer the discount rate is applied, the more the value of money is worn away. The discount rate can be thought of as the yield on an investment. A discount rate should be equal to the yield on investments of comparable risk.

The equation for computing the present value of a sum of money can be derived from the Future Value Formula, equation Eq.13.2.

$$FV = PV \times (1 + i)^n \qquad \text{Eq.13.2}$$

Using a little algebra, this can be re-arranged to yield equation Eq.13.5.

$$PV = \frac{FV}{(1 + i)^n} \qquad \text{Eq.13.5}$$

There is one additional convention to observe. When talking about Present Value, use k which stands for the discount rate, instead of i which is used for interest. This final adjustment gives equation Eq.13.6.[3, 4]

$$PV = \frac{FV}{(1 + k)^n} \qquad \text{Eq.13.6}$$

Suppose a company promises an employee a bonus of $20,000 if he or she stays with the company until a project is completed in three years. The employee might want to know what that bonus is worth in today's dollars, so he or she could compare it to a signing bonus offered by another company. Suppose the discount rate for investments of similar risk is 15%. What is the present value of the bonus?

$$PV = \frac{\$20,000}{(1 + 15\%)^3}$$

$$= \frac{\$20,000}{1.5209}$$

$$= \$13,150$$

Most of the time, future payments are only discounted once per year. However, sometimes, for example when computing the value of corporate bonds, future payments are discounted more than once per year. When there is more than one discounting period a year, equation Eq.13.7 must be

---

[3] Vance, David E. 2003. Financial Analysis and Decision Making. McGraw-Hill Companies. New York. pp.91-94.
[4] Mayo, Herbert B. 1998. Financial Institutions, Investments and Management. The Dryden Press. Harcourt Brace College Publishers. Fort Worth. pp.18-20.

used to find the period discount rate. Whenever a discount rate is adjusted, the number of periods must also be adjusted, using equation Eq.13.4.

k = Annual Discount Rate/Number of Periods per Year      Eq.13.7

Suppose a corporate bond had a yield (market rate of interest) of 8%, and like most corporate bonds, it pays interest semi-annually. The discount rate, k, would be:

k = 8% yield / 2 payments per year

= 4% per period

## Functional Notation

A function is a shorthand way of writing an equation. Functions are mathematical machines. Put variables (data) into the machine, turn the crank, and a result comes out.[5] The future value equation Eq.13.2 can be written in functional notation, as shown in equation Eq.13.8.

FV = PV x FVIF (i, n)                          Eq.13.8

FV is the Future Value, the value to be received when the investment matures. PV is the Present Value; the amount of cash to be invested now. FVIF is the name of the function which computes the Future Value Interest Factor. The data input into the function are placed in parentheses after the function name. The variables i and n are the period interest rate and the number of periods. Using an X-ray machine, one can see that equation Eq.13.9 is inside the function FVIF (i, n).

$$FVIF\ (i, n) = (1 + i)^n$$                          Eq.13.9

The Present Value equation written in functional notation is shown as equation Eq.13.10.

PV = FV x PVIF (k, n)                          Eq.13.10

PV is the present value of the money to be received in the future. FV is the amount to be received in the future. PVIF is the name of the Present

---

[5] Vance, David E. 2009. Ratios: For Analysis, Control and Profit Planning. Global Professional Publishing. Slip Mill Lane, Cranbrook, Kent U.K. pp.107-108.

Value Interest Factor function and the variables k and n are the period discount rate and the number of periods. Using an X-ray machine, one can see that equation 13.11 is inside the function PVIF (k, n).

$$PVIF (k, n) = \frac{1}{(1 + k)^n} \qquad \text{Eq.13.11}$$

## Future Value Interest Factor of an Annuity

An annuity is an even stream of payments. The stream of payments can be coming in or going out. The point is, that each payment, whether daily, weekly, monthly or annually, is the same amount.

How much money would you have if you saved the same amount over some period and got compound interest on the amount saved? Sounds like a tricky calculation, and it is. Fortunately, a method to simplify the calculation has been worked out.[6, 7] This calculation is called the Future Value Interest Factor for an Annuity. Equation Eq.13.12 is the functional notation for this calculation.

$$FV = Pmt \times FVIFA (i, n) \qquad \text{Eq.13.12}$$

FV is the value that one will have after all payments and compound interest on those payments has been added together. Pmt is the amount of each payment. FVIFA is the Future Value Interest Factor of an Annuity function; i, and n are the period interest rate and the number of periods respectively. The equation inside the function FVIFA (i, n) is shown in equation Eq.13.13.

$$FVIFA (i, n) = \frac{(1 + i)^n - 1}{i} \qquad \text{Eq.13.13}$$

Suppose Alice saved $300 per month for three years at 6% interest compounded monthly. How much would she have?

The first step in any time value of money calculation is to determine the period interest rate, i, and the number of periods, n. Since money is

---

[6] Vance, David E. 2003. Financial Analysis and Decision Making. McGraw-Hill Companies. New York. pp.98-100.
[7] Mayo, Herbert B. 1998. Financial Institutions, Investments and Management. The Dryden Press. Harcourt Brace College Publishers. Fort Worth. pp.20-23.

being saved monthly, and there are twelve months in a year, i and n will have to be adjusted, using equations Eq.13.3 and Eq.13.4.

$$i = \text{Annual Percentage Rate/Periods per Year} \qquad \text{Eq.13.3}$$

$$= 6\%/12 \text{ months per year}$$

$$= 0.5\%$$

$$n = \text{Number of years x Periods per Year}$$

$$= 3 \text{ years x } 12 \text{ months per year}$$

$$= 36$$

$$FV = \$300 \text{ x } \frac{(1 + 0.5\%)^{36} - 1}{0.5\%}$$

$$= \$300 \text{ x } \frac{1.005^{36} - 1}{.005}$$

$$= \$300 \text{ x } \frac{1.19668 - 1}{.005}$$

$$= \$300 \text{ x } \frac{.19668}{.005}$$

$$= \$300 \text{ x } 39.336$$

$$= \$11,800.80$$

While this calculation might seem somewhat difficult at first, it is far easier than calculating the interest from the time of deposit to the ending date on 36 payments, and then adding up the 36 deposits with their accumulated interest.

## Present Value Interest Factor of an Annuity

Sometimes, people are promised an even stream of payments in exchange for something. Bob has a hundred acres of land in Montana that he wants to sell for $120,000. Ted wants to buy it, but he doesn't have the cash for an outright purchase. Instead, Ted offers to pay $1,200 per month for ten years. Is this a good deal or a bad deal?

At first glance, this may seem like a good deal. Ted is willing to write checks totaling $144,000 (10 years x 12 months per year x $1,200). But, the dollars in those future payments will be worth less than today's dollars, so a prudent person would discount those payments to determine their value in present dollars.

Conceptually, one could discount every monthly payment to the present and then add up those present values. There are several problems with this. The first, it is tedious. Second, as the number of calculations grows, the risk of error grows. Fortunately, this type of problem is encountered so often that a short cut method has been devised. This shortcut uses a function called the Present Value Interest Factor of an Annuity.[8], [9] Equation Eq.13.14 shows how to compute the present value of an even stream of payments using the function PVIFA (k, n).

$$PV = Pmt \times PVIFA \ (k, n) \qquad\qquad Eq.13.14$$

PV is the present value of all the payments in the payment stream. Pmt is the amount of each payment. PVIFA is the name of the Present Value Interest Factor of an Annuity function, and the variables k, and n are the period discount rate and number of periods respectively. The equation inside the function PVIFA (k, n) is shown in equation Eq.13.15.

$$PVIFA \ (k, n) = \frac{1}{k} - \frac{1}{k} \times \frac{1}{(1+k)^n} \qquad\qquad Eq.13.15$$

Before proceeding, a discount rate must be selected. The discount rate and interest rate are intimately related, and often turn on whether one is paying or receiving payments. The discount rate represents, among other things, the degree of riskiness of a deal. For example, one might ask whether the deal is more or less risky than putting money in a bank. Obviously, sale to a private buyer is riskier, so the discount rate should be higher than the interest rate promised by a bank. Is this deal more or less risky than bonds issued by a large, well-known, company? It is probably riskier, so the discount rate should be higher than the yield on good quality

---

[8] Vance, David E. 2003. Financial Analysis and Decision Making. McGraw-Hill Companies. New York. p.94.
[9] Mayo, Herbert B. 1998. Financial Institutions, Investments and Management. The Dryden Press. Harcourt Brace College Publishers. Fort Worth. pp.23-25.

corporate bonds. This deal is probably even riskier than a used car loan, so let's use a discount rate of 15% per year.

Since payments are being made monthly, the annual discount rate must be converted to the period discount rate using equation Eq.13.7.

$$k = \text{Annual Discount Rate/Number of Periods per Year} \quad \text{Eq.13.7}$$

$$= 15\%/12 \text{ payments per year}$$

$$= 1.25\%$$

The number of periods, n, is computed using equation Eq.13.4. In the case of the Montana land sale, payments are to be made monthly for ten years.

$$n = 10 \text{ years x } 12 \text{ months per year}$$

$$= 120$$

The Present Value can then be computed.

$$PV = \$1,200 \times \left[ \frac{1}{1.25\%} \quad \frac{-1}{1.25\%} \quad x \quad \frac{1}{(1 + 1.25\%)^{120}} \right]$$

$$= \$1,200 \times \left[ 80 \quad - 80 \times (1 / 4.440213) \right]$$

$$= \$1,200 \times \left[ 80 - 18.01753 \right]$$

$$= \$1,200 \times 61.98247$$

$$= \$74,378.96$$

Even though the buyer is willing to write checks totaling $144,000 (120 payments of $1,200 each) the present value of those dollars is only $74,378.96. If the asking price of $120,000 is fair, the seller should decline the offer.

## Time Value of Money Tables

Tables have been worked out for common time value of money problems and values. Table 13.2 is a list of the time value of money functions, their functional notations, and the Appendices at the end of the book where each table may be found.

**Table 13.2 Time Value of Money Tables**

| Function Name | Functional Notation | Appendix |
|---|---|---|
| Future Value Interest Factor | FVIF (i, n) | Appendix A |
| Present Value Interest Factor | PVIF (k, n) | Appendix B |
| Future Value Interest Factor of an Annuity | FVIFA (i, n) | Appendix C |
| Present Value Interest Factor of an Annuity | PVIFA (k, n) | Appendix D |

The four tables are all read the same way. Compute the period interest or discount rate and number of periods. Find the correct table. Then read down the left side of the table to get the correct n, then read across to the correct period interest or discount rate. The value in that cell is the value of the function.

To find PVIFA (1.25%, 120), use Table 13.3 PVIFA Partial Table. Read down the left column to find n = 120. Then read across to the column 1.25%. The value at this location should be 61.9828.

**Table 13.3 PVIFA Partial Table**

| N | 0.50% | 0.75% | 1.00% | 1.25% | 1.50% | 2.00% |
|---|---|---|---|---|---|---|
| 1 | 0.99502 | 0.99256 | 0.9901 | 0.98765 | 0.98522 | 0.98039 |
| 2 | 1.9851 | 1.97772 | 1.9704 | 1.96312 | 1.95588 | 1.94156 |
| 3 | 2.97025 | 2.95556 | 2.94099 | 2.92653 | 2.9122 | 2.88388 |
| 60 | 51.7256 | 48.1734 | 44.955 | 42.0346 | 39.3803 | 34.7609 |
| 120 | 90.0735 | 78.9417 | 69.7005 | **61.9828** | 55.4985 | 45.3554 |
| 240 | 139.581 | 111.145 | 90.8194 | 75.9423 | 64.7957 | 49.5686 |
| 360 | 166.792 | 124.282 | 97.2183 | 79.0861 | 66.3532 | 49.9599 |

We can recalculate the present value of Ted's promise to pay $1,200 per month for ten years using equation Eq.13.14 and the value from the PVIFA table.

$$= \$1,200 \text{ x PVIFA } (1.25\%, 120)$$

$$= \$1,200 \text{ x } 61.9828$$

$$= \$74,379.36$$

Tables can be, and are, used for convenience. The equations inside functions are used when additional precision is required, or a computer program is doing the computation. It is easier for a computer program to do the calculation than to look up a value in a two-dimensional table.

## Reasonableness Checking

Every mathematical calculation, whether the time value of money or any other calculation, ought to be checked for reasonableness. After making a calculation, try to estimate the highest number the answer could be, and the lowest number it could be. If the computed answer isn't between these two limits, there is probably an error in the calculation.

### Future Value

Future value is an estimate of the amount of money one will have in the future if a certain sum of money is invested today at a given interest rate. What is the minimum amount this future value could be? The minimum value is at least the amount initially invested. This implies an interest rate of zero. The maximum value is probably ten times what was invested. If the calculated answer isn't between these two limits, there is probably an error in the calculation.

### Present Value

The present value is the value in today's dollars of some amount promised in the future. The most that the present value could possibly be is the amount promised in the future. This would imply a discount rate of zero. But, it is very unlikely that the present value will be less than one tenth of the amount promised.

# Future Value of an Annuity

The future value of an annuity is the value that will accrue if an even stream of deposits is made into an interest-bearing account. The minimum value for such a calculation is the amount of each payment, times the number of payments. This would be true even if the interest rate were zero. But if the amount calculated is greater than ten times the number of payments, times the amount of each payment, the answer is probably incorrect.

# Present Value of an Annuity

The present value of an annuity is the value, in today's dollars, of an even stream of payments received over time. The absolute maximum this could be is the number of payments, times the amount of each payment. This implies a discount rate of zero. But if the present value of an annuity is less than one tenth of the number of payments, times the amount of each payment, there is probably an error in the calculation.

# Common Errors

The most common errors in time value of money calculations are (i) failure to adjust for the period interest or discount rate, (ii) failure to adjust the number of periods, and (iii) use of the wrong formula or table. Reasonableness checks will identify most of these errors. Problem-solving accuracy can be significantly improved by performing reasonableness checks.

---

### Reasonableness Checks

Every calculation, whether related to the time value of money or not should be checked for reasonableness.

After a calculation is complete, take a few seconds to ask, what are the highest and lowest values the answer can reasonably have?

If the answer is outside these limits, recheck the calculations and the data used in them.

The most common types of time value of money errors are failure to properly adjust i, k, and n, and use of the wrong formula or table.

---

# Loan Payments

Computing loan payments is a common financial problem. People know the cost of what they want to buy, the interest rate being charged and how long they plan to finance a purchase. What they want to know is the amount of the payment. Frequently, the decision to buy a car, house, boat or airplane turns not just on the price, but on the monthly payment. Equation Eq.13.14 can be used to compute payments.[10]

$$PV = Pmt \times PVIFA\ (k, n) \qquad \text{Eq.13.14}$$

Assume a purchase is being 100% financed, with no down payment. Then PV, the present value of all the payments, must equal the purchase price of whatever is being bought. Customers know the annual interest rate and the length of a loan. This provides everything needed to figure out the value of PVIFA (k, n). With the purchase price and a value for PVIFA (k, n), the only unknown in equation Eq.13.14 is the amount of the payment. Pmt is the symbol for payment.

Suppose one wants to purchase a car that cost $25,000, to be financed over five years, at 9% annual percentage rate. What would the monthly payment be?

First compute the period interest rate i, and the number of periods n. Unless there is specific information to the contrary, assume loan payments are made monthly. Note that the interest rate from the point of view of the buyer is the discount rate from the point of view of the lender. So, we can use the annual interest rate as the annual discount rate.

k  = Annual interest rate/12 months per year.

= 9% / 12

= 0.75%

n  = number of years x 12 months per year

= 5 x 12

= 60

---

[10] Vance, David E. 2003. Financial Analysis and Decision Making. McGraw-Hill Companies. New York. pp.94-96.

Look up PVIFA (.75%, 60) in the Present Value Interest Factor of an Annuity Table, Appendix D, and get 48.1734. Applying this to Eq.13.14 gives

$$\$25,000 = \text{Pmt} \times 48.17325$$

$$\text{Pmt} = \$25,000/48.17325$$

$$= \$518.96 \text{ per month.}$$

---

### Car Loans

Debt is one of great killers of companies. Debt can also be a serious drain on personal finances. One way to minimize the impact of car loans is to make a substantial down payment. Even those happy with their current car should start systematically making deposits into an account dedicated solely to purchasing a new car.

A small but growing number of people believe a person should put 50% down on a car. If they can't, then either they are considering a car that is too expensive, or they must save longer.

Most people make car loan or lease payments all their lives. A better plan is to buy a car you like and drive it until it is rust.

There is no reason why a well-made, well cared for car cannot last 10 years and 200,000 miles, and still be in very good condition.

The author bought a Nissan 300ZX, a very fast car, and drove it 17 years and 300,000 miles. It was still one of the fastest cars on the road when traded in. The car was paid off in four years which meant 13 years without car payments. You can do the same. Who deserves that money more, you or car companies and banks?

---

A prudent car buyer would have a trade-in, or substantial down payment, which will change the monthly payments. Suppose a buyer put $7,500 down. Then the present value of the payments must equal the amount financed, not the purchase price.

| Price | $25,000 |
|---|---|
| Less down payment | $7,500 |
| Amount financed | $17,500 |

Using the amount financed as PV in equation Eq.13.14 gives
$$\$17,500 = \text{Pmt} \times 48.17325$$

$$\text{Pmt} = \$17,500 / 48.17325$$

$$= \$363.27$$

Loan payment analysis can be applied to mortgages, boat loans, and any loan with an even monthly payment.

## Loan Amortization

Every loan payment can be deconstructed into two parts, principal and interest. Principal reduces the loan balance, the amount still owed. Interest is burned up and vanishes. Amortization schedules are important to those who (i) want to pay off their loan early, (ii) take an interest deduction, or (iii) develop financing strategies.[11]

Suppose a person has a $200,000, thirty-year mortgage with a 6% annual percentage rate. What would their amortization schedule look like? The period interest rate would be 0.5% (6% annual percentage rate/12 months per year), and the number of periods would be 360 (30 years x 12 months per year). Using equation 13.14, the payment for this loan would be $1,199.10 per month.

In the first month, the interest on the $200,000 loan balance would be $1,000 ($200,000 x 0.5%). This means $1,000 of the first monthly loan payment of $1,199.10 is burned up as interest. Only $199.10 of the first month's payment reduces the loan balance. After paying $1,199.10, the loan balance is now $199,800.90 ($200,000 - $199.10).

In the second month, the interest on the new balance of $199,800.90 would be $999.00 ($199,800.90 x 0.5%). Only $200.10 of the second payment goes towards paying down the loan balance, $999.00 is burned up as interest. The second payment of $1,199.10 would only reduce the loan balance to $199,600.80. See Table 13.4 Amortization Schedule.

---

[11] Vance, David E. 2003. Financial Analysis and Decision Making. McGraw-Hill Companies. New York. pp.96-97.

**Table 13.4 Amortization Schedule**

This amortization table is for the first twelve months of a thirty-year, $200,000 loan with a 6% rate.

| -----Payment---- | | | Principal | Loan |
|---|---|---|---|---|
| No. | Amount | Interest | Repaid | Balance |
| | | | | 200,000.00 |
| 1 | 1,199.10 | 1,000.00 | 199.10 | 199,800.90 |
| 2 | 1,199.10 | 999.00 | 200.10 | 199,600.80 |
| 3 | 1,199.10 | 998.00 | 201.10 | 199,399.70 |
| 4 | 1,199.10 | 997.00 | 202.10 | 199,197.60 |
| 5 | 1,199.10 | 995.99 | 203.11 | 198,994.49 |
| 6 | 1,199.10 | 994.97 | 204.13 | 198,790.36 |
| 7 | 1,199.10 | 993.95 | 205.15 | 198,585.21 |
| 8 | 1,199.10 | 992.93 | 206.17 | 198,379.04 |
| 9 | 1,199.10 | 991.90 | 207.20 | 198,171.84 |
| 10 | 1,199.10 | 990.86 | 208.24 | 197,963.36 |
| 11 | 1,199.10 | 989.82 | 209.28 | 197,754.08 |
| 12 | 1,199.10 | 988.77 | 210.33 | 197,543.75 |
| | *14,389.20* | *Totals* | *2,456.01* | |

This amortization schedule shows that after making $14,389.20 of payments, the loan balance has only been reduced $2,456.01. In this example, almost 83% of the first year's loan payments were consumed in interest. The balance payoff is so gradual, that a borrower will be in great debt for a very long time. But is there a better way?

Suppose, rather than paying $1,199.10 for the first payment, $1,399.20 was paid, which is the first payment of $1,199.10, plus the next month's loan principal of $200.10. If 1,399.20 was paid, then interest on payment two could be skipped, and the next payment would be number three. By skipping payment two, the borrower saves $999 of interest.

If the next amount paid is $1,401.20, that is regular payment three of $1,199.10 plus the fourth month's principal of $202.10, the next payment due would be number five. By skipping payment four, $997 of interest would be saved. To achieve savings by paying the next month's principal in advance, **a payment must be made every month.** Paying each next month's principal in advance will enable a borrower to pay off a 30-year mortgage in 15 years and save a considerable amount of interest.

Suppose one is about to make payment number five and has an additional $822.65 from a bonus, and makes a payment in the amount of $2,021.75 ($1,199.10 + $822.65). The $822.65 is equal to the principal for payments six, seven, eight and nine. That means these payments are skipped, saving about $3,973.75 in interest. The payment due the following month would then be number 10 putting the borrower five months closer to paying off the loan.

---

**Loan Interest**

For the first few years of a mortgage, most of each month's payment is burned up in interest. Relatively little of each payment goes toward paying down the loan balance.

Loans can be shortened and interest saved if, in addition to the regular loan payment, an additional amount is paid on loan principal. For this to work a payment must be made every month.

Many people pay their regular mortgage payment each month plus next month's principal, which cuts loan length in half.

---

## Conclusion

It is often necessary to make decisions concerning the amount of money to be received or paid in the future. Such decisions are complicated, because the value of dollars decreases over time. The value of future dollars is less than the value of dollars in hand now, because dollars received in the present can be invested to grow; inflation erodes the value of money; and there is some risk that promised future dollars will not be paid. Four functions address most issues when dealing with money over time.

The future value interest factor addresses how much one will have if an amount is invested today, at interest for a certain period. The present value interest factor estimates the value in today's dollars of some amount of money promised in the future. The future value interest factor of an annuity is a way to compute the amount one would have, if one saved the same amount every period for a number of years and accumulated interest on the savings. The present value interest factor of an annuity estimates the value in today's dollars of an even stream of payments to be received over a period of years.

When there is more than one period in a year, the interest or discount rate must be adjusted by dividing annual rate by the number of periods in a year. When interest or discount rates are adjusted, the number of periods must be adjusted. The number of periods is the number of years, times the number of periods per year. Tables have been developed to facilitate computation of time value of money functions. One drawback to tables is that they only help for a selected number of periods, interest and discount rates. Where tables do not work, formulae are available.

Every calculation should be checked for reasonableness. The future value should be more than the amount invested, but not ten times as much. The present value should be less than the amount promised, but not less than a tenth as much. When saving a regular amount and investing it at interest, the future value should be at least the amount saved each period, times the number of periods, but if the amount is ten times this amount, there is probably an error in the computation. The present value of an even stream of payments should be less than the amount of each payment, times the number of payments, but probably not less than a tenth of that amount.

Loan payments can be computed using the present value interest factor of an annuity. The amount financed must equal the present value of all payments.

An amortization table analyzes how much of every loan payment is interest and how much reduces the loan balance. A loan amortization table can also be used to see how prepayment of principal can reduce the length of the loan and the amount of interest paid.

# Terms and Concepts

**Amortization Table** – A loan amortization table analyzes the amount of each payment that is interest and the amount that reduces the loan balance.

**Car Loans** – Most people make car loan or lease payments their entire lives. A better strategy is to buy a car you like and keep it as long as possible. There is no reason why a well-made, well cared for car cannot last ten years and 200,000 miles.

**Compound Interest** – When interest is computed on interest that has already accumulated, it is said to be compound interest.

**Discount Rate** – A discount rate is used to translate the value of future promised money into today's dollars. A discount rate is like sandpaper wearing away the value of money. Select a discount rate that is equal to the yield on a comparable investment.

**Functional Notation** – Functional notation is a compact way of describing a formula. A function is a mathematical machine. One or more variables are input into the machine and a single number is output.

**Future Value** – This function answers the question, "If a person invested a sum of money at a certain interest rate for a certain number of years, how much would that person have in the future?"

**Future Value Interest Factor of an Annuity** – This function is used to compute the amount one would have if one saved a given amount on a regular basis and accumulated interest on those savings.

**Loan Payments** – Loan payments can be computed using the Present Value Interest Factor of an Annuity function. Usually, the amount financed, interest rates and length of the loan are known. The remaining unknown, the payment, can be computed.

**More Than One Period in a Year** – When there is more than one period in a year, the interest, or discount rate must be divided by the number of periods in the year to get the period interest or discount rate. Whenever the interest or discount rate is adjusted, the number of periods must be adjusted by multiplying the number of years, times the number of periods in a year.

**Present Value** – The present value is the value in today's dollars of an amount promised in the future. Future money is worth less than money in hand today, because today's money can be invested to grow, inflation erodes the value of money over time, and there is a risk that promised money will never be received.

**Present Value Interest Factor of an Annuity** – This function is used to estimate the value, in today's dollars, of a stream of payments to be received in the future. This function can also be used to compute payments.

**Reasonableness** – Every calculation should be checked for reasonableness.

**Time Value of Money Tables** – To facilitate time value of money calculations, tables have been worked out for commonly-used values of interest and discount rates, and for various numbers of periods.

# References

Mayo, Herbert B. 1998. Financial Institutions, Investments and Management. The Dryden Press. Harcourt Brace College Publishers. Fort Worth.

Vance, David E. 2009. Ratios: For Analysis, Control and Profit Planning. Global Professional Publishing. Slip Mill Lane, Cranbrook, Kent U.K.

—. 2003. Financial Analysis and Decision Making. McGraw-Hill Companies. New York.

# CHAPTER FOURTEEN

# COMPANY VALUATION

---

When you complete this chapter, you should be able to:

14.1 Discuss the importance of company valuation.

14.2 Know the difference between a public and private company and the advantages and disadvantages of each.

14.3 Compute market capitalization and find book value.

14.4 Compute value based on discounted cash flow.

14.5 Estimate value using various multiplier methods.

14.6 Know how to improve value estimates by adjusting for debt load.

14.7 Adjust value estimates based on common premiums and discounts.

14.8 Estimate the stock price for a company going public.

---

## Introduction

Bruce Johnson, is a 53-year-old engineer, and the founder and owner of Sun Energy, a solar panel manufacturer with $30 million in sales. Johnson founded the company when he was 28 and is now ready to sell out and retire. Walter Winston is a 38-year-old consultant who wants to buy a company. He has been analyzing Sun Energy and is considering making an offer.

If Johnson asks $100 million for his company when it is only worth $10 million, potential buyers will think he is unreasonable and they won't talk to him. If he asks $10 million for a company worth $20 million he will be giving away half the value he created over a lifetime. How can Johnson estimate the real value of his company?

Winston has a similar problem. How does he know what to offer? If he offers $10 million for a company worth $20 million, the seller will think him ill-prepared to negotiate for the company. But if he offers $40 million for a company worth only $20 million he will be giving away investors' capital and taking on more debt than necessary to finance the acquisition. How can anyone know the fair value of a company?

There are many reasons to value a company other than for an outright purchase or sale. Companies must be valued when they sell shares to private investors. For example, if a business is worth $100,000 and someone invests $25,000 they will expect about a quarter of the stock. If the company is worth $2,500,000 and they invest $25,000, they should only expect about 1% of the stock.

Companies must be valued before an initial public offering. An initial public offering is selling stock to the public for the first time. Companies must be valued for estate taxes, and when company stock is being used as collateral for a loan.

Just as there are many reasons to value a company, there are many ways to value a company; among the most common are the book value, discounted cash flow, market capitalization, and several multiplier methods. Data used in these methods are frequently adjusted to back out one-time events. A company's value may also be adjusted with premiums and discounts. All in all, company valuation is both an art and a science requiring the application of quantitative methods and business judgment.

## Book Value

Accounting is about measurement, and one accounting report, the Balance Sheet, provides a measure of a company's value. Equity, found on the Balance Sheet, is the theoretical amount that would be available to owners if all assets were sold for their book value, and all liabilities were paid off. Equity represents the owners' interest in a company. A company's book value is Assets less Liabilities, as shown in equation Eq.14.1.

Book Value = Assets – Liabilities                    Eq.14.1

An operating company is dynamic and can grow. An operating company is expected to produce income into the foreseeable future. In contrast, book value is based on the value assets would have if they were stacked up in a warehouse. They have no value beyond their physical value. For this reason, book value is thought to represent a company's minimum value.[1, 2, 3]

Suppose Sun Energy had assets of $28 million, liabilities of $11 million and equity of $17 million. The minimum estimated value of Sun Energy is probably at least $17 million. Book value can be computed using Eq.14.1.

$$\text{Book Value} = \$28M - \$11M$$

$$= \$17M$$

## Market Capitalization

Market capitalization, often referred to as 'market cap', is the share price, times the number of shares outstanding as shown in equation Eq.14.2.

$$\text{Market Cap} = \text{Share Price} \times \text{Shares Outstanding} \qquad Eq.14.2$$

Market cap is the theoretical value of a company if all outstanding shares were purchased at once at the market price. The number of shares outstanding can be found on the income statement below Net Income. The market price is the price reported on a stock exchange. For large companies, stock price information is available in the Wall Street Journal. Stock price is available for public companies, large and small, on finance.yahoo.com. Market cap is theoretical, because as big blocks of a company's stock are purchased, the price will rise on the remaining shares, which would push up the overall market cap. Likewise, if large blocks of a company's stock are dumped on the market, the overall market cap will drop.

---

[1] Laiw, K. Thomas. 1999. John Wiley & Sons. New York. p.34.
[2] Daves, Philip R., Michael C. Ehrhardt, Ronald E. Shrieves. 2004. Corporate Valuation: A Guide for Managers and Investors. Thompson South-Western. Mason, Ohio. p.8.
[3] Mayo, Herbert B. 1998. Financial Institutions, Investments and Management, 6th Ed. Dryden Press Harcourt Brace College Publishers. Fort Worth. p.56.

There are a few limitations to using market cap as a valuation method. First, the company must be publicly traded. Second, market cap is a volatile measure of value.[4]

Suppose a television network reports that an Air Iowa plane crashed, killing all aboard. The price of Air Iowa stock might drop by a third. That would instantly lower the market cap of Air Iowa by a third. Now, suppose an hour later the same television network corrected their report, and said it wasn't an Air Iowa plane, but an Air Ohio plane which crashed. The stock price of Air Iowa would probably rebound to its original price and with it, the market cap of the company. Was the intrinsic value of Air Iowa less after the first television report? Probably not, so while market cap is a highly regarded measure of value, it sometimes understates or overstates a company's value in terms of earning power.

Suppose Sun Energy has four million shares of stock outstanding, it is listed on the NASDAQ stock exchange, and its price is $5.10 per share. Its market cap may be computed using equation Eq.14.2.

$$\text{Market Cap} = \$5.10 \times 4,000,000$$

$$= \$20,400,000$$

## Price Earnings Ratio

Most people don't buy companies; they buy shares of stock in companies. A company's price earnings (PE) ratio is the price of a stock on a given day, divided by one year's earnings per share (EPS) as shown in equation Eq.14.3. A PE ratio can be thought of as the cost to buy $1 of earnings. The EPS is usually the last annual EPS. However, some analysts compute a moving four quarter EPS. The PE ratio is a dimensionless number.

$$\text{PE} = \text{Current Stock Price} / \text{EPS} \qquad \text{Eq.14.3}$$

Example: A stock has $2 earnings per share. Its price is $32 on the day it is measured.

$$\text{PE} = \$32 / \$2 \qquad = 16.$$

---

[4] Vance, David E. 2009. Ratios for Analysis, Control and Profit Planning. Global Professional Publishing. Cranbrook, Kent, U.K. p.122, 142.

A company's average PE ratio over a period of years is thought to provide a baseline indicator of value. If a company's PE ratio drops below its average, some say it becomes a bargain. For example, suppose a stock has a three-year PE ratio of 16 and the PE drops to 12. That means it is possible to buy a dollar of earnings in that company for $12 rather than the typical $16. This might signal a buying opportunity. On the other hand, if a stock has a historical PE ratio of 16 and its PE jumps to 22, that might mean it is temporarily overpriced and may indicate it's time to sell out and harvest profits. Sophisticated investors think PE analysis is naive. However, sophisticated investors also invested in sub-prime mortgage bonds, Enron, and Venezuelan government bonds.

## Discounted Cash Flow

Academics widely agree that the discounted cash flow (DCF) method is the most theoretically sound method of valuing a company. The DCF value of a company is the sum of the present value of the future cash flows generated by a company in perpetuity, as shown in equation Eq.14.5.

$$\text{DCF Value} \quad = \Sigma_n \text{ PVIF } (k, n) \text{ x Cash Flow}_n \qquad \text{Eq.14.5}$$

The symbol $\Sigma$ is the Greek letter Sigma. It means sum, or add up, everything to the right of the sign. In this case, the present value of the cash flow for year $n=1$ is added to the present value of the cash flow for the year $n=2$, and so forth.

To be theoretically correct, **free cash flow** (FCF) should be used to value a company, not just cash flow. Free cash flow is the cash available after a company reinvests in working capital, plant and equipment, and pays dividends.[5, 6, 7, 8]

A draw back to DCF is that it requires a **large number of assumptions**. To estimate free cash flow, it is necessary to project sales, expenses, dividend payments, and changes in working capital, many years

---

[5] Laiw, K. Thomas. 1999. John Wiley & Sons. New York. p.33.

[6] Daves, Philip R., Michael C. Ehrhardt, Ronald E. Shrieves. 2004. Corporate Valuation: A Guide for Managers and Investors. Thompson South-Western. Mason, Ohio. pp.4-5.

[7] Weston, J. Fred, Mark L. Mitchell, J. Harold Mulherin. 2004. Takeovers, Restructuring and Corporate Governance. Pearson Prentiss Hall. Upper Saddle River, N.J. pp.248-249.

[8] Vance, David E. 2005. Raising Capital. Springer Science +Business Media. New York. pp.169-171.

into the future. Technology, products, customer tastes and competition are all dynamic, and may change over the course of a year. This raises a question as to whether estimates beyond three or four years are mere guess-work. Another issue is the number of years of free cash flow that should be used. In theory, an infinite number of years should be summed, but no company lasts forever. As a practical matter, ten to fifteen years is generally summed.

After that, a **terminal value** is used to estimate all future discounted cash flows. Terminal value can be estimated using equation Eq.14.6.

$$\text{Terminal Value} = FCF_{n+1} / (k - g) \qquad \text{Eq.14.6}$$

Where $FCF_{n+1}$ is the Free Cash Flow for the year after the last one estimated, k is the discount rate, and g is the estimated growth rate, out to infinity. Suppose a discount rate of 20% is used, and a company has an estimated growth rate to infinity of 7% per year. Given its FCF for year n=12 is $7.3 million; its FCF for the next year, n+1 is $7.8 million ($7.3 million x (1+7%)). Use equation Eq.14.6 to compute the terminal value.

$$\text{Terminal Value} = \$7.8 \text{ million} / (20\% - 7\%)$$

$$= \$7.8 \text{ million} / 13\% \qquad = \$60.0 \text{ million}$$

This terminal value is then discounted to the present value using the discount rate of 20% per year. The discounted terminal value is added to the present value of each years' free cash flow. In this example, it would be added to 12 years of discounted cash flow.

The DCF valuation model is very sensitive to the discount rate selected. The discount rate embraces issues like inflation and the riskiness of getting paid. When using the DCF model, part of the risk is that a company won't be able to produce its estimated free cash flow. The DCF model is also very sensitive to the growth rate used to compute the terminal value. In the example which follows, the terminal value accounts for more than a quarter of company value. This puts a lot of weight on the assumptions made by the analyst computing a company's DCF value.

The mechanics of the DCF method are to: (i) estimate free cash flow for several years; (ii) select a discount rate; (iii) use the discount rate to compute the present value of each annual free cash flow; (iv) compute the terminal value, and discount that terminal value to present dollars; and (v) sum all of that, and the result is an estimate of the value of the company.

Suppose Sun Energy projects the free cash flows shown in Table 14.1 Discounted Cash Flow Valuation, and those cash flows are discounted at a 20% per year. Free cash flow (FCF) a year from now (Year 1) is estimated at $2.0 million. The Present Value Interest Factor at 20% per year for 1 year, PVIF (20, 1), is 0.833. Year 1 FCF is multiplied times 0.833 to get the present value of next year's FCF which is $1.7 million. The FCF in year 2 of $2.3 million is multiplied times PVIF (20%, 2) or .694 to get $1.6 million and so forth.

The value of the terminal year has already been estimated at $60.0 million. Multiplying this times PVIF (20%, 13) or 0.094 discounts it back to its present value of $5.6 million. See Table 14.1 for an example. Summing all the discounted cash flows, Sun Energy would be valued at about $20.3 million.

**Table 14.1 Discounted Cash Flow Valuation**

| Year | Free Cash Flow Millions | Present Value Interest Factor PVIF (20%, Year) | Present Value Millions |
|---|---|---|---|
| 1 | 2.0 | 0.833 | 1.7 |
| 2 | 2.3 | 0.694 | 1.6 |
| 3 | 2.6 | 0.579 | 1.5 |
| 4 | 2.9 | 0.482 | 1.4 |
| 5 | 3.3 | 0.402 | 1.3 |
| 6 | 3.7 | 0.335 | 1.2 |
| 7 | 4.2 | 0.279 | 1.2 |
| 8 | 4.7 | 0.233 | 1.1 |
| 9 | 5.3 | 0.194 | 1.0 |
| 10 | 5.9 | 0.162 | 1.0 |
| 11 | 6.6 | 0.135 | 0.9 |
| 12 | 7.3 | 0.112 | 0.8 |
| Terminal Value | 60.0 | 0.094 | 5.6 |
| | | *Company Value =* | *20.3* |

# Multiplier Methods

The most common way to value an asset is to analyze what similar assets have sold for. This is done all the time in real estate. If one needs to value a home in a particular neighborhood, look at what other homes in the neighborhood have sold for. But, every home is a little different. Some are a little larger than others and some have more bedrooms or bathrooms than others. So, a common denominator is needed to adjust for these differences. Price per square foot might be one way to adjust. If the average price per square foot in a neighborhood is $140 and one is valuing a home with 1,500 square feet, one might expect its value to be around $210,000 (1,500 square feet x $140 per square foot).

Companies are considered similar if they are in the same industry and provide similar goods and services to similar customers. Every company in America has a four-digit Standard Industrial Classification (SIC) code. SIC codes are one indication of whether two companies are in the same industry. Financial statements for all publicly-traded companies are posted on the SEC's website: www.sec.gov. This is an excellent source of information on comparable companies.

Just as houses are all a little different, companies are different. No two companies are exactly the same size. Multipliers are used to adjust for those differences. Public company data is used to compute multipliers, because private company data is hard to get, and it is difficult to estimate a private company's market value except when it is sold.

There are two cautions when using multiplier methods. First, confirm that comparable companies provide substantially the same goods and services as the one being valued. Even within a SIC code, products vary widely. For example, SIC code 3715 is for trailers, but Great Dane, which makes the large cargo trailers used by Wal-Mart is not comparable to Featherlite, Inc., which makes utility and horse trailers.

The second caution is that, where possible, companies should be of relatively comparable size. If one company is a hundred times larger than another they aren't comparable, even if they provide the same goods and services. It's best if comparable companies are less than five times larger or smaller than each other. Ten times larger or smaller is acceptable, but not recommended. Beyond this, questions arise as to whether companies are different in type and not just in size. Unfortunately, publicly-traded companies are usually much, much larger than private companies, so when valuing a private company, differences in size must be tolerated.

# EBITDA Multiplier Method

To compare companies of different sizes requires some common denominator. Earnings before Interest and Taxes plus Depreciation and Amortization (EBITDA) is the preferred common denominator of many analysts. It is an estimate of a company's cash flow from operations before variables like financing or tax strategy are introduced.

Usually, income statements have a subtotal, which says something like 'Operating Income', or 'Earnings before Interest and Taxes'. This subtotal will appear above interest expense. To get EBITDA, depreciation, amortization and depletion must be added to operating income. Depreciation, amortization and depletion can be found on the Statement of Cash Flows.

**The company being valued is the target company.** Rather than comparing the target company to one or two other companies, it is better to compare the target to half a dozen or more companies. The EBITDA Multiplier may be computed using equation Eq.14.7. The EBITDA Multiplier is dimensionless.[9]

EBITA Multiplier = Σ Market Cap / Σ EBITDA          Eq.14.7

Table 14.2 EBITDA Multiplier is an example of how the EBITDA Multiplier may be computed. The number of outstanding shares (OS) and the current share price are used to compute the market cap for comparable companies.

**Table 14.2 EBITDA Multiplier**

| Comparable Company | EBITDA | Outstanding Shares | Share Price | Market Cap |
|---|---|---|---|---|
| Bob's Solar | $110M | 8,000,000 | $48.13 | $385M |
| Sun Silicon | $90M | 4,000,000 | $85.50 | $342M |
| Sun Electric | $200M | 8,000,000 | $800M | $100.00 |
| Light Power | $20M | 1,000,000 | $64.00 | $64M |
| Threshold | $30M | 20,000,000 | $5.10 | $102M |
| Power Co | $50M | 10,000,000 | $17.00 | $170M |
| | | | | |
| *Totals* | *$500M* | | | *$1,863M* |

---

[9] Vance, David E. 2009. Ratios for Analysis, Control and Profit Planning. Global Professional Publishing. Cranbrook, Kent, U.K. p.128.

EBITDA Multiplier = $1,863M / $500M

= 3.726

**The EBITDA Multiplier is the number of dollars the market will pay for one dollar of EBITDA.** Suppose, for example a company has $1 million of EBITDA, its value would be $3.726 million ($1 million x 3.726). If a company had $10 million of EBITDA, the market would value the company at $37.26 million ($10 million x 3.726), and so forth. The EBITDA multiplier is used to estimate the value of the target company using equation Eq.14.8.

Target Value = Target EBITDA x EBITDA Multiplier          Eq.14.8.

Given a Sun Energy EBITDA of $6.5 million. Its value can be estimated using equation Eq.14.8.

Target Value = $6.5M x 3.726

= $24.2M

One limitation on the EBITDA Multiplier Method, is that it cannot be used when the target company's EBITDA is zero, negative, or close to zero. Another limitation is that companies used for comparison cannot have an EBITDA which is zero, negative, or close to zero. Finally, the companies used to develop the industry EBITDA multiplier must be publicly traded, and their stocks must be traded on a daily basis, so that a reliable market cap can be computed.

## Sales Multiplier Method

Many analysts consider the EBITDA Multiplier Method the best method of valuing a company. However, other analysts worry that the options permitted by Generally Accepted Accounting Principles could be used to manipulate EBITDA. An alternative is to use the Sales Multiplier Method. The Sales Multiplier Method uses sales as the common denominator for valuing companies. Sales leaves few opportunities for accounting manipulation.

**The Sales Multiplier** can be thought of as **the number of dollars it takes to purchase one dollar of sales** in the target company's industry.

The Sales Multiplier can be computed using equation Eq.14.9. The Sales multiplier is dimensionless.[10, 11]

$$\text{Sales Multiplier} = \Sigma \text{ Market Cap} / \Sigma \text{ Sales} \qquad \text{Eq.14.9}$$

Table 14.3 Sales Multiplier is an example of how a sales multiplier can be used to estimate the value of Sun Energy.

**Table 14.3 Sales Multiplier**

| Comparable Company | Sales | Outstanding Shares | Share Price | Market Cap |
|---|---|---|---|---|
| Bob's Solar | $600M | 8,000,000 | $48.13 | $385M |
| Sun Silicon | $450M | 4,000,000 | $85.50 | $342M |
| Sun Electric | $1,000M | 8,000,000 | $100.00 | $800M |
| LightPower | $80M | 1,000,000 | $64.00 | $64M |
| Threshold | $120M | 20,000,000 | $5.10 | $102M |
| PowerCo | $200M | 10,000,000 | $17.00 | $170M |
| *Totals* | *$2,450M* | | | *$1,863M* |

$$\text{Sales Multiplier} = \$1,863M / \$2,450M$$

$$= 0.7604$$

The market is willing to pay $0.7604 per dollar of sales in this industry. If a company has $10 million in sales, its market value would be $7.604 million ($10 million x 0.7604). Company value may be estimated using equation Eq.14.10.

$$\text{Target Value} = \text{Target Sales} \times \text{Sales Multiplier} \qquad \text{Eq.14.10}$$

Suppose Sun Energy has $30M in sales. Its value can be estimated using the Sales Multiplier and equation Eq.14.10.

$$\text{Target Value} = \$30M \times 0.7604 \qquad = \$22.8M$$

---

[10] Laiw, K. Thomas. 1999. John Wiley & Sons. New York. p34.
[11] Vance, David E. 2009. Ratios for Analysis, Control and Profit Planning. Global Professional Publishing. Cranbrook, Kent, U.K. p129.

The company value based on the EBITDA Multiplier Method (EMM) is $24.2 million, whereas the company value based on the Sales Multiplier Method (SMM) is $22.8 million. There is no reason why the two methods should yield the same result. A sophisticated analyst would probably consider estimates from several methods when valuing a company.

## Net Income Multiplier Method

Some analysts use the Net Income Multiplier to value companies. Their argument is that lots of companies have sales, but they are unable to translate those sales into profits. Since profits are the ultimate goal, perhaps companies should be valued based on profitability.[12] The counter argument is that the Net Income Multiplier method is less reliable than either the EBITDA or Sales Multiplier methods, because differences in financing and tax strategy make it more difficult to compare net income from company to company. One way to reduce these differences is to use adjusted net income as shown in equation Eq.14.11. Adjusted net income adds interest net of taxes back to net income, so that all companies can be compared on a 'pre-financing' basis.

Adjusted Net Income = Net Income + Interest x (1 – Tax Rate)    Eq.14.11

Suppose a company has net income of $4,000,000, net interest expense of $200,000 and it is in the 21% tax bracket. Applying equation Eq.14.11, adjusted net income is:

Adjusted Net Income = $4,000,000 + $200,000 x (1 -21%)

= $4,000,000 + $200,000 x 79%

= $4,000,000 + $158,000

= $4,158,000

Adjusted net income can then be used to compute the Net Income Multiplier. The Net Income Multiplier cannot be used when target company's adjusted net income is zero, negative, or close to zero. Further,

---

[12] Vance, David E. 2009. Ratios for Analysis, Control and Profit Planning. Global Professional Publishing. Cranbrook, Kent, U.K. p130.

companies with an adjusted net income that is zero, negative, or close to zero cannot be used as comparable companies to estimate the Income Multiplier. The Net Income Multiplier can be estimated using equation Eq.14.12.

Net Income Multiplier = Σ Market Cap / Σ Adjusted Net Income   Eq.14.12

Table 14.4 Net Income Multiplier is an example of how the net income multiplier can be computed.

**Table 14.4 Net Income Multiplier**

| Comparable Company | Adjusted Net Income | Outstanding Shares | Price per Share | Market Cap |
|---|---|---|---|---|
| Bob's Solar | $100M | 8,000,000 | $48.13 | $385M |
| Sun Silicon | $50M | 4,000,000 | $85.50 | $342M |
| Sun Electric | $120M | 8,000,000 | $100.00 | $800M |
| Light Power | $13M | 1,000,000 | $64.00 | $64M |
| Threshold | $12M | 20,000,000 | $5.10 | $102M |
| Power Co | $20M | 10,000,000 | $17.00 | $170M |
| | | | | |
| *Totals* | *$315M* | | | *$1,863M* |

Net Income Multiplier = $1,863M / $315M

= 5.91

This means the market is willing to pay $5.91 for every dollar of adjusted net income in this industry. Target company valuation may be estimated using equation Eq.14.13.

Eq.14.13

Target Value = Target Adjusted Net Income x Net Income Multiplier

Suppose Sun Energy has adjusted net income of $4,130,000. Using the Net Income Multiplier, Sun Energy's adjusted net come and equation Eq.14.13 gives the following estimate of company value.

Target Value = $4.13M x 5.91

= $24.4M

## Customer Multiplier Method

Companies in the electric, gas, water, sewer, cell phone and cable industry, have large numbers of similar customers. In such industries, the number of customers can be used to estimate company value. A Customer Multiplier is computed by dividing the sum of the market cap of comparable companies by the sum of the number of customers for those companies,[13] as shown in equation Eq.14.14.

Customer Multiplier = Σ Market Cap / Σ Customers          Eq.14.14

Table 14.5 Customer Multiplier is an example of how a multiplier might be computed for companies in the water industry. When computing the Customer Multiplier, be sure to state market cap in dollars, and not thousands or millions of dollars.

**Table 14.5 Customer Multiplier**

| Comparable Company | Customers | Outstanding Shares | Share Price | Market Cap |
|---|---|---|---|---|
| United Water | 400,000 | 20,000,000 | $15.00 | $300,000,000 |
| Fargo Water | 90,000 | 1,500,000 | $46.67 | $70,000,000 |
| Lehigh Valley | 250,000 | 5,000,000 | $40.00 | $200,000,000 |
| Maine Water | 110,000 | 4,000,000 | $20.00 | $80,000,000 |
| Stratton Water | 150,000 | 5,000,000 | $24.00 | $120,000,000 |
| *Totals* | *1,000,000* | | | *$770,000,000* |

Customer Multiplier  = $770,000,000 / 1,000,000

= $770 per customer

This means the market is willing to pay $770 for each customer. For example, if a company has 100,000 customers, the market will value it at $77,000,000 (100,000 x $770). The value of a target company can be estimated by multiplying the number of customers, times the Customer Multiplier, as shown in equation Eq.14.15. Suppose a buyer is trying to value the Harrison Water Company, and Harrison has 72,000 customers.

---

[13] Vance, David E. 2009. Ratios for Analysis, Control and Profit Planning. Global Professional Publishing. Cranbrook, Kent, U.K. p131.

Eq.14.15.

Target Value = Target Number of Customers x Customer Multiplier

= 72,000 x $770

= $55,440,000

## Refinements to Value Estimates

### Adjustments for One-Time Items

Valuations focus on the future, even though the methods discussed in this chapter are usually based on historical data. But, if it is known that the future will not be like that past in some way, there should be an adjustment for that difference. For example, one might want to eliminate one-time events that affect EBITDA, Sales or Net Income.

One-time effects from Discontinued Operations and Extraordinary Items are already backed out of Sales and Operating Income which is used to compute EBITDA. They are also backed out of the subtotal 'Income from Continuing Operations', so use this subtotal in place of net income when computing adjusted net income.

There may also be significant, but less dramatic, one-time events that should be eliminated when estimating company value. For example, the cost or benefit of settling a significant lawsuit or tax dispute might be eliminated. A significant one-time write-down of accounts receivable, or inventory, might also be a reason to adjust financial statement data. Any event that is unlikely to be repeated should be eliminated before the Sales, EBITDA or Net Income Multiplier methods are used.

### Adjustments for Debt Level

Another way to refine the estimate of company's value is to take debt into consideration. When a company is purchased, the purchaser assumes responsibility for the company's debt. How does a company's debt effect its value? Consider companies A and B, with the following characteristics:

|                    | A     | B     |
|--------------------|-------|-------|
| Sales              | $50M  | $50M  |
| EBITDA             | $10M  | $10M  |
| Adjusted Net Income | $4M   | $4M   |
| **Debt**           | **$10M** | **$30M** |
| Market Cap         | $40M  | $20M  |

The Revenue, EBITDA and Net Income values are the same for both companies, but would you pay the same amount for both companies? In this example, company B is burdened with more debt than company A, and its market cap is lower.

The EBITDA, Sales, Adjusted Net Income and Customer Multipliers assume companies have an **average** amount of debt. Assuming debt is average across comparable and target companies masks a lot of detail.

Suppose companies A and B were publicly traded with market capitalizations of $40M and $20M respectively. If these companies are the only two in the industry, the industry Sales Multiplier would be .6 (($40M +$20M) Market Cap / ($50M +$50M)) sales.

**The Total Value (TV) is the value a company would have if it were debt free.** If a company were debt free, all value would be allocated to the shareholders (owners.) For publicly traded companies the owner's value is the market value. If every dollar of debt reduces a dollar allocated to the shareholders, we can use equation Eq.14.16 to compute a company's total, debt free value. TV stands for Total Value.

$$TV = \text{Market Cap} + \text{Debt} \qquad \text{Eq.14.16.}$$

We can use this to generate a new set of multipliers that should be more accurate than the commonly used multipliers. The Total Value Sales, EBITDA, Adjusted Net Income and Customer Multiplier equations are shown in equations Eq.14.17, Eq.14.18, Eq.14.19 and Eq.14.20 respectively.

$$\text{TV Sales Multiplier} = \Sigma\,TV\,/\,\Sigma\,\text{Revenue} \qquad \text{Eq.14.17}$$

$$\text{TV EBITDA Multiplier} = \Sigma\,TV\,/\,\Sigma\,\text{EBITDA} \qquad \text{Eq.14.18}$$

$$\text{TV Adj. Net Income Multiplier} = \Sigma\,TV\,/\,\Sigma\,\text{Adj. Net Income} \quad \text{Eq.14.19}$$

$$\text{TV Customer Multiplier} = \Sigma\,TV\,/\,\Sigma\,\text{Customers} \qquad \text{Eq.14.20}$$

Table 14.6 Total Value Analysis demonstrates computation of total value multipliers. This example assumes A and B constitute all comparable companies in their industry.

**Table 14.6 Total Value Analysis**

|  | A | B | Industry |
|---|---|---|---|
| Market Value | $40M | $20M | $60M |
| Debt | $10M | $30M | $40M |
| Total Value (TV) | $50M | $50M | $100M |
| Sales | $50M | $50M | $100M |

*TV Sales Multiplier* = *TV/Sales* = *$100M/$100M* =   *1.0*

| EBITDA | $10M | $10M | $20M |
|---|---|---|---|

*TV EBITDA Multiplier* = *TV/EBITDA* =*$100M/$20M*   =   *5.0*

| Adjusted Net Income | $4M | $4M | $8M |
|---|---|---|---|

*TV Adj. Net Inc. Multiplier* =*TV/Adjusted Net Inc.* =*$100M/$8M* =*12.5*

When using total value multipliers, each target company would be valued as though it had no debt. After its debt free, or Total Value is calculated, adjust for debt by subtracting the target company's debt from its total value to get the debt adjusted value.

Suppose companies C and D are acquisition targets, have sales of $20M and $25M, and debt of $5M and $12M respectively. Table 14.7 Company Valuations Panel A shows the valuations with the debt adjustment and Panel B shows company valuations without the debt adjustment.

**Table 14.7 Company Valuations**

**Panel A Company Valuation Adjusted for Debt**

|  | C | D |
|---|---|---|
| Sales | $20M | $25M |
| x TV Sales Multiplier | x 1.0 | x 1.0 |
| Total Value (TV) | $20M | $25M |
| Less Debt | -5M | -12M |
| TV Sales Multiplier Method Value | $15M | $13M |

**Panel B Company Valuation without Adjustment for Debt**

|                             | C       | D       |
| --------------------------- | ------- | ------- |
| Sales                       | $20M    | $25M    |
| x Sales Multiplier          | x  0.6  | x  0.6  |
| Sales Multiplier Method Value | $12M  | $15M    |

In this example, company C looks $3 million more valuable after adjusting for debt, and company D looks $2 million less valuable after adjusting for debt.

## When to use Valuation Methods

No valuation method is perfect. Each method has its own strengths and weaknesses. As a rule, a target company should be valued using several methods. However, not all methods are equally well regarded.

There is a strong inclination to say that a company is worth what someone will pay for it, so that implies that the market cap is the best indicator of value. Market cap depends on share price, and share price is volatile.

Academics favor the discounted cash flow (DCF) method of valuing companies. It is less susceptible to momentary fluctuations in stock price than market cap. On the other hand, it requires forecasts of sales, expenses, changes in working capital, and other variables far into the future. This is difficult to do with any degree of precision. The DCF method is extremely sensitive to the discount rate selected. The number of years forecast using the DCF method will change a company's estimated value. Finally, valuation is sensitive to assumptions about future growth.

The EBITDA Multiplier method is favored by many analysts and investors because it requires far fewer assumptions than the DCF method and is not as volatile as the market cap method. EBITDA stands for Earnings Before Interest, Taxes, Depreciation and Amortization. It is a rough estimate of the cash flow from operations independent of financing or tax strategy. However, it cannot be used where EBITDA is zero, negative, or close to zero.

Analysts skeptical of the accounting assumptions needed to compute EBITDA, favor the Sales Multiplier Method. The Sales Multiplier Method can be used whether or not EBITDA is zero, negative or close to zero.

A few analysts favor the Adjusted Net Income Multiplier method because there is a long road between making a sale and making a profit.

Many companies are good at making sales, but poor at making profits. Critics of the Adjusted Net Income Multiplier method argue performance can be masked by financing and tax strategy. These objections are partly overcome by using adjusted net income, rather than just net income, in valuations. This method cannot be used when adjusted net income is zero, negative, or close to zero.

Many analysts favor the Customer Multiplier method. It is a rough estimate of the present value of the cash flows generated by a company's customers. Critics of this method argue that customers don't automatically generate cash flows, and a few large customers can skew results.

The criticisms of the EBITDA, Sales, Net Income and Customer Multiplier methods also apply when using their Total Value variants. However, the Total Value variants should be more accurate because they account for a company's debt load rather than assuming an average debt load for an industry.

An analyst might use three, four or five methods to compute a weighted average estimate of a company's value as shown in equation Eq.14.21. Book value is generally considered a minimum value and not averaged with other methods. In this equation $V_i$ is the value of the ith valuation method and $w_i$ is the weight assigned to the ith valuation method.

$$\text{Weighted Average} = \frac{\Sigma \, w_i \times V_i}{\Sigma \, w_i} \qquad \text{Eq.14.21}$$

Company valuation requires professional judgment. For example, the selection of valuation methods and the selection of appropriate comparable companies requires judgement. Professional judgement is also required when deciding whether all methods should be equally weighted, or whether some are considered more reliable, and should therefore carry a greater weight.

In Table 14.8 Company Valuations, the analyst shows a clear preference for the EBITDA Multiplier because he or she gave it a weight of 5. And, they seem to think the Adjusted Net Income Multiplier is the least reliable, because they gave it a weight of 1. Every analyst will give methods different weights depending on their experience and judgement.

**Table 14.8 Company Valuations**

|   | Valuation Method | Weight wi | Value Vi | wi x Vi |
|---|---|---|---|---|
| 1 | Sales Multiplier | 3 | $35M | $105M |
| 2 | EBITDA Multiplier | 5 | $32M | $160M |
| 3 | Adjusted Net Income Multiplier | 1 | $25M | $25M |
| 4 | Customer Multiplier | 2 | $30M | $60M |
|   | *Totals* | *11* |  | *$350M* |

Using equation Eq.14.21, a weighted average company valuation can be computed.

Weighted Average  = $350 / 11

                  = $31.8M

## Public Company vs. Private Company

All companies start out as private companies. Private companies can do business in their own name, buy and sell merchandise, manufacture goods, and provide services. They can do all the things they need to do to make a profit.

Public companies are companies that have registered their securities with the Securities and Exchange Commission (SEC). Almost any evidence of ownership in a profit-making organization may be considered a security under the law. The most common securities are common stock, preferred stock and corporate bonds.

Private companies cannot sell their securities to the public and cannot list their securities on a stock exchange. Those who buy securities in a private company are often restricted as to whether, and to whom, they may resell those securities. This makes the securities of private companies illiquid. Something is illiquid if it is difficult to convert to cash.

Once a company has **registered** its securities with the SEC it becomes a public company. Registered securities can be sold to the public and listed on stock exchanges. Registration is complex and expensive so 'going public' is a big deal. Public companies must have audited financial statements, report results on a quarterly and annual basis, and file reports when any material change occurs. Compliance, auditing and reporting costs for a public company are high. Most companies are not public companies.

Why go public? It is easier for public companies to raise money because they have access to stock exchanges. Owners can sell small slices of their ownership without giving up control of a company. And, investors are more willing to buy shares in a public company, because they know they can easily resell them.[14]

## Premiums and Discounts

After a company's estimated value is computed, other adjustments may have to be made to account for special conditions.

### Private Company Discount

The value of private companies is usually 20% to 25% less than the value of a comparable public company because shares of private companies are illiquid. To value a privately-held company, first value it as though it were a public company. Then discount the 'public value' by 20% to 25% to estimate the fair value of the private company as shown in equation Eq.14.22.[15, 16]

Private Company Value = Public Value x (1 –Discount)          Eq.14.22

If Sun Energy were a public company its estimated value would be $24.9 million. But, suppose Sun Energy was a private company and the private company discount in it industry is 23%. Estimate Sun Energy's value as a private company using equation Eq.14.22.

Private Company Value = $24.9M x (1 – 23%)

= $24.9M x 77%

= $19.2M

[14] Vance, David E. 2005. Raising Capital. Springer Science +Business Media. New York. pp.215-219.
[15] —. 2005. Raising Capital. Springer Science +Business Media. New York. p.169
[16] —. 2009. Ratios for Analysis, Control and Profit Planning. Global Professional Publishing. Cranbrook, Kent, U.K. pp.136-137.

## Control Premium

To buy a public company, or even a controlling interest in a public company, one must usually pay a control premium. Prices quoted on stock exchanges are for passive investments in companies. Companies produce income, pay dividends and hopefully their share price increases. But individual investors rarely have a chance to influence or control the company or send additional benefits in their direction.

When one gains control of a company that provides the opportunity to benefit oneself through salaries, bonuses, special dividends, consulting contracts, and other situations. As one begins to acquire stock in a company, the price of that stock will rise. Control premiums of 30% to 40% are not uncommon.[17, 18]

## Minimum Price

Sometimes, when a company falls on hard times and its price declines, a company's market cap may fall below what some believe is its intrinsic value. This may make it an acquisition target. Boards of directors are reluctant to approve the sale of a company if the offer price is less than the highest price a company has traded for in the last year. Suppose a stock has a current price of $20 per share, but within the last year it sold for $30 per share, the directors would probably be reluctant to sell the company for less than $30 per share.

Sometimes this reluctance causes shareholders to miss an opportunity to get the best price for their stock. For example, Yahoo traded at $18.87 on January 31, 2008 and on February 1, 2008 Microsoft offered $31.00 per share for the company. This represented a 64% premium over the prior day's trading price. But on October 29, 2007 just 94 days earlier, Yahoo's price hit $34.07 per share.[19, 20] Yahoo rejected Microsoft's offer. It took 69 months, over five and a half years, for Yahoo's stock to recover to the

---

[17] Laiw, K. Thomas. 1999. John Wiley & Sons. New York. p.35.
[18] Weston, J. Fred, Mark L. Mitchell, J. Harold Mulherin. 2004. Takeovers, Restructuring and Corporate Governance. Pearson Prentiss Hall. Upper Saddle River, N.J. p.202.
[19] Ballmer, Steven A. 2008. "Microsoft Proposes Acquisition of Yahoo! for $31 per Share," Feb. 1. http://www.microsoft.com/presspass/press/2008/feb08/02-01corpnewspr.mspx
[20] ___. 2011. "Yahoo Historical Prices," *Yahoo Finance*. http://finance.yahoo.com/q/hp?s=YHOO&a=00&b=1&c=2007&d=01&e=1&f=2008&g=d&z=66&y=0

amount Microsoft offered in 2008. For most of that time Yahoo traded for less than $20 per share. In business, time is money.

## Conclusion

When buying or selling a company it is important to have a method for valuing it. Proper valuation is important when raising capital, when using company stock as collateral, for estate planning and for tax purposes.

Publicly traded companies may be valued by market cap which is the number of shares outstanding, times share price. A drawback of this method is that share price, and therefore valuations, are volatile. Market cap may overvalue or undervalue a company, compared to its intrinsic value. The discounted cash flow method is preferred by academics. It is the present value of the free cash flows a company will generate far into the future. The disadvantage of this method is that it requires many assumptions about future sales, expenses, changes in working capital, plant investments, dividends, discount rates and future growth rates.

Multiplier methods attempt to value companies by comparing them to similar companies. Companies are considered similar if they are in the same industry and provide similar goods and services. Differences in size are accounted for through ratios. For example, the EBITDA Multiplier is the price the market will pay for a dollar of EBITDA in a certain industry. The Sales Multiplier is the price the market will pay for a dollar of sales. The Income Multiplier is the price the market will pay for a dollar of income. The Customer Multiplier is the price the market will pay for one customer.

EBITDA is earnings before interest, taxes, depreciation and amortization. The EBITDA Multiplier is considered one of the best indicators of value, because it is a rough estimate of cash flow from operations, independent of tax or financing strategy. The Sales and Customer Multipliers are less well regarded, because there is a long road between sales, or customers, and profits. The Income Multiplier has been criticized because companies have different financing and tax strategies. Adjusted net income minimizes these problems by adding interest, net of taxes, back to net income prior to applying multiplier methods.

Several adjustments can be made to improve the accuracy of valuation estimates. Before using the discounted cash flow or multiplier methods, one-time sales or expenses should be eliminated. Multiplier methods assume average debt loads across an industry. Individual debt loads can be accounted for by first valuing companies as though they were debt free. That means adding their debt to their market cap, then constructing a set of multipliers based on the debt free value of comparable companies. Value the target company as though it were debt free, then subtract the target company's actual debt.

There is no perfect way to value a company. Each method has its strengths and weaknesses. A prudent analyst should use several methods and then take a weighted average of valuations.

A private company's value might have to be adjusted because shares in a private company are illiquid. Private companies frequently sell at a 20% to 25% discount from what they would sell for if they were public companies. When a public company is being purchased, the buyer usually pays a control premium that can be 30% to 40% above market cap. Finally, boards of directors are reluctant to sell companies for less than their highest share price in the last twelve months. In summary, company valuation is both an art and a science, but many techniques are available to help rationally estimate value.

## Appendix 14a Initial Public Offering Price

A private company becomes a public company by registering its shares with the Securities and Exchange Commission (SEC). The first time they offer securities to the public after registration is called an Initial Public Offering (IPO). When shares are issued in an IPO, there is no market price because the shares have never before been on the market. The question is: **What is a fair value for newly issued shares?**

When a company issues new stock, an underwriter, usually an investment banker, buys all the new stock at a discount and then resells it. Obviously, if the stock price is low, it is easy to sell. So, underwriters want to set a low price. But, the lower the price, the less money a company gets from the IPO to invest in new products, sales, marketing and expansion. So, a company should do its own calculation to make sure the underwriter isn't selling the stock below its fair value.[21, 22, 23, 24]

The pre-IPO company value (CV) can be estimated using the techniques discussed in this chapter. When companies go public, they usually raise a certain amount of capital (Amt) by issuing new shares to the public. The pre-IPO company value (CV), plus the net amount of cash

---

[21] Laiw, K. Thomas. 1999. John Wiley & Sons. New York. pp.55-56, 58, 129, 284.
[22] Weston, J. Fred and Eugene F. Brigham. 1975. Managerial Finance, 5th Ed. Dryden Press. Hinsdale Ill. 399-407.
[23] Mayo, Herbert B. 1998. Financial Institutions, Investments and Management, 6th Ed. Dryden Press Harcourt Brace College Publishers. Fort Worth. pp.140-148.
[24] Vance, David E. 2005. Raising Capital. Springer Science +Business Media. New York. pp.253-257.

generated by selling new shares (Amt), must be spread over the old outstanding stock (OS), plus the number of new shares (NS) issued, to get the estimated stock price (P), as shown in equation Eq.14.23.[25]

$$P = \frac{CV + Amt}{OS + NS} \qquad\qquad Eq.14.23$$

The amount raised (Amt) is based on price, (P) times the number of new shares issued (NS) less underwriting and stock issuance fees, as shown in equation Eq.14.24. Think of fees as the investment banker's discount.

$$Amt = P \times NS \times (1\text{-Fees}) \qquad\qquad Eq.14.24$$

Re-write equation Eq.14.24 as equation Eq.14.25.

$$P = Amt / NS \times (1 - Fees) \qquad\qquad Eq.14.25$$

Since equations Eq.14.23 and Eq.14.25 both equal price, set them equal to each other to get equation Eq.14.26.

$$\frac{CV + Amt}{(OS + NS)} = \frac{Amt}{NS \times (1 - Fees)} \qquad\qquad Eq.14.26$$

Cross multiply both sides to eliminate the denominators, as shown in equation Eq.14.27.

$$(CV + Amt) \times NS \times (1\text{-Fees}) = Amt \times (OS + NS) \qquad\qquad Eq.14.27$$

$$(CV + Amt) \times NS \times (1\text{-Fees}) = Amt \times OS + Amt \times NS$$

Subtract Amt x NS from both sides which gives equation Eq.14.28.

$$(CV + Amt) \times NS \times (1\text{-Fees}) - Amt \times NS = Amt \times OS \qquad\qquad Eq.14.28.$$

Factor NS from the terms on the left side of equation to get equation Eq.14.29.

---

[25] Vance, David E. 2005. Raising Capital. Springer Science +Business Media. New York. pp.247-251.

$$NS \times ((CV + Amt) \times (1\text{-Fees}) - Amt) = Amt \times OS \qquad Eq.14.29$$

Divide both sides of the equation by $((CV + Amt) \times (1 - Fees) - Amt)$ to get equation Eq.14.30.

$$NS = \frac{Amt \times OS}{((CV + Amt) \times (1 - Fees) - Amt)} \qquad Eq.\ 14.30$$

Suppose a company valued at \$25M has 5M shares outstanding. It wants to raise an additional \$6M when it goes public by selling new shares. Underwriting fees and other costs of going public, such as audits and legal fees, are about 8% of the amount to be raised. How many shares should it issue and what should be their price? The number of new shares can be estimated using equation Eq.14.30

$$NS = \frac{\$6M \times 5M}{(\$25M + \$6M) \times (1\text{-}8\%) - \$6M}$$

$$= \frac{\$30MM}{(\$31M) \times 92\% - \$6M}$$

$$= \frac{\$30MM}{\$28.52M - \$6M}$$

$$= \$30MM \,/\, \$22.52M$$

$$= 1.3321M \text{ shares}$$

$$= 1{,}322{,}100 \text{ shares}$$

Since the price per share is given by equation Eq.14.25, share price can be estimated once NS is known.

$$P = Amt \,/\, NS \times (1 - Fees) \qquad Eq.14.25$$

$$= \$6M \,/\, 1.33221M \times (1\text{-}8\%)$$

$$= \$6M \,/\, 1.22563M$$

$$= \$4.90$$

As with most valuation calculations, this price per share is only an estimate. If an underwriter wanted to price shares at $4.70, or $5.10, that would be reasonable under the circumstances. However, if the underwriter wanted to price shares at $3.00 each, that might be unreasonably low.

## Terms and Concepts

**Board of Directors** – A board of directors is the principal governing body of a corporation. The board is elected by shareholders.

**Book Value** – This is the value of a company if all assets are sold at their book value and liabilities are paid off. This is the same as a company's equity. Book value is generally considered a company's minimum value.

**Common stock** – Common stock is evidence of a fractional ownership interest in a corporation.

**Control Premium** –When one purchases enough stock to gain control of a company, one expects to pay a premium over and above the market price. With control, one can direct benefits to oneself in the form of salary, consulting fees and dividends. Control premiums are often 30% to 40%.

**Customer Multiplier** – the Customer Multiplier is the amount the market is willing to pay for a customer in a given industry. The Customer Multiplier = Σ Market Cap / Σ Customers. It is used to value service companies where all customers are more or less alike. Examples include cable, gas, and water companies.

**DCF** – see Discounted Cash Flow.

**Debt Load, Adjustment for** – Multiplier methods assume both comparable companies and target companies have an average level of debt for their industry. To adjust for debt load, value the comparable companies as though they were debt free. Then create a series of multipliers based on debt free comparables. These are called Total Value or TV Multipliers. Use TV Multipliers to value the target, then subtract the target's debt.

**Discontinued Operations** – These are operations that have been sold or closed. Use Income from Continuing Operations instead of Net Income when using the Adjusted Net Income Multiplier method.

**Discount, Private Company** – Stock in private companies is less liquid than stock in public companies. That means that private companies usually sell at a 20% to 25% discount to similar public companies.

**Discounted Cash Flow (DCF)** – The free cash flow of companies is projected far into the future. Then cash flows are discounted back to the present. The sum of the present value of all free cash flows is an estimate of the company's value. The major drawbacks to the DCF valuation method are that (i) it requires assumptions about future sales, expenses and changes in working capital far into the future, and (ii) it is highly sensitive to the discount rate selected.

**Dividends** – Companies may pay dividends to stock holders out of earnings. Typically, companies pay only a fraction of Earnings per Share in dividends.

**Earnings per Share** – This is a company's net income, less preferred dividends, divided by the number of outstanding shares.

**EBITDA** – This is Earnings before Interest, Taxes, Depreciation and Amortization. EBITDA is a rough estimate of a company's ability to generate cash from operations.

**EBITDA Multiplier** – the EBITDA Multiplier is the amount the market is willing to pay for a dollar of EBITDA in a given industry. The EBITDA Multiplier = $\Sigma$ Market Cap / $\Sigma$ EBITDA. A limitation on the EBITDA Multiplier Method is that it cannot be used with companies that have an EBITDA that is zero, negative, or close to zero.

**EPS** – see Earnings per Share.

**Extraordinary Items** – These are items which are both rare and unusual. Valuations are about a company's future performance, so where there are extraordinary items use 'Income from Continuing Operations' instead of net income, when valuing a company.

**Free Cash Flow** – This is the cash generated by a company that is available for any purpose. It is net income, plus depreciation, amortization and depletion, plus or minus changes in working capital, less investment in plant and equipment, less dividends.

**Liquidity** – This is the ease with which something can be converted to cash. An asset is illiquid if it is hard to convert to cash. Illiquidity makes an asset less valuable.

**Market Capitalization** – Also referred to as Market Cap, this is the number of shares outstanding, times the market price per share. Market Cap is volatile.

**Multiplier Methods** – This is a group of valuation methods that attempt to value a company by finding companies comparable to the target company. Some common denominator is needed to adjust for size differences. Common methods of adjusting for size include EBITDA, sales, net income and the number of customers.

**Net Income Multiplier** – The Net Income Multiplier, more correctly the Adjusted Net Income Multiplier, can be thought of as the value the market is willing to pay for a dollar of adjusted net income. A criticism of this method is that financing and tax strategy make companies less comparable. Using Adjusted Net Income, which is Net Income plus Interest, times 1 – Tax Rate, scrubs out most of the variation based on financing strategy, and some of the variation based on tax strategy. The Adjusted Net Income Multiplier = Σ Market Cap / Σ Adjusted Net Income for a group of comparable companies. The Net Income Multiplier Method cannot be used with companies that have an Adjusted Net Income that is zero, negative, or close to zero.

**One-time Events** – Valuations are about a company's future value, so one-time events should be eliminated before a target company is valued.

**PE** – see Price Earnings Ratio.

**Preferred stock** – Preferred stock is a type of stock created by contract. It is only issued in special circumstances, for example when a company is just starting, or if a company is in trouble and cannot sell common stock. Preferred stock has a stated face value, and a stated interest rate.

**Price Earnings Ratio** - The Price Earnings Ratio (PE) is a share's current price, divided by its Earnings per Share. When a company's PE ratio dips below its historical norms, some suggest the company is a bargain, and it represents a buying opportunity. On the other hand, when a company's PE ratio is higher than its historic norms, some believe that it is time to sell.

**Price, Minimum for Acquisition** – Company boards are reluctant to sell for less than a company's highest stock price in the last twelve months.

**Private Company** – All companies start as private companies. Companies become public companies when they register their securities with the Securities and Exchange Commission (SEC). Those buying shares in a private company are usually restricted as to whom, if anyone, they can sell shares to, and a private company cannot be listed on a stock exchange. These restrictions make shares of private companies illiquid.

**Private Company Discount** – see Discount, Private Company.

**Public Company** – A public company is one that has registered its securities with the Securities and Exchange Commission (SEC). The advantages of being a public company are that shares can be sold to anyone, and can be listed on stock exchanges, shares are more liquid than private company shares, and it is easier to raise capital. Public companies must have audited financial statements and report financial performance to the SEC annually, quarterly, and whenever there are any material changes in the business.

**Sales Multiplier** – The Sales Multiplier is the amount the market will pay for a dollar of sales in a given industry. The Sales Multiplier = Σ Market Cap / Σ Sales for a group of comparable companies.

**Securities and Exchange Commission (SEC)** – The SEC is the United States federal government agency that oversees securities and stock exchanges. It posts the financial statements of public companies on its website: www.sec.gov.

**Security** – Almost any evidence of an investment in a common enterprise where the investor relies on the efforts of others to make a profit is a security. The most common types of securities are common stock, preferred stock and bonds.

**Standard Industrial Classification (SIC)** – All companies in the United States are classified by their SIC code. The first step in finding companies that are comparable to the target company is to look for companies with the same four-digit SIC code.

**Target Company** – This is the company being valued.

# References

Ballmer, Steven A. 2008. "Microsoft Proposes Acquisition of Yahoo! for $31 per Share," Feb. 1.
http://www.microsoft.com/presspass/press/2008/feb08/02-01corpnewspr.mspx

Daves, Philip R., Michael C. Ehrhardt, Ronald E. Shrieves. 2004. Corporate Valuation: A Guide for Managers and Investors. Thompson South-Western. Mason, Ohio.

Laiw, K. Thomas. 1999. John Wiley & Sons. New York.

Mayo, Herbert B. 1998. Financial Institutions, Investments and Management, 6th Ed. Dryden Press Harcourt Brace College Publishers. Fort Worth.

Vance, David E. 2009. Ratios for Analysis, Control and Profit Planning. Global Professional Publishing. Cranbrook, Kent, U.K.

—. 2005. Raising Capital. Springer Science +Business Media. New York.

Weston, J. Fred, Mark L. Mitchell, J. Harold Mulherin. 2004. Takeovers, Restructuring and Corporate Governance. Pearson Prentiss Hall. Upper Saddle River, N.J.

Yahoo Historical Prices. 2011. "Yahoo Historical Prices," *Yahoo Finance*.
http://finance.yahoo.com/q/hp?s=YHOO&a=00&b=1&c=2007&d=01&e=1&f=2008&g=d&z=66&y=0

# APPENDIX A

# FUTURE VALUE INTEREST FACTOR FVIF (i, n)

| n | 0.25% | 0.333% | 0.417% | 0.50% | 0.75% | 1.00% | 1.25% |
|---|---|---|---|---|---|---|---|
| 1 | 1.003 | 1.003 | 1.004 | 1.005 | 1.008 | 1.010 | 1.013 |
| 2 | 1.005 | 1.007 | 1.008 | 1.010 | 1.015 | 1.020 | 1.025 |
| 3 | 1.008 | 1.010 | 1.013 | 1.015 | 1.023 | 1.030 | 1.038 |
| 4 | 1.010 | 1.013 | 1.017 | 1.020 | 1.030 | 1.041 | 1.051 |
| 5 | 1.013 | 1.017 | 1.021 | 1.025 | 1.038 | 1.051 | 1.064 |
| 6 | 1.015 | 1.020 | 1.025 | 1.030 | 1.046 | 1.062 | 1.077 |
| 7 | 1.018 | 1.024 | 1.030 | 1.036 | 1.054 | 1.072 | 1.091 |
| 8 | 1.020 | 1.027 | 1.034 | 1.041 | 1.062 | 1.083 | 1.104 |
| 9 | 1.023 | 1.030 | 1.038 | 1.046 | 1.070 | 1.094 | 1.118 |
| 10 | 1.025 | 1.034 | 1.042 | 1.051 | 1.078 | 1.105 | 1.132 |
| 11 | 1.028 | 1.037 | 1.047 | 1.056 | 1.086 | 1.116 | 1.146 |
| 12 | 1.030 | 1.041 | 1.051 | 1.062 | 1.094 | 1.127 | 1.161 |
| 13 | 1.033 | 1.044 | 1.056 | 1.067 | 1.102 | 1.138 | 1.175 |
| 14 | 1.036 | 1.048 | 1.060 | 1.072 | 1.110 | 1.149 | 1.190 |
| 15 | 1.038 | 1.051 | 1.064 | 1.078 | 1.119 | 1.161 | 1.205 |
| 16 | 1.041 | 1.055 | 1.069 | 1.083 | 1.127 | 1.173 | 1.220 |
| 18 | 1.046 | 1.062 | 1.078 | 1.094 | 1.144 | 1.196 | 1.251 |
| 20 | 1.051 | 1.069 | 1.087 | 1.105 | 1.161 | 1.220 | 1.282 |
| 24 | 1.062 | 1.083 | 1.105 | 1.127 | 1.196 | 1.270 | 1.347 |
| 28 | 1.072 | 1.098 | 1.123 | 1.150 | 1.233 | 1.321 | 1.416 |
| 30 | 1.078 | 1.105 | 1.133 | 1.161 | 1.251 | 1.348 | 1.452 |
| 32 | 1.083 | 1.112 | 1.142 | 1.173 | 1.270 | 1.375 | 1.488 |
| 36 | 1.094 | 1.127 | 1.161 | 1.197 | 1.309 | 1.431 | 1.564 |
| 40 | 1.105 | 1.142 | 1.181 | 1.221 | 1.348 | 1.489 | 1.644 |
| 48 | 1.127 | 1.173 | 1.221 | 1.270 | 1.431 | 1.612 | 1.815 |
| 50 | 1.133 | 1.181 | 1.231 | 1.283 | 1.453 | 1.645 | 1.861 |
| 60 | 1.162 | 1.221 | 1.283 | 1.349 | 1.566 | 1.817 | 2.107 |
| 72 | 1.197 | 1.271 | 1.349 | 1.432 | 1.713 | 2.047 | 2.446 |
| 84 | 1.233 | 1.323 | 1.418 | 1.520 | 1.873 | 2.307 | 2.839 |
| 96 | 1.271 | 1.376 | 1.491 | 1.614 | 2.049 | 2.599 | 3.296 |
| 108 | 1.310 | 1.432 | 1.567 | 1.714 | 2.241 | 2.929 | 3.825 |
| 120 | 1.349 | 1.491 | 1.647 | 1.819 | 2.451 | 3.300 | 4.440 |
| 240 | 1.821 | 2.223 | 2.713 | 3.310 | 6.009 | 10.893 | 19.715 |
| 360 | 2.457 | 3.313 | 4.468 | 6.023 | 14.731 | 35.950 | 87.541 |

## APPENDIX A (CONTINUED)

# FUTURE VALUE INTEREST FACTOR FVIF (i, n)

| n | 1.5% | 2.0% | 3.0% | 4.0% | 5.0% | 6.0% | 10.0% |
|---|------|------|------|------|------|------|-------|
| 1 | 1.015 | 1.020 | 1.030 | 1.040 | 1.050 | 1.060 | 1.100 |
| 2 | 1.030 | 1.040 | 1.061 | 1.082 | 1.103 | 1.124 | 1.210 |
| 3 | 1.046 | 1.061 | 1.093 | 1.125 | 1.158 | 1.191 | 1.331 |
| 4 | 1.061 | 1.082 | 1.126 | 1.170 | 1.216 | 1.262 | 1.464 |
| 5 | 1.077 | 1.104 | 1.159 | 1.217 | 1.276 | 1.338 | 1.611 |
| 6 | 1.093 | 1.126 | 1.194 | 1.265 | 1.340 | 1.419 | 1.772 |
| 7 | 1.110 | 1.149 | 1.230 | 1.316 | 1.407 | 1.504 | 1.949 |
| 8 | 1.126 | 1.172 | 1.267 | 1.369 | 1.477 | 1.594 | 2.144 |
| 9 | 1.143 | 1.195 | 1.305 | 1.423 | 1.551 | 1.689 | 2.358 |
| 10 | 1.161 | 1.219 | 1.344 | 1.480 | 1.629 | 1.791 | 2.594 |
| 11 | 1.178 | 1.243 | 1.384 | 1.539 | 1.710 | 1.898 | 2.853 |
| 12 | 1.196 | 1.268 | 1.426 | 1.601 | 1.796 | 2.012 | 3.138 |
| 13 | 1.214 | 1.294 | 1.469 | 1.665 | 1.886 | 2.133 | 3.452 |
| 14 | 1.232 | 1.319 | 1.513 | 1.732 | 1.980 | 2.261 | 3.797 |
| 15 | 1.250 | 1.346 | 1.558 | 1.801 | 2.079 | 2.397 | 4.177 |
| 16 | 1.269 | 1.373 | 1.605 | 1.873 | 2.183 | 2.540 | 4.595 |
| 18 | 1.307 | 1.428 | 1.702 | 2.026 | 2.407 | 2.854 | 5.560 |
| 20 | 1.347 | 1.486 | 1.806 | 2.191 | 2.653 | 3.207 | 6.727 |
| 24 | 1.430 | 1.608 | 2.033 | 2.563 | 3.225 | 4.049 | 9.850 |
| 28 | 1.517 | 1.741 | 2.288 | 2.999 | 3.920 | 5.112 | 14.421 |
| 30 | 1.563 | 1.811 | 2.427 | 3.243 | 4.322 | 5.743 | 17.449 |
| 32 | 1.610 | 1.885 | 2.575 | 3.508 | 4.765 | 6.453 | 21.114 |
| 36 | 1.709 | 2.040 | 2.898 | 4.104 | 5.792 | 8.147 | 30.913 |
| 40 | 1.814 | 2.208 | 3.262 | 4.801 | 7.040 | 10.286 | 45.259 |
| 48 | 2.043 | 2.587 | 4.132 | 6.571 | 10.401 | 16.394 | 97.017 |
| 50 | 2.105 | 2.692 | 4.384 | 7.107 | 11.467 | 18.420 | |
| 60 | 2.443 | 3.281 | 5.892 | 10.520 | 18.679 | 32.988 | |
| 72 | 2.921 | 4.161 | 8.400 | 16.842 | 33.545 | 66.378 | |
| 84 | 3.493 | 5.277 | 11.976 | 26.965 | 60.242 | | |
| 96 | 4.176 | 6.693 | 17.076 | 43.172 | | | |
| 108 | 4.993 | 8.488 | 24.346 | 69.120 | | | |
| 120 | 5.969 | 10.765 | 34.711 | | | | |
| 240 | 35.633 | | | | | | |
| 360 | | | | | | | |

# APPENDIX B

# PRESENT VALUE INTEREST FACTOR PVIF (k, n)

| n | 0.50% | 0.75% | 1.00% | 1.25% | 1.50% | 2.00% | 3.00% |
|---|-------|-------|-------|-------|-------|-------|-------|
| 1 | 0.995 | 0.993 | 0.990 | 0.988 | 0.985 | 0.980 | 0.971 |
| 2 | 0.990 | 0.985 | 0.980 | 0.975 | 0.971 | 0.961 | 0.943 |
| 3 | 0.985 | 0.978 | 0.971 | 0.963 | 0.956 | 0.942 | 0.915 |
| 4 | 0.980 | 0.971 | 0.961 | 0.952 | 0.942 | 0.924 | 0.888 |
| 5 | 0.975 | 0.963 | 0.951 | 0.940 | 0.928 | 0.906 | 0.863 |
| 6 | 0.971 | 0.956 | 0.942 | 0.928 | 0.915 | 0.888 | 0.837 |
| 7 | 0.966 | 0.949 | 0.933 | 0.917 | 0.901 | 0.871 | 0.813 |
| 8 | 0.961 | 0.942 | 0.923 | 0.905 | 0.888 | 0.853 | 0.789 |
| 9 | 0.956 | 0.935 | 0.914 | 0.894 | 0.875 | 0.837 | 0.766 |
| 10 | 0.951 | 0.928 | 0.905 | 0.883 | 0.862 | 0.820 | 0.744 |
| 11 | 0.947 | 0.921 | 0.896 | 0.872 | 0.849 | 0.804 | 0.722 |
| 12 | 0.942 | 0.914 | 0.887 | 0.862 | 0.836 | 0.788 | 0.701 |
| 13 | 0.937 | 0.907 | 0.879 | 0.851 | 0.824 | 0.773 | 0.681 |
| 14 | 0.933 | 0.901 | 0.870 | 0.840 | 0.812 | 0.758 | 0.661 |
| 15 | 0.928 | 0.894 | 0.861 | 0.830 | 0.800 | 0.743 | 0.642 |
| 16 | 0.923 | 0.887 | 0.853 | 0.820 | 0.788 | 0.728 | 0.623 |
| 18 | 0.914 | 0.874 | 0.836 | 0.800 | 0.765 | 0.700 | 0.587 |
| 20 | 0.905 | 0.861 | 0.820 | 0.780 | 0.742 | 0.673 | 0.554 |
| 24 | 0.887 | 0.836 | 0.788 | 0.742 | 0.700 | 0.622 | 0.492 |
| 28 | 0.870 | 0.811 | 0.757 | 0.706 | 0.659 | 0.574 | 0.437 |
| 30 | 0.861 | 0.799 | 0.742 | 0.689 | 0.640 | 0.552 | 0.412 |
| 32 | 0.852 | 0.787 | 0.727 | 0.672 | 0.621 | 0.531 | 0.388 |
| 36 | 0.836 | 0.764 | 0.699 | 0.639 | 0.585 | 0.490 | 0.345 |
| 40 | 0.819 | 0.742 | 0.672 | 0.608 | 0.551 | 0.453 | 0.307 |
| 48 | 0.787 | 0.699 | 0.620 | 0.551 | 0.489 | 0.387 | 0.242 |
| 50 | 0.779 | 0.688 | 0.608 | 0.537 | 0.475 | 0.372 | 0.228 |
| 60 | 0.741 | 0.639 | 0.550 | 0.475 | 0.409 | 0.305 | 0.170 |
| 72 | 0.698 | 0.584 | 0.488 | 0.409 | 0.342 | 0.240 | 0.119 |
| 84 | 0.658 | 0.534 | 0.434 | 0.352 | 0.286 | 0.189 | 0.083 |
| 96 | 0.620 | 0.488 | 0.385 | 0.303 | 0.239 | 0.149 | 0.059 |
| 108 | 0.584 | 0.446 | 0.341 | 0.261 | 0.200 | 0.118 | 0.041 |
| 120 | 0.550 | 0.408 | 0.303 | 0.225 | 0.168 | 0.093 | 0.029 |
| 240 | 0.302 | 0.166 | 0.092 | 0.051 | 0.028 | 0.009 | 0.001 |
| 360 | 0.166 | 0.068 | 0.028 | 0.011 | 0.005 | 0.001 | |

# APPENDIX B (CONTINUED)

## PRESENT VALUE INTEREST FACTOR PVIF (k, n)

| n | 4.00% | 5.00% | 6.00% | 9.00% | 10.00% | 12.00% | 15.00% |
|---|-------|-------|-------|-------|--------|--------|--------|
| 1 | 0.962 | 0.952 | 0.943 | 0.917 | 0.909 | 0.893 | 0.870 |
| 2 | 0.925 | 0.907 | 0.890 | 0.842 | 0.826 | 0.797 | 0.756 |
| 3 | 0.889 | 0.864 | 0.840 | 0.772 | 0.751 | 0.712 | 0.658 |
| 4 | 0.855 | 0.823 | 0.792 | 0.708 | 0.683 | 0.636 | 0.572 |
| 5 | 0.822 | 0.784 | 0.747 | 0.650 | 0.621 | 0.567 | 0.497 |
| 6 | 0.790 | 0.746 | 0.705 | 0.596 | 0.564 | 0.507 | 0.432 |
| 7 | 0.760 | 0.711 | 0.665 | 0.547 | 0.513 | 0.452 | 0.376 |
| 8 | 0.731 | 0.677 | 0.627 | 0.502 | 0.467 | 0.404 | 0.327 |
| 9 | 0.703 | 0.645 | 0.592 | 0.460 | 0.424 | 0.361 | 0.284 |
| 10 | 0.676 | 0.614 | 0.558 | 0.422 | 0.386 | 0.322 | 0.247 |
| 11 | 0.650 | 0.585 | 0.527 | 0.388 | 0.350 | 0.287 | 0.215 |
| 12 | 0.625 | 0.557 | 0.497 | 0.356 | 0.319 | 0.257 | 0.187 |
| 13 | 0.601 | 0.530 | 0.469 | 0.326 | 0.290 | 0.229 | 0.163 |
| 14 | 0.577 | 0.505 | 0.442 | 0.299 | 0.263 | 0.205 | 0.141 |
| 15 | 0.555 | 0.481 | 0.417 | 0.275 | 0.239 | 0.183 | 0.123 |
| 16 | 0.534 | 0.458 | 0.394 | 0.252 | 0.218 | 0.163 | 0.107 |
| 18 | 0.494 | 0.416 | 0.350 | 0.212 | 0.180 | 0.130 | 0.081 |
| 20 | 0.456 | 0.377 | 0.312 | 0.178 | 0.149 | 0.104 | 0.061 |
| 24 | 0.390 | 0.310 | 0.247 | 0.126 | 0.102 | 0.066 | 0.035 |
| 28 | 0.333 | 0.255 | 0.196 | 0.090 | 0.069 | 0.042 | 0.020 |
| 30 | 0.308 | 0.231 | 0.174 | 0.075 | 0.057 | 0.033 | 0.015 |
| 32 | 0.285 | 0.210 | 0.155 | 0.063 | 0.047 | 0.027 | 0.011 |
| 36 | 0.244 | 0.173 | 0.123 | 0.045 | 0.032 | 0.017 | 0.007 |
| 40 | 0.208 | 0.142 | 0.097 | 0.032 | 0.022 | 0.011 | 0.004 |
| 48 | 0.152 | 0.096 | 0.061 | 0.016 | 0.010 | 0.004 | 0.001 |
| 50 | 0.141 | 0.087 | 0.054 | 0.013 | 0.009 | 0.003 | 0.001 |
| 60 | 0.095 | 0.054 | 0.030 | 0.006 | 0.003 | 0.001 | |
| 72 | 0.059 | 0.030 | 0.015 | 0.002 | 0.001 | | |
| 84 | 0.037 | 0.017 | 0.007 | 0.001 | | | |
| 96 | 0.023 | 0.009 | 0.004 | | | | |
| 108 | 0.014 | 0.005 | 0.002 | | | | |
| 120 | 0.009 | 0.003 | 0.001 | | | | |
| 240 | | | | | | | |
| 360 | | | | | | | |

# APPENDIX C

# FUTURE VALUE INTEREST FACTOR OF AN ANNUITY FVIFA (i, n)

| n | 0.25% | 0.50% | 0.75% | 1.00% | 1.25% | 1.50% | 2.00% |
|---|-------|-------|-------|-------|-------|-------|-------|
| 1 | 1.000 | 1.000 | 1.000 | 1.000 | 1.000 | 1.000 | 1.000 |
| 2 | 2.002 | 2.005 | 2.008 | 2.010 | 2.013 | 2.015 | 2.020 |
| 3 | 3.008 | 3.015 | 3.023 | 3.030 | 3.038 | 3.045 | 3.060 |
| 4 | 4.015 | 4.030 | 4.045 | 4.060 | 4.076 | 4.091 | 4.122 |
| 5 | 5.025 | 5.050 | 5.076 | 5.101 | 5.127 | 5.152 | 5.204 |
| 6 | 6.038 | 6.076 | 6.114 | 6.152 | 6.191 | 6.230 | 6.308 |
| 7 | 7.053 | 7.106 | 7.159 | 7.214 | 7.268 | 7.323 | 7.434 |
| 8 | 8.070 | 8.141 | 8.213 | 8.286 | 8.359 | 8.433 | 8.583 |
| 9 | 9.091 | 9.182 | 9.275 | 9.369 | 9.463 | 9.559 | 9.755 |
| 10 | 10.113 | 10.228 | 10.344 | 10.462 | 10.582 | 10.703 | 10.950 |
| 11 | 11.139 | 11.279 | 11.422 | 11.567 | 11.714 | 11.863 | 12.169 |
| 12 | 12.166 | 12.336 | 12.508 | 12.683 | 12.860 | 13.041 | 13.412 |
| 13 | 13.197 | 13.397 | 13.601 | 13.809 | 14.021 | 14.237 | 14.680 |
| 14 | 14.230 | 14.464 | 14.703 | 14.947 | 15.196 | 15.450 | 15.974 |
| 15 | 15.265 | 15.537 | 15.814 | 16.097 | 16.386 | 16.682 | 17.293 |
| 16 | 16.304 | 16.614 | 16.932 | 17.258 | 17.591 | 17.932 | 18.639 |
| 18 | 18.388 | 18.786 | 19.195 | 19.615 | 20.046 | 20.489 | 21.412 |
| 20 | 20.482 | 20.979 | 21.491 | 22.019 | 22.563 | 23.124 | 24.297 |
| 24 | 24.703 | 25.432 | 26.188 | 26.973 | 27.788 | 28.634 | 30.422 |
| 28 | 28.966 | 29.975 | 31.028 | 32.129 | 33.279 | 34.481 | 37.051 |
| 30 | 31.113 | 32.280 | 33.503 | 34.785 | 36.129 | 37.539 | 40.568 |
| 32 | 33.272 | 34.609 | 36.015 | 37.494 | 39.050 | 40.688 | 44.227 |
| 36 | 37.621 | 39.336 | 41.153 | 43.077 | 45.116 | 47.276 | 51.994 |
| 40 | 42.013 | 44.159 | 46.446 | 48.886 | 51.490 | 54.268 | 60.402 |
| 48 | 50.931 | 54.098 | 57.521 | 61.223 | 65.228 | 69.565 | 79.354 |
| 50 | 53.189 | 56.645 | 60.394 | 64.463 | 68.882 | 73.683 | 84.579 |
| 60 | 64.647 | 69.770 | 75.424 | 81.670 | 88.575 | 96.215 | 114.052 |
| 72 | 78.779 | 86.409 | 95.007 | 104.710 | 115.674 | 128.077 | 158.057 |
| 84 | 93.342 | 104.074 | 116.427 | 130.672 | 147.129 | 166.17 | 213.87 |
| 96 | 108.347 | 122.829 | 139.856 | 159.927 | 183.641 | 211.72 | 284.65 |
| 108 | 123.809 | 142.74 | 165.48 | 192.89 | 226.02 | 266.18 | 374.41 |
| 120 | 139.741 | 163.88 | 193.51 | 230.04 | 275.22 | 331.29 | 488.26 |
| 240 | 328.302 | 462.04 | 667.89 | 989.26 | 1497.24 | 2308.9 | 5744.4 |
| 360 | 582.737 | 1004.52 | 1830.74 | 3494.96 | 6923.28 | 14113.6 | 62328.1 |

# APPENDIX C (CONTINUED)

# FUTURE VALUE INTEREST FACTOR
# OF AN ANNUITY FVIFA (i, n)

| n | 3.00% | 4.00% | 5.00% | 6.00% | 7.00% | 8.00% | 9.00% |
|---|---|---|---|---|---|---|---|
| 1 | 1.000 | 1.000 | 1.000 | 1.000 | 1.000 | 1.000 | 1.000 |
| 2 | 2.030 | 2.040 | 2.050 | 2.060 | 2.070 | 2.080 | 2.090 |
| 3 | 3.091 | 3.122 | 3.153 | 3.184 | 3.215 | 3.246 | 3.278 |
| 4 | 4.184 | 4.246 | 4.310 | 4.375 | 4.440 | 4.506 | 4.573 |
| 5 | 5.309 | 5.416 | 5.526 | 5.637 | 5.751 | 5.867 | 5.985 |
| 6 | 6.468 | 6.633 | 6.802 | 6.975 | 7.153 | 7.336 | 7.523 |
| 7 | 7.662 | 7.898 | 8.142 | 8.394 | 8.654 | 8.923 | 9.200 |
| 8 | 8.892 | 9.214 | 9.549 | 9.897 | 10.260 | 10.637 | 11.028 |
| 9 | 10.159 | 10.583 | 11.027 | 11.491 | 11.978 | 12.488 | 13.021 |
| 10 | 11.464 | 12.006 | 12.578 | 13.181 | 13.816 | 14.487 | 15.193 |
| 11 | 12.808 | 13.486 | 14.207 | 14.972 | 15.784 | 16.645 | 17.560 |
| 12 | 14.192 | 15.026 | 15.917 | 16.870 | 17.888 | 18.977 | 20.141 |
| 13 | 15.618 | 16.627 | 17.713 | 18.882 | 20.141 | 21.495 | 22.953 |
| 14 | 17.086 | 18.292 | 19.599 | 21.015 | 22.550 | 24.215 | 26.019 |
| 15 | 18.599 | 20.024 | 21.579 | 23.276 | 25.129 | 27.152 | 29.361 |
| 16 | 20.157 | 21.825 | 23.657 | 25.673 | 27.888 | 30.324 | 33.003 |
| 18 | 23.414 | 25.645 | 28.132 | 30.906 | 33.999 | 37.450 | 41.30 |
| 20 | 26.870 | 29.778 | 33.066 | 36.786 | 40.995 | 45.762 | 51.16 |
| 24 | 34.426 | 39.083 | 44.502 | 50.816 | 58.177 | 66.765 | 76.79 |
| 28 | 42.931 | 49.968 | 58.403 | 68.528 | 80.698 | 95.339 | 112.97 |
| 30 | 47.575 | 56.085 | 66.439 | 79.058 | 94.461 | 113.283 | 136.31 |
| 32 | 52.503 | 62.701 | 75.299 | 90.890 | 110.218 | 134.214 | 164.04 |
| 36 | 63.276 | 77.598 | 95.836 | 119.121 | 148.913 | 187.102 | 236.12 |
| 40 | 75.401 | 95.03 | 120.80 | 154.76 | 199.64 | 259.06 | 337.88 |
| 48 | 104.408 | 139.26 | 188.03 | 256.56 | 353.27 | 490.13 | 684.28 |
| 50 | 112.797 | 152.67 | 209.35 | 290.34 | 406.53 | 573.77 | 815.08 |
| 60 | 163.053 | 237.99 | 353.58 | 533.13 | 813.52 | 1253.21 | 1944.79 |
| 72 | 246.667 | 396.06 | 650.90 | 1089.63 | 1850.09 | 3174.78 | 5490.19 |
| 84 | 365.88 | 649.1 | 1184.8 | 2209.4 | 4184.7 | 8013.6 | 15462.2 |
| 96 | 535.85 | 1054.3 | 2143.7 | 4462.7 | 9442.5 | 20198.6 | 43510.1 |
| 108 | 778.19 | 1703.0 | 3865.7 | 8996.6 | 21284.3 | 50883 | 122400 |
| 120 | 1123.7 | 2741.6 | 6958.2 | 18119.8 | 47954.1 | 128150 | 344289 |
| 240 | 40128.4 | 306130 | 2434771 | | | | |
| 360 | 1394021 | | | | | | |

# APPENDIX D

# PRESENT VALUE INTEREST FACTOR OF AN ANNUITY PVIF (k, n)

| n | 0.25% | 0.50% | 0.75% | 1.00% | 1.25% | 1.50% | 2.00% |
|---|-------|-------|-------|-------|-------|-------|-------|
| 1 | 0.998 | 0.995 | 0.993 | 0.990 | 0.988 | 0.985 | 0.980 |
| 2 | 1.993 | 1.985 | 1.978 | 1.970 | 1.963 | 1.956 | 1.942 |
| 3 | 2.985 | 2.970 | 2.956 | 2.941 | 2.927 | 2.912 | 2.884 |
| 4 | 3.975 | 3.950 | 3.926 | 3.902 | 3.878 | 3.854 | 3.808 |
| 5 | 4.963 | 4.926 | 4.889 | 4.853 | 4.818 | 4.783 | 4.713 |
| 6 | 5.948 | 5.896 | 5.846 | 5.795 | 5.746 | 5.697 | 5.601 |
| 7 | 6.931 | 6.862 | 6.795 | 6.728 | 6.663 | 6.598 | 6.472 |
| 8 | 7.911 | 7.823 | 7.737 | 7.652 | 7.568 | 7.486 | 7.325 |
| 9 | 8.889 | 8.779 | 8.672 | 8.566 | 8.462 | 8.361 | 8.162 |
| 10 | 9.864 | 9.730 | 9.600 | 9.471 | 9.346 | 9.222 | 8.983 |
| 11 | 10.837 | 10.677 | 10.521 | 10.368 | 10.218 | 10.071 | 9.787 |
| 12 | 11.807 | 11.619 | 11.435 | 11.255 | 11.079 | 10.908 | 10.575 |
| 13 | 12.775 | 12.556 | 12.342 | 12.134 | 11.930 | 11.732 | 11.348 |
| 14 | 13.741 | 13.489 | 13.243 | 13.004 | 12.771 | 12.543 | 12.106 |
| 15 | 14.704 | 14.417 | 14.137 | 13.865 | 13.601 | 13.343 | 12.849 |
| 16 | 15.665 | 15.340 | 15.024 | 14.718 | 14.420 | 14.131 | 13.578 |
| 18 | 17.580 | 17.173 | 16.779 | 16.398 | 16.030 | 15.673 | 14.992 |
| 20 | 19.484 | 18.987 | 18.508 | 18.046 | 17.599 | 17.169 | 16.351 |
| 24 | 23.266 | 22.563 | 21.889 | 21.243 | 20.624 | 20.030 | 18.914 |
| 28 | 27.010 | 26.068 | 25.171 | 24.316 | 23.503 | 22.727 | 21.281 |
| 30 | 28.868 | 27.794 | 26.775 | 25.808 | 24.889 | 24.016 | 22.396 |
| 32 | 30.717 | 29.503 | 28.356 | 27.270 | 26.241 | 25.267 | 23.468 |
| 36 | 34.386 | 32.871 | 31.447 | 30.108 | 28.847 | 27.661 | 25.489 |
| 40 | 38.020 | 36.172 | 34.447 | 32.835 | 31.327 | 29.916 | 27.355 |
| 48 | 45.179 | 42.580 | 40.185 | 37.974 | 35.931 | 34.043 | 30.673 |
| 50 | 46.946 | 44.143 | 41.566 | 39.196 | 37.013 | 35.000 | 31.424 |
| 60 | 55.652 | 51.726 | 48.173 | 44.955 | 42.035 | 39.380 | 34.761 |
| 72 | 65.817 | 60.340 | 55.477 | 51.150 | 47.292 | 43.845 | 37.984 |
| 84 | 75.681 | 68.453 | 62.154 | 56.648 | 51.822 | 47.579 | 40.526 |
| 96 | 85.255 | 76.095 | 68.258 | 61.528 | 55.725 | 50.702 | 42.529 |
| 108 | 94.545 | 83.293 | 73.839 | 65.858 | 59.087 | 53.314 | 44.110 |
| 120 | 103.562 | 90.073 | 78.942 | 69.701 | 61.983 | 55.498 | 45.355 |
| 240 | 180.311 | 139.581 | 111.145 | 90.819 | 75.942 | 64.796 | 49.569 |
| 360 | 237.189 | 166.792 | 124.282 | 97.218 | 79.086 | 66.353 | 49.960 |

## APPENDIX D (CONTINUED)

## PRESENT VALUE INTEREST FACTOR OF AN ANNUITY PVIF (k, n)

| n | 3.00% | 4.00% | 5.00% | 6.00% | 10.00% | 12.00% | 15.00% |
|---|-------|-------|-------|-------|--------|--------|--------|
| 1 | 0.971 | 0.962 | 0.952 | 0.943 | 0.909 | 0.893 | 0.870 |
| 2 | 1.913 | 1.886 | 1.859 | 1.833 | 1.736 | 1.690 | 1.626 |
| 3 | 2.829 | 2.775 | 2.723 | 2.673 | 2.487 | 2.402 | 2.283 |
| 4 | 3.717 | 3.630 | 3.546 | 3.465 | 3.170 | 3.037 | 2.855 |
| 5 | 4.580 | 4.452 | 4.329 | 4.212 | 3.791 | 3.605 | 3.352 |
| 6 | 5.417 | 5.242 | 5.076 | 4.917 | 4.355 | 4.111 | 3.784 |
| 7 | 6.230 | 6.002 | 5.786 | 5.582 | 4.868 | 4.564 | 4.160 |
| 8 | 7.020 | 6.733 | 6.463 | 6.210 | 5.335 | 4.968 | 4.487 |
| 9 | 7.786 | 7.435 | 7.108 | 6.802 | 5.759 | 5.328 | 4.772 |
| 10 | 8.530 | 8.111 | 7.722 | 7.360 | 6.145 | 5.650 | 5.019 |
| 11 | 9.253 | 8.760 | 8.306 | 7.887 | 6.495 | 5.938 | 5.234 |
| 12 | 9.954 | 9.385 | 8.863 | 8.384 | 6.814 | 6.194 | 5.421 |
| 13 | 10.635 | 9.986 | 9.394 | 8.853 | 7.103 | 6.424 | 5.583 |
| 14 | 11.296 | 10.563 | 9.899 | 9.295 | 7.367 | 6.628 | 5.724 |
| 15 | 11.938 | 11.118 | 10.380 | 9.712 | 7.606 | 6.811 | 5.847 |
| 16 | 12.561 | 11.652 | 10.838 | 10.106 | 7.824 | 6.974 | 5.954 |
| 18 | 13.754 | 12.659 | 11.690 | 10.828 | 8.201 | 7.250 | 6.128 |
| 20 | 14.877 | 13.590 | 12.462 | 11.470 | 8.514 | 7.469 | 6.259 |
| 24 | 16.936 | 15.247 | 13.799 | 12.550 | 8.985 | 7.784 | 6.434 |
| 28 | 18.764 | 16.663 | 14.898 | 13.406 | 9.307 | 7.984 | 6.534 |
| 30 | 19.600 | 17.292 | 15.372 | 13.765 | 9.427 | 8.055 | 6.566 |
| 32 | 20.389 | 17.874 | 15.803 | 14.084 | 9.526 | 8.112 | 6.591 |
| 36 | 21.832 | 18.908 | 16.547 | 14.621 | 9.677 | 8.192 | 6.623 |
| 40 | 23.115 | 19.793 | 17.159 | 15.046 | 9.779 | 8.244 | 6.642 |
| 48 | 25.267 | 21.195 | 18.077 | 15.650 | 9.897 | 8.297 | 6.659 |
| 50 | 25.730 | 21.482 | 18.256 | 15.762 | 9.915 | 8.304 | 6.661 |
| 60 | 27.676 | 22.623 | 18.929 | 16.161 | 9.967 | 8.324 | 6.665 |
| 72 | 29.365 | 23.516 | 19.404 | 16.416 | 9.990 | 8.331 | 6.666 |
| 84 | 30.550 | 24.073 | 19.668 | 16.542 | 9.997 | | |
| 96 | 31.381 | 24.421 | 19.815 | 16.605 | 9.999 | | |
| 108 | 31.964 | 24.638 | 19.897 | 16.636 | 10.000 | | |
| 120 | 32.373 | 24.774 | 19.943 | 16.651 | | | |
| 240 | 33.306 | 24.998 | 20.000 | | | | |
| 360 | 33.333 | 25.000 | | | | | |

# INDEX